THE ENGLISH JACOBIN NOVEL
1780–1805

THE ENGLISH
JACOBIN NOVEL
1780–1805

GARY KELLY

OXFORD
AT THE CLARENDON PRESS
1976

Oxford University Press, Walton Street, Oxford OX2 6DP

OXFORD LONDON GLASGOW NEW YORK
TORONTO MELBOURNE WELLINGTON CAPE TOWN
IBADAN NAIROBI DAR ES SALAAM LUSAKA ADDIS ABABA
KUALA LUMPUR SINGAPORE JAKARTA HONG KONG TOKYO
DELHI BOMBAY CALCUTTA MADRAS KARACHI

ISBN 0 19 812062 1

© *Oxford University Press 1976*

*Printed in Great Britain
at the University Press, Oxford
by Vivian Ridler
Printer to the University*

TO
MY MOTHER

PREFACE

The following chapters comprise an essay in literary history. I have tried to combine history with criticism, using materials from biography as well as the history of philosophy, politics, economics, society, art, and literature wherever and in whatever way seemed necessary. The English Jacobin novel, indeed most of the polemical and engaged literature of the 1790s, has long been misprized and misunderstood, but the imagination works through these forms of writing too, and I have simply tried to provide the information necessary to read the fiction correctly and therefore provide for its revaluation.

What I argue is that the four major English Jacobin novelists— Robert Bage, Elizabeth Inchbald, Thomas Holcroft, and William Godwin—took the form and matter of the English novel from the eighteenth into the nineteenth century. They consciously developed the legacy of Richardson, Fielding, Smollett, and Sterne, and passed it on to later and more talented generations of novelists. At the same time I have tried to respect, and even to emphasize, individual differences. Comparison is as useful as informed analysis, and since the history of the English Jacobin novel is part of the history of the imagination, a study of four very different minds during an age of great political and intellectual crisis may help to advance the understanding of that history.

However, these chapters would not have been written but for the support of the Canada Council and the University of New Brunswick, and the advice and encouragement of Rachel Trickett and Stephen Gill. I have also benefited from the criticisms of James T. Boulton and Jonathan Wordsworth and from discussions with Kenneth MacLean, Marilyn Butler, and Fred Cogswell. I am grateful to Lord Abinger and to the Pforzheimer, Duke University, and Birmingham Public Libraries for permission to use material in their possession. Finally, very little of my research would have been possible, let alone as agreeable as it has been, were it not for the friendly assistance of the staffs of the Bodleian, British Museum, Victoria and Albert Museum, Birmingham, Pforzheimer, and University of New Brunswick Libraries.

CONTENTS

INTRODUCTION

I. THE ENGLISH JACOBINS

There were no great novels published in England during the 1790s, but there were many interesting ones. The decade of the French Revolution was one of great achievement in polemical prose, of new developments in graphic satire, and of a temporary recrudescence of verse satire. It was the decade in which Jane Austen and Walter Scott, Wordsworth and Coleridge, reached their maturity as individuals; it was a decade in which the foundations for new tastes in all the arts were being laid; but it does not seem to have been a period of great advance in the art of the novel. But that the popular novel was taken up by men and women of ingenuity, skill, and good intentions has already been proven by J. M. S. Tompkins, Edith Birkhead,[1] and other historians of the novel; and the chapters which follow are an attempt to carry the inquiry some way further and, by concentrating on four authors of decided connections, views, aims, and achievements, to deepen understanding of the relation of literature and history during the Revolutionary decade of the 1790s.

First, however, it is necessary to describe who and what the English Jacobins were. They were not simply all those who, in the 1790s, held liberal views and greeted the French Revolution with joy. Nor were the English Jacobins simply English sympathizers with the French Jacobins, although there were some of these, mostly amongst the artisan class. Nor, on the other hand, were the English Jacobins only those who saw the French Revolution merely as the long overdue imitation by France of England's Glorious Revolution of 1688, for many who supported Government repression in 1794 applauded the fall of the Bastille in 1789. All of the above groups existed in England in the early 1790s; but ultimately it was the *Anti*-Jacobins, the supporters of the *status quo* in Church and State, those who joined the Association for Preserving Liberty and Property against Republicans and Levellers in

---

[1] *The Popular Novel in England 1770–1800* (1932, repr. Lincoln, Nebraska, 1961); *The Tale of Terror, A Study of the Gothic Romance* (1921, repr. New York, 1963).

1793, those who saw the French Revolution as a repetition of the
bloody English Civil War and detested it as a revival of Presby-
terianism in politics—it was they who singled out the enemy and
attempted to smear them with the mud of French politics. And so
at the end of 1793, Daniel Isaac Eaton reprinted in his periodical
Politics for the People, or Hog's Wash, the following ironical account
of 'The Origin of Jacobinism':

The DEVIL was the *first Jacobin*, for which he was hurled neck and
heels out of heaven.

ADAM and EVE were *Sans Culottes*, consequently *Jacobins*, for which
they were kicked out of Paradise.

NOAH, was the next *Jacobin*, for when all the world followed their
own noses, *he followed his own Conscience.*

MOSES and ARON, were *Jacobins*, because they *abolished the Slave
Trade* in Egypt.

SAMUEL, was a *Jacobin*, because when the Israelites demanded a
King he pulled down thunder from the Clouds and almost frightened
them out of their wits.

In the latter ages the TWELVE FISHERMEN were terrible *Jacobins*,
though they called themselves *Apostles.*—Does not the scriptures say
they were *accused of Sedition*?[1]

One of the Anti-Jacobins' principal victims, John Thelwall,
saw that the only defence against such a smear was to accept it
and wear it as a badge of honour, because 'it is fixed upon us, as
a stigma, by our enemies'.[2] But English Jacobinism—the 'us' of
Thelwall's remark—was neither a monolithic party nor a creation
of the Anti-Jacobin papers and pamphleteers. The most recent
historian of the movement has described it as 'a state of mind, a
cluster of indignant sensibilities, a faith in reason, a vision of the
future. It was also individuals and groups among whom Thelwall
admitted there were "many different opinions . . . as to the extent"
of change that was needed.'[3]

English Jacobinism manifested itself, therefore, in different
ways. Some Jacobins were organized in societies, such as the
London Corresponding Society, founded in January 1792 mainly

---

[1] *Politics for the People*, ed. Daniel Isaac Eaton, 4th edn. (London, 1794), part i,
p. 173. The article was reprinted from *The Oracle* in number xii of *Politics for the
People*, advertised in number xi for publication on 28 December 1793.

[2] Quoted in Carl B. Cone, *The English Jacobins* (New York, 1968), p. iii.

[3] Cone, *The English Jacobins*, p. v.

for artisans,[1] and led by Thomas Hardy, with whom Thomas Holcroft was charged with treason in 1794. Their gospel was *The Rights of Man*, the second part of which Godwin and Holcroft had helped to have published in February 1792;[2] but they also seem to have read and admired the works of Holcroft and Godwin themselves.[3] Then there was the Society for Constitutional Information, which Holcroft attended regularly for two years from October 1792.[4] This organization, which had a more genteel membership than the Corresponding Societies, was founded in 1780 to promote political knowledge and gradual reform, but when Holcroft joined it was taking a more radical turn.[5] The Dissenters or those of Dissenting background, such as a great many of William Godwin's friends of the 1780s and early 1790s, belonged to the Revolution Society, which aimed to celebrate the Glorious Revolution but also celebrated the Revolution in France. Godwin had dined with the Society on the day after Richard Price delivered the famous *Discourse on the Love of Our Country* which was the occasion of Burke's *Reflections*,[6] and at a subsequent dinner Godwin had been told, 'We are particularly fortunate in having you among us; it is having the best cause countenanced by the man, by whom we most wished to see it supported.'[7] In January 1793 Godwin had even written to the French National Convention as the representative of the Revolution Society, expressing the hope that there would be no hostilities between their two countries.[8] Finally, there was the Whig politicians' club, the

---

[1] P. A. Brown, *The French Revolution in English History* (1918, repr. London, 1965), pp. 70–1.

[2] Charles Kegan Paul, *William Godwin, His Friends and Contemporaries* (London, 1876), i. 70. The date is wrongly given there as 1791.

[3] Francis Place, *The Autobiography of Francis Place (1771–1854)*, ed. Mary Thale (Cambridge, 1972), p. 136 n.

[4] William Hazlitt, *The Life of Thomas Holcroft*, ed. Elbridge Colby (London, 1925), ii. 27 n.

[5] Gwyn A. Williams, *Artisans and Sans-Culottes* (London, 1968), p. 67. Cf. G. S. Veitch, *The Genesis of Parliamentary Reform* (1913, repr. London, 1965), p. 71, where Veitch declares that the S.C.I. 'could not by any stretch of the imagination be called popular'.

[6] Godwin's MS. Journal, in the Bodleian Library. The *Discourse* was delivered as a sermon on 4 November 1789, and Godwin dined with the Revolution Society on 5 November.

[7] Kegan Paul, i. 65. According to the MS. Journal the remark was made to Godwin at a dinner on 14 July 1790.

[8] The letter is in the Godwin MSS. in the collection of Lord Abinger, available on microfilm from the Bodleian and Duke University Libraries.

Friends of the People (founded April 1792), of which Fox and
Sheridan were the leading ornaments, and it was to them that
Holcroft and Godwin had delivered their hortatory 'Letters' in
April 1791.[1]

Godwin and Holcroft were obviously directly involved in
organized English Jacobinism in the early 1790s, that English
Jacobinism which believed in parliamentary reform and which
saw the French Revolution merely as a stimulus to extend the
battle for liberties which had begun and ended, they hoped
temporarily, in the seventeenth century. But they were not
revolutionaries. They were certainly more extreme in 1791 than
they later became, or than they were later to admit, judging by the
tone of Holcroft's 'Letter to Fox':

'Lift your voice in the cause of eternal justice; familiarise to our ears
those truths that to convince need only to be spoken, satisfy your
fellow beings that you are unequivocally the friend of their cause: and
you may then fill the important office of mediator between the political
monopolies that must gradually withdraw their pretensions, and the
political justice that either by tranquil or violent means must succeed.'[2]

But they abhorred violence, and even in the early 1790s saw it
only as a last resort. They made that distinction between principle
and practice which Godwin enunciated in the last of his novels
to be considered here:

A thousand things might be found excellent and salutary, if brought
into general practice, which would in some cases appear ridiculous,
and in others be attended with tragical consequences, if prematurely
acted upon by a solitary individual. The author of Political Justice,
as appears again and again in the pages of that work, is the last man in
the world to recommend a pitiful attempt, by scattered examples to
renovate the face of society, instead of endeavouring by discussion and
reasoning, to effect a grand and comprehensive improvement in the
sentiments of its members.[3]

It was by 'discussion and reasoning' that the heroes and heroines
were to reform the villains of English Jacobin novels. Like most
nineteenth-century reformers, the English Jacobins stopped short
of advocating violence, which in any case they thought was not

---

[1] The 'Letters' were unpublished, but are found in the Abinger collection. Holcroft wrote to Fox, and Godwin to Sheridan (Kegan Paul, i. 67).

[2] The 'Letter to Fox' is in Godwin's handwriting in the Abinger collection, but
enclosed in quotation marks, which suggests that it is merely Godwin's copy.

[3] *Fleetwood*, vol. i, p. xii.

vindicated by history. As Godwin told Lady Caroline Lamb in 1819, 'I am in principle a Republican, but in practice a Whig.'[1]

In spite of their various connections with organized English Jacobinism, the English Jacobin novelists were sceptical of the real benefits of political association, and in fact Godwin argued against political societies in *Political Justice* (1793) and in his pamphlet, *Considerations on Lord Grenville's and Mr. Pitt's Bills, Concerning Treasonable and Seditious Practices, and Unlawful Assemblies* (1795).[2] The literary Jacobins worked best for reform within their own informal circles, which allowed them to theorize and argue without the irritating necessity of facing real political action.

On the fringes of the organized societies, then, 'philosophers' such as Holcroft and Godwin felt they could play an important part in this crisis of human history. They saw themselves as Shelley later saw poets, as the true legislators of mankind, and in 1793 Godwin noted his friend Jardine's complaint 'that Holcroft and I had our heads full of plays and novels and then thought ourselves philosophers'.[3] At the same time, they could rub shoulders with the ever shifting crowd of supporters of one or more liberal cause, or even with supporters of Government. Godwin's connection with public life in the early 1790s was mainly through the Dissenters and 'Commonwealthmen' amongst and by whom he had been educated. But as his fame spread, so too did his acquaintance with those in high society, often liberal young scions of ancient stock, who later remembered him with affection when they ascended to full possession of their social and political privileges. Mrs. Inchbald too enjoyed a wide range of social connections. Owing to her celebrity as an actress and playwright, and also to her wit and beauty, she always had more fashionable acquaintance than she needed, and more than some of her more rigid friends, such as Holcroft and Godwin, thought good for her. But owing to her East Anglian origins she also had extensive connections amongst that astonishing collection of Dissenting intelligentsia centred in Norwich, and active in every branch of religion, industry, and the arts. Holcroft was not so happy in his connections: always a vindicator of the privileges of talent over those

[1] Kegan Paul, ii. 266.
[2] The title-page gave the author as 'A Lover of Order'.
[3] Abinger collection. Note of a conversation at Wimbledon, where Horne Tooke lived, and dated 24 Mar. 1793.

of birth, he kept within the world of the arts, to which he was passionately devoted. Nevertheless, through these connections he was in contact with every new development in drama, music, and painting, and he passed his knowledge and his friends to Godwin, who was always more preoccupied with the problems of history and philosophy. Even Robert Bage, a man of narrow domestic habits, engaged in one of the oldest mass-production industries, paper-making, was, through the Derby Philosophical Society, in touch with the leaders in science and industry, as well as with the English disciples of the French Enlightenment, such as Erasmus Darwin, Richard Lovell Edgeworth, and members of the Lunar Society of Birmingham.[1] Bage remained outside the turmoil of London political and literary life (although he paid at least two visits to London in the 1790s[2]), and yet the turmoil managed to find him out, retired as he was. On 25 July 1791 he wrote to his friend William Hutton, who had been one of the victims of the Birmingham Riots only a few days before:

Since the riots, in every company I have had the misfortune to go into, my ears have been insulted with the bigotry of 50 years back—with, damn the presbyterians—with church and king huzza—and with true passive obedience and nonresistance—and may my house be burned too, if I am not become sick of my species, and as desirous of keeping out of its way, as ever was true hermit.[3]

A year and a half later he wrote again:

No man's ear is open to anything but Church and king—and Damn the french—and damn the presbyterians. I abstain from all society, because respect for my moral principles is scarce sufficient to preserve me from insult on account of my political—[4]

And as late as 1800, he found it necessary to ask Godwin's aid in finding a place for a clergyman friend who had suffered because of his political unorthodoxy.[5]

---

[1] Eric Robinson, 'The Derby Philosophical Society', in A. E. Musson and Eric Robinson, *Science and Technology in the Industrial Revolution* (Manchester, 1969), pp. 190–9.
[2] Bage Correspondence (Birmingham Public Library), letter to William Hutton, 26 Apr. 1792; letter to Thomas Hutton, 4 Aug. 1796.
[3] Ibid.
[4] Ibid., letter dated 24 Jan. 1793.
[5] Abinger collection; Robert Bage to William Godwin, 1 June 1800.

2. ENGLISH JACOBINISM

One way and another, then, the four English Jacobins considered here were as vexed and exhilarated by the events of the
decade as anyone. They all had connections with one or other of
the aspects of organized English Jacobinism, and they all suffered
in some degree from the inevitable reaction against it. But more
significantly in terms of their novels, they were also English
Jacobins by virtue of their beliefs. They did not, of course, hold
identical views on every subject, and the term 'Jacobin' itself is
misleading, since most of those in Britain who bore that label
were in fact Girondins in their principles and beliefs, and took
their political thought from native rather than French precedents.
Holcroft, Godwin, Bage, and Mrs. Inchbald all came to share in
a complex of values and beliefs formed from the empirical psychology of Locke and Hartley, the republican politics of the eighteenth-century 'Commonwealthmen',[1] the rational religion of the
Scottish philosophers, and the historical optimism of the French
Enlightenment. They too took the motto *écraser l'infâme*, often
because they too had direct personal experience of social, moral,
or legal oppression. They opposed tyranny and oppression, be it
domestic, national or international, spiritual or temporal; they
were against all distinctions between men which were not based
on moral qualities, or virtue; and they were utterly opposed to
persecution of individuals, communities, or nations for their
beliefs on any subject. Most important of all, they saw history,
both past and present, as an account of the efforts of some men to
establish the rule of reason against its enemies, which were not
imagination and feeling, but error and prejudice.

Their Reason was, it is true, at times rather severe of visage,
not a humane judge, but a persecutrix not very different from the
Evangelical super-ego which was already treading down the libido
of 'merry England', and attempting to force the national ego into
a new Puritanism. But the coldness of their reason has been
exaggerated, and their passion for it ridiculed. Bage's favourite
authors after all were Voltaire, Fielding, and Smollett; Holcroft's
were Butler, Fielding, Smollett, and the comic dramatists; and
both writers carried on the tradition they loved with vigour and

---

[1] Described in Caroline Robbins, *The Eighteenth-Century Commonwealthman* (1959,
repr. New York, 1968).

panache. Mrs. Inchbald contributed to a new naturalness in her
acting, her play-writing, and her fiction, and she showed in both
her novels a wit and irony worthy of Jane Austen. Godwin certainly pursued truth with the kind of earnest devotion only
possible in a lapsed Calvinist: when, in writing *St. Leon* (1799),
he wished to portray the character of a dog, he had to consult
Buffon's *Lettres sur les animaux*,[1] and whilst visiting his friend
Horne Tooke at Wimbledon in 1793, he recorded the following
specimen of moral philosophy: 'Singular character of Captain
Gawler, as a black leg and sensualist—. . . says there is more pleasure in f—g one's self, considered merely in a sensual view; and
that the superior pleasure in the other case consists in outwitting
a woman, taking from her what she does not like to part with.'[2]
And yet in 1796 Mary Wollstonecraft, the most outstanding
woman of her day, found it possible both to admire and love the
man Charles Lamb referred to affectionately as 'the Professor'.

What the English Jacobins and the English Jacobin novelists
insisted on was simply that reason should decide the issue in
human affairs and human government, not power based on money,
age, rank, sex, or physical strength. The necessities of their argument in support of this kind of reason led them to some absurdi-
ties no doubt, which subsequent events in France and Britain
exposed only too cruelly. But, as will emerge in the chapters
which follow, one of the chief aims of the English Jacobins as
novelists was to depict, somewhat hopefully, the struggle and
eventual triumph of reason over *l'infâme*.

3. FROM REVOLUTION TO ROMANTICISM

Apart from the common pool of ideas which they inherited from
the French Enlightenment on the one hand and the native political
and philosophical tradition on the other, the most important influence on English Jacobin novels was simply the events of the
1790s. Although English Jacobins were often reluctant second
parties to controversy, there was, at least in the 1790s, a certain
community of reaction towards the events and issues of the time,
which in turn shaped their community of ideas in common ways.

The first euphoria over the fall of the Bastille was, of course,

---

[1] MS. Journal; entry for 4 June 1799, 'Buffon, le chien'.
[2] Abinger collection.

shared by many, but thereafter the process of winnowing began, as events in France and Britain gradually reduced the English Jacobins to the hardiest few. As Godwin wrote in 1810, 'My fellow labourers have . . . fallen off from me on every side.'[1] Up to 1794 and the Treason Trials, however, hopes remained high. The first serious blow against the English Jacobins was struck by Burke's *Reflections on the Revolution in France* (November 1790), but that was followed by a plethora of replies ranging from reasoned to indignant, and ultimately Godwin's *Political Justice* (published on St. Valentine's Day, 1793) took its place in this catalogue,[2] the most philosophical of the replies and, amongst those above the artisan class, probably more influential than Paine's *Rights of Man*.

This 'paper war' was soon being fought on two fronts: the question of reform in Britain, often referred back to the English Civil War and the Glorious Revolution; and the progress of the Revolution in France. Ultimately, of course, the two battles were only parts of a single campaign, fought through every period of human history, and when Louis XVI spent his last hours reading the account of the execution of Charles I in Hume's *History of England*,[3] he was simply proving the century's belief that history was prophecy. But at first the English Jacobins, with their enthusiasm and their novels, pamphlets, plays, poems, and philosophical treatises, had the best of the action, until the Government, or the Association for Preserving Liberty and Property against Republicans and Levellers, silenced them.[4]

The creation of a popular government in the National Assembly (1789), the establishment of civil and religious liberty (1790), the attempted escape and 'treachery' of Louis XVI (1791), marked a steady rise in English popular enthusiasm for the Revolution, of which the beating back of the 'leagued despots' at Valmy, and the declaration of the Republic in September 1792, were the culmination. It was in this year that Holcroft joined the Society for Constitutional Information and published the most complete

[1] Abinger collection. Draft essay on mystery, religion, and death, dated 6 Oct. 1810. The echo from the New Testament suggests both Godwin's Calvinist training, and the millenarism of the age.

[2] A catalogue listed in James T. Boulton, *The Language of Politics in the Age of Wilkes and Burke* (London and Toronto, 1963), pp. 265–71.

[3] Jean-Baptiste Cléry, *A Journal of the Occurrences . . . During the Confinement of Louis XVI*, trans. R. C. Dallas (London, 1798), p. 216.

[4] In *The Morning Chronicle* (3 Feb. 1793) Godwin addressed John Reeves, the founder of the Association, as 'the assassin of the Liberties of Englishmen'.

and most optimistic of English Jacobin novels, and in the same year Bage contributed a prophecy of a new age of equality and justice in the last pages of *Man As He Is*.

But the English Jacobins had let their early enthusiasm get out of hand, and they had allowed their cause to become too closely identified with the fate of France. The establishment of the French clergy as a branch of the state had upset many in England, and the French declaration of war on Austria in April 1792 seemed full of menace for all the Establishments of Europe. The Paris mob exceeded past excesses with the attack on the Tuileries (August) and the massacre of Royalist prisoners (September), which inspired Mrs. Inchbald to write a play in which present reality was disguised as events during the St. Bartholemew Massacres of 1572. The persecutions of revolutionary and reactionary zeal were already being seen in terms of the religious persecutions of the Reformation, Counter-Reformation, and wars of religion, and it was an analogy which Godwin was to explore further in *Things As They Are* (1794)[1] and his historical novel, *St. Leon* (1799). The execution of Louis XVI and the outbreak of war between France and England early in 1793 made sympathy with France virtual treason. Finally, the war hysteria in France threw power into the hands of the extremists, and the destruction of the Girondins, with whose political philosophy the English Jacobins had most in common, added a new wave to the refugees flocking to England. In Robespierre's Paris even Mary Wollstonecraft was in danger, and Tom Paine barely escaped the guillotine.

Events in England too soon left the English Jacobins with no political ground to stand on. The Birmingham Riots of July 1791, in which friends of Bage and Godwin were direct sufferers, were seen as a severe setback to the advance of reason: the people did not seem worthy of true political justice. Slowly but inexorably the government began to track down political dissidents, many of whom were also Dissenters, and to try them for real or trumped-up crimes. The founding of the Association for Preserving Liberty and Property against Republicans and Levellers in December 1792 placed a new, unofficial weapon in the hands of repression. The trials following the Edinburgh Convention of December 1792 and the prosecution of Paine's *Rights of Man* brought political

---

[1] Better known as *Caleb Williams*; I have retained the original title in order to keep the novel's polemical purpose in the foreground of the discussion.

persecution even closer to Holcroft and Godwin. Then, in May 1793, the prosecution of Godwin's *Enquiry Concerning Political Justice* was debated in parliament, only a few months after its publication. The conviction of Joseph Gerrald also struck both Holcroft and Godwin deeply, since they had come to know him personally. Their reaction to Gerrald's martyrdom was much like that of Coleridge—'Such is Joseph Gerald [sic]! Withering in the sickly and tainted gales of a prison, his healthful soul looks down from the citadel of his integrity on his impotent persecutors.'[1] The final blow fell in 1794, the year in which *Things As They Are* and the first part of *Hugh Trevor* were published, and in which Mrs. Inchbald finished writing *Nature and Art* (published 1796). In May, the same month as the suspension of Habeas Corpus, Holcroft, Thelwall, and Horne Tooke, three of Godwin's closest friends, were arrested along with a number of others. Their acquittal in November was a hollow victory—by the end of the next year the establishment of the Directory in France and the passing of the 'Two Acts'[2] in Britain signalled the indefinite postponement of all the sanguine hopes of the early 1790s.

Alternatives were sought, and began to penetrate the system of rational optimism which had been seized so zealously in the early 1790s and which the English Jacobins hoped would soon advance humanity to the last age of moral, physical, and social perfection. Pantisocracy was mooted and abandoned, although traces of it appear at the end of Mrs. Inchbald's *Nature and Art*. The older English Jacobins—Godwin and Holcroft—began to realize that dogmatism would not succeed. Holcroft had already paid a tribute to Fox in the first part of *Hugh Trevor*, and Godwin too realized that Fox's geniality and temperate perseverance in the cause he felt to be right were more productive than the precipitate dogmatism of the English Jacobins.[3] Holcroft and Godwin also began to emphasize the value of sympathy rather than argument in achieving individual moral reform, and to appreciate the power of imagination and feeling, ideas vital to the young ex-Jacobins who were now becoming Romantics.

[1] In *Conciones ad Populum* (1795), in *Lectures 1795 on Politics and Religion*, ed. Lewis Patton and Peter Mann (London and Princeton, 1971), p. 41.
[2] i.e. the acts against which Godwin wrote *Considerations* . . . (1795).
[3] Abinger collection. MS. notes on a 'character' of Fox, undated, but apparently written before Fox's death, and not the 'Character of Mr. Fox' published in the *London Chronicle* in November 1806.

In the second part of *Hugh Trevor* (1797) and in *St. Leon* (1799) there is a new emphasis on sympathy, but there is also a note of pessimism, even an elegiac note suggesting that the heroic age of public action was past. In their novels of 1805, *Bryan Perdue* and *Fleetwood*, Holcroft and Godwin concentrate on domestic man and individual moral reform. The English Jacobin novel is transformed into the Romantic novel or the novel of sentimental satire, prototypes of Scott and Bulwer Lytton, just as the English Jacobin politics are transformed into nineteenth-century radical and liberal politics as the young followers[1] of Holcroft, Godwin, and Paine in the 1790s carry the struggle forward into the new century. The English Jacobin novel was born, flourished, and died with English Jacobinism itself.

4. THE ENGLISH JACOBIN NOVELISTS

Robert Bage, Elizabeth Inchbald, Thomas Holcroft, and William Godwin shared a variety of common associations, beliefs, and experiences; but they were not the only writers of English Jacobin novels. There were other novelists who were as interesting, particularly those women such as Mary Wollstonecraft, Mary Hays, and Helen Maria Williams, who tried to bring new attitudes to female experience to the popular novel. And there were other novelists, such as Charlotte Smith and Mary Robinson, who could display some talent and who also partook of that 'brisk traffic in opinions'[2] around William Godwin. With all of these novelists Holcroft, Godwin, and Mrs. Inchbald were also acquainted. But whatever their achievement as women, 'philosophers', or writers, either their talent or their Jacobinism soon faded[3] and they did not share that philosophically motivated search for 'unity of design' which was central to the technique of the major English Jacobin novelists.

Above all, the special relationship between Bage, Holcroft, Godwin, and Mrs. Inchbald had several dimensions—literary and formal, as well as personal and ideological. Holcroft, for example,

---

[1] Those were the liberal politicians and peers who obtained Godwin his sinecure as Yeoman Usher of the Exchequer in 1833. Kegan Paul, ii. 321–2.

[2] B. R. Pollin, *Education and Enlightenment in the Works of William Godwin* (New York, 1962), p. 219.

[3] Philippe Séjourné, *Aspects généraux du roman féminin en Angleterre de 1740 à 1800* (Aix-en-Provence, 1966), pp. 420–1.

was one of Godwin's 'four principal oral instructors' (the others were Joseph Fawcett, George Dyson, and Coleridge),[1] and Godwin was clearly the major influence on Holcroft. Together they were the Castor and Pollux of literary English Jacobinism, and Godwin's MS. Journal shows that there was not a subject of importance on which they did not confer in the 1790s. Moreover, both were seriously interested in Mrs. Inchbald, both as a novelist and as a woman, and it would seem they both attempted to formalize the relationship with her into marriage.[2] But she was by no means their disciple. Through her novel *A Simple Story* she demonstrated to them the possibilities which the abused popular novel could offer to the writer of serious views, and through personal knowledge of the relation between her life and her fiction they saw new opportunities for using autobiography to give that form both originality and the authenticity of real life. Her critical acumen and fine literary tact influenced the particulars of their novels, and years later Godwin wrote to her on the publication of his *Mandeville* (1817):

I cannot appear before the world in my old character of a novelist, without recollecting with some emotion the sort of intercourse that passed between us, when Caleb Williams was in his nonage, and in the vigour of his age. Particularly I have looked a hundred times with great delight at the little marginal notes and annotations with which you adorned the pages of my writings of that period.[3]

It has to be admitted that the personal connection between these three and Robert Bage was slight. Holcroft and Mrs. Inchbald never met him, although Godwin took the trouble to seek him out twice, in 1797 and 1800.[4] There was of course a degree of reciprocal literary influence, which connected Bage with Holcroft in particular; and there was, in the greater economy and higher sense of purpose of *Hermsprong*, an indication that Bage had learned something from the novels of the others. There was also a personal if indirect connection between Bage and the London Jacobins through common friends such as Joseph Priestley and

[1] Kegan Paul, i. 17.
[2] Godwin's MS. Journal entry for 16 Sept. 1793: 'Call on Inchbald, talk of marriage.'
[3] Letter to Mrs. Inchbald, 1 Dec. 1817. Forster Collection, Victoria and Albert Museum, no. 226.
[4] Godwin's MS. Journal.

Erasmus Darwin,[1] and especially through a common inheritance
of ideas which was represented by those friends, the inheritance
from the French Enlightenment on the one hand, and the English
Revolution of the seventeenth century on the other. Through the
impact of the French Revolution of 1789–92 these two influences
were combined and given new life. From that new complex of
ideas and attitudes all four of these English Jacobin novelists
drew their fictional subjects and fashioned their formal techniques.

5. ENGLISH JACOBINISM AND THE NOVEL

Such was the involvement of the English Jacobin novelists with
each other and with the events and issues of the decade of Revolution, and it is not surprising that the course of events in that
decade should be reflected in their novels. The wildest fancies of
the Gothic novelist, the deepest emotions delineated by the senti-
mentalist, could hardly exceed the real terrors and passions released by Revolution. But for the English Jacobin novelists the
relation of fiction to history and human nature went deeper than
this. Their English Jacobin philosophy went beneath the mere
surface of character and incident to affect their technique at every
level.

Their manifesto appeared as early as 1780, in the preface to
Holcroft's *Alwyn*. Holcroft, in a manner which would have been
familiar to readers of 'philosophical' history, traced the progress
of civilization in the development of works of the imagination,
and ended by distinguishing the romance, a product of the age of
'Gallantry',[2] from the novel of his own time:

> MODERN writers use the word Romance, to signify a fictitious history
> of detached and independent adventures; and, under that idea, call
> the Telemaque of Fenelon, and the Cyrus of Ramsay, Romances. Le
> Sage's Gil Blas, and Smollett's Roderick Random, though of a dif-
> ferent species, come under the same denomination. A Novel is
> another kind of work. Unity of design is its character. In a Romance,
> if the incidents be well marked and related with spirit, the intention is

---

[1] On 17 August 1800 Godwin met the Bages at Darwin's (MS. Journal). Cf. P.
Faulkner (*Notes and Queries*, ccxxii, Apr. 1967, p. 144), who states that there is no
direct evidence that Bage actually knew Darwin.

[2] The Romance was therefore associated with the feudal and chivalric culture
which Burke was to defend, and which was to be smashed by the French Revolution.

answered; and adventures pass before the view for no other purpose than to amuse by their peculiarity, without, perhaps, affecting the main story, if there should be one. But in a Novel, a combination of incidents, entertaining in themselves, are made to form a whole; and an un-necessary circumstance becomes a blemish, by detaching from the simplicity which is requisite to exhibit that whole to advantage. Thus, as in dramatic works, those circumstances which do not tend, either to the illustration, or forwarding the main story, or, which do not mark some character, or person in the drama, are to be esteemed un-necessary.

HENCE it appears, the legitimate Novel is a work much more difficult than the Romance, and justly deserves to be ranked with those drama-tic pieces whose utility is generally allowed. Novels have fallen into disrepute. Love-sick girls and boys are supposed to be the only persons capable of being amused by them: and, while a poverty of stile, a want of knowledge of the human heart, of men and manners; while a puny tale of love and misfortune, cross fathers, and unhappy children, un-natural rigour, and unaccountable reconciliation, without discrimina-tion of character, without variety of incident, with but one set of phrases, one languid, inanimate description, with scarce a single ray of imagination to comfort the disconsolate reader, are their great charac-teristics, Novels shall continue to want admirers: but Tom Jones shall never want admirers. (vol. i, pp. vi–viii.)

Over fifty years later, Godwin made the same point, in an account of the composition of *Things As They Are*, when he declared that 'the unity of spirit and interest in a tale truly considered, gives it a powerful hold on the reader, which can scarcely be generated with equal success in any other way'.[1]

Holding certain political and moral views is of course no claim to special attention as a novelist. Nevertheless, the very nature of some of the views of the English Jacobin novelists made them consider the problem of technique as something more than the problem of planning and ornamentation. In particular, their belief in the 'doctrine of necessity', expressed in the principle that 'the characters of men originate in their external circumstances',[2] led them to consider the integration of character and plot as

---

[1] In the preface to the Standard Novels edition of *Fleetwood* (1832), in William Godwin, *Caleb Williams*, ed. David McCracken (London, New York, and Toronto, 1970), p. 337.

[2] The chapter heading of Book i, Ch. iv of *Political Justice* (2nd edn. 1796). In the first edition of 1793 this was Book i, Ch. iii, entitled 'The Moral Characters of Men Originate in their Perceptions'. William Godwin, *Enquiry Concerning Political Justice*, ed. F. E. L. Priestley (Toronto, 1946), iii. 141.

essential to the nature of the true novel. And, as will become apparent in the following chapters, the English Jacobin novelists all tried in various ways to achieve this 'unity of design'. They tried to show how their characters had been formed by circumstances, and how character and incident were linked together like the parts of a syllogism. The conclusion to be drawn from their novels therefore would have a logical truth and necessity which would make them simply the imaginative enactments of a philosophical argument. The English Jacobin novels were doubly 'philosophical' therefore: they contained many dialogues, monologues, and 'perorations' on serious and weighty topics; and they were 'philosophical' in structure and technique.

Obviously such a militant sense of purpose could cause problems. A story which moves inexorably to a certain conclusion, no matter how valid in its own terms, will lose a certain interest unless there are compensating features—the unpredictableness of 'entertainment'. Perhaps for this reason Godwin, all too aware of how Holcroft had erred in trying to construct a novel as an argument in *Anna St. Ives*, threw all his energy into creating striking characters, and also invented the end of his novel first, and then found the necessary events to support his conclusion.[1] His emphasis was on character, but it was not the Theophrastan 'Character' which was used by Bage, Holcroft, and Mrs. Inchbald in their Jacobin satires. In an undated MS. essay on tragedy and fiction Godwin wrote, 'The real essence of every story of human affairs is character. Without this it is all rottenness and dust. It is by character that I understand a story, and come to feel its reality.'[2] By concentrating on character he hoped to achieve that 'overpowering interest' which the others, in their pursuit of the right conclusion, often failed to obtain. Godwin attained his end, and his 'unity of spirit', but he did not achieve 'unity of design', and none of his novels has the same sense of impulsion in the plot as *Anna St. Ives*. Only Bage wholly neglected this necessitarian 'unity of design', but his novels have a unity of their own, a thematic unity which transcends their picaresque form, and which is certainly intensified in *Hermsprong*, written after he had had a chance to absorb the achievement of Holcroft and Godwin.

---

[1] Account of the composition of *Things As They Are* in preface to the Standard Novels edition of *Fleetwood* (1832). *Caleb Williams*, ed. D. M. McCracken, p. 337.

[2] Abinger collection.

The real difference between Bage and the rest, however, is that he is interested in human nature, as it was understood in the eighteenth century; they are interested in human psychology. Holcroft and Mrs. Inchbald, it is true, slackened their interest in psychological realism after writing their first English Jacobin novels, but even in their subsequent works they made some attempt to follow what for Godwin was the overriding concern. It is this difference which places Bage at the end of the eighteenth century and Godwin at the beginning of the nineteenth, Bage as a product of the Enlightenment and Godwin as a forerunner of Romanticism. Psychological realism was also the key to the English Jacobin novelists' attempt to weld plot to character: the course of every incident in the novel, and the succession of incidents, must be seen to originate in the characters of the protagonists. Hence their interest in Richardson, Rousseau, and the sentimental novel, alongside an interest in Defoe, Fielding, Smollett, and the picaresque; and hence the central importance in their novels of some kind of development of character.

Holcroft, in particular, owed a great deal of his theory and practice to the well-wrought picaresque of Fielding and Smollett, but even higher in his esteem stood Samuel Richardson. In 1784 Godwin published *Italian Letters*, an obvious imitation of *Clarissa*,[1] and in Holcroft's first Jacobin novel, *Anna St. Ives*, he presented the public with what seemed to be a *sans-culotte* Clarissa. In the 1790s Godwin too turned to Richardson's greatest work several times for guidance, and the original epistolary form in which he read Mrs. Inchbald's *A Simple Story* suggests that it too took a lead from Richardson. It was not any particular character, theme, or incident from *Clarissa* which interested the English Jacobin novelists, but the combination of all three, the detailed analysis of human emotion and passion which they hoped to combine with their own militant and radical philosophy of man.

One aspect of the critical debate over Richardson which the English Jacobin novelists found particularly germane to their necessitarian philosophy concerned the portrayal of virtuous and 'mixed' characters.[2] Their aims were as moral as Richardson's,

---

[1] In some autobiographical notes (undated, but probably written in August 1797) Godwin wrote, '1770 Abridgements of Richardson—compose an imitation from day to day in walking.' Abinger collection.

[2] A debate initiated by Johnson's remarks on the novel in *The Rambler*, no. 4, in which his criterion was Richardson's characterization.

and the problem of making vice real and yet virtue triumphant
proved as intractable for them as it had done for their predecessors.
Try as he might Holcroft could not avoid making Anna St. Ives
seem a prude some of the time, Frank Henley a Grandisonian prig
most of the time, and the 'villain' Coke Clifton by far the most
interesting character in the whole of the novel. But Clifton was
a model of the 'mixed' character which many novel-writers and
critics thought too risky for presentation to the weak-minded
creatures who were assumed to be the typical novel-readers.[1] To
give Holcroft his due, he learned from his failure in *Anna St. Ives*,
and in his next novel, *Hugh Trevor* (1794-7), made his hero less
of a paragon, and his 'mixed' character less central to the action.
Finally, in *Bryan Perdue* (1805) the hero is himself an 'acquitted
felon'.[2] Unfortunately even the heroes of these two novels become
progressively more priggish as they become more virtuous.

Mrs. Inchbald, Bage, and Godwin, however, did manage to
solve the problem, in different ways. Mrs. Inchbald's skill in the
portrayal of suppressed emotion makes Dorriforth, the hero of
A Simple Story, interesting even though he is a priest, and when
he becomes the tyrannical Lord Elmwood she manages to invest
him with the same emotional complexity with which Godwin,
undoubtedly following her lead, endowed his misanthropes—
Falkland in *Things As They Are* (1794), and the hero of *Fleetwood*
(1805). But Caleb Williams, although he is a complex character
because of his 'criminal' curiosity, does not always avoid the
same self-satisfaction of the martyr to 'things as they are' which
characterizes Frank Henley. Bage in his novels and Mrs. Inchbald
in *Nature and Art* also tended to make moral distinctions seem all
black and white, but at least they have the saving grace of humour.
Even so, their characters tend to be two-dimensional, either
witty or sentimental, and the 'mixed' characters are all minor ones.

Ultimately it was only Godwin's *Things As They Are* and *Fleetwood*, and Mrs. Inchbald's *A Simple Story*—the English Jacobin
novels which have most in common with the novels of the nineteenth century—which solved the problem of characterization in
overtly didactic fiction. It would be comforting to believe that

---

[1] See the remarks of Henry Mackenzie, from *The Lounger*, xx (18 June 1785), in
Novel and Romance 1700-1800, A Documentary Record, ed. Ioan Williams (London,
1970), p. 331.
[2] The tag was applied to Holcroft and others by the Anti-Jacobins after the
Treason Trials of 1794.

this was because their authors were, in writing these works, somehow *entêtés*,[1] carried away by their autobiographical imaginings or by some subconscious compulsion to write novels which were more personal and hence more real than they knew. But the examination of the origins and intent of these novels in the chapters which follow will indicate that this is only partly so. The truth is, the English Jacobin novelists were, for a variety of reasons, *entêtés* with the philosophy of English Jacobinism, and at most important points their choice of characters and characterization can be seen to have been made according to its principles.

Since most critics in the late eighteenth century tended to regard the novel as merely the sum of its parts[2]—plot, character, description, style, dialogue—it is the more significant to find the English Jacobins treating technique as of the utmost importance. Their 'unity of design' had reference of course to a certain observance of decorum in fashioning the novel's parts—'design' in the sense of plan, disposition of elements to make up a whole which has an artistic harmony. But they also aimed for unity of intent, a design in which their various 'designs' on the reader were integrated with one another, with the autobiographical impulse, and with the novel's artistic character. Only in this way could their fiction effect a moral revolution in its readers, and it was through this design that the English Jacobins effected a revolution in the art of the novel.

---

[1] The word Godwin used to describe his various literary and philosophical passions (MS. autobiographical notes in the Abinger collection, probably written in August 1797).

[2] *Novel and Romance 1700–1800, A Documentary Record*, ed. Ioan Williams, p. 23.

CHAPTER I

ROBERT BAGE

I. 'POLITICAL AND PHILOSOPHICAL OPINIONS'

In what remains the best single essay on Robert Bage, Walter Scott rightly emphasizes the novelist's interest in both character and 'political and philosophical opinions'.[1] More recently J. M. S. Tompkins has included Bage in her chapter on 'new life in the novel' precisely because of his seriousness about social and political issues;[2] and Harrison R. Steeves has described Bage's chief merit as 'an unobscured outlook upon contemporary social and political conventions, illusions, and inequities'.[3]

In spite of this unanimity regarding Bage's seriousness as a novelist, no one has yet indicated the precise nature and depth of the political and social interest in his work, or shown how his view of society actually directs his choice of characters, themes, and plots. For the *Ballantyne's Novelist's Library* Scott chose the least provocative of Bage's novels,[4] and G. Barnett Smith suggested that the 'philosophy' of all of them could safely be considered apart from their value as entertainment.[5] But it was Bage's aim to make serious views an essential part of the novel and its entertainment, and his novels were interesting to the other English Jacobin novelists precisely because their political and philosophical themes could not be considered apart from their characters and plots. If Bage's works lack the 'unity of design' which Holcroft and Godwin considered the distinguishing feature of the novel, they still have a kind of unity of their own, a thematic unity, and before attempting to define this unity it is necessary to consider the historical and intellectual milieu which gave Bage his themes.

Little is known about Bage himself, apart from the excellent

---

[1] *Ballantyne's Novelist's Library*, ed. Walter Scott (Edinburgh, 1824), vol. ix, pp. xxv–vi. [2] *The Popular Novel in England 1770–1800*, p. 193.
[3] *Before Jane Austen* (London, 1966), p. 274.
[4] *Mount Henneth* (1781), *Barham Downs* (1784), and *James Wallace* (1788).
[5] *Dictionary of National Biography*, s.v. Robert Bage.

memoir by Catherine Hutton, daughter of Bage's great friend William Hutton, which Scott inserted in his Preface. Bage was the son of a paper-maker at Darley, near Derby, and his mother died soon after his birth. He was educated at a 'common school' in Derby and gave early evidence of considerable intellectual ability. He learned his father's trade and at twenty-three married a young woman very much like one of the heroines in his novels, possessed of 'beauty, good sense, good temper, and money'.[1]

The great friends of Bage's youth were William Hutton, historian of Derby, and John Whitehurst, a Derby watch-maker and author of miscellaneous technical works. Hutton was also a publisher and bought almost the whole of the paper production of the mill which Bage owned at Tamworth, and it was to Hutton that Bage frequently complained about the Scylla and Charybdis of his existence, the rapacious excisemen on the one hand, and the continual demands of his workmen for higher pay on the other.[2] Like manufacturers ever since, Bage found himself squeezed between government and labour. He seems to have been able to face both with a certain degree of humour.

In religious matters Bage was a materialist.[3] There is ample evidence in his novels that he sympathized with the Dissenters, although Scott was probably incorrect in assuming that he had had a Quaker upbringing.[4] As William Hutton put it, Bage was 'barely a Christian, yet one of the best'.[5] To everyone, including his servants and domestic animals, but excluding perhaps those excisemen, he showed the greatest benevolence.[6]

Although far from the world of literary London, Bage was at the centre of the literary-scientific world of Birmingham and Derby. He did, however, feel himself deprived of a library suitable for more serious literary tasks. 'He believes he should not have written novels, but for want of books to assist him in any other literary undertaking.'[7] And yet Godwin, who had met the cream

---

[1] *Ballantyne's Novelist's Library*, vol. ix, p. xvii. The Memoir comprises pp. xvii–xxv of the Preface.

[2] Letters from Bage to Hutton, 1782–1801, in the Local Studies Library, Birmingham Public Library. [3] Kegan Paul, i. 263.

[4] *Ballantyne's Novelist's Library*, vol. ix, p. xxvi. Cf. John H. Sutherland, 'Bage's Supposed Quaker Upbringing', *Notes and Queries*, cxcviii (Jan. 1953), 32–3.

[5] *Monthly Magazine*, xii (Jan. 1802), 479. William Hutton's Memoir of Bage.

[6] *Ballantyne's Novelist's Library*, vol. ix, p. xxiv.

[7] Letter from William Godwin to Mary Wollstonecraft, 15 June 1797, in Kegan Paul, i. 263.

of London's intellectual and literary society, paid high tribute to the qualities of Bage's mind and conversation: 'When we met him, I had taken no breakfast; and though we had set off from Burton that morning at six, and I spent the whole morning in riding and walking, I felt no inconvenience on waiting for food till our dinner time at two, I was so much interested with Mr. Bage's conversation.'[1] In fact, it is possible to argue that Bage was in touch with a wider spectrum of eighteenth-century thought than Godwin himself. 'Trade, which is thought to corrupt the mind, made no such impression upon his', wrote William Hutton.[2] As the owner of a paper-mill and member of the Derby Philosophical Society Bage was the friend of scientists and entrepreneurs who were creating a revolution in industry that was to equal in importance the revolution in late eighteenth-century politics. An interest in theoretical science was combined with practical application of new knowledge to manufacturing techniques, and the initiative in scientific study was moving away from the established institutions—the Royal Society and its allies the Universities of Oxford and Cambridge—to the centres of provincial manufacture and *their* allies, the Dissenting Academies. 'The important role of the Dissenting Academies in introducing more liberal, scientific and utilitarian studies into English education is well known, and Warrington provided one of the most illustrious examples.'[3]

Science, religious Dissent, and political reform met in the person of one of Warrington's most celebrated members, Joseph Priestley. Priestley also belonged to the best of the new philosophical societies, the Lunar Society of Birmingham.[4] But there were others at Norwich, Northampton, Exeter, Bristol, Bath, Plymouth, Derby, Manchester, Newcastle, and many other places.[5] The Derby Philosophical Society of which Bage was a member did not have quite the diversity of the Lunar Society, but it was an interesting group nevertheless, and included Erasmus Darwin and his son Robert, Josiah Wedgwood and his inventor cousin

[1] Kegan Paul, i. 263.
[2] *Monthly Magazine*, xii. 478.
[3] A. E. Musson and Eric Robinson, *Science and Technology in the Industrial Revolution* (Manchester, 1969), pp. 31, 36–7, 90.
[4] Described in full in Robert Schofield, *The Lunar Society of Birmingham* (Oxford, 1963).
[5] Musson and Robinson, p. 89.

Ralph, William Strutt, eldest son of Jedediah Strutt and inheritor of much of his father's mechanical genius, William Duesbury the great Derby china manufacturer, three mayors of Derby, and Sir Brooke Boothby,[1] formerly considered a 'pretty gentleman du premier ordre',[2] but subsequently a member of the Lichfield circle, intimate of Rousseau, and critic of Burke during the 1790s.

The Derby Society met to discuss scientific matters and perform experiments, and they possessed a fine library which contained *The Wealth of Nations*, Howard on Prisons, and Paley's *Moral and Political Principles*, in addition to books on travel, politics, economics, and science.[3] The members clearly did not restrict themselves to discussing scientific matters. But in the 1780s, when the society began, it was still possible for men of goodwill to agree to disagree. When some members of the Society sent a message of sympathy to Priestley after the Birmingham Riots, a split resulted when other members felt that the Society was overstepping its role by engaging in controversial politics.[4] The Derby Philosophical Society was not the only group to be so divided in the 1790s.

Nevertheless, through his association with these men Bage had contact with the most liberal thought of the late eighteenth century, as well as with the intellectual life of France and London. Occasionally the rather eccentric scientific interests of these friends appear in Bage's novels, especially in *James Wallace*, written about the time the Society came into existence and published in 1788. When Bage describes the attempts of Paracelsus Holman's father to use electricity to increase the fertility of his land,[5] he was perhaps mocking the experiments of an associate of the Society (though not actually a member), Abraham Bennet, F.R.S., who published *New Experiments on Electricity* at Derby only a year after the appearance of *James Wallace*.

The scientific interests of the Society's members do not play much part in Bage's novels, however. Much more important was the Society's role in bringing together men of many interests, some of whom were Dissenters and many of whom could be

---

[1] Musson and Robinson, p. 193.
[2] *D.N.B.*, s.v. Sir Brooke Boothby.
[3] Musson and Robinson, pp. 196, 194.
[4] Musson and Robinson, p. 197.
[5] *James Wallace*, in *Ballantyne's Novelist's Library*, ix. 390.

expected to have a stake in the movement for political and social reform. In one letter written very early in the Society's life the founder, Erasmus Darwin, referred to it as a kind of Freemasonry.[1] But the Freemasons, along with debating clubs, benefit societies, and probably the scientific societies as well, were regarded by the forces of conservative reaction in the 1790s as hotbeds of Jacobinism, or at least as potential centres for political dissent. In *Proofs of a Conspiracy* (1797) John Robison, Professor of Natural Philosophy at the University of Edinburgh, had claimed to show that there was an international conspiracy, 'carried on in the secret meetings of Free Masons, Illuminati, and Reading Societies', to subvert liberty and monarchy, and had cited Priestley as an open advocate of 'the detestable doctrines of Illuminatism'.[2]

The Birmingham rioters had already carried this view into practical effect in July 1791, and carefully destroyed Priestley's library and scientific apparatus, while shouting 'No Philosophers— Church and King forever'.[3] A co-sufferer in those riots was Bage's friend, William Hutton, who discovered in the midst of his flight from the mob that the mere mention of Bage's name was sufficient to procure him instant credit.[4] When Hutton, along with others, tried to recover damages from the Government, Bage was one of his witnesses in court,[5] facing the same George Hardinge who was later to take such a violent dislike to Mrs. Inchbald's friends Holcroft and Godwin, and to her Jacobin satire *Nature and Art*. But Bage himself, although a man of retired habits, found the political temperature too hot. It is not surprising that critics have found a more bitter tone in the novel Bage wrote after these sad events, *Hermsprong; or, Man As He Is Not* (1796). Godwin too depicted the Riots, as late as 1799, in his second major novel, *St. Leon.*

Living far from the English Jacobin circles of London, Bage was nevertheless in the forefront of most liberal ideas and activities in the late eighteenth century, and managed to write novels which pleased the critics, influenced the most celebrated of

[1] Musson and Robinson, p. 191.
[2] Op. cit. (Edinburgh, 1797), pp. 481–2.
[3] Schofield, *The Lunar Society of Birmingham*, p. 360.
[4] *Monthly Magazine*, xii. 479.
[5] Note to a copy of letters from Bage to Hutton regarding the Riots and the trials, evidently by Hutton's daughter Catherine. Hutton Beale Collection 29A–B, in the Local Studies Library, Birmingham Public Library.

English Jacobin writers, and eventually won for himself the scorn
of *The Anti-Jacobin Review and Magazine*.[1]

2. BAGE AND THE TRADITION OF THE NOVEL

Bage was connected with the vanguard of innovation in science,
industry, religion, and politics, and yet the most immediately
striking fact about his fiction is its continuity with the great
eighteenth-century tradition of the novel.

There is, first of all, the seriousness without solemnity which
is found in Fielding and Smollett, but which had been lacking in
their imitators during the heyday of the 'English Popular Novel'.
In fact, so unusual was this serious moral purpose that J. M. S.
Tompkins has included Bage in her chapter on 'new life in the
novel'. Scott, who was a conservative, included Bage in *Ballantyne's Novelist's Library* not because of his Jacobinical views, but
because he both 'instructed' and amused.[2] In short, Bage fulfilled
the traditional role of the author according to neo-classical
standards of criticism—he could both teach and delight.

Bage's early reviewers were also unanimous in praising his
acceptance of the moral function of literature, for it was a barren
period for the English novel, and reviewers had little to rejoice
over. *The Monthly Review* praised Bage's first novel, *Mount Henneth*
(1781)[3] in terms which might have been used as a motto for the
English Jacobin novelists of the 1790s: 'Its sentiments are liberal
and manly, the tendency of it is perfectly moral; for its whole
design is to infuse into the heart, by the most engaging examples,
the principles of honour and truth, social love, and general
benevolence.'[4] And later the same periodical was to describe
Bage's third novel, *The Fair Syrian* (1787), as 'a performance in
which instruction and entertainment are blended in a manner that
is rarely to be found; and which, in the present state of novel
writing, we cannot too much commend'.[5]

The important point, however, is that Bage blended instruction
and entertainment, in a way seldom found since the days of
Fielding and Smollett, whereas other 'serious' novelists, including

---

[1] Op. cit. v (Feb. 1800), 152, in a review of *St. Leon*.
[2] Op. cit., p. xxxiii.
[3] Cf. *Notes and Queries*, ccx (Jan. 1965), 27, where H. R. Steeves argues for
a publication date of 1782.
[4] Op. cit., 1st Ser., lxvi (Feb. 1782), 130.
[5] Ibid. lxxvi (Apr. 1787), 329.

other English Jacobin novelists, tended to alternate the two. Bage's 'engaging examples' also managed to blend comedy with satire, for he delighted in attacking every form of social and political abuse and, as his son Charles emphasized, Bage could easily become 'indignant at the wantonness of pride and power'.[1] Yet his view of the proper objects of satire was serious and responsible; in a letter to his friend William Hutton, who had just published a 'Dissertation on Juries', Bage wrote: 'I received thy pamphlet; and am not certain whether I have not read it with more pleasure than any of thy former works. It is lively and the reasoning just. Only remember it is sometimes against the institution itself of Juries and County courts that you have directed your satire— which I think ought to be confined to the Abuse of them.'[2]

But if Bage was serious, he was not grave or severe, as the other English Jacobin novelists often were. His comic satire did not have the animus of the early Augustans or the French Enlightenment satirists, but was more in line with the 'general' satire acceptable to late eighteenth-century readers and critics, and found for example in Cowper and Goldsmith. Only in his last novel, *Hermsprong* (1796), did Bage's satire acquire the harshness found in Holcroft's *Hugh Trevor* (1794–7) and Mrs. Inchbald's *Nature and Art* (1796), a harshness derived from Swift and La Rochefoucauld, La Bruyère and Voltaire. But in spite of his evident admiration for the French opponents of *l'infâme*, there was something peculiarly English about Bage, especially in his early works. It was from these that Scott, who was a great student of eighteenth-century literature, chose the selection for the *Ballantyne's Novelist's Library*, emphasizing Bage's 'rich and truly English vein of humour'.[3] Holcroft too, with his interest in the idea of ruling passions, was in the line of humour which began to take over from the line of wit sometime around the middle of the century,[4] and, like Bage, he aimed at first to reform rather than censure. A recent critic has gone so far as to describe Bage as 'an eighteenth-century Shaw' and has remarked that 'Bage's social

[1] *Ballantyne's Novelist's Library*, ix. xxv.

[2] Letter from Bage to Hutton, dated 29 Apr. 1789, in the Local Studies Library, the Birmingham Public Library. The text is slightly different in the version in Scott's memoir (p. xxi).

[3] *Ballantyne's Novelist's Library*, ix. xxvi.

[4] James Kinsley and James T. Boulton, edd., *English Satiric Poetry Dryden to Byron* (London, 1966), pp. 17–18.

satire at its best shows the bland spirit of Chaucer, not the flame of Swift'.[1] Bage's comedy is also softened by borrowings from Richardson and Rousseau, Prévost and Mackenzie (although he could also make fun of sensibility), and his novels are, like Mrs. Inchbald's *Nature and Art*, Holcroft's *Hugh Trevor* and *Bryan Perdue*, and Godwin's *Fleetwood*, a mixture of satire and sentiment. The result, occasionally, was a farrago, but it was highly original. As J. M. S. Tompkins puts it, Bage partook of 'that attitude of benignant irony, based on an equal sense of man's frailty and his worth, which was, indeed, natural to the age, though Fielding gave it its most perfect expression'.[2]

In fact, Bage's humour is almost too disarming; it conceals the real radicalism of his underlying views, a radicalism which grows as his fiction develops in maturity. Even in the 1790s he escaped the censure heaped on other novelists with similar views simply because his fiction possessed the saving grace of humour. The Fieldingesque denial of seriousness, achieved at times even by exaggerated mock-seriousness, leaves his social and political criticism in an advantageously ambiguous light. He could be read and enjoyed by everyone, whereas conservative readers and reviewers gave only grudging praise to the achievements of Godwin and Holcroft, or condemned them outright for their pernicious views. It is only when the contemporary allusions and themes in Bage's novels are examined in detail, and the humour, of necessity, left out of the analysis, that his radicalism becomes apparent.

Even the techniques employed in Bage's novels seem to suggest a fundamental lack of seriousness. In terms of structure, plot, and characterization Bage belonged to the tradition of Smollett rather than of Fielding. His characters, for example, are mostly Theophrastan 'Characters', and in his last novel he jokingly referred to the fact.[3] His plots, too, are Smollettian, being diffuse, digressive, and cumulative in incident and moral effect, gathering events and characters and conversations around certain ideas, rather than working logically to a conclusion like the plots of Holcroft and Godwin. Occasionally a reviewer even complained that Bage's story was *too* close to his model, and *The Critical Review* said of

[1] Steeves, *Before Jane Austen*, pp. 272, 289.
[2] *The Popular Novel in England*, p. 40.
[3] [Robert Bage,] *Hermsprong; or, Man As He Is Not* (London, 1796), i. 43.

James Wallace: 'The adventures of Wallace, as a footman, are so nearly copied from the Roderick Random of our incomparable Smollett, as to displease by a too close imitation . . . .'[1] In the rambling structure of his novels Bage was untypical of the English Jacobin novelists who believed in philosophical necessity and who therefore sought to avoid coincidence and show the *necessary* links in action and the development of character. Holcroft, for example, also drew on Smollett for his second major novel, *Hugh Trevor*, but tried to introduce the same high degree of logic to his plot which he had essayed in *Anna St. Ives*.

Even Bage's borrowings from the novel of sensibility are in a light-hearted vein, and pertain more to Rousseauistic pathos than to Richardsonian domestic tragedy. If Bage's novels abound in depraved aristocrats, fashionable ladies, young rakes, and the occasional bawd, they are also full of virtuous and loyal servants, chaste young women, and incredibly noble lovers. Bage never wrote a fully Richardsonian novel such as Holcroft's *Anna St. Ives*. He was not an 'enthusiast' either in his politics or his literary work. He defies labels such as Richardsonian or Smollettian, and combines influences in a way thoroughly original, if somewhat synthetic. And so once again Bage leaves the impression of lack of seriousness, of indifference to maintaining the purity of his models. In fact he is the most thoroughly 'popular' of all the English Jacobin novelists.

Yet Walter Scott, and the reviewers of the 1790s, considered Bage to be a Jacobin. In 1800 *The Anti-Jacobin Review and Magazine* classed *Man As He Is* and *Hermsprong* with vicious novels such as *Desmond*, *Nature and Art*, and 'the trash of Mrs. Robinson'.[2] Even though four of his six novels were published before 1789, Bage shared most of the assumptions and values of other English Jacobin novelists, whose important novels were almost entirely a response to the crisis of the 1790s. Like them, Bage was deeply affected by the French Revolution debate in England, and his novels only seem to have more continuity because little attention is usually paid to the plays which Holcroft and Mrs. Inchbald produced during the 1780s. Their work as a whole shows the same fairly continuous development from liberalism to radicalism which can be traced through the novels of Bage.

[1] Op. cit., 1st Ser., lxvii (Jan. 1789), 76.
[2] Op. cit. v (Feb. 1800), 152.

In fact the French Revolution itself created little that was new; it accelerated changes which were already taking place, and gave new stimulus to a debate which had been going on ever since the English Civil War and the Settlement which followed the Glorious Revolution.[1] Even in the decade before 1789 the issues of constitutional and social reform, brought to a head by the crisis of the American Revolution, had begun to be discussed with a new earnestness.[2] That this intensification of controversy should affect the novel is not surprising; it was after all a popular form of entertainment and depended more than is now realized on a certain level of topicality. Bage merely extended the range of this kind of reference in the novel.

A similar development has been traced by Dorothy George in graphic satire from the time of Hogarth to that of Gillray: 'The new look was a product of changing techniques and of a more realistic approach to politics.'[3] The 'Classic Age of English Caricature' which she describes is explicable in terms of political rather than artistic history: 'Not only do prints multiply in times of crisis, but their forcefulness varies with the intensity of convictions and passions.'[4] It was a period when, in certain quarters at least, 'intensity of convictions and passions'—enthusiasm—was once more regarded with approval.[5]

In his novels Bage satirizes 'enthusiasm' along with all sorts of other excesses; but it is entirely wrong to see him therefore as a secret conservative,[6] sympathetic to that Establishment which had been fending off Dissenters' and other enthusiasts' demands for reform ever since the Revolution Settlement. Though not a Dissenter himself,[7] Bage knew many, and his own intellectual milieu was amongst those who found that liberal studies produce liberal views. From a circle of men whose sympathies and financial interests were hurt by a war with the American colonies, Bage sent forth novels which admirably expressed their views on Old

---

[1] Cone, *The English Jacobins*, Ch. iii.

[2] See Ian R. Christie, *Wilkes, Wyvill and Reform* (London and New York, 1962), Chapters iii–vi.

[3] M. D. George, *English Political Caricature* (Oxford, 1959), i. 171.

[4] George, i. 176.

[5] Susie Tucker, *Protean Shape* (London, 1967), p. 233.

[6] P. S. Denenfeld, 'Social Criticism in the Novels of Robert Bage', unpublished Ph.D. dissertation, Northwestern University, 1957, p. 276.

[7] John H. Sutherland, 'Bage's Supposed Quaker Upbringing', *Notes and Queries*, cxcviii (Jan. 1953), 32–3.

Corruption and its immoral wars. When events and themes
changed, Bage's novels changed too, but they remained a link
between the earlier period of crisis and the period of the French
Revolution, because the same fundamental issues were at stake.
It is in 'intensity and passion' rather than in chronological prece-
dence that Bage differs from the other English Jacobin novelists.

3. 'UNITY OF DESIGN': THE THEMES OF BAGE'S FICTION

Aristocrats versus 'The Middling Sort'

It used to be a commonplace, before the rise of social history, that
the eighteenth century was an age of aristocrats, and its novelists
certainly delighted in creating hundreds of new peers, almost all
villainous. Bage's aristocrats are no exception: they are rapacious,
boorish, lustful, arrogant, and impecunious. Except for the gruff
but kindly Lord Konkeith, who is moreover a Scot, all of the
nobles from Sir Richard Stanley in *Mount Henneth* to Lord Grondale in *Hermsprong* are unfeeling tyrants, whose desire to recoup
the losses of a life of gaming and dissipation sends them, and their
sons, in search of title-hungry merchants and squires with
eligible daughters. In *Barham Downs* (1784) Lord Winterbottom,
the best of Bage's early villains, tries to avoid the necessity of
retrenchment by forcing himself on the daughter of Justice
Whitfield, a kindly man who is blinded by a coat of arms and the
desire to be called grandfather by a peer.

Scott, naturally enough, disagreed with Bage's picture of the
higher ranks of society, but for rather peculiar reasons of his own:
'Men of rank, in the present day, are too indifferent, and too
indolent, to indulge any of the stormy passions, and irregular, but
vehement desires, which create the petty tyrant, and perhaps
formerly animated the feudal oppressor.'[1] He was probably re-
acting against literary conventions himself in this remark, and
thinking of the exaggerated ennui of the 'silver fork' novels of
the early nineteenth century, but as far as novel readers were
concerned it was always the convention and not reality which
mattered. Such readers wanted to applaud the characters whom
Bage depicted as the natural enemies of his depraved aristocrats,
the merchants and wealthy farmers, or at least their less work-

---

[1] *Ballantyne's Novelist's Library*, ix. xxviii.

soiled and more handsome sons. Such characters, with their
suspicion of the vices of the city and the town, contempt for
fashion, and respect for the middle-class domestic virtues, were
the front line of what can only be described as the class-war.[1]
When Lord Winterbottom is called out by young Henry Osmond,
a former merchant, though a genteel one, he merely retorts, 'You
cannot call yourself a gentleman, when you reflect upon your
past-gone occupation.'[2] Significantly, Winterbottom is also a member of the Government, and thus associated with Lord North's
administration, which had been attacked by the independent
members and country interest in Parliament for its wasteful
expenditure and disastrous policy of war with France. In fact
Winterbottom's name may even be a sly reference to North.

If so, Bage's linking of a stock novel character with real and
pressing political issues was not unique. During the heyday of
'Wilkes and Liberty' Charles Johnstone had dressed contemporary
events in a very thin disguise of fiction in *Chrysal, or The Adventures
of a Guinea* (1760-5) and *The Reverie; or, A Flight to the Paradise of
Fools* (1762). Nor was Bage the only author in the 1780s to associate the frivolity of the nobility with the decline of empire. In
1783 Cowper addressed the country's aristocratic rulers:

> There is a public mischief in your mirth;
> It plagues your country. Folly such as your's,
> Grac'd with a sword, and worthier of a fan,
> Has made, what enemies could ne'er have done,
> Our arch of empire, stedfast but for you,
> A mutilated structure, soon to fall.[3]

Bage's friends were merchants and industrialists, and they were
being hurt by a war waged, so it seemed, solely by the aristocratic
oligarchy who held the reins of power by means of extensive
political corruption. It is but natural, then, for Lord Winterbottom and Henry Osmond to be enemies. But Bage also satirized
the *nouveaux arrivés* who, once wealth had procured the coronet,
sought to shed all trace of the origin of that wealth. In *Hermsprong*

---

[1] Cf. Frank Henley, the hero of *Anna St. Ives*, whose father is the steward of
Sir Arthur St. Ives, father of the heroine.
[2] [Robert Bage,] *Barham Downs* (London, 1784), i. 199.
[3] William Cowper, *The Task*, i, lines 769-74, in *Poetical Works*, ed. H. S. Milford,
4th edn., with corrections and additions by Norma Russell (London, 1967).

Sir Philip Chestrum seeks to impress Miss Campinet with his
partly ancient lineage:

'My family, Miss Campinet, is very great and noble by my mother's
side. She was a Raioule, a great name in English history. I have some
thoughts of changing my name to it, by act of parliament; for Chestrum
is but an odd sort of name. Beside, my father was in trade once, and his
title a new one; so people looking more at his side than my mother's,
I don't get so much respect on account of my family as is my due.
Should not you like Raioule better than Chestrum, Miss Campinet?'
(ii. 141.)

The fact that Sir Philip is deformed physically to match his mental
and moral smallness is perhaps an indication of a more Swiftean
element in Bage's satire in this last of his novels.

   In an earlier novel such as *The Fair Syrian* (1787) his satire on
the vanity of high birth retains a more humane warmth. The comic
French aristocrat St. Claur protests, when his tyrannical mother
finds a rich *bourgeoise* for him, that

Madame Prévigny was nothing more than the widow of a *Fermier-
General*; of no blood; no alliance; nothing to support her in the *grand
monde*, but a million or two of livres—yet did this mother of mine, the
Marchioness de St. Claur, Prince of Grex, with an *et cetera* half as long
as a Spanish title, condescend to court her acquaintance, and to propose
the head of the house of St. Claur as a husband for *Mademoiselle*, born
and educated at the foot of the Pyrenees, and newly arrived at Paris.[1]

The object of attack in both these examples is the same, and the
technique is similar: Bage merely lets the characters talk, and as
snobs usually do, they condemn themselves. The character of
St. Claur, however, is a reminder that Bage's aristocrats, although
they usually have English names, are in fact borrowing a French
attitude in their contempt for the lower orders. Bage must have
known that, in the north of England especially, the high-born
were as actively engaged and interested in commerce and industry
as his own self-made friends. The truth is that Bage's villainous
lords are drawn mostly from satire and novels rather than from
real life.

   It is also true that Bage probably wished to satirize the tendency
of the English nobility to ape the fashions and attitudes of their
European cousins. He was also expressing a real social animus

---

[1] [Robert Bage,] *The Fair Syrian* (Dublin, 1787), ii. 46.

which, however, remained latent until some crisis—the American and French Revolutions—heightened social tensions. As to the real state of 'the middling sort' even Scott agreed with Bage that the golden mean in society offered most opportunity for happiness and virtue:

> Those . . . who weigh equally, will be disposed to think that the state of society most favourable to virtue, will be found amongst those who neither want nor abound, who are neither sufficiently raised above the necessity of labour and industry, to be satiated by the ready gratification of every wild wish as it arises, or so much depressed below the general scale of society, as to be exasperated by struggles against indigence, or seduced by the violence of temptations which that indigence renders it difficult to resist.[1]

Bage's view was a moral and egalitarian one, that nobility was dependent on virtue, not birth. In *Barham Downs* (1784) the Quaker apothecary replies to a demand for the respect due to rank: 'Give me leave to inform thee in my turn, that I am Isaac Arnold, by birth a man, by religion a Quaker, taught to despise all titles that are not the marks of virtue; and of consequence—thine. I rank above thee' (i. 330–1). The idea is hardly original, but it is certainly radical; and Bage held it consistently before 1789.

It is significant that Arnold makes the riposte while defending Kitty Ross from the aristocrat's lust, for sex is the battlefield on which aristocratic *ton* and middle-class morality fight for supremacy. The outcome is always a foregone conclusion. Earlier in *Barham Downs* Sir Ambrose Archer[2] puts the case for middle-class sense when he tells Whitfield that the latter's daughter is not impressed by Lord Winterbottom's titles and appurtenances 'because she thinks well of certain other things, which your great folks who delight in wealth and grandeur seldom think of at all. She thinks well of piety, benevolence, humility, social affection, and the peaceable virtues of domestic life' (i. 155). Sir Ambrose is himself a reformed profligate, and knows what he is talking about.

Bage's novels characteristically proceed by such short pithy speeches as the above. Although not a dramatist like Holcroft and Mrs. Inchbald, Bage could match them for crisp and witty conversation in his novels, and he develops the larger themes of his

---

[1] *Ballantyne's Novelist's Library*, ix. xxviii.

[2] In popular novels, and English Jacobin ones, the line of demarcation between classes seems to lie between baronet and baron. Cf. Sir Vavasour Firebrace's views on the special virtues of baronets in Disraeli's *Sybil* (1845), Book ii, Ch. ii.

novels, not by plot, as the other English Jacobin novelists tried to do, but by character and short comments, conversations, or encounters. Bage's novels accumulate points by means of short scenes, dialogues, or satiric Characters, in all of which he reveals his debt to the periodical essay and the seventeenth-century Theophrastan 'Character'. Bage condenses his larger themes into smaller anecdotes, and at times even sets them apart with the heading 'Story'. The tale of Sir Howell Henneth in *Mount Henneth* (1781) is such a vignette, illustrating the themes discussed above, and showing why the ideals cherished by Annabella Whitfield in *Barham Downs* could never be fulfilled in marriage to a vicious noble. Henneth inherits a large fortune, and the rest follows naturally. 'Twelve years he spent in all the pride and pomp of equipage; gave the *ton* to the *beau monde*, and became the fashion of the fair. Half a dozen trips to Paris, two to Italy, a score or two of *volant amours*, and a couple of duels, raised him to the summit of reputation.'[1] Gaming leads to a rapid fall, and a rigid economy advocated by the faithful family steward (one of Bage's favourite types) eventually turns Sir Howell into a misanthrope, miser, and hermit—in short, a negation of the neo-Classical ideal of man.

Throughout Bage's fiction the aristocrats follow the *ton* to financial ruin, while 'the middling sorts' pursue love, morality, benevolence, and sobriety; and are rewarded with love, usually a fortune, and occasionally a title. With the poor Bage is not concerned, except as objects of charity for his heroes and heroines, and there are only two references in his novels to the effects of the Poor Law.[2] Both lords and paupers exist in Bage's novels only as foils to middle-class virtues and attitudes. His novels are not only for, they are almost exclusively about the well-to-do 'middling sort'. Although Bage loads his argument by stacking all the advantages on one side, he is not really writing tracts for the class war, because 'the middling sort' had not yet become the middle classes. Bage's novels describe a process of social change which was only just beginning in earnest, but which had been shaping up for some time;[3] and Bage's own view of social conflict is cross between that of Fielding, with his distinction between

---

[1] [Robert Bage,] *Mount Henneth*, 2nd edn. (London, 1788), i. 90.
[2] *James Wallace* (1788), p. 485; *Hermsprong* (1796), i. 6.
[3] See E. N. Williams, ' "Our Merchants are Princes": The English Middle Classes in the Eighteenth Century', *History Today*, xii (Aug. 1962), 548–57.

nobility, gentry, and commonalty,[1] and that of nineteenth-century supporters of gradual reform, who sought to detach the politically unprivileged 'middle classes' from the artisan and working men's reform movement.[2] Bage's novels display the confidence of the middle-classes, but not in terms of class consciousness, a phrase which was not even used earlier than an English translation of *Kapital* in 1887.[3] Bage in fact phrases his argument in familiar eighteenth-century moral-philosophical terms rather than social or economic ones, and his characters belong to the world of Fielding and Smollett, rather than that of Disraeli, Kingsley, and Mrs. Gaskell; and Bage's moral-philosophical terms are those of Gibbon and Hume, Swift and Voltaire.

'Fashion, leader of a chatt'ring train'

The evidence of this moral-philosophical inheritance is seen in the issues over which his middle-class heroes and upper-class villains disagree, and to a large extent the plots of Bage's novels, such as they are, involve the middle-class protagonists in temptation by the corruptions of the aristocratic world. Sensible heroines, like Annabella Whitfield in *Barham Downs* and Julia Foston in *Mount Henneth*, detest the city and its courts, crowds, fops, masquerades, gamesters, and titled debauchees. Lady Bembridge, on the other hand, once the simple Emilia Amington, has married a title and become a leader of the *ton*. She advises her brother Sir John to forget his dislike and moral disapproval of the frivolous and fashionable lord her husband:

you would have him harangue the house upon the dignity and integrity of past times; and oppose the court; and make protests: Waste the midnight lamp in projects for his country's good; banish luxury, taste, and fashion; build churches, or endow an hospital; and restore the reign of miracles and mince-pyes. Dear Brother, banish these whims; come amongst us, and enjoy your five senses. Do as other people do. Above all, lend my lord this *6000l.* (*The Fair Syrian*, i. 146–7.)

The opposition of the stoic and the epicurean outlook here was to be developed in other Jacobin novels, notably Holcroft's *Anna St. Ives*; but in Bage's novel it is clearly a comment, similar to the lines of Cowper quoted earlier, on the supposed connection between aristocratic frivolity and the loss of an American empire.

---

[1] Asa Briggs, 'Middle-class Consciousness in English Politics, 1780–1846', *Past and Present*, ix (Apr. 1956), 66.   [2] Briggs, p. 70.   [3] Ibid., p. 67.

Fashion becomes politically significant because it is the means by which the aristocracy defend their exclusiveness. The more expensive the fashion, the more effective it is likely to be in shutting out the *canaille* (even the use of French is part of the process). Sir Antony Havelley the fop in *James Wallace*, for example, prefers a good tailor to liberty and good laws (p. 435). Again and again Bage emphasizes one of the favourite ideas of Augustan England, that luxury breeds decadence, and marks the approaching end of a civilisation.[1] The relation of luxury to politics becomes obvious, for with inexorable logic, political corruption becomes the necessary means of supporting the extravagant projects dictated by fashion.

Moreover, fashion corrupts the whole of society, not just those who indulge in it, and the novels are studded with vignettes which portray humbler versions of Sir Howell Henneth, ruined by fashion and their wives' vanity. The most interesting example, for the light it throws on other Bagean themes, is also in *Mount Henneth* (ii. 63).[2] Hugh Griffiths is a prosperous shoemaker who is ruined by his family's desire to ape a higher level of society: their ambition, by an inexorable chain of cause and effect, produces the need for improvements in the house and furnishings, better apparel and equipage—all leading to less shoemaking, poorer quality work, bankruptcy, and arrest for debt. What is interesting is the form Sir James Foston's benevolence takes when he decides to intervene: he allows only enough to restore Griffiths to his original humble status. It is a *prudent* kindness. One recalls Bage's assertion that he was compelled to take up his pen in order to pay for his daughters' new gowns, and the droll Scot Dr. Gordon probably speaks for Bage when he denies that *all* such domestic disasters as that suffered by the Griffiths family are due to the rage for fashion: 'No, I am not so unreasonable; nine in ten only' (*Mount Henneth*, ii. 76-7).

The Use of Riches

Since fashion diverts money from virtuous to selfish uses it is related to another theme familiar in the moral literature of the earlier half of the eighteenth century, the idea of the use of riches.

[1] Cf. James W. Johnson, *The Formation of English Neo-Classical Thought* (Princeton, New Jersey, 1967), pp. 48-9.
[2] The account is placed under the title '*Story of* HUGH GRIFFITHS'.

The example of Sir James Foston's prudential benevolence is not followed in the later novels. Bage was susceptible enough to the influence of the novel of sentiment to make most of his heroes prodigal in this respect. James Wallace spends his wedding-day, not in enjoying the society of his bride, but in clearing the sponging-houses of Liverpool of debtors (p. 506).

However, to a man in Bage's position, closer to the life of the land than the London Jacobins, another aspect of the use of riches would be of wider relevance. As Cowper wrote:

> Improvement too, the idol of the age,
> Is fed with many a victim [*The Task*, iii, lines 764–5].

There are several 'improving' lords of the manor in Bage's novels, and the activities of Squire Garford in *Man As He Is* may have suggested those of Sir Arthur St. Ives in Holcroft's *Anna St. Ives*. Squire Garford is soon forced to live abroad because of these extravagant projects at home, as one of his workmen relates:

> 'Squire Garford married before he came of age, a very pretty young lady from Londonwards. Neither house nor ground was like what it is now; for the ground would have done you good to look at, it was in such condition; but the house was old. Now the ground's old and the house new. Then you see a mort of obelisks they call 'em, and temples up and down; and six hundred acres of prime land as crow e'er flew over, was turned into pleasure ground.'[1]

In the same novel, in which fashion is more than an occasional theme, there is another character who may have been taken up by Holcroft in his portrayal of the difficulties of Sir Arthur St. Ives, Mr. Haubert, a man with architectural projects, like Gray's Lord Holland, but who is ruined and eventually becomes a debtor to his steward.

Bage makes many of his points by means of parallel or contrasting characters—a technique which received its fullest flourish from Mrs. Inchbald in *Nature and Art* (1796)—and against the examples of poor stewardship he sets a sufficient number of counter-examples. Particular acts of benevolence are so numerous in the novels as to have made the Poor Law superfluous had they been carried out in reality. In his emphasis on good stewardship Bage was not only remembering Pope's Man of Ross and attacking aristocratic wastefulness, he was also promoting a tenet of

---

[1] [Robert Bage,] *Man As He Is* (London, 1792), i. 70.

considerable importance to liberal, non-Calvinistic Dissenters, with their stress on works as well as faith. Certainly the Dissenters whom Bage knew personally were of this persuasion.

The positive contrast to the destructive 'improver' is the benevolent landlord, who realizes that concern for his tenants' welfare is both humane and profitable. In *Barham Downs*, for example, the reformed Sir George Osmond restrains his harsh steward Yates from prosecuting several tenants who are in difficulties due to the American war (ii. 188); and in *Man As He Is* the eventual reform of the temporarily wayward Sir George Paradyne is foreshadowed by his indulgence in allowing his (always honest and deserving) tenants to recover from their difficulties (iii. 10). In *Hermsprong* the hero comes to the aid of Mr. Wrigley, who is being persecuted by his former patron Lord Grondale, embodiment of every private and social vice (vol. iii, Ch. xii). Finally, there is the example of the Marquis de St. Claur, who decides to try to become that rarity, a French landlord who is as kind to his tenants as an English one would be (*The Fair Syrian*, ii. 322–3).

Such characters represent Bage's version of that ideal of eighteenth-century liberals, the independent country gentleman, and it would be wrong to see them as evidence that Bage was really a conservative in his view of society.[1] He concentrated on individual virtue, as did the other English Jacobins, and, in any case, there were very few in England in the 1790s who advocated the complete redistribution of wealth and land. The same ideal of benevolent landlordism, based on Biblical traditions of the stewardship of riches, is also found in the novels of Holcroft and Mrs. Inchbald, and even Godwin, who originally felt that charity could not be justified philosophically, came to see the importance of benevolence in the light of his revised attitudes to sympathy and the 'domestic affections'. And, like the other Jacobin novelists too, Bage showed the opposite side of the question by depicting servants giving the lead in honesty and kindness to their masters. In *Mount Henneth* the steward Smith opens Sir Richard Stanley's eyes to his tyranny in trying to force his daughter to marry money (ii. 233–4). In *The Fair Syrian* Wood points out to

[1] Philip Stanley Denenfeld, 'Social Criticism in the Novels of Robert Bage', unpublished Ph.D. dissertation, Northwestern University, 1957, p. 276. Perhaps Bage did have the writings of Bolingbroke in mind, but the ideal of the independent country gentleman was a general one, a rallying banner for opponents of Walpole and his system rather than a monopoly of the Tories.

Sir John his folly in putting too much credit in the 'World's' view of the distance between himself and the lowlier-born Miss Warren (i. 226–7). And in *Barham Downs* the loyal old steward Timothy Thistle acts as a counter to the iniquitous Yates (ii. 187–8). Bage's ideas of the relations between classes may be based on reverence for order and example, but his basic interest is still in the *moral* equality of men.

However, in the novels before *Man As He Is* much of the material which has to do with the opposing themes of fashion and the use of riches is used only in the digressions and 'stories'; the main plots usually concern some sort of lover's test, and resistance to the temptations of fashion and devotion to benevolence are only two aspects of the whole sequence of adventures. But in the two novels published in the 1790s these two themes actually become a shaping force. *Man As He Is* is still basically a 'lover's test' plot, but it is also a humorous study of the moral education of a young man of fortune. Unlike the perfect hero of Bage's previous novel, James Wallace, whom Judith Lamounde described as 'the preceptor, who taught me the proper use of fortune' (p. 453), Sir George Paradyne is literally 'man as he is', and he struggles from falsehood to *faux pas*, from folly to *folie*, through four volumes, in an effort to merit the hand of the idealized heroine. In many ways this is Bage's best novel,[1] because it is less schematic, more crowded with ideas, diversions, and minor characters than *Hermsprong*. As Mrs. Barbauld put it, '*Man as He Is* has more of a story, and more variety of character.'[2] The plot is as rambling as that of any of Bage's earlier novels, but there is more of a congruence of plot and subject. Sir George's life is in fact, as in narration, a series of digressions and temptations, until Miss Colerain saves him at the end. Many of the digressions in the other novels have an appropriate moral parallel with the main story, but only in *Man As He Is* does the variety of incident and character have a point in itself. In this novel Bage's usual anarchy of plot is both appropriate for the 'adventures' described, and more consistently related to the old central theme, which is the conflict of fashionable corruption—'worldliness' as a negative moral outlook—and the proper aim of life, to use one's

---

[1] J. M. S. Tompkins considers it Bage's best work. See *The Popular Novel in England*, p. 196.

[2] *The British Novelists*, vol. xlviii (London, 1820), p. ii.

possessions, both personal and material, for the benefit of others. The only difference between this view, posited in *Man As He Is* with humour and vivacity, and Godwin's position in *Political Justice*, posited with the utmost philosophical rigour, is that Godwin attempts to make benevolence a matter of justice and reason rather than of human sympathy.

Women

But sympathy became increasingly important in Godwin's life and philosophy, largely because of the importance of women, and the virtuous feelings associated with them, the 'domestic affections'. Bage had already anticipated Godwin, simply by relying on popular novel conventions and an idealized view of the importance of women, expressed in Cowper's lines 'Addressed to Miss —':

> And dwells there in a female heart,
> By bounteous heav'n design'd
> The choicest raptures to impart,
> To feel the most refin'd. (lines 1–4.)

Bage's plots are wholly conventional in that they lead eventually to a marriage as the reward of virtue. For middle-class readers the conjugal rites sealed the moral and material progress of hero and heroine, and reconciled the conflict of love with whatever value had been set up in opposition to it in the rest of the novel. However, one of the ways in which Bage's novels were original was in the portrayal of that essential element in these love-plots, the women. Bage's son Charles asserted that his father 'seems, almost always, to have been fonder of the company of ladies than of men'.[1] In several novels Bage directly addresses his 'fair readers', and is not above a few winks and nods over the conventions expected in a product of the Minerva Press.[2] Nevertheless, he took women seriously, and seems, like the other English Jacobins, to have believed strongly in the equality of women. The characters of women, however unrealistically presented, are the main turning-points of his plots.

However Bage was also like the other English Jacobin novelists

---

[1] *Ballantyne's Novelist's Library*, ix. xxv.

[2] Perhaps it is ironical that Bage's most Jacobinical novels, *Man As He Is* and *Hermsprong*, actually received the Minerva Press imprint. The previous novel, *James Wallace*, bore the imprint of William Lane. See E. A. Osborne, 'A Preliminary Survey for a Bibliography of the Novels of Robert Bage', *Book Handbook*, no. 1 (1947), 30–6.

in that his heroines are not usually impressive or even successful creations. The fact that the same woman will bring out the worst in one man and the best in another has nothing to do with her individual character. Love is a moral litmus paper in Bage's novels, and women are merely part of the test apparatus. However much he preferred the company of women, and consciously wrote for them, he seems to have been incapable of making any of his female characters, apart from the secondary ones, as interesting and vivacious as an Elizabeth Inchbald or a Mary Wollstonecraft.

Bage's love plots are conventional and briefly dealt with. There is full-blown romantic love between heroes and heroines, obstructed by fashionable follies or parental pride and tyranny. The themes tend to radiate out from these simple plot lines, rather than being bound up with them. On the other hand there is the full-blown lust and avarice which the rakes and aristocrats feel towards the same objects which attract the James Wallaces and Henry Osmonds. Initially the sensual lords have the upper hand, because they enjoy the temporary alliance of parental pride; and the pursuit of lust and money allows Bage to indulge in a few Richardsonian elements, with abductions, waiting coaches, and secluded mansions. But eventually the conspiracy of arranged marriage, that cardinal iniquity of women's romantic fiction ever since *Clarissa*, is overthrown, not by rebellion, but by stoic endurance and virtuous candour, the traditional recourse recommended to women.

However, as is often the case, it is Bage's variations which give new life to the old conventions. The most important of his revisions of the schemes of the popular novel has to do with the 'ruined' woman.[1] Bage includes scenes of seduction or near seduction which have that undertone of prurience which Fielding exposed in *Shamela*. At the same time Bage shows an awareness of sexual realities that is far more frank and sophisticated than anything to be found in any of the other Jacobin novelists, and Scott confessed to having cleaned up the three novels which he chose for the *Novelist's Library*.[2]

[1] There was, of course, the great example of Rousseau's Julie, but Bage's treatment is humorous rather than sentimental.

[2] *Ballantyne's Novelist's Library*, ix. xxx. Crouch asserts however, 'There are no important expurgations in any one of the novels.' W. C. A. Crouch, 'The Novels of Robert Bage', unpublished Ph.D. dissertation, Princeton University, 1937, p. 272.

The most complete example of the 'ruined' woman is in the story of Kitty Ross in *Barham Downs*. She is seduced as a young innocent by the young and equally indiscreet Corrane. After various narrow escapes the couple finally succumb to common frailty: 'Kitty unable to resist the flood of tumultuous sensations, gave herself up to be plundered without resistance; his honour's penitence and virtue were lost in the conflict; and the scene was— Ruin' (i. 73). Ruin of course only for Kitty. Yet she recovers from the slip, with the aid of the kindly Quaker apothecary Arnold. She earns her right to reclaim the title of virtuous woman (she conveniently miscarries while on her way to continue her liaison), and although Corrane later returns to claim her as his mistress by some sort of natural right, she escapes at the last moment from a fate worse than death, maintains her life of virtue, inherits Arnold's fortune, and marries her lawyer Mr. Wyman.

Other young ladies, with no disinterested patron and less determination, fare worse. As Sir George Osmond observes on the fate of Molly Patterson, who was seduced by his steward Yates, 'The custom of society, punishes woman too much for this offence, and man too little' (*Barham Downs*, ii. 189). In the middle of the story of Honoria Warren's escape from the perilous state of slavery in the Levant there is a nice contrast, both to the prevailing social attitude and to the suppressed eroticism of Honoria's situation, in the story of a Georgian slave girl who looks back on her previous eleven masters with a certain amount of affection (*The Fair Syrian*, ii. 68–70); but then she at least need not exhibit the delicacy expected of a European woman.

So while Bage criticizes the literary and social convention of the ruined woman, he still avails himself of the tension caused by the possibility that a woman might be ruined. The outstanding example is the story of Camitha Melton in *Mount Henneth*. An American maiden of fiery independence she had been captured in a sea-battle and sent to Mrs. P—'s fashionable brothel. Bage had a fairly liberal view of prostitution as a necessary social evil, and one of the novel's 'good' characters, Henry Cheslyn, tells the old bawd, 'You are a useful woman, in your way, Mrs. P—, I own; populous cities, for ought [sic] I know, might be worse without you; but certainly you should only beat up for volunteers; and not be allowed to *press* into the service' (i. 97). Like Honoria Warren, Miss Melton escapes with her virtue intact, but not before Bage has derived a useful amount of titillation from her plight. Were it not for the saving grace of his humour such hypocrisy might be seen as the kind of thing which gave the Minerva Press a bad name. It is fitting therefore that the most lively of Bage's heroines in peril, Miss Fluart, appeared in his most Jacobin novel, and one which also appeared in the lists of the Minerva Press, *Hermsprong; or, Man As He Is Not.*

Sensibility and Benevolence

Bage exploits conventional sensibility in his novels in the same way he exploits the convention of female 'ruin'. Judith Lamounde tells her correspondent Miss Edwards that one day, whilst reading a novel, James Wallace burst in upon her with the exclamation 'O madame! . . . whilst you are weeping the fictitious distresses of a Catharine, did you but know what real calamities are around you!' (p. 427.) Judith suffers at first from an excess of sensibility and it is none other than her footman, James Wallace, who, with his naïvely practical view of the world's ills, eventually teaches her 'the proper use of fortune' (p. 453). So that eventually a charming degree of sensibility is reconciled with a healthy recognition of the real world's ills and enjoyments.

At the end of the novel Judith Lamounde marries her former footman, and another aspect of the sentimental romance or stage comedy, the conflict of love and duty, is developed and reconciled. Some of the examples already cited in this chapter will indicate that Bage felt that duty and love had to be merited before they were received. In opposing love and duty Bage does not accept the normal plot conventions entirely at face value however; although as usual he retains enough of the convention, like that of the 'ruined' woman, to keep his stories moving. This opposition of two values, which he accepts when convenient, but rejects in theory and occasionally uses as the butt of humour, is similar to Bage's use of another feature of eighteenth-century fiction, the opposition of prudence and benevolence, sense and sensibility.

One of Bage's many inset 'stories' will illustrate this point. In *Mount Henneth* Bage uses another of his favourite devices, contrasting characters, in the 'Story' of two Athenian maids whose father is killed in a battle which also deprives the state of some territory on which the family wealth depends. Both ladies are of marriageable age, but the elder sister feels that there is now nothing left for their inheritance but sorrow. 'I give up my portion,' says the younger and trips away to find a husband (ii. 226). She marries, and lives happily, while her sister pines away for young Alcandor, who has suddenly lost interest in the impoverished maid. She dies, while the younger sister lives to enjoy the family prosperity that results from the recovery of their land.

The story has a point in itself, but it also marks the difference of outlook between Laura Stanley, who tells it, and Julia Foston. In many ways they are lineal descendants of Anna Howe and Clarissa. In *The Fair Syrian* there is a similar contrast between the resilient Amelia Clare and the hypersensitive Honoria Warren, and in *Barham Downs* between Annabella Whitfield and her sister Peggy. The contrast between the outspoken Maria Fluart and the retiring Caroline Campinet in *Hermsprong* is even more schematic, and the line of development can also be traced through Holcroft's heroine and her correspondent in *Anna St. Ives*. Bage criticizes oversensibility, then, by the economical means of contrasting characters, a device obviously developed from *Clarissa*. Yet he also makes most of his leading ladies into just the type of saintly symbol which he mocks through their witty and satirical friends. It is only the secondary characters which Bage tempers with Jacobinical rebelliousness, and he nowhere portrays a major female character similar to Mrs. Inchbald's Miss Milner, unless it is in the Miss Fluart of *Hermsprong*, who was created, perhaps significantly, after Mrs. Inchbald published the vicissitudes of her independent heroine.

It remains true that in his treatment of sensibility, as in his treatment of the 'ruined' woman, Bage manages to eat his cake and have it. The same ambiguity is found in his examples of a subject close allied to sensibility, namely benevolence.

Villains and villainesses always have an eye for the main chance, while the heroes are characterized by the sort of imprudent benevolence displayed by James Wallace on his wedding-day. Aristocrats, of course, have no conception of benevolence; Lord Grondale and Dr. Blick agree in condemning Hermsprong's kindness to the village struck by a severe storm:

'I suppose he has exerted himself to-day, in order to eclipse the lord of the parish.'

'I dare say your lordship is right. I saw at once his charity did not flow from Christian benevolence.'

'For my part, I have no opinion of these charitable ebullitions.'

'Your lordship is perfectly happy in your terms. Yes, ebullitions,—bubbles.'

'Indiscriminate giving is not my taste: I chuse to consider my objects' [i. 227].

Although Sir James Foston also liked to consider his objects, his motives were still disinterested. The Bage clearly liked to keep the vices all on one side: that Lord Grondale should also be the most thorough-going of the parental tyrants, and a man who has received his peerage for the delivery of his Cornish boroughs into the Government interest, are not incidental traits of his character. The opposing values of passion and prudence, love and duty, benevolence and self-interest arrange themselves along the same lines as those taken up by good or bad characters. And a liberal purse, if directed to good ends, is a sign of a liberal heart. A character's attitude to benevolence is therefore tied up with wider issues and an over-all moral pattern in Bage's novels. And so, in spite of the fact that his novels appear to be rambling structures, full of delightful irrelevancies, Bage still manages to give a unified impression by linking all his moral themes to one central issue, the nature and limitations of freedom and restraint.

Domestic and Social Tyranny

The conflict of freedom and restraint is dealt with most fully in Bage's handling of the conventional plot device of parents' obstruction of the romantic designs and views of the younger generation. Clearly, Bage could not deal with such a subject without having to consider the influence of Richardson. In his very first novel Bage depicts the struggle of poor Julia Foston against the attempts by her father and brother to force her into a marriage with the gross and canting hypocrite, Abraham Pymnel. Julia, of course, is torn between duty and revulsion, and the parallel to *Clarissa* is obvious.

Bage carried this situation right into his last novel, in showing how Lord Grondale tries to force his daughter into a similarly unsuitable match, but his approach is too much tempered with humour for it to develop into a Richardsonian study of the struggle for psychological domination. Bage simply does not allow matters, or the sense of evil, to go so far. But his choice of this by now standard romance plot, with its arranged marriages, threatened or real abductions, and other attempts to treat women as chattels, is more than just acceptance of a popular and commercially successful Richardsonian formula. Every novel has its young lady under parents' house-arrest, but the characters also sit down regularly to the type of round-table discussion typical of Bage's novels,[1] and debate the problems of filial duty and parental oppression. But this rather hackneyed issue is in itself given new impetus and wider relevance by Bage, because he treats parental oppression of romantic lovers as a domestic variety of the same tyranny that led to persecution of individuals such as Wilkes at home, and the American colonies abroad.[2]

He does this by having his characters discuss the matter in the most general terms, thereby leaving them in their particular situation, while at the same time allowing the reader to make the wider application. In this way Bage avoids the didacticism of the discussions in *Anna St. Ives* and *Hugh Trevor*. In his first novel, *Mount Henneth*, Bage already exhibits this method. James Foston tells the story of Miss Winter to Lady Stanley in order to make the latter realize that 'the effect of persecution, whether for love, or faith, is generally contrary to the design' (ii. 268). The observation conjures up a weight of historical reflection to illuminate a mere problem of love, and Sir Ambrose Archer in *Barham Downs* tries to bring Justice Whitfield to his senses by a similar kind of argument. He tells Lord Winterbottom, after Annabella has disappeared from her home-made prison, 'I mean to oppose oppression, by equity' (i. 189). Justice Whitfield's proprietorial attitude, however, is similar to that of Captain Suthall towards Miss Melton in *Mount Henneth*, when he tries to force his other, more high-spirited daughter to reveal where Annabella has fled:

'Suppose I had lost a horse, and the thief had trusted you with the place where it was concealed; you would not tell me because it would be a breach of trust?'
'My sister is not a horse, Papa; nor has she been stolen.'
'But is not she my property, Miss? Answer me that.'
'She is your *daughter*, Sir' [i. 252].

Where all these remarks tend is finally revealed in *Man As He Is*,

---

[1] J. H. Sutherland, 'Robert Bage: Novelist of Ideas', *Philological Quarterly*, xxxvi (1957), 214.
[2] Bage may also have had in mind the condition of India under Warren Hastings, an issue also dealt with by Mrs. Inchbald in her play *Such Things Are* (1787).

when one character tries to dissuade another from indulging in parental autocracy, by the reminder that 'too peremptory a tone lost us America' (i. 40).

It is significant that the parallel between domestic and public tyranny is made explicit in the first of Bage's novels of the 1790s. In *Man As He Is* Lady Mary Paradyne tries to enforce some sort of filial obedience in her son, and fails simply because he does not respect her views or feel that she is right. Lady Mary also tries to impose her will on her daughter, and succeeds, with disastrous consequences. She arranges for her tender and obedient daughter Emilia to marry Mr. Birimport, a repatriated nabob who defends Warren Hastings's actions in India (ii. 141–2), and who is himself of marked tyrannical tendencies. The association of ideas and ideals here is obvious: reason can be the only legitimate persuader, and children should have the right to invoke it against the irrational prejudices of their parents.

In *Hermsprong* the conflict of love and duty is made even more schematic. Lord Grondale is a complete monster, like Mr. Birimport associated with political corruption and tyrannical attitudes to domestic and public affairs. Caroline Campinet's intention to obey him at all costs is opposed by Miss Fluart, who controls Lord Grondale by teasing him, as Bage perhaps hoped to control oppression by his humour and satire. Miss Fluart remonstrates with Caroline over her excessive dutifulness, and the latter replies:

'In pity to me, my dear, . . . you should restrain your lively genius. Lord Grondale is my father; he may have his failings, but is it fit for a daughter to see them? In short, my dear Maria, he is my father; I say every thing in that.'

Miss Fluart, with composed gravity, answered, 'Yes, my dear—that—that sanctifies him.'

'How can you, Maria, so pervert my meaning? I refer to the duty I owe; a duty which forbids my giving him offence.'

'Very true, child,' Miss Fluart replied, with continued gravity. 'Yes, about this high transcendent duty—yes, it is all true. Pray, my dear, did you ever hear, or see in the dictionary, the word reciprocity? I assure you, the politicians make great rout about it' [ii. 11–12].

Miss Fluart is making a general point as well as a particular one, and it is the same one made in the last of Bage's novels published before the French Revolution, *James Wallace*. Paracelsus Holman tells the hero: 'There are many bad men in the world, James

Wallace; many of them are fathers. Now, according to you, they are entitled to reverence and respect from their children: But imitation follows reverence; so your pietyship is only propagating immorality by your patriarchal maxims' (p. 505). Bage's argument is the same one he used against aristocratic pride: authority will receive its due if it is worthy, and seen to be worthy. For those who reverence titles and power must be sure that homage will not be abused, whether at home or in public life.

Behind this argument is the liberal Whig view of the social contract, and the parallel between the family and the state went back, in English political writing, at least as far as Hobbes and the writers of the Commonwealth period.[1] The idea of contract was especially important to the eighteenth-century Commonwealthmen,[2] and Bage's thoroughgoing application of this principle in his fiction suggests that his intellectual roots were in some ways very close to Godwin's. It would not be stretching a point to see behind Paracelsus Holman's rejection of 'patriarchal maxims' the attack by Locke, Tyrrell, and Algernon Sydney on Filmer's paternalistic monarchism, and behind ideas such as Miss Fluart's 'reciprocity' support for the Commonwealthman's ideal of mixed and therefore stable government in the state.[3] This is not to say that Bage is offering the old plot convention of parental tyranny as a political allegory; but it is significant that his two novels written and published when Commonwealth political literature was being rifled for its contemporary relevance should both contain overt discussion of the parallels between private and public moralities.

Religion

But Bage also owed a large debt to the French Enlightenment. Through the pages of his novels breathes the same spirit that animated the *Philosophical Dictionary* and *D'Alembert's Dream*, and this is nowhere more apparent than in his treatment of religion. His condemnation of established religion is universal. Delane, the proud priest in *Barham Downs*, for example, had been a hack

---

[1] See especially Hobbes's *Leviathan*, ed. C. B. Macpherson (Harmondsworth, 1968), pp. 253 ff. (Pt. ii, Ch. 20).

[2] Caroline Robbins, *The Eighteenth-Century Commonwealthman*, p. 8.

[3] Z. S. Fink, *The Classical Republicans*, 2nd edn. (Evanston, Illinois, 1962), p. 27 n.

journalist in his younger days; and the culminating example of the churchman is, not surprisingly, in *Hermsprong*. Dr. Blick plays the sycophant to Lord Grondale the debauchee and superannuated politician, and he preaches a sermon on the Birmingham Riots which is an accurate representation of the way Dissent and sedition were associated by supporters of Church and King. The sermon, moreover, is an obvious reference to that preached by Bishop Horsley 'Before The Lords Spiritual And Temporal' on 30 January 1793, the anniversary of the 'martyrdom' of Charles I. Horsley's text had been Romans 13 : 1 : 'Let every soul be subject unto the higher powers', and it contributed greatly to the apprehension felt by all Dissenters and their friends when conservative reaction made itself manifest in the aftermath of the Birmingham Riots.

Against Blick's intolerant sermon is set Hermsprong's tolerant scepticism, an attitude which in 1796 would undoubtedly have been seen to have a political application as well. Once again events had turned one of Bage's favourite themes into a piece of provocative radicalism, for views similar to Hermsprong's had been expressed even in the earliest of Bage's novels (*Mount Henneth*, i. 174). It was established religion of any kind which Bage opposed. The Church of Scotland pastor in *James Wallace*, for example, is inevitably a man 'of great bigotry, and sma' humanity' (p. 461), and Bage also criticized the excessive religious prejudices of Roman Catholics and Jews (*Barham Downs*, ii. 351; *The Fair Syrian*, i. 171), and even on occasion mocked the enthusiasm of Dissenters. There is Arnold the virtuous Quaker apothecary, but there is also Paracelsus Holman's zany father, a Dissenter who is critical of Bage's friend Priestley (*James Wallace*, p. 398). While Mr. Holman devotes himself to ridiculous scientific projects his orthodox wife devotes herself to fashion (p. 381). There is, Bage implies, little to choose between them.

His views on established religion, like those of the English Jacobin Commonwealthmen, can no doubt be traced back to writers such as Milton. But on the subject of religion in general Bage was obviously influenced by the French *philosophes*. Quakers such as Isaac Arnold had been admired ever since Voltaire's *Philosophical Letters*,[1] and Bage must have agreed with the emphasis placed by writers such as Montesquieu on virtuous living rather than the mere outward forms of religion. In the *Persian Letters*

[1] G. R. Havens, *The Age of Ideas* (New York, 1955), p. 396.

Montesquieu had argued that all religions were good if they made men better, and Bage's friend William Hutton had taken a similar line in his pamphlet on the Birmingham Riots: 'Every species of religion tends to improve the man, otherwise it is not religion. Should a Jew cheat me, I have no right to charge it to his religion, but to his *want* of religion: he must have fallen short of its principles.'[1] Perhaps the influence of the *Persian Letters* may also be traced in the particular way in which Bage expresses his views on the subject of religion: in *Mount Henneth* it is an old Indian priest who declares that 'we are all, the universe I mean, brethren of the same faith' (i. 199), and in *The Fair Syrian* Abu Taleb is praised for being a Muslim by action rather than precept (ii. 36). These parallels with eastern religion were a commonplace of Enlightenment thought by the time Bage came to write his novels, but they may suggest at least one line of his intellectual inheritance.

There is more than just a general moral argument behind Bage's views on religion, however. Ever since the Revocation of the Edict of Nantes in 1685 religious intolerance had been institutionalized in France, and an attack on the Revocation was an attack on the established powers of the land. The case had been the same in Britain; the pressure for the removal of religious tests was linked with pressure for a wider political reform, since it came to be felt that the former could not be achieved without the latter. The subject was revived after the September Massacres of 1792, which were compared with the St. Bartholemew Massacres even by English Jacobin writers, such as Mrs. Inchbald.[2] Now the plea for tolerance became a desperate attempt to lower the temperature of controversy, lest the terrible events of September 1792 be repeated in Britain. But Bishop Horsley's sermon marked the point of no return; increasingly pleas for religious and civic toleration were seen as a veil for sedition.

Bage had not changed his ground in any way, but by the 1790s real life Dr. Blicks began to preach that legal emancipation for Dissenters was a threat to liberty and property, and Bage inevitably became associated with those who held more extreme views. It was no coincidence that when Holcroft chose the customary extract for inclusion in his review of *Man As He Is* for *The Monthly*

---

[1] [William Hutton,] *The Life of William Hutton, written by himself* (London, 1816), p. 165.

[2] In *The Massacre*, which she suppressed at the desire of Holcroft and Godwin.

Review, it should be the lively discussion on religious toleration.[1] Bage's example, and his characterization of Churchmen and Dissenters, was followed by Holcroft in *Hugh Trevor* and Mrs. Inchbald in *Nature and Art*, and the association of political and religious oppression was eventually treated by Godwin in a truly grand manner in *St. Leon* (1799). Bage, perhaps unintentionally, set a pattern for the rest of the English Jacobin novelists to follow. The liberal of 1780 was transformed by events far from his little bailiwick of Tamworth into a model for the English Jacobins, and an object of detestation to *The Anti-Jacobin Review and Magazine*.

Politics

A similar process seems to have taken place in the development of the political themes and references in Bage's novels. At least one historian has felt that the English reaction to the American Revolution, which was just approaching its conclusion in defeat for Britain when Bage first appeared in print, marks the real watershed in eighteenth-century politics.[2] The defeat at Yorktown made the fall of Lord North's ministry inevitable, and the advent of Fox to power also brought the consitutional issue of the king's influence to a head. At the same time, the threat of invasion from France had produced the Volunteer Movement in Ireland, which in turn led to greater vociferousness in Irish demands for an independent parliament. The growth of extraparliamentary associations for reform, such as the Petitioning Movement, was partly caused by disgust with the inability of opposition in the House of Commons to prevent what the country interest considered to be wasteful expenditure, or to end an unpopular war which clearly could not be won. All of these issues find their way into Bage's novels of the 1780s.

It has already been noted that Lord Winterbottom in *Barham Downs* is associated with the ministry of the day. This novel, Bage's second, abounds with political incidents and allusions, and this is only natural, for it was published in 1784, during that period which Dorothy Marshall has described as the forcing-house of late eighteenth-century English politics. Winterbottom is a complete ministerial man: 'And Opposition, poor devils, says

[1] Op. cit., 2nd Ser., x (Mar. 1793), 298.
[2] Dorothy Marshall, *Eighteenth Century England* (London, 1962), p. 448.

the Justice. Are silenced and put to flight, replies my Lord. And how should it be otherwise? For wisdom and fine parts, his Majesty's cabinet, although I have the honour to be of it, is absolutely superior to anything the universe has yet beheld' (i. 80). As a member of the Government he naturally looks askance at demands for economy made by advocates of reform, such as Edmund Burke:

Well but my Lord, says the Justice, is not it pity the King's Friends should not attend a little bit more than they do to œconomy?

National œconomy, my dear Sir, is a very childish term. How can it have escaped the penetration of a man of your sagacity, that the more government spend, the greater circulation is produced; and the greater the circulation, the wealthier and happier, the body of the people [i. 82–3].

Justice Whitaker is appropriately concerned with public expenditure: he is a member of the country interest who abandoned Toryism only when the malt tax was raised (i. 47). We are reminded not only of Bage's running battle with the excisemen, but of the general tendency of the country and mercantile interests, with which of course Bage must have been to some extent associated, to see national politics in terms of shillings and pence.

In the character of Delane there is another object of Opposition abuse since the days of Grub Street, the Government hack, who also appears in Holcroft's *Hugh Trevor*. Lawyer Wyman tells Harry Osmond in Bage's novel: 'The bulk of authors now are become political; and seem to have adapted the precept of Doctor Swift, "Suit your words to your music well." The sweetest of music to an author, is undoubtedly the jingle of guineas; the exchequer furnishes the greatest number of concertos, and requires nothing more but to "suit your words to your music well" ' (ii. 34).

Barham Downs also contains references to other leading issues of the 1780s. There is a glance at the Volunteer Movement in Ireland, which, under the sympathetic Lord Lieutenant the Earl of Buckinghamshire, had developed from an organization of Irish Protestants to resist an invasion from Catholic France, into an unofficial militia backing the restless Irish parliament's demands for greater independence and free trade (ii. 340).

References to Irish problems are also plentiful in *The Fair Syrian*, which is partly set in Ireland, and more space is devoted to showing the plight of the unhappy islanders in the face of rapacious landlords and rack-renters such as Lord Cronnot, whose views are similar to those of the autocratic Corrane in *Barham Downs* (i. 320). In *The Fair Syrian* Honoria Warren writes to her friend Miss Clare that she cannot fear death: 'Born and educated in a country where pestilence and famine destroy a large portion of mankind, and where the hand of tyranny plays wantonly with the lives and felicities of those who remain, I have been made familiar with death' (i. 89). In the same novel the Marquis de St. Claur describes the lively debates in an Irish coffee-house: 'Three topics of dispute were distinguishable. Whether the Irish ought to insist upon the English parliament renouncing all right of legislature over them, or be content with renouncing it themselves? Whether the scheme of the Fencibles was or was not insidious? And whether it was possible to entertain a doubt of Miss Warren's guilt?' (i. 124). This amounts to a potted version of the main controversies in Ireland since the achievement of independence for the Irish parliament in January 1783; and only one of the issues mentioned belongs to the fiction of Bage's novel. In November 1783 the Convention of Volunteers met in Dublin, a meeting which was attended by Richard Lovell Edgeworth, who was a member, along with others of Bage's friends, of the Lunar Society of Birmingham.[1] No doubt Edgeworth's reactions to this period of turmoil found their way back to Bage in some form or another. Bage may also have received information from another source, a Mr. Archdale, who was a fellow member of the Derby Philosophical Society, and whom Erasmus Darwin described as one 'who is going to make speeches in the Irish parlament [sic]'.[2]

Irish demands for independence had been accelerated by events in America. As Sir George Osmond tells the comic Irish Captain O'Donnell—who incidentally is forced into French and hence anti-British service because under the Test Act Catholics could not hold the King's commission—'your country is going to recover her lost rights; America restores them to her' (*Barham Downs*, ii. 290). In fact the American war and the example of American independence figure more in these early novels than does the Irish question. In *Mount Henneth* John Cheslyn's fable of Carthage and her colonies is an obvious allegory for the revolt of

---

[1] Musson and Robinson, p. 163.   [2] Ibid., p. 193.

the American colonies (i. 58). There are even American characters
in the book, in the persons of Mr. Melton and his daughter
Camitha. *The Fair Syrian* begins in America, where St. Claur is
captured by John Amington after some comic skirmishes in the
American countryside. As he often does, Bage sets his views aside
in a section which is only superficially integrated with the plot.
St. Claur describes his encounter with the prosperous American
farmer whose wife he had tried in vain to seduce, and who elabo-
rates on some of the paradoxes of the war:

'Thou knowest the Americans are struggling for liberty. Thy King,
and the King of Spain, who dote upon it so, that they keep it all to
themselves, and tell their people it is not for common wear, help us
forward in the obtaining it with all their might; and the King of
England, who lives but to extend and secure this blessing to all his
subjects, is labouring as lustily to deprive us of it. . . .
    '. . . Let them give their own people that liberty they endeavour to
procure us, and they will be as high in my esteem, almost as William
Penn' [i. 28–9].[1]

Such political sermons are frequently set aside in this way; but
just as the minor moral themes in Bage's novels are related to the
wider issue of freedom and restraint, so the particular political
issues which are discussed are also related to the moral themes.
The prime example is in *Barham Downs*. Annabella Whitaker
expresses her distaste for London life by a fable of the search of
Fashion for its mother, Folly. The search leads from a Masquerade
ball through the offices of the secretaries of state, the Guildhall,
and the House of Commons, where the whole story turns into
a denunciation of the American war. The conclusion is as liberal
as it could be: folly produces fashion which can be supported only
by the fortunes to be acquired through political corruption and
the fat pickings available in war-time. It is a conclusion that can
be drawn from all of Bage's novels. He casts his satire in a genial
mode it is true—he does not lash folly, he laughs at it; but behind
the romance and the comedy is a consistent and liberal view of the
ills of the time. If Bage says little about the remedy for these ills,
apart from the unexceptionable advocacy of high standards of
personal virtue, he at least manages to cover the widest range of
abuses and corruptions, which clearly must be removed before

---

[1] The American farmer is obviously a Quaker.

men can live happily together, free from *l'infâme*, and therefore free to express the best of human nature.

4. THE DEVELOPMENT OF BAGE'S FICTION

It is obvious that there is a great deal of contemporary politics in all of Bage's novels, not just in those written in the 1790s; and yet the first modern critic of the English Jacobin novel, Allene Gregory, has felt that *Man As He Is* and *Hermsprong* are different in kind from his earlier work: 'The sharp conflicts of ideas arising from the political crisis have at last crystallized Bage's very liberal sentiments into a genuine radicalism.'[1] *The Anti-Jacobin Review and Magazine* made a similar judgment as early as 1800;[2] such a view, however, needs some qualification.

Contemporary criticism is often a better guide to the important aspects of controversial works than that written by the historian far removed from the passions of the time; and in 1792 *The English Review* greeted the first of Bage's post-Revolutionary novels, *Man As He Is*, with the remark that, 'In this age of disquisitions, religious and political, it was not to be expected that the author of *Man as he is* would omit an opportunity of declaring his opinion.'[3] It was indeed an age of disquisitions and Bage was merely responding to the controversies of the day as he had responded to the Irish controversy, the American controversy, and all the other public issues of the 1780s. In fact the examples already chosen to illustrate the various aspects of Bage's fiction have been taken from all of his novels, and demonstrate the essential continuity of his moral and social satire. If there is any change in Bage's last two novels it is due as much to the change in the times and the normal development of Bage's talents as to any sudden change in his outlook on life.

Man As He Is, for example, was obviously conceived in the context of pre-Revolutionary problems. Bage retains his familiar easy-going air, in a Smollettian fable about the progress of a wealthy young baronet, Sir George Paradyne, towards moral independence and a virtuous bride. There are a large number of

[1] Allene Gregory, *The French Revolution and the English Novel* (New York, 1915), p. 168.
[2] Op. cit. v (Feb. 1800), 152.
[3] *The English Review*, xx (Dec. 1792), 438.

serious dialogues and round-table discussions, it is true, but these
were also to be found in Bage's earlier novels. Even the political
background of the novel is pre-Revolutionary. Bage still attacks
Old Corruption, and shows Lord Auschamp trying to buy the pen
of Lindsay for the service of the Ministry (i. 49), as Lord Winterbottom had successfully bought Delane's in *Barham Downs*, and
as Lord Idford was to buy Hugh Trevor's in Holcroft's novel of
1794. When Lord Auschamp learns that Sir George is going
abroad with Lindsay as his tutor, he expresses the hope that the
baronet will return with an enlarged affection for his native land.
When Lindsay concurs in this hope Auschamp asks him in what
he conceives the superiority of England to consist:

'In good laws, my Lord; by which personal liberty is as well secured,
and private property as well guarded, as is consistent with civil society.'

'These blessings, says Lord Auschamp, we owe to the indulgent
family upon the throne; to which I suppose you will think it just to
inculcate a peculiar loyalty.'

'I hope my Lord, I have the proper sentiments of a subject to this
illustrious family; to which all loyalty will be due so long as it continues the faithful guardian and executor of our laws. As to the civil
blessings we enjoy, I humbly conceive we owe them to our own good
sense and manly exertions; nor do I know that liberty like ours ever
flowed, with design at least, from any throne on earth' [i. 29–30].

Behind Lindsay's views is of course the idea of social contract so
dear to Commonwealthmen and Jacobins, and given classic expression in that sermon by Richard Price which had set Burke
to writing his *Reflections*, and in which Price had described as one
of the 'rights' established by the Glorious Revolution, 'the right
to chuse our own governors; to cashier them for misconduct; and
to frame a government for ourselves'.[1] Even the title of Price's
sermon has an obvious connection with the conversation of
Lindsay and Lord Auschamp. And yet views of this kind can be
found in Bage's novels before 1789, and were no different from
the claims which Fox and the Whigs had been advancing for years.
It was the French Revolution and the reaction to it in Britain
which radically changed the context of such views, and made
them provocative or profoundly true, depending on which side
of the growing controversy one took.

[1] Richard Price, *A Discourse on the Love of Our Country, delivered on November 4,
1789, at the Meeting House in the Old Jewry, to the Society for Commemorating the Revolution
in Great Britain* (London, 1789), p. 34.

There are a few references to the Revolution in the novel, but Lord Auschamp is drawn on essentially the same lines as Lord Winterbottom, only his objects of fear and contempt have changed. He now fears 'democratic anarchy' rather than the boorish manners of the *canaille*, and observes that young men tend too much to 'maxims of liberty' (i. 43). He and Lady Mary are forced to recall, when contemplating some new attempt to coerce Sir George, that 'too peremptory a tone lost us America'. The novel really belongs in the context of the debate on the American rather than the French Revolution, and in fact the novel is set partly in pre-Revolutionary France. There is a whole chapter devoted to Sir George's encounter in the Tuileries Gardens with the Marquis de Lafayette and the Marquis de Lally Tollendal, and the conversation which results (iii. 110 ff.) is a comparison of French oppression with English liberty that no doubt drew on the reading of Montesquieu and other French writers which Bage had exhibited in his earlier novels.

No doubt Bage inserted some references to more recent events, but on the whole *Man As He Is* represents only a superior example of the fiction Bage had developed in the 1780s, and only on the last page of the novel does he deliver a Jacobinical parting shot as he sends his happily married couples off

to see if the nation of Francks, so merry when governed by folly, are not grown grave, since wisdom has had a share in the administration. This, I find, is partly the case; but when an English senator had said in a book . . . 'That man has no rights,'—the whole French people fell into a violent fit of laughter, which continues to this day. Some rights, at least, they said, might be allowed to man; the rights of suffering, and of paying taxes; these no courts would dispute.—But if, said they, men have no rights, they have wills at least; and Kings, Lords, and Priests, shall know it [iv. 272].[1]

When *Man As He Is* came out, in September 1792, Bage could still afford this kind of optimism and humour. Revolutionary enthusiasm in England was reaching a peak with the declaration of the French republic and the checking of the armies of the 'leagued despots' at Valmy. And not too far from Bage's Tamworth five or six thousand members of the Sheffield Constitutional Society celebrated Valmy in a great public demonstration.[2] The

---

[1] The 'English senator' referred to is Burke.
[2] Gwyn A. Williams, *Artisans and Sans-Culottes* (London, 1968), p. 58.

September Massacres were a disturbing portent, but could be attributed to reaction against foreign intervention and royalist treachery.[1] War with France and the conservative reaction in Britain still lay in the future. But events had already occurred which were to place such things as Bage's fictionalized conversation on toleration in an entirely new context by the time Holcroft came to quote it in his review of *Man As He Is*.

By the time *Hermsprong* was published in 1796 the Directory ruled France, and Pitt's policy of repression had already sent several men to Botany Bay and driven others, such as Joseph Priestley, into exile. In Ireland Richard Lovell Edgeworth found himself associated with Irish rebels by the undiscriminating prejudice of loyalists.[2] The suspension of Habeas Corpus, the Treason Trials of 1793 and 1794, and the 'Two Acts' of 1795 had stifled English Jacobinism. The experience of Wordsworth and Coleridge with 'Spy Nosy' was soon to show that Bage was not wide of the mark when he depicted Lord Grondale trying to get rid of the troublesome hero by having him taken up as a French spy (*Hermsprong*, iii. 24–5).

Bage's new novel, like Mrs. Inchbald's *Nature and Art* published in the same year, was an open and vehement attack on this organized repression. There are signs too that Bage was now taking his avocation much more seriously: *The Monthly Review* detected influences from the French philosophical as well as the English Jacobin novel, in the character of Hermsprong: 'This noble character has much originality: but its features may be traced back partly to the native openness and resources of the ingenuous *Huron* of Voltaire, and partly to the systematic sincerity and philosophic courage of *Frank Henley* in Holcroft's *Anna St. Ives*.'[3] *Nature and Art* also had its naïvely wise hero, in the character of young Henry, whose simple common sense and lack of 'civilized' preconceptions enable him to expose, as Hermsprong does, the vanities and illusions of society.

None of the Jacobin novels of the middle 1790s strives for naturalism. *Hugh Trevor*, *Nature and Art*, and *Hermsprong* are all designed to unfold the errors of 'things as they are' in a kind of satirical procession of vices. Bage's hero, for example, gets

---

[1] Williams, p. 38.
[2] Desmond Clarke, *The Ingenious Mr. Edgeworth* (London, 1965), pp. 156, 159–60.
[3] Op. cit., 2nd Ser., xxi (Sept. 1796), 21.

embroiled with the law when Lord Grondale tries to have him arrested for treason because he has read *The Rights of Man* (iii. 125), a crime of unquestionably contemporary relevance. Bage makes a distinction drawn at some point by all the English Jacobins after the Treason Trials of 1794, when he describes the plotting of Grondale and his cohorts: 'It was not of justice they talked; it was of law' (iii. 174). The remark also suggests that Bage was familiar with the most philosophical expression of English Jacobinism, Godwin's *Political Justice*.

Hermsprong is also like most of the other English Jacobin novels in that it contains surprisingly little direct reference to the French Revolution. This is partly because such reference was not only dangerous after 1793, it was increasingly embarrassing; but it was also in part because Bage and the other English Jacobin novelists expressed their views in ways acceptable to readers of the 'English popular novel' and these ways included general moral types as well as a high proportion of moral argument, but not, as yet, the attempt to depict the actual 'condition of England'. In any case the English Jacobins saw particular political and social abuses only as outward signs of the deeper moral issues.

Even so, there is a high degree of allusion and indirect reference to particular issues and personalities in the various English Jacobin novels, although this element has not unfortunately been brought out in recent annotated editions of these works. The contrast between the fat pluralist and the poor curate, for example, was a commonplace, and Bage contrasts the toadying Dr. Blick with good parson Brown and the worthy curate Mr. Woodcock. Hermsprong takes the opportunity to discuss with the narrator of the novel the state of the clergy, and emphasizes that the actions of men like Blick are abuses in the clerical office, not the rule (i. 108). This point reminds one immediately of Bage's views on his friend William Hutton's pamphlet on juries. But Blick is also clearly meant to be a caricature of Bishop Horsley—both preach sermons on the Birmingham Riots which are identical for arguments in defence of the *status quo* and intemperance against Dissenters and other advocates of reform. Other English Jacobin novelists too were quick to take up the subject of Horsley's sermon, but Bage had merely developed the contrast between religious Dissent and the established church, present in his earlier novels, into the wider context of the French Revolution debate of the 1790s. It was events themselves and not any change in Bage's outlook, which had created this new context. It was one of Bage's friends, Joseph Priestley, after all, who had been one of the chief victims of the Riots which provided the subject for Dr. Blick's sermon.

Bage's treatment of politics in *Hermsprong* is even more continuous with that found in his earlier novels. Lord Grondale is a politician of the old school—in his youth a leader of the *ton*, he caught politics like a disease. With several Cornish boroughs in his pocket he was soon bought up by the Government; he abandons political independence as Lord Idford had done in *Hugh Trevor*, and like Sir Barnard Bray in the same novel his price is a coronet. It also comes as no surprise to discover that Lord Grondale is an oppressor of the poor like Lord Bendham, another placeman portrayed in Mrs. Inchbald's *Nature and Art*. When the wife of one of his tenants refuses to submit to his foul designs, Grondale persecutes the miserable family, as Tyrrel persecuted his tenants in Godwin's *Things As They Are*. Clearly the English Jacobin novelists all had the same picture of what Holcroft was later to call 'official or pestilential rogues'.[1]

Bage also brings his treatment of the plight of women into line with the latest English Jacobin thought of the 'nineties. He depicts Grondale as the sort of domestic tyrant by now familiar in his novels, but Grondale's attempt to force his dutiful daughter into a marriage with the jumped-up and physically deformed Sir Philip Chestrum allows Bage to insert references to Mary Wollstonecraft (ii. 168) and a conversation in which Miss Fluart argues strenuously for equality of choice in marriage (iii. 94). Finally Hermsprong himself sums up this particular argument of the novel with a plea for complete equality of the sexes (iii. 230). He is a fictional hero of whom Mary Wollstonecraft would have approved—a complete Jacobin hero in fact—but his views had always been present in some form or another in Bage's novels, and in *Hermsprong* he was merely bringing his 'popular novel' material up to date.

The moral argument of Bage's novels had not, in fact, changed at all. Hermsprong makes a distinction to be found at the base of all of Bage's fiction when he declares, after having saved the life of Lord Grondale's daughter, 'As to rank,—I have been taught

[1] *Bryan Perdue* (1805), i. 15.

only to distinguish men by virtue' (i. 62). What has changed is what might be called the author's moral expectations for the future of mankind. It is true enough that *Hermsprong* has its happy ending and that virtue triumphs over villainy; but the revolutionary parting shot of *Man As He Is* is transformed into Hermsprong's vision of Pantisocracy on the banks of the 'Potowmac'. It is a vision almost identical to the description of the communal life at the end of Bage's first novel, *Mount Henneth*.

Perhaps it is too convenient to see Bage's fiction travelling full circle, but the moral of his last novel—'Give me, heaven! any life, but the life of grandeur!' (ii. 223)—belies the radical views and serious satire to be found in *Man As He Is*, and in most of *Hermsprong* itself. It is a withdrawal from commitment to contemporary issues which is also found in *Nature and Art* (1796) and, even more significantly, in the increasing Romanticism of Godwin's *St. Leon* (1799). By 1796 it was obvious that English Jacobinism had been defeated, and Bage was only following in fiction the path which friends such as Priestley had already followed in fact. The regions of the 'Potowmac' was where Priestley and many others had already gone.

Bage's last two novels seem to be more radical than their predecessors only because the crisis of the 1790s made men speak out more plainly than before. By 1800 Bage's novels, in spite of their most un-Jacobinical humour, could be classed by *The Anti-Jacobin Review and Magazine* along with 'the trash of Mrs. Robinson' and Mrs. Inchbald's *Nature and Art*. On the whole, however, Bage escaped from the opprobrium heaped on the other English Jacobin novelists, partly due to his humour, but partly no doubt because he was harmlessly removed from the centre of political passions in London. And yet Bage's views, as expressed in his novels ever since 1781, were very little different from those of the most outspoken London radicals. *Hermsprong* in particular had a sharper edge to its satire, and although *Man As He Is* had its influence on Holcroft, it was really *Hermsprong*, the least 'typical' of Bage's novels, which made Godwin, in the summer of 1797, so anxious to meet this obscure Midlands paper-manufacturer.[1] *Man As He Is*, with its Smollettian vigour, appealed to Holcroft; *Hermsprong*, with its greater severity and closeness to the French

[1] The meeting is described in Godwin's letter to Mary Wollstonecraft, Kegan Paul, i. 262-3.

philosophical novel, appealed to Godwin; but neither novel was essentially different from the kind of fiction which Bage had been producing since 1781. As the public issues changed, so too did Bage's incorporation of those issues into his novels. As the more philosophical of the English Jacobins might have put it, following the argument of *Political Justice*, circumstances made character, both in life and in fiction.

It is somewhat of a paradox, then, that Bage was so uninterested in that issue of fundamental importance to the other English Jacobin novelists, the causal relation between circumstances and character. Except to a very small degree in *Hermsprong*, he was only interested to show how a character, already formed, managed the issues that were always at stake in the conflict between coercion and free will, social requirements and the necessities of individual choice and independence. It was, basically, an interest in the eighteenth-century debate on ethics, but it was also, in its way, as much a 'Protestant' or Dissenting interest as anything to be found in the more serious novels of William Godwin. Moreover, Bage's humour and his ability to draw eccentric characters have obscured the fact that he has his own kind of seriousness, and that his novels have their own kind of unity. The view of G. B. Smith has been the dominant one:

As novels they may not interest strongly by their plot, but there is a distinct originality about them. They were chiefly intended to inculcate certain political and philosophical opinions . . . . Considered altogether apart from their moral and social bearings, the novels of Bage display an unquestionable power in drawing and developing character, while their style is always entertaining and frequently incisive.[1]

By now it should be clear that their 'moral and social bearings' cannot be separated from their ability to entertain. It is true that in theme, structure, and characterization Bage's fiction is often highly conventional; he relied, after all, on the great tradition of the eighteenth-century English novel, as did all of the English Jacobin novelists—it is one sign of their high seriousness. But for Bage the conventions took on new life when invested with his systematic moral purpose; and so the unity of his novels is not that of a syllogism which demonstrates the causal relationship between circumstances and moral character, as in the novels of Holcroft and Godwin, but that of a certain moral 'atmosphere'.

[1] *D.N.B.*, s.v. Robert Bage.

He works not in a straight line, but by parallels and digressions which all, eventually, contribute to the 'political and philosophical' view of man which he wished to 'inculcate'.

And in a way Bage's characters are the plots. Ideas and incidents, debates and controversies, adhere to individuals rather than to any concatenation of events which works out a meaning in itself. It is in this way that Bage can make ideas and politics both serious and amusing. The machinery of character and plot is united with the social and moral criticism in a way that is to be found in all of Bage's novels. He came from a part of the country where eccentric and extraordinary individuals were creating a revolution in industry and society; it is not surprising that the characters in his novels should reflect his own circumstances.

The themes of Bage's novels are all the same, the interest in political issues remains the same. Only the particular issues, and the technical skill, change and develop. In turning to the popular novel at the advanced age of fifty-two, Bage tried to correct a situation which one of his own characters described in *James Wallace*:

My uncle remembers well . . . when no young people of a decent appearance were regarded, unless they could speak upon the publications in vogue—novels then were not—and even make moral sentiments in a tolerable manner.

But then it must be owned, there was sometimes a horrible clash of opinion in very good company, especially when religion or politics were the subject; the two grand sources of disputation. By degrees it became the fashion never to introduce those spoilers of peace; and hence we are said to have now a most gentleman-like religion, never offensive by exuberance of zeal, and a most accomodating public spirit, perfectly acquiescent in every measure of every minister. In short, the good English people, with some exceptions, choose rather to be ignorant and polite, than learned and contentious [p. 492].

Robert Bage, the paper-maker from Elford, was one of the exceptions, and there were soon to be many more. He made it seem right that novels should be concerned with the social and political problems of the day. It was a suggestion which other English Jacobin writers were not to miss.

CHAPTER II

ELIZABETH INCHBALD

I. A SIMPLE STORY

'The Living Pressure of a Human Passion'

If Bage showed that novels could use 'a horrible clash of opinion' for more than mere topical decoration, Mrs. Inchbald and the other women novelists of the 1790s demonstrated that novels could use personal experiences to give a greater intensity—a personal animus—to the treatment of public issues. For all his humour and vivacity and seriousness Bage investigated moral issues rather than individual psychology. But from the very beginning of the revolutionary decade of the 1790s the English Jacobins had, in *A Simple Story*, a model of psychological self-examination on which they could pattern their own studies of the influence of society and its institutions on the development of individual character. By providing such a model, Mrs. Inchbald was establishing the other pole, as it were, to the humorous satire of Bage, and between the two the English Jacobin novel tended to oscillate during the rest of the decade.

In treating of the influence of education, upbringing, and social position on the character of her heroine in *A Simple Story* Mrs. Inchbald not only helped to shape this element of the English Jacobins' contribution to the nineteenth-century novel, but she influenced other novelists, such as Maria Edgeworth, who were also interested in the relationship between society and the individual, but who were not Jacobins. Moreover, she made her influence felt by working in a vein of much interest to the English Jacobin as well as nineteenth-century novelists—the nature of woman's experience, and her role in society—and by working in that vein so well she induced admiring imitation, for the tracing of influences of this kind must take account of art as well as ideology.

Her first and only important biographer wrote of Mrs. Inchbald

that she 'was all heart'.[1] Certainly both her life and her novels
have usually been considered in the context of '*le roman féminin*',[2]
and so well did she depict the range of female sensibility in *A
Simple Story* that she escaped from the animosity aroused by other
English Jacobin novelists and became, in the later years of the
decade, the natural interpreter of Kotzebue for English theatre
audiences. Although *The Anti-Jacobin Review and Magazine* described her in 1800 as '*the scavenger of democracy*',[3] her adaptation of
Lovers' Vows was a subject of controversy in Jane Austen's *Mansfield Park* (1814) because of the impropriety of its social *mores*
rather than the Jacobinism of its political views.

Like most women novelists, Mrs. Inchbald did not really fuse
her personal experience with her politics, and it was the polemical
Nature and Art (1796) rather than the autobiographical *A Simple
Story* (1791) which evoked the wrath of *The Anti-Jacobin Review*.
Mrs. Inchbald's first novel is better described as 'pre-Jacobin',
and yet it was this novel which had the most profound influence
on the other English Jacobin novelists. As an intelligent woman of
wide social experience she was aware of the falsities of language
and gesture to be found in the usual novel of female life, and
of the misleading exaggerations of character which critics were
unanimous in condemning. She avoided the excessive and rebellious sensibility of the heroines of Mary Wollstonecraft, Helen
Maria Williams, and Mary Hays, but she also avoided the unliving
and uninteresting virtue portrayed in non-Jacobin novels. The
novel then had a status not unlike that of Hollywood films today.
A month after her own lively contribution to Prince Hoare's
journal *The Artist*, in which she set forth her views on novel
writing,[4] the placeman-turned-laureate, Henry James Pye, expressed concern over the trend towards greater realism, of which
A Simple Story had formed such an important part: 'The Romance
held up an example, which set exact imitation at defiance; but the
Novel presents scenes that we seem all likely to be engaged in,
and by drawing not so much exaggerated as deceptive pictures of
actions and manners, they have in many cases a pernicious influence on morals, especially in the female mind.'[5] Pye did not, it

---

[1] James Boaden, *Memoirs of Mrs. Inchbald* (London, 1833), ii. 237.
[2] Philippe Séjourné, *Aspects généraux du roman féminin en Angleterre de 1740 à 1800*
(Aix-en-Provence, 1966), *passim*. [3] Op. cit. v (Feb. 1800), 152.
[4] *The Artist*, vol. i, no. 14 (June 13, 1807), 9–19.
[5] *The Artist*, vol. i, no. 18 (July 11, 1807), 10.

seems, have Mrs. Inchbald in mind when he made his criticisms, but there is no question that the example which she set in *A Simple Story* induced other women writers to go several steps further.

At least part of the influence of *A Simple Story* on Holcroft and Godwin must be ascribed to the fact that they knew the author well and knew that the heroine of the novel, Miss Milner, was really a self-portrait. Alexandra Kollontai has remarked that 'most of the novels and short stories that have been written by women are autobiographical',[1] and it is no surprise to discover that during the 1780s, when she was working over the novel which was to become the first half—the first two volumes—of *A Simple Story*, Mrs. Inchbald was also continuously at work on her autobiography. But she was a conscious artist as well as a woman, and it is obvious that the fiction was not only drawn from real experience, but represented a judgement on that experience: 'From the knowledge she has supplied of her progress and feelings through life, the instances are abundant in which Miss Milner may be said to be fashioned out of the indiscretions with which the fair authoress's judgment reproaches her own inequality of temper, and pertinacious adherence to her self-will' (Boaden, i. 141). For, as other women novelists of the decade were to discover, it is the peculiar advantage of fiction that autobiographical judgements can be accepted in a novel as mere invention, when they would remain unacceptably direct and candid in autobiography. *A Simple Story* was more to Mrs. Inchbald than a product of her pen; it was the product of her deepest feelings about her life. The novel allowed her to be candid as she could never be in autobiography, and candour had a very special place amongst the English Jacobin virtues. As early as June 1778 John Kemble, the pattern for the young Dorriforth, had made facetious enquiries after the new work: 'Pray how far are you advanced in your novel?—what new characters have you in it—what situations? how many distressed damsels and valorous knights? how many prudes, how many coquettes? what libertines, what sentimental rogues in black and empty cut-throats in red?' (Boaden, i. 93). Mrs. Inchbald certainly dressed the incidents of real life in some of the conventional guises which Kemble's letter suggests; but the important point is that the novel was not finally published

---

[1] Alexandra Kollontai, 'The New Woman', in *The Autobiography of a Sexually Emancipated Communist Woman*, trans. Salvator Attanasio (New York, 1971) p. 73 n.

until 1791, and for over a decade its author had been able to let her imagination, tempered by reflection, play over the most important events and characters in her life, over those things which had shaped her character. It is not surprising that when she finally allowed the novel into the world it should be seen to contain an unusually detailed and consistent account of character and of feeling.

The aspect of the novel which had the most obvious influence on Holcroft in his writing of *Anna St. Ives* was precisely this detail of psychological observation. While yet a girl Mrs. Inchbald had conceived a near-disastrous passion for an actor named Richard Griffiths (Boaden, i. 9), and once she had become an actress herself she had several narrow escapes from the particular occupational hazard of women in the eighteenth-century theatre (Boaden, i. 29). For her own protection as much as anything she had married a much older man, Mr. Inchbald, when only eighteen, and the marriage had been a stormy one, mainly due to Mrs. Inchbald's tendency to attract many, and older, admirers. The young wife was, in any case, of an independent disposition. In January 1777 she met John Philip Kemble, then only twenty, who paid her daily visits, which resulted, it seems, in daily quarrels between Mrs. Inchbald and her husband; in February she began writing her novel (Boaden, i. 74–5).

When her husband died just over a year later in June 1778, she found much to reproach herself with, although Boaden discreetly suggests that her remorse was over her outbursts of fiery temper rather than the fires of passion for Kemble, or anyone else (i. 95–6). That Boaden was not entirely wide of the mark is proved, however, by the portrayal of Miss Milner's pride in *A Simple Story*:

'There shall be no longer a doubt,'—cried Miss Milner, 'I'll put him to the proof.'

'For shame, my dear! you talk inconsiderately—what do you mean by proof?'

'I mean, I will do something that any prudent man ought *not* to forgive; and yet, with that vast share of prudence he possesses, I will force him still to yield to his love.'

'But suppose you should be disappointed, and he should not yield?' said Miss Woodley.

'Then, I have only lost a man who had no regard for me.'

'He may have a great regard for you, notwithstanding.'

'But for the love I have, and do still bear my lord Elmwood, I will have something more than a *great regard* in return.'

'You have his love, I am sure.'

'But is it such as mine?—I could love *him* if he had a thousand faults.—And yet,' said she, recollecting herself, 'and yet, I believe, his being faultless, was the first cause of my passion.'[1]

Mrs. Inchbald had obviously observed herself well, and the way in which Miss Milner drives her vanity towards an excessive sensibility, a refinement of vanity, points towards Jane Austen's characterization of the same vice. At the same time it is remarkable how much Miss Milner's character resembles that of the jealous heroines of the heroic 'she-tragedies' of the late seventeenth century. Like Mary Robinson, Elizabeth Inchbald took to herself many of the characteristics of roles she had played on the stage; like Mary Wollstonecraft, she often saw herself in the lines of Lee and Rowe, Otway and Dryden.

The rather paradoxical combination of sensibility and pride was one with which Mrs. Inchbald was afflicted herself: that is why she could describe it so well. But because she had also reflected long and earnestly on her own conduct, because of her peculiar gift of candour, she also came to understand the self-deluding sophistry of injured pride. The conclusive engagement in the battle for power in love between Miss Milner and her guardian Dorriforth takes place over that classic *locus* for exposition of the theme of liberty and libertinism in fiction and drama, the masquerade.[2] Even the unimaginative Boaden could see that the incident in which Miss Milner dresses in buskins, an immodest costume for a lady, in order to personate Chastity, was based on an incident in which Mrs. Inchbald had also dressed in what was taken to be male attire (i. 140–1). As Harriette Wilson, a woman who shared Mrs. Inchbald's spirit of independence but not her unsullied reputation, was to write many years later, 'I love a masquerade; because a female can never enjoy the same liberty anywhere else.'[3]

Mrs. Inchbald too enjoyed her liberty—after the death of Inchbald her Roman Catholic friends had several times to warn her

---

[1] Elizabeth Inchbald, *A Simple Story*, ed. J. M. S. Tompkins (London, New York, and Toronto, 1967), pp. 148–9.

[2] See Jean Starobinski, *L'Invention de la liberté 1700–1789* (Geneva, 1964), p. 90.

[3] [Harriette Wilson,] *Harriette Wilson's Memoirs of Herself and Others* (London 1929), p. 588. Originally published 1825.

about her behaviour (Boaden, i. 109), and in 1780 and 1781, when her novel was probably in its early stages, frequent visits from the recently-divorced Marquis of Carmarthen gave them further cause for alarm (i. 141). Although Mrs. Inchbald did not succumb to the temptations of wealth and fashion, she indeed knew and understood the dangers with which Miss Milner flirted. But, unlike Holcroft, Mrs. Inchbald did not usually just transfer material *en bloc* from life to fiction. She develops the incident described above, for example, into an acute observation on the hollowness of vanity's self-deceptions: though Miss Milner 'perceived she was the first object of admiration in the place, yet there was one person still wanting to admire; and the remorse at having transgressed his injunctions for so trivial an entertainment, weighed upon her spirits, and added to its weariness' (*A Simple Story*, p. 161). Miss Milner learns, the hard way, that beauty, to be a benefit to its possessor, must be tempered by judgement. It is a moral which could have come from *The Spectator*.

Such moral observations, whatever their origin, are common in *A Simple Story*, but critics and biographers alike have tried to play down certain aspects of Mrs. Inchbald's seriousness and to minimize her connections with the other English Jacobins. So perceptive a critic as J. M. S. Tompkins has, in editing the novel, gone as far as to reject the considerable labour which the novelist expended in revising her text, and preferred 'the flavour of the wild berry' to 'the fruits of her attentive self-culture' (*A Simple Story*, p. xvii). This judgement is surely right, but it adds to the impression that Mrs. Inchbald was somehow a native genius who fell into the wrong hands—those of Holcroft and Godwin—and so acquired an alarming and adventitious earnestness of purpose. Like Mary Wollstonecraft, she was an ardent autodidact, and proud of her hard-won knowledge. Like many women novelists, she sought consciously to combine this knowledge with the fruits of her imagination and experience.

There is no reason, then, to suppose that Mrs. Inchbald did not have a serious moral purpose, as well as an autobiographical one, right from the beginning. She undertook a study of the craft of the novel for example, and in 1778 read *Julia Mandeville* 'as bearing on her work', as well as Melmoth's *Liberal Opinions, Julia de Roubigné, Louisa Mildmay, The Vicar of Wakefield*, and the letters of Swift. And in the same year she was being courted by the Marquis of Carmarthen, she 'studied attentively the works of Pope, diverging from his poem to the translated letters of Abelard and Eloisa' (Boaden, i. 93–4, 137). That she chose to interest herself in the most sentimental of Pope's works is revealing, but the fact remains that Mrs. Inchbald was, throughout the 1780s, assiduous in her pursuit of 'self-culture'. In fact, so far had this pursuit gone that by 1782 she was studying geography, astronomy, and natural philosophy, and Boaden had to confess that 'her mind was acquiring, not so much a Protestant, as a free or philosophical character' (i. 159).

She immersed herself in the moral and philosophical literature of the preceding age, but she reflected as well as read, and, more important, she experienced much of society and its vanities through her increasing social and theatrical success. Reflection on the literary, philosophical, and historical classics of the Augustan age was combined with reflection on the vicissitudes of her own life—the best combination for an author who intended to take up the classical responsibility of the writer, to both please and instruct.[1]

Mrs. Inchbald was both beautiful and intelligent, and she recognized the paradox of being so blessed. She was woman enough to be vain of her person, and to despair at its decline. Vanity was also the chief cause of her frequent disputes with her husband, and the other men in her life, for 'she had always a very teasing love of admiration and attention' (Boaden, i. 89). And so, in the novel as in her own experience, pain and anguish result when pride is allowed to stifle candour. There often seems to be something of La Rochefoucauld in Mrs. Inchbald's treatment of this theme, although she tempers somewhat his cynicism. She could have been recalling his observation that 'la vérité est le fondement et la raison de la perfection et de la beauté',[2] when she recorded Lady Evans's description of Dorriforth's eighteen-year-old ward:

'And she is very beautiful, that I can assure you,' replied her ladyship.

'Which I call no qualification,' said Dorriforth, rising from his seat in evident uneasiness.

---

[1] In 1783 she read Johnson carefully, in order to learn something of criticism (Boaden, i. 180).

[2] La Rochefoucauld, *Réflexions . . . et maximes morales*, ed. D. Secretan (Geneva, 1967), Maxim 626.

'But where there is nothing else,' returned Lady Evans, 'let me tell you, beauty is something.'

'Much worse than nothing, in my opinion,' returned Dorriforth [p. 9].

The Roman Catholic priest evidently knew his *Spectator* and his moral maxims as well as the women novelists of the century did. But if the first two volumes of *A Simple Story*, the novel at which Mrs. Inchbald toiled throughout the 1780s, concern themselves with the struggle of pride against sensibility in Miss Milner, then the second half of the novel, originally conceived as a separate work (Boaden, i. 264), concerns itself in large part with the struggle of Dorriforth (now Lord Elmwood) to reconcile his pride with his sensibility. It may have been this very similarity or parallelism which first gave Mrs. Inchbald the idea of joining her two novels into one.

'*A Proper Education*'

Her treatment of the conflict of pride and sensibility—essentially a woman novelist's theme—reveals a thoroughgoing moral seriousness based on a wide and intense study of the most important moral writers of the century, and also unites the two halves of Mrs. Inchbald's novel. Her treatment of the related theme of the conflict of beauty and education can be placed in a similar context. Like most women writers Mrs. Inchbald blamed the degraded condition of women on their education. The debate on female education and reading had been gathering volume and immediacy ever since *The Spectator* had devoted several essays to the subject.[1] Mere fashionable accomplishments, of the sort taught Miss Milner at her boarding school, were also attacked by Mary Wollstonecraft in *A Vindication of the Rights of Woman* (1792), by Maria Edgeworth in *Practical Education* (1798), and by Hannah More in *Strictures on the Modern System of Female Education* (1799). Maria Edgeworth was also a great admirer of *A Simple Story* and perhaps she actually had Miss Milner in mind when she wrote, in her first published work, 'The common fault of ignorant and ill-educated women is a love for dominion: this they show in every petty struggle where they are permitted to act in private life.'[2] The remark would serve admirably as an epigraph for

[1] e.g., numbers 38, 92, 96, 242, 278.
[2] Maria Edgeworth, *Letters for Literary Ladies* (London, 1795), pp. 53-4.

Mrs. Inchbald's first novel, and for more than one of Maria Edgeworth's own works.

The first two volumes of *A Simple Story* dwell on the errors of an 'ill-educated woman', but the second part of the novel restores the balance, as Mrs. Inchbald clearly intended, by showing the positive results of an academic and stoical training in Miss Milner's daughter Matilda.[1] It was the positive benefits of education which were in fact of increasing interest to various women authors amongst the English Jacobins, as they strove to raise the dignity of Woman above the merely domestic circle. And although such writers were castigated in the Anti-Jacobin reviews and novels for advocating libertinism instead of liberty, the real import of their work was in exactly the opposite direction. As Mary Wollstonecraft had written as early as 1787 in her first published work, 'Whatever tends to make a person in some measure independent of the senses, is a prop to virtue.'[2]

Although James Boaden, Mrs. Inchbald's biographer, was only the first of many to scoff at the didactic element in *A Simple Story*, he was merely attempting to obscure the real connections between her novels and those of the other English Jacobins.[3] *A Simple Story* is not just a re-working of experience, it is an attempt to relate that experience to broad moral issues; and in the growing debate on the condition of women no issue was so important or central as that of education. The last sentence of this novel, for all its portentousness, does in fact unite the histories of mother and daughter under one moral head, and places the two halves of the novel in the context of a single 'argument':

> Mr. Milner, Matilda's grandfather, had better have given his fortune to a distant branch of his family—as Matilda's father once meant to do—so he had bestowed upon his daughter

A PROPER EDUCATION [p. 338].

There is no reason to suppose that this conclusion was simply the blatant hand of Holcroft interfering with Mrs. Inchbald's native

---

[1] Mrs. Inchbald thus anticipates Mary Wollstonecraft's *Vindication of the Rights of Woman* (1792) in advocating the same education for both girls and boys.

[2] Mary Wollstonecraft, *Thoughts on the Education of Daughters* (London, 1787), pp. 26–7.

[3] In fact, the whole tendency of his *Memoirs* is to underplay any seriousness on her part, whether it is her early passion for self-improvement, her English Jacobinism or her later religiosity.

literary tact. Something of the serious bent of her mind has already been seen in the lists of her reading in the 1780s and it cannot be accidental that just before she began writing her novel she had read, in French, the *Télémaque* of Fénelon (Boaden, i. 83), source of so many of the English Jacobins', and indeed the century's, views on education.

In the novel itself there are constant reminders of Miss Milner's lack of moral self-discipline, the affair of the masquerade being only the culminating example. Without Miss Woodley as confidante or Dorriforth as Mentor and husband—the ideal combination which Mrs. Inchbald sought herself, but in vain—the heroine's fall is inevitable; and when Lord Elmwood is called away to visit his estates in the West Indies,[1] his wife is left without a guide to preserve her from the effects of her resurgent vanity and lack of intellectual resources: 'Lady Elmwood, at first only unhappy, became at last provoked; and giving way to that impatient, irritable disposition she had so seldom governed, resolved, in spite of his injunctions, to divert the melancholy hours his absence caused, by mixing in the gayest circles of London' (p. 196). When she eventually takes her former suitor, Lord Frederick, as a lover, it is out of *ennui*.

Lady Elmwood's fall is recounted at the beginning of the third volume as an event of the past, but the story of this and the last volume concerns Matilda's attempt to atone for her mother's error and regain her father's love, alienated from her by Lady Elmwood's crime. Matilda too is beautiful, but unlike her mother she has not been corrupted by the fashionable education of the day. She is raised, significantly enough, by her mother's virtuous confidante Miss Woodley, and by her father's former tutor and confessor, Sandford. From the latter, Matilda even receives the classical education which Mrs. Inchbald, fervent autodidact that she was, must have envied. Matilda's character is formed entirely outside of society, in those ideal conditions—'good company, good books, experience, and the misfortunes of others' (pp. 10–11) —which Miss Woodley had once hoped would mitigate the evil effects of Miss Milner's sojourn at boarding school. On this point *A Simple Story* anticipated the rampant Rousseauism of Mrs. Inchbald's next novel, *Nature and Art* (1796).

[1] Cf. a similar kind of incident, without such grave consequences, in Jane Austen's *Mansfield Park*, ed. John Lucas and James Kinsley, p. 28.

There is obviously an autobiographical source for the adventures of Miss Milner and Matilda. While the first half of the novel is a comment on Mrs. Inchbald's turbulent youth and undisciplined sensibility, the second half is an idealized reparation for the emotional excesses of the first. The conflict of beauty and sensibility with virtue and education becomes a structural principle as well as a moral theme, and as a result Mrs. Inchbald's fictionalization of her own experience is presented with a lack of the special pleading and hysterical incoherence that is all too frequent in the work of other women Jacobin novelists who also tried to use personal experience to animate their popular novels.

It was not until the nineteenth century that women novelists managed to use such experience with restraint, but in *A Simple Story* Mrs. Inchbald anticipated in a modest way the achievements of Maria Edgeworth, Mrs. Gaskell, the Brontës, and George Eliot. In *Felix Holt, The Radical* (1866), for example, the portrait of Miss Lingon,[1] one day to become Mrs. Transome, is remarkably similar to that of Miss Milner; and in *Daniel Deronda* the willful Gwendolen Harleth—'The Spoiled Child'—combines Miss Milner's beauty, charm, vanity, and ignorance with a great desire for power.[2]

Mrs. Inchbald never achieved the same weightiness of style or breadth of subject found in George Eliot's novels, but both authors strove to bring greater intensity and authenticity to the portrayal of woman's experience, and both stressed the importance of education in the widest sense to the formation of that experience. Not surprisingly, some of Mrs. Inchbald's achievement rubbed off onto the men who were Jacobin novelists, especially Holcroft and Godwin, when they came to describe how women *did* think and feel and act, instead of how they *ought* to. *Anna St. Ives* (1792) and *Fleetwood* (1805) in particular, show the Jacobinical uses to which others could put Mrs. Inchbald's achievement.

'A Novel in lieu of Biography'

Mrs. Inchbald also showed the other Jacobin novelists the use which could be made of personal experience. As late as 1805 she wrote to Godwin sending a work in manuscript, and asked if she should suppress it, compress it, or merely supply fictitious names

---

[1] Op. cit., Illustrated Copyright edn. (London, n.d.), i. 40 ff.
[2] Op. cit., Illustrated Copyright edn. i. 53.

for the real ones, 'and so render it a novel in lieu of biography'.[1]
She had already shown Holcroft and Godwin, in *A Simple Story*,
how fiction could be used as an outlet for the kind of disturbing
emotions which the English Jacobins, with their emphasis on
rationalism, tended to repress. Fiction could be used for confession, and even for atonement, for few of the English Jacobins
possessed Rousseau's astonishing candour, though they all admired it. For example, if Miss Milner, like Gwendolen Harleth,
represents the 'Spoiled Child', the unspoiled child in *A Simple
Story* is Matilda; but she is more than just the counter of 'Nature'
to her mother's 'Art'; she is, like Miss Milner herself, a direct
expression of some of the deepest feelings in Mrs. Inchbald's
experience.

Just as the romance of Miss Milner and Dorriforth is a parallel
to the real romance of Mrs. Inchbald and Kemble, so the desire
of Matilda to regain her father's love in the second part of the
novel is a parallel both to Miss Milner's love for her guardian and
the young Elizabeth Simpson's loss of her father. The girl who
lost her father at the age of seven (Boaden, i. 5) became the young
woman who married a man old enough to be her father, and she
in turn became the widow who was constantly becoming involved
with men who, like Holcroft and Godwin, were to her as some
kind of Mentor. The fable of Telemachus could come to have a
very personal application.

Matilda's sense of the deprivation of her father's affection is
described with an authenticity quite lacking from the other relationships in this part of the novel. She is allowed to live in Elmwood House with Miss Woodley and Sandford after her mother's
death, but only on condition that she never leave her own apart-
ments whilst Lord Elmwood is there. This taboo naturally stimu-
lates in the girl an almost morbid curiosity about everything to do
with her estranged parent: ' "How strange is this!" cried Matilda,
when Miss Woodley and she were alone, "My father within a few
rooms of me, and yet I am debarred from seeing him!—Only by
walking a few paces I might be at his feet, and perhaps receive his
blessing!" ' (p. 226). Her situation is an artificial one and seems,
like that of Caleb Williams in *Things As They Are*, to have been
devised primarily as a psychological outlet or analogue for intense

---

[1] Letter from Mrs. Inchbald to Godwin, dated 8 Mar. [1805], in the Abinger
collection.

and recurring emotions in the author herself. That this was so may be confirmed by the fact that this second part of *A Simple Story* verges at times on tear-jerking, as when Miss Woodley returns to tell Matilda of her dinner with Lord Elmwood: 'After listening with anxiety and joy to all she told, Matilda laid hold of that hand she said Lord Elmwood had held, and pressed it to her lips with love and reverence' (p. 288).

Such moments occur seldom, however, and Mrs. Inchbald reveals an astonishing penetration into deep psychological disturbance and its symptoms which had to wait over a century for fully scientific exposition. The elaborate precautions taken by Lord Elmwood to prevent accidental contact with a daughter 'contaminated' by her mother's 'crime', his warm behaviour to Miss Woodley the friend of both his wife and his child, his frequent abstraction and melancholy, all show the true direction of his thoughts, and Mrs. Inchbald need offer no explanations. Mrs. Inchbald is really at her best in depicting the struggle to suppress deep feeling, and such passages are among the best things in the second part of the novel. Lord Elmwood cannot conceal his interest when he finds Miss Woodley selecting some books from his library. 'One author he complained was too light, another too depressing, and put them on the shelves again; another was erroneous and he changed it for a better; and thus he warned her against some, and selected other authors; as the most cautious preceptor culls for his pupil, or a fond father for his darling child' (pp. 272–3). The final simile in the passage is a kind of deliberate Freudian slip: it both describes Lord Elmwood's behaviour, and draws attention to the fact that it is in fact the reverse of 'fond'. By an innocent-seeming comparison Mrs. Inchbald penetrates to the heart of Elmood's futile attempts to repress feeling.

The climax, indeed the conclusion, of volume three is an incident of a similar kind, the accidental meeting of Lord Elmwood and his daughter, which is described in terms which narrowly escape bathos, but do escape because of the author's usual sense of literary tact:

She had felt something like affright before she saw him—but her reason told her she had nothing to fear, as he was far away.—But now the appearance of a stranger whom she had never before seen; an air of authority in his looks as well as in the sound of his steps; a resemblance to the portrait she had seen of him; a start of astonishment which he gave on beholding her; but above all—her *fears* confirmed her. It was him.—She gave a scream of terror—put out her trembling hands to catch the balustrades on the stairs for support—missed them—and fell motionless into her father's arms.

He caught her, as by that impulse he would have caught any other person falling for want of aid.—Yet when he found her in his arms, he still held her there—gazed on her attentively—and once pressed her to his bosom.

At length, trying to escape the snare into which he had been led, he was going to leave her on the spot where she fell, when her eyes opened and she uttered, 'Save me.'—Her voice unmanned him.— His long-restrained tears now burst forth—and seeing her relapse into the swoon again, he cried out eagerly to recall her.—Her name did not however come to his recollection—nor any name but this—'Miss Milner—Dear Miss Milner' [pp. 273–4].

The fainting scene, stock in trade of every romance-writer and discreet substitute for the swoon of sexual ecstasy, is here given new and complex meaning. For once tears rightly 'burst' forth, for at a single stroke Mrs. Inchbald has uncovered the deep and complex psychological realities which insist on bursting the bounds of a rational and authoritarian restraint. It was just this aspect of the achievement of *A Simple Story* which was to be of use in Holcroft's *Anna St. Ives* and Godwin's *Things As They Are*.

There can be little doubt that Matilda's sad exile from her father's love is in fact a finely controlled transmutation of the author's own experience. Until the dramatic meeting on the stairs, Matilda's recollection of her father is distant indeed. 'She was just three years old when her father went abroad, and remembered something of bidding him farewell; but more of taking cherries from his hand as he pulled them from the tree to give to her' (pp. 220–1). She saw him again when she was six, and he had returned from the West Indies to find himself a cuckold. When John Simpson died and deprived his daughter Elizabeth of his paternal love forever, she was only seven, and in this fact, and in Mrs. Inchbald's life-long involvement with men much older than herself,[1] there is perhaps sufficient evidence that in the most interesting part of the second half of *A Simple Story* she was once again expressing her deepest feelings in fictional form.

Of course other women novelists, such as Mary Wollstonecraft,

---

[1] And see her interest in the romance of Abelard and Eloise (Boaden, i. 137).

Mary Hays, and Helen Maria Williams did much the same, and yet their novels are difficult to read today because they indulged freely in a kind of psychological explicitness which Mrs. Inchbald avoided entirely. Ultimately it was Mrs. Inchbald's approach to such experiences which was vindicated by the development of the novel in the nineteenth century. Maria Edgeworth was one of the first to admire *A Simple Story* prodigiously, and to put her finger on the core of the novel's achievement.

I hope you will not suspect me of the common author practice of returning praise for praise, when I tell you that I have just been reading, for the third—I believe for the fourth time—the 'Simple Story.' Its effect upon my feelings was as powerful as at the first reading; I never read *any* novel—I except *none*—I never read any novel that affected me so strongly, or that so completely possessed me with the belief in the real existence of all the people it represents. I never once recollected the author whilst I was reading it; never said or thought, *that's a fine sentiment*—or, *that is well expressed*—or *that is well invented.* I believed all to be real, and was affected as I should be by the real scenes if they had passed before my eyes : it is truly and deeply pathetic. I determined, this time of reading, to read it as a critic—or rather, as an author, to try to find out the secret of its peculiar pathos. But I quite forgot my intention in the interest Miss Milner and Dorriforth excited : but *now it is all over*, and that I can coolly exercise my judgment, I am of opinion that it is by leaving more than most other writers to the imagination, that you succeed so eminently in affecting it. By the force that is necessary to repress feeling, we judge of the intensity of the feeling; and you always contrive to give us by intelligible but simple signs the measure of this force. Writers of inferior genius waste their words in *describing* feeling; in making those who pretend to be agitated by passion describe the effects of that passion, and talk of the *rending of their hearts, &c.* A gross blunder! as gross as any Irish blunder; for the heart cannot feel, and describe its own feelings, at the same moment.

And as an example of this genius Maria Edgeworth cited a passage examined already in this chapter, and declared, 'Nothing can be finer than the scene upon the stairs, where Dorriforth meets his daughter, and cannot unclasp her hand, and when he cannot call her by any name but Miss Milner—dear Miss Milner.'[1] If practitioners of any literary art make the best critics it is because they have an eye for what is best in another author. It is indeed the finest achievement, perhaps the only *major* achievement of Mrs.

---

[1] Maria Edgeworth to Elizabeth Inchbald, 14 Jan. 1810. Boaden, ii. 152–3, 154.

Inchbald the novelist to show, 'by intelligible but simple signs', the repression and the force of powerful but natural feelings. She avoids describing too much on the one hand, and the Gothic indulgence in morbid and unnatural emotion on the other. And it is obvious that in both parts of *A Simple Story*, as well as in *Nature and Art*, Mrs. Inchbald derived her understanding of real feelings largely from her own real experience.

'Intelligible but Simple Signs'

Ultimately it was this achievement of psychological realism—an artistic achievement rather than English Jacobin ideology— which explains Mrs. Inchbald's influence on writers so different as Holcroft and Maria Edgeworth. Compared to their novels *A Simple Story* certainly had but a narrow range both of characters and setting; but the ground which it does cover is carefully worked over, and by filling a small compass with strong but measured psychological conflicts Mrs. Inchbald achieves a degree of intensity lacking from all English Jacobin novels except *Things As They Are*. If her understanding of human feelings was obtained largely from her own experience, then her manner of expressing that understanding in her fiction was due largely to her great experience, as both actress and playwright, of the theatrical conventions of expression which prevailed in her day. In a way, Mrs. Inchbald could be said to have translated the new naturalistic style of acting introduced by the Kembles, and particularly by Mrs. Inchbald's friend Sarah Siddons, into the techniques of fiction.

Like many a successful dramatist, Mrs. Inchbald had been an actress but no outstanding one. Nevertheless, in her novels she displayed a fine awareness of the importance of gesture and 'business', and gave the lie to Johnson's assertion, in his life of Otway, 'that the attention of the poet and the player have been differently employed—the one has been considering thought, and the other action; one has watched the heart, and the other contemplated the face'.[1] As Maria Edgeworth recognized it was largely through gesture or the simple telling phrase that Mrs. Inchbald's characters revealed their feelings. This aspect of the actor's art it was which made *A Simple Story* seem so original to

---

[1] *Lives of the English Poets* ed. G. Birkbeck Hill (Oxford, 1905), i. 242.

contemporary readers; as *The Critical Review* put it, 'the workings of the passions are inimitably displayed'.[1]

But *A Simple Story* is more than just a triumph of art revealing nature. In a very real sense it is a 'philosophical' novel. The strength of *A Simple Story* is in the simple accuracy of its psychological observations, an accuracy derived from both experience and study. Although the evidence already presented to show the autobiographical bases of the novel would tend to confirm Godwin's—and J. M. S. Tompkins's—view that Mrs. Inchbald's was a kind of native and natural genius, there is also a great deal in the novel to suggest that she learned how to express her insights on female experience partly by way of the enormous amount of study which she got through during the decade in which she wrote and re-wrote her novel.

Her description of states of mind and feeling is, in effect, 'philosophical' in a way which anticipates the English Jacobin novel without participating in its didactic excesses. Mrs. Inchbald is often at her best, for example, on what might be called the psychology of love. In Miss Milner we see in detail the birth, growth, and success of love, traced through all the gradations of vanity, interest, affection, love, hope, despair, and triumph, very much as it is traced by Holcroft in the heroine of *Anna St. Ives*. There is a touch of autobiographical authenticity, for example, in the description of the purity of Miss Milner's newly awakened love for Dorriforth:

Sincere love, (at least among the delicate of the female sex) is often gratified by that degree of enjoyment, or rather forbearance, which would be torture in the pursuit of any other passion—real, delicate, and restrained love, like that of Miss Milner's, was indulged in the sight of the object only; and having bounded her wishes by her hopes, the height of her happiness was limited to a conversation in which no other but themselves partook a part [p. 81].

'Restrained love' is the special subject of *A Simple Story* in both the adventures of Miss Milner and Matilda—artificial restraints imposed from without, by the fact that Dorriforth is Miss Milner's guardian, and a priest, in the one case; and by the tyrannical injunctions of Lord Elmwood in the other. But in both cases the restraints are similar to those Mrs. Inchbald must have felt when, as a married woman and an actress whose conduct was open to

[1] Op. cit., 2nd Ser., i (Feb. 1791), 208.

everyone's scrutiny, she indulged in what must have seemed to her an innocent relationship with the young Kemble, when she passed hours daily alone in his company 'without', as Boaden puts it, 'fear of her fame' (i. 81).

Nevertheless, at the bottom of this simple description of Miss Milner's earliest feelings for Dorriforth there is something which may in fact be called 'philosophical'. There is just a hint of Augustan moral sentiment in the short phrase which gives direction to the passage quoted above, the observation that Miss Milner had 'bounded her wishes by her hopes'; and the balance of wishes against hopes with the aid of unobtrusive repetition re-enacts syntactically the moral import of the phrase. And yet the whole sentence runs to almost eighty words, conveys a complex observation, and still retains that simple intelligibility which is the characteristic of Mrs. Inchbald's style.

At the same time Mrs. Inchbald relates Miss Milner's particular feeling for her guardian to more general themes in the novel. She is not content with telling a 'simple story' of love, but is continually mindful of the moral dimension of feeling. Although Miss Milner's ill-education is the ultimate cause of her downfall, for example, it also enables her to fall in love with her guardian-priest in the first place: 'had she been early taught what were the sacred functions of a Roman ecclesiastic, though all her esteem, all her admiration, had been attracted by the qualities and accomplishments of her guardian; yet education would have given such a prohibition to her love, that she had been precluded from it, as by that barrier which divides a sister from a brother' (p. 74). There is more here than just a fine observation on the psychological origins and limitations of love; the final comparison suggests a dimension of inhibition and restraint which is at the core of the novel's peculiar authenticity, and which is developed throughout both its sections. In the second part of the novel, for example, it is Rushbrook, originally rescued by Miss Milner from just the sort of exile which is inflicted on Matilda, who must endure the heavy demands of self-restraint (pp. 286–93). Not only does Mrs. Inchbald give her psychological insights a simplicity and directness suited to the 'English Popular Novel', then; she also creates a moral dimension in this particular kind of realism, and creates an over-all pattern of development within the whole novel.

Whenever she comes close to treating an aspect of Miss Milner's love which may have some autobiographical basis Mrs. Inchbald's remarks are tinged occasionally with a kind of irony that may be derived from La Rochefoucauld's well-known maxims on the power of vanity and pride in affairs of the heart. In her second novel in particular Mrs. Inchbald borrowed heavily from La Rochefoucauld's somewhat cynical view of the tender feelings, but in *A Simple Story* too the sharp edge of self-criticism seems to be attained by imitating his ironical distancing from suscepti-bility. When Mrs. Inchbald describes the ambition of Miss Milner as 'the dear-bought experiment of being beloved in spite of her faults, (a glory proud women ever aspire to)' (p. 138), she was looking at her heroine's feelings from the viewpoint of La Roche-foucauld's definition of love—'c'est une passion de régner' (Maxim 68).

The whole second volume of *A Simple Story* can be seen as an exemplification of La Rochefoucauld's definition, and the extra 'philosophical' weight which the novel gains from such elements was no doubt one source of its appeal to Holcroft and Godwin. But if some critics have made too little of this 'serious' aspect of the novel's art, neither should too much be made of it. In the last analysis it was probably Mrs. Inchbald's simple mastery of technique in the laying out of her admittedly limited moral themes which impressed her friends Holcroft and Godwin, and perhaps spurred them to turn her achievements to their own Jacobin ends.

Certainly both *Anna St. Ives* and *Things As They Are* deal to a very great extent with the restraints placed upon feeling and the individual character's desire to achieve that ideal of simple candour in personal relationships which was cherished by Dissenters and English Jacobins alike, and which was to become of great im-portance in the fiction of the next century. Candour is only the social manifestation of the philosophical demand for truth, and it is, inevitably, in conflict with pride and vanity which conceal the truth at the cost of ultimate moral disaster. This conflict is the real moral and philosophical theme of *A Simple Story*, and its technical instruments are all those penetrating details of restraint imposed on feeling for which Maria Edgeworth, herself a great master of technique, justly praised her precursor.

There is a further aspect to the appeal of *A Simple Story* to

those novelists, such as the English Jacobins and Maria Edgeworth, to whom education and the formation of character were
important subjects. *A Simple Story*, as much as *Anna St. Ives* and
the novels of Godwin, bears out one of the central tenets of the
English Jacobin philosophy, that 'the characters of men originate
in their external circumstances'.[1] The adventures of two women
in *A Simple Story* are a consistent illustration of the principle
which Godwin was to formulate as one of the basic arguments in
Political Justice, published two years after Mrs. Inchbald's novel.
Both Miss Milner and Matilda are, for all their spontaneity and
charm, shown to be the products of their 'education' in the widest
sense, the whole range of circumstances and experiences which
surround their youth. But *A Simple Story* is accurately described
as a 'pre-Jacobin' novel because the 'philosophical' basis of
character is not yet the centre of the novel's interest, but only an
organizing principle for the two love stories, and for the 'intelligible but simple signs' by which the feelings involved are
made both interesting and real. The test of the English Jacobin
novel, as of any novel, is not its philosophy but its artistic
realization of whatever 'philosophy' it chooses to promulgate. It
is this test which establishes the superiority of *A Simple Story*
to almost all other English Jacobin novels, and which sets it
above other novels of the period which attempt to describe real
rather than idealized female experience.

Several English Jacobin novelists shared the autobiographical
intensity of *A Simple Story*, and a few occasionally came up to
Mrs. Inchbald's level of psychological penetration, but most
lacked her sense of structure and simple mastery of technique.[2]
A Simple Story was being written and re-written throughout the
decade in which Mrs. Inchbald was learning her literary craft, as
a successful playwright. From this experience, not accurately described as an apprenticeship since it formed part of a separate
career which outlasted that of novelist, Mrs. Inchbald derived
the obvious benefits—a sense of structure and distribution of
material over an arc of dramatic action, a knowledge of how to
construct a scene so that its development revealed its meaning

---

[1] *Political Justice* (1796 edn.), Book i, Ch. iv.
[2] For example the novels of Mary Hays, Mary Wollstonecraft, and Helen Maria
Williams. Amongst women novelists it was non- or Anti-Jacobin writers who made
the most of Mrs. Inchbald's achievement.

simply and efficiently, and an actress's understanding of appropriate gesture and the 'business' which often renders dialogue superfluous. It was this art, whatever its source, which ultimately made whatever 'philosophy' her novel did possess persuasive to both Jacobin and Anti-Jacobin readers alike.

Dramatic Contrasts

The principle which informs all of the elements of Mrs. Inchbald's craftsmanship is the simple and economical one of contrast. It was a principle vital to sorting out the large number of characters and intricate plots of the 'sentimental comedy' of which Mrs. Inchbald and Holcroft were such apt practitioners. It was a kind of comedy admirably suited to adaptation to fiction, and it could be presented in terms of the simple moral opposites found in literature written by autodidacts (Holcroft was one too) for a popular audience, but which nevertheless allowed the writer of ability—a Mrs. Inchbald or a Jane Austen—considerable scope to cover an astonishing number of subtle moral discriminations.

Like the large theme of education and the growth of character, the moral contrasts of the novel are built up by an accretion of details rather than by the moral disquisition more characteristic of Holcroft and Godwin. A simple device for displaying such contrasts, and at the same time for introducing some humour, is to show a series of reactions to the same incident. When Sandford comes to tell the assembled ladies that Dorriforth has gone to fight a duel with Lord Frederick over a supposed insult to Miss Milner, the various reactions show the depths, or shallows, of their respective feelings:

> 'Murder!' exclaimed all the ladies.
> 'Yes,' answered he, addressing himself to Miss Fenton, 'your betrothed husband is a party concerned; he is going to be second to Mr. Dorriforth, who means this very evening to be killed by my lord Frederick, or to kill him, in addition to the blow he gave him last night.'
> Mrs. Horton exclaimed, 'If Mr. Dorriforth dies, he dies a martyr.'
> Miss Woodley cried with fervour, 'Heaven forbid!'
> Miss Fenton cried, 'Dear me!'
> While Miss Milner, without uttering one word, sunk speechless on the floor [p. 67].

This is theatrical in the best sense, mitigates a melodramatic conclusion with comedy, and presents characters in contrast with an economy worthy of Jane Austen.

The effect of this technique is more militant in *Nature and Art*, Mrs. Inchbald's thoroughly Jacobin novel, because the characterizations aimed at are limited to their functions within the satiric strategy of the novel. When young Henry arrives at his uncle's house for the first time, the feelings of the various members are also arranged so as to culminate in the only approved response:

While young Henry was walking up the stairs, the dean's wife was weighing in her mind, in what manner it would most redound to her honour to receive him; for her vanity taught her to believe that the whole inquisitive world pried into her conduct even upon every family occurrence.

Young William was wondering to himself what kind of an unpolished monster his beggarly cousin would appear; and was contemplating 'how much the poor youth would be surprised, and awed by his superiority.'

The dean felt no other sensation than an impatient desire of beholding the child.[1]

This series of reactions is noticeably less dramatic in the technical sense than the example from *A Simple Story*. The situation is explained to us, as Maria Edgeworth would say, rather than being left to the reader's imagination. The quality of the example from *Nature and Art* is closer to the satire of *Northanger Abbey* than the humour of *Pride and Prejudice*, since in Mrs. Inchbald's earlier novel, as in Jane Austen's later ones, satire is a method rather than a shaping purpose—it is absorbed into a wider frame of values in *A Simple Story*, and adapted to a narrative technique that is broader than any single device that it employs. In *Nature and Art* explanation takes the place of, or vitiates, the economy of dramatic contrast found in *A Simple Story*.

Another variety of dramatic contrast which Mrs. Inchbald exploits in *A Simple Story* is a sort of dramatic irony ideally suited to a novel which is largely about characters dwelling in ignorance of their own and each other's feelings. Such scenes are often described in terms of some kind of tableau in which the situation of the characters makes dialogue unnecessary.[2] An example has already been noticed in the encounter of Matilda and her father

---

[1] Elizabeth Inchbald, *Nature and Art* (London, 1796), i. 60–1.
[2] A technique learned perhaps from Rousseau's *La Nouvelle Héloïse*.

on the stairs in the second part of the novel, a scene picked out for special praise by Maria Edgeworth. Another example she chose for special mention concerns the attempt by Miss Milner to reconcile her guardian to his ostracized young nephew Harry Rushbrook: 'What a beautiful stroke is that of the child who exclaims, when Dorriforth lets go his hands [on discovering this child is his nephew], "*I had like to have been down*" ' (Boaden, ii. 153). No doubt there is something over-dramatic in the contrast of the child's natural expression of fear with Dorriforth's sudden repression of feeling on discovering that the child who has so delighted him is the same one he has banished from his sight forever, as the offspring of a sister who had ignored family views and married for love. But the characterization receives its justification in the second part of the novel when Dorriforth, now Lord Elmwood, banishes Matilda and nominates Rushbrook as his heir, in a much more severe and terrible denial of natural affection. The consequences of this second effort of repression we have already witnessed, in the scene upon the stair in which Elmwood's instinctive move to catch Matilda as she swoons is a direct reversal of his earlier move in suddenly releasing little Harry Rushbrook. The most important scenes in the novel are of just this kind, dramatic in the sense that the action is the meaning, but also dramatic in contrasting one character's reaction against another's. Her characters' gestures are a 'language of signs' which, like their speech, is both idiosyncratic and intelligible, and which, for once, takes seriously the sentimental convention that there are some things words cannot express.

No doubt J. M. S. Tompkins is right to suggest that this aspect of Mrs. Inchbald's art came from her experience as an actress (*A Simple Story*, p. viii), and complemented her playwright's gift for telling dialogue. But Mrs. Inchbald's technique is more than mere embellishment. If gestures tell more than speech it is because hers is a story of inner rather than outer conflict, and for such a story gesture is the most 'natural'[1] and the most telling language. Dorriforth, Miss Milner, Sandford, are all locked in a moral and psychological bastille built by reason and pride, and since words are the language of this super-ego, only gestures can elude the

---

[1] On the distinction between 'natural' and 'conventional' language see Jean Starobinski, *J.-J. Rousseau. La transparence et l'obstacle* (revised, Paris, 1971), pp. 179–80.

censorship of conscience to tell the story of the heart's imprison-ment. The novel's real dramatic contrast, the one that reveals the novel's moral meaning, is the contrast between word and deed.

A dramatic technique better suited to the purpose of *Nature and Art* is the juxtaposition of contrasting scenes. In her Jacobinical play *Next Door Neighbours* (1791), which foreshadowed many of the themes of the Jacobin novel of 1796, the first scene changes from the preparations of Sir George Spendorville for an evening of fashionable dissipation, to 'An Apartment, which denotes the Poverty of the Inhabitants', wherein Henry[1] and his sister Eleanor are heard to lament that 'the noise of carriages and link-boys at Sir George Splendorville's, next door, would keep us awake, if our sorrows did not'.[2] The same kind of transition, in reverse, is made between Chapters thirty-three and thirty-four in *Nature and Art*. After a touching description of Hannah Primrose's de-light in her illegitimate child, the following chapter opens, 'From the mean subject of oxen, sheep, and peasants, we return to per-sonages—*i.e.* persons of rank and fortune' (ii. 93).

There are contrasts of a similar kind in *A Simple Story*, but they are played down. In Rushbrook and Margrave, for example, we have one of those 'valorous knights' and one of the 'senti-mental rogues dressed in black' about which Kemble had teased Mrs. Inchbald when she was just beginning her novel.[3] In a scene in the last volume Rushbrook and Elmwood dine together in strained silence; Rushbrook loves Matilda but may not even name her, much less ask for her hand, while Elmwood has re-treated into a similar restraint because of Rushbrook's refusal to accept a match he has proposed for him, and because of Rush-brook's misguided attempt to discuss the guilt he feels as the usurper of Matilda's rightful place (pp. 289–90). The next chapter opens with an implicit contrast to this spectacle of excessive delicacy and self-restraint as the necessarily *un*restrained Margrave plans to abduct Matilda. The contrast goes unremarked by the author, and the reader is left to draw his own conclusions. If such effects are dramatic only in the widest sense, they are still a sign of the greater subtlety of technique in the earlier novel.

[1] Rushbrook's first name is also Henry, and the name is representative of simple virtue in *Nature and Art* as well.

[2] Op. cit., p. 10.

[3] Margrave is probably modelled on Sir Hargrave Pollexfen in *Sir Charles Grandison*.

Reversals and Parallels

The dramatic use of contrast in characterization and the disposition of scenes was a technique Mrs. Inchbald brought from her
theatrical experience, and, in *A Simple Story* at least, was a technique highly suited to the matter in hand. In *Nature and Art* contrast, as the form of the title suggests, becomes the essence of
the novel's satire, as the adventures of Henry and William, and
their sons of the same name, are contrasted to show the success
of vice in the world, and the failure of virtue. In the earlier novel
contrast also works as a structural principle, but in a different
way. The reversals of the second half of *A Simple Story* may have
originated in Mrs. Inchbald's decision to amalgamate two separate
novels, but the skill with which she performed the task resulted
in a multiplication rather than an amalgamation of meaning.

The obvious model for a work in two parts separated by the
age of a generation was, as J. M. S. Tompkins notes, *The Winter's
Tale*.[1] Even the title of Mrs. Inchbald's novel is somewhat similar
in import to that of Shakespeare's play. Certainly Mrs. Inchbald
was aware of the problem of effecting just the right sort of transition. She begins volume three with a rare philosophical reflection
on the transitoriness of things, but relates the observations to a
desire to inform the 'reflective reader' of the changes which have
taken place in the characters he has come to know in the first two
volumes. To give a solid basis to this transition she takes care to
establish the continuities which underlie change.

The transformation of Dorriforth the sensitive lover and
guardian into the tyrannical Lord Elmwood, for example, is
a simple and direct one: 'Lord Elmwood's love to his lady had
been extravagant—the effect of his hate was extravagant likewise'
(p. 194). By the repetition of the one word 'extravagant', a word
which may be used for either praise or blame, Mrs. Inchbald
indicates precisely the transition from the beneficent extravagance
of love to the destructive extravagance of hate. The use of a single
word indicates the even-handedness of the judgement Mrs. Inchbald applies to her characters, and at the same time seems to suggest a moral as well as an artistic logic in what might otherwise
seem like a retreat into Gothic peripeteia.

The reversal in the character of Sandford follows a pattern

[1] *The Popular Novel in England, 1770–1800*, p. 339.

very much like that of Dorriforth his master. As an enemy of Miss Milner Sandford is frank, with an undertone of self-righteousness because the first half of the novel 'belongs' to the proud Miss Milner; as the protector of Matilda Sandford is frank, with an undertone of sensibility because the second half of the novel belongs to the 'sensible' Matilda. So skilfully had Mrs. Inchbald married her two separate stories that Sandford's character, like Dorrifoth's, seems to change only within the rules of the English Jacobin view of character—one based on the rules of philosophic necessity. It may be true that the other English Jacobin novelists, and Mrs. Inchbald herself in *Nature and Art*, went on to consider the operation of necessity in a social context, and attempted to show how the nature of society determined the nature of the individual. This, apart from the rather sparse treatment of Dorriforth's training for priesthood, Mrs. Inchbald admittedly neglected to do in *A Simple Story*. But then most of the English Jacobin novelists, whatever their intentions, settled for presenting individual cases—a Coke Clifton, a Falkland, a Belmont, a St. Leon—of what they asserted, but did not *show* to be general and prevailing social conditions. In her Lord Elmwood and her Sandford Mrs. Inchbald did almost as much, and if she neglected the general assertions about society, it has probably benefited her reputation as a novelist with posterity.

Clearly Mrs. Inchbald reworked her second story carefully to accord with the material already covered in the story of Miss Milner. The result is that the dramatic technique of showing inner conflict is translated into a structure of parallels and reversals, and the neatness of construction reflects the neatness of the novel's moral argument. The death-bed of Lady Elmwood, for example, in the first chapter of volume three, is explicitly compared to that of her father in the novel's very first chapter:

At the commencement of this story, her father is described in the last moments of his life, with all his cares fixed upon her, his only child—how vain these cares! how vain every precaution that was taken for her welfare! She knows, she reflects upon this; and yet, torn by that instinctive power which a parent feels, Lady Elmwood on her dying day has no worldly thought, but that of the future happiness of *her* only child [p. 195].

Even when the parallel is not pointed out as explicitly as this, the moral is revealed by significant changes in the parallel. At the end of volume one Miss Woodley forces her young friend to leave Dorriforth and exile herself in Bath in order to prevent her extravagant passion for her guardian from revealing itself. Such a precaution is necessary because Miss Milner's improperly educated mind and heart would be incapable of concealing their true sentiments. At the beginning of volume four there is a similar exile, imposed by Lord Elmwood on his daughter, after the meeting on the stair has revealed to him the true state of his feelings. In both incidents a womanly resolve to endure the inevitable almost breaks when the coach is at the door; but unlike her mother, Matilda does not weep at leaving Elmwood House: her sensibility has been chastened by adversity and a proper education, and she can rationally hope for an eventual alteration in her father's sternness. The difference between these two parallel incidents is a sign of the difference between mother and daughter, and not just an arbitrary device of structuring.

In fact, *A Simple Story* conveys its moral by the same sort of structural technique that is found in *Nature and Art*, the first novel contrasting the characters and fates of mother and daughter; the second virtues and vices, material and moral success and failure, of two brothers and their sons. Contrasts of this kind were, of course, characteristic of didactic fiction such as *Sandford and Merton* and Hannah More's Cheap Repository. By joining two highly autobiographical tales so as to bring out similar moral contrasts, Mrs. Inchbald had, by 1791, anticipated some of the leading features of the Jacobin and Anti-Jacobin fiction of the rest of the decade.

The contrast of Miss Milner's education with that of her daughter becomes a structural principle of too great importance to be merely a late revision inspired by the influence of Holcroft and Godwin. Apart from the obvious moral conclusions to be drawn from this contrast itself, there is the undeniable fact that many of the lesser themes and morals of the novel are also linked to the difference in the characters of Miss Milner and Matilda. The villains fit into this pattern of difference, for example: Lord Frederick succeeds with Lady Elmwood because he knows how to use her vanity and *ennui* against her; while Margrave fails, or must resort to force, because Matilda has no vanity. Her education, directed by Sandford, has given her the intellectual resources that Miss Milner, for all her fashionable accomplishments, fatally

lacked. The contrast, if simple and direct, is founded on the difference of education, and therefore argues rather than states the
moral.

It is also worth remembering that Dorriforth's education forms
an important aspect of the novel's treatment of the theme. Like
Godwin, Dorriforth is rendered unfit for the nice balancing of
reason and sentiment which daily contact with frail mortals
requires, by his training for the priestly vocation. Like Godwin,
too, he conceives of justice in rational and abstract terms, and
will not temper the wind of his wrath to the shorn lamb. As he
banishes Harry Rushbrook from his presence in the first part of
the novel, simply because he is the child of a sister whose marriage
Dorriforth did not approve, so in the second part of the novel
Dorriforth, transformed into Lord Elmwood, banishes his daughter simply because she is the child of a woman—his wife—whose
sin of adultery has rendered her forever damned in his memory.
It is only poetic justice that the exile of the first part, Harry Rushbrook, replaces Matilda as Elmwood's natural heir in the second
part and then falls in love with her, rebuking Elmwood's unfeeling
justice with an excess of feeling on his own part.

The priest-like austerity of Dorriforth leads him to judge
severely, but also to deny the forgiveness which God himself
would not deny to his repentant creatures. The very education of
a priest, Mrs. Inchbald implies, renders him unfit to communicate
God's mercy to his spiritual wards. It is only a natural consequence
of Dorriforth's education, therefore, that he cannot show mercy
to those who are his natural wards. Only Miss Milner, the ward
with whom he is entrusted at the very beginning of the novel, can
penetrate his monk-like detachment from the world of real feelings and passions; but she only succeeds in breaking down the
walls of his retreat, leaving him a prey to whatever passions may
sweep over him, and not leading him to a truly secular view of
human weakness. Dorriforth, it has been claimed, is Kemble in
disguise; it is not too much to suggest that he is also an anticipa-
tion of another of Mrs. Inchbald's suitors, Godwin the philosopher of abstract justice, the lapsed Calvinist, but not yet the
lover and husband of the philosopher of the natural passions,
Mary Wollstonecraft.[1]

[1] Although he read the MS. of *A Simple Story* in 1790, Godwin did not meet Mrs.
Inchbald until 1792. She would, of course, have heard of him before that through

Whatever the mixture of real personages that went into *A Simple Story*, there can be little doubt that Mrs. Inchbald tried, by means of contrasts and parallels, to give a degree of credibility and logical consistency to her characters which was, for the popular novel of the time, quite out of the ordinary. Nor can there be any doubt that this logic and symmetry was quite impressive to Holcroft and Godwin, and that it showed them new possibilities for the use of fiction for Jacobin ends. But just as an exaggerated logic of plot and characterization leads to a slackening of interest, and even to the need for illogical and coincidental resolutions in *Anna St. Ives*, *Things As They Are*, and *Hugh Trevor*, so too the neatness of Mrs. Inchbald's construction in *A Simple Story* results in slackening of interest, and the apparent need for the Gothic novel machinery of abduction, in the second part. In volumes three and four there is no sense that anything might happen, there are no rampant passions which are interesting because of their very unpredictableness. Instead of the fire of passion there is the glow of sensibility, a substitution which Mrs. Inchbald may have yearned for in her own somewhat turbulent life. Moreover, the human interest in the second part of the novel has little to do with the felicities of parallel situations and reversals of character; it has to do with the yearning of Matilda for her father, and his ill-concealed yearning for her. The rest is fine enough, neat and careful workmanship; but the art cannot conceal that the best of the novel comes from nature. The symmetrical plan of the book, with its parallels of incident and reversals of character and situation, becomes not only an element of the book's achievement, but also, as with many of the English Jacobin novels, a sign of its limitations. There is change, but no development.

Although she had not yet written an overtly Jacobinical novel, then, Mrs. Inchbald anticipated in *A Simple Story* the difficulties which the other Jacobin novelists were yet to face. It is tempting, in view of the superiority of the pre-Jacobin *Simple Story* to the Jacobin *Nature and Art*, to see Mrs. Inchbald as a natural talent spoiled by the earnest dogmatism of her bespectacled friends Holcroft and Godwin. But an analysis of the earlier novel's structure and moral themes shows that in a very real sense *A Simple Story* is the beginning and the basis of the English Jacobin

Holcroft. It would seem that Godwin proposed to her on 16 September 1793, according to his MS. Journal.

novel. It is also a presage of the difficulties which were to afflict the Jacobin novel throughout that development. Almost all English Jacobin novels were based on a fine or original conception, and most managed to be interesting for at least half their length. But their authors had to eschew that inconsequence which was often the sole saving grace of the popular novel (it was the whole grace of Bage's early novels, for example). English Jacobin fables had to be 'arguments', since they shared a common view of the necessary chain of circumstance in art and life; but this view ran dead against the common pursuit of entertainment, which meant suspense or at least a sense of possibility. When they made their intentions plain in their fictions, as they usually did, the English Jacobin novelists killed this interest. And so they were, for a variety of reasons, put to a variety of shifts, usually coincidence or some other straining of credibility, in an attempt to stay within the bounds of popularity which had to be respected if they were to use fiction for the spread of truth. Even so, few of the Jacobin novelists succeeded in keeping alive the impetus and freshness of the original idea through the later parts of their novels. And to this pattern of failure, for all her skill, Mrs. Inchbald was no exception.

Perhaps it is just that, as with Mary Wollstonecraft, the life which provided the best elements of fiction should ultimately imitate the novel's art. One might say of the latter part of Mrs. Inchbald's life as one could say of her fiction, that restraint quelled impulse, and the girl who ran away to become an actress eventually declined into the diligent and dedicated authoress whose sensibility foundered into religious sentimentalism. Harris, her manager at Covent Garden, may have been expressing both praise and regretful criticism when he said, 'That woman, Inchbald, has solemnly devoted herself to *virtue* and a *garret*' (Boaden, i. 192).

2. NATURE AND ART

'Satire upon the Times'

When Mrs. Inchbald next appeared as a novelist in 1796, the English Jacobin novel had already run through half its course. The very title of *Nature and Art* indicates its author's change of purpose from writing a 'simple story' to mounting a 'Satire upon the Times'.[1] Mrs. Inchbald's second novel was inspired not by her personal experience as a woman, wife, and daughter, but by her experiences amongst the liberals and men of letters of London in the 1790s. It is public and intellectual experience which went into *Nature and Art* rather than the private feelings which shaped *A Simple Story*. It is in fact a kind of 'sentimental comedy' like the dramatic writings which had made Mrs. Inchbald's literary reputation and introduced her to Holcroft and Godwin in the first place.

When, in 1800, Mrs. Inchbald found herself described in *The Anti-Jacobin Review and Magazine* as 'the scavenger of democracy',[2] it was not because, in the novel published four years earlier, she had suddenly revealed a new and radically subversive streak in her writings. The social and moral satire found in the pages of *Nature and Art* was not much different from that to be found in many of her popular 'humanitarian comedies'[3] of the 1780s and '90s. Admittedly, Mrs. Inchbald had changed somewhat from the liberal dramatist of the previous decade, but by 1796 the state of official public opinion had changed much more. As early as 1787 she had displayed her own peculiar blend of satire and sentiment in a play based at once on the trial of Warren Hastings and on the work of Howard the prison reformer. Thomas Vaughan's prologue to the play set the tone:

> This play was *tragi-comically* got,
> Those sympathetic sorrows to impart
> Which harmonize the feelings of the heart . . . .

Even the title of the play, *Such Things Are*, was a harbinger of such later titles as *Man As He Is* and *Things As They Are*. In other respects, too, the play anticipates Mrs. Inchbald's 'Satire upon the Times'. Although it is set in the East Indies and shows a tyrannical Sultan terrorizing his subjects, the main satire in the play is against the flattering and subservient courtier, such as Lord Flint, a predecessor of Lord Bendham in *Nature and Art*, who is 'the slave of every great man, and the tyrant of every poor one'.[4]

The play also anticipates a favourite theme of English Jacobin

---

[1] The novel's title when first completed. See Boaden, i. 328.
[2] Op. cit. v (Feb. 1800), 152.
[3] Allardyce Nicoll, *A History of English Drama, 1660–1900*, vol. iii, *Late Eighteenth Century Drama 1750–1800* (London, 1952), p. 144.
[4] Elizabeth Inchbald, *Such Things Are* (London, 1788; produced 1787), p. 4.

novels of the next decade, the reconciling and ennobling power of love and sympathy—what the English Jacobin philosophers called philanthropy. While the rest of the characters are involved in intrigues which eventually rebound on their own heads, the hero, Haswell, attempts to spread the spirit of compassion. Where successful, he does so by example rather than precept. While visiting the prison to relieve the needs of the inmates his pocket-book is stolen by Zedan. But when Haswell offers him help and sympathy, Zedan is moved to return the wallet, expressing feelings that are completely new to him:

> *Has.*: You like me then?
> *Zed.*: (*Shakes his head and holds his heart.*) 'Tis something that I never felt before—it makes me like not only you, but all the world besides—the love of my family was confined to them alone; but this makes me feel I could love even my enemies.
> *Has.*: Oh, nature! grateful! mild! gentle! and forgiving!—worst of tyrants they who, by hard usage, drive you to be cruel! [p. 28].

The moral of the play is not far from Godwin's argument, expressed six years later in *Political Justice*, that tyranny corrupts a whole nation and spreads itself to every level of society. Haswell acts, however, not from pre-Jacobin philanthropy, but in accordance with 'The Christian Doctrine' (p. 39). Finally, the Sultan is himself revealed to be a Christian, who had impersonated a slain rebel prince years before, and found himself compelled into acts of tyranny in order to maintain his position once the rebellion had been successful. Moreover, the Sultan's love Arabella was supposed killed in the rebellion, but when Haswell reveals that she is alive and immured in the Sultan's own prison, the ruler throws away his tyrannic appearance which he had taken up partly out of disappointed love and partly for reasons of state. Thus the political allegory, typically for Mrs. Inchbald's work, is combined with a love story and love is in this sentimental comedy the liberating force which it also becomes in the later English Jacobin novels *St. Leon, Hugh Trevor* (vols. iv–vi), and *Fleetwood*.

But the play is also, as plays then often were, highly topical, and it is, like *Nature and Art*, to some extent at least a 'Satire upon the Times'. Set in the East Indies and depicting the effects of tyranny on courtiers and subjects alike, the play had obvious reference to the Warren Hastings affair, which had been simmering since the late 1770s and now boiled over. In June 1786

Burke had opened the first charge against Hastings in the House of Commons, but was defeated. Fox had succeeded in passing the second charge, rather unexpectedly. The third charge 'was entrusted to Sheridan, who brought it before the House on February 7, 1787, in a speech of nearly six hours' duration, which was universally agreed at the time to constitute the final consummation of English eloquence, and has certainly not been rivalled since'.[1] Mrs. Inchbald's play, written no doubt while the first two charges were occupying the public attention, was presented with precise timing by Harris on Saturday, February 10, 1787. Naturally enough it was a success and received the Royal Command (Boaden, i. 243).

Although topical, the play was not very original, and the solution it offers to the ills of mankind, love and humanitarianism as represented by the character of Haswell, is hardly a radical one. On the other hand, the Sultan's motives for tyranny are shown with understanding. Mrs. Inchbald was clearly more interested in sensibility than reform, a preference she did not alter even in the much more radical decade of the 1790s. The rest of her plays of the 1780s do not show the same interest in political events or topical themes. Even *The Child of Nature* (1788) had little connection with the ideas of Rousseau or Voltaire, and was remarkable only for its repetition of the January–May theme which almost amounted to an obsession in Mrs. Inchbald's life and writings.

However, in 1791, when she had already come under the influence of Holcroft, she produced another 'Satire upon the Times', a successful play entitled *Next Door Neighbours*, which foreshadowed many of the themes and situations to be found in *Nature and Art*, as even the normally unperceptive Boaden noticed:

The *interest* seems to have struck the author as capable of far greater expansion, and she accordingly remembered the filial piety and honour of Henry Wilford, ready to accept a prison to release his father, when, in 'Nature and Art,' she sends the Henry of her novel to the coast of Africa, to perish, or redeem his father. The heartless profligacy of Splendorville is remembered also in the Bishop's son, who, as a judge, passes sentence of death on the victim of his early lust; and Eleanor, however slightly, lends some few points of interest to her [i.e. Mrs. Inchbald's] Rebecca and Agnes. The *turns* of opposition in the *dialogue*,

---

[1] Christopher Hobhouse, *Fox*, 2nd edn. (London, 1947), p. 172.

appear reflected, too, in the *conversations* which so abound in the romance; and we could easily show their almost immediate proximity
to each other [i. 294].

In the next year, shocked, as were many English Jacobins, by the
September Massacres and the increasing bitterness of party an-
tagonisms in France, she produced a historical tragedy based on
the St. Bartholemew Massacres, entitled *The Massacre*. The play
was refused by Harris, for obvious reasons, and Holcroft and
Godwin also persuaded Mrs. Inchbald to withdraw the printed
edition.[1] The real interest of the play however is that it goes
back to the French religious wars for a parallel to the 1790s;
Godwin was to go to the same period for some of his parallels
in *St. Leon* (1799).

By now Mrs. Inchbald was clearly of the party of English
Jacobinism. In 1792 she read *Anna St. Ives* (Boaden, i. 308),
a fictionalized version of the principles which Godwin himself
had not yet completely formulated into his *Enquiry Concerning
Political Justice*. But if cautious voices had persuaded her to suppress *The Massacre* in 1792, she now found that notoriety was not
without its benefits. Just three months after the founding of the
Association for Preserving Liberty and Property against Republicans and Levellers, she published her play *Every One Has
His Fault* (produced at the end of January 1793), and immediately
drew down the fire of a Government paper founded expressly
to denounce sedition.[2] But, as often happens, denunciation only
increased public interest, and the sale of the play was 'immense'
(Boaden, i. 310).

These were early days, however. Later in the year the tide began
to turn against liberals and reformers, after the outbreak of war
enabled the Government to bring the charge of treason to bear
on dissidents. Mrs. Inchbald discovered that those dependent on
the favour of the public were particularly exposed to changes in
public opinion, however manipulated that opinion might be by
those in power, and John Taylor 'with great sincerity told her
to beware of her politics, as their apparent leaning might injure
her fortune' (Boaden, i. 314). Possibly Taylor was aware of the

---

[1] Boaden, i. 304. Colman also rejected the play, and so Mrs. Inchbald's claim in
the preface that the play was never intended for the stage is disingenuous.
[2] Boaden, i. 310; P. A. Brown, *The French Revolution in English History*, p. 85.

contents of her novel, which was to be published eventually as *Nature and Art*. According to Boaden she had begun copying out the novel for the press in January 1794 (i. 315), and Godwin read through her 'Romance, ms' on the twenty-seventh and thirtieth of the same month.[1] She also showed the new work to Holcroft and George Hardinge (Boaden, i. 315). But the novel did not appear in 1794, nor in 1795, and was finally published only in 1796, long after it might have had any practical effect on the debate on the French Revolution and English reform.

It is easy to guess why this delay took place. Early in 1794 the Government was preparing its assault on the English Jacobins, an assault of which the Treason Trials later in the year were only one part. As one of the Queen's attorneys-general Hardinge was perhaps so situated as to be able to warn his friend that it was a most inauspicious time to publish a novel expressing liberal views. Hardinge himself liked the novel at first, but soon turned violently against it. He accused Mrs. Inchbald of having 'the head of bigotry and the soul of Holcroft' and of having abused him in a manner which would have shocked even 'G***, the little atheist': 'As to your *abuse*, you have taught me to value it. Oh that I may for ever be called *stupid* by the person who wrote a *Satire upon the Times*, by setting a ship on fire, and burning every soul in the book except a Lord of the Bedchamber—by whom she meant the K——' (Boaden, i. 328–9). Boaden did not realize it, but the 'Satire upon the Times' was the provisional title of *Nature and Art*, and Lord Bendham, the Lord of the Bedchamber, was intended to be George III. No wonder Hardinge was shocked and alarmed. If Holcroft was to be arrested for treason as a member of a society seeking reform and as the author of *Anna St. Ives*, there might be some danger in daring to satirize the King himself.

Mrs. Inchbald took the better part of valour in these perilous times—her only publication in 1794 was a truncated, two-act play, entitled *The Wedding Day*, which was produced at the very moment (1 November 1794) when public attention was monopolized by the outcome of the Treason Trials, but which contained only one unexceptionable reference to political affairs. Mrs. Inchbald did not obtrude herself on the public again until *Nature and Art* was published in 1796, and she did not hazard

[1] Godwin's MS. Journal.

her dramatic reputation with a possibly Anti-Jacobin audience until March of 1797.[1]

'The Prejudice of Education'

Although it was suppressed for a time and was published when such 'Satire upon the Times' could be of little real value in the English Jacobin spread of truth, *Nature and Art* was written at the height of liberal ferment in England and remains a document of fundamental interest in the history of the English Jacobin novel. In particular, the new novel develops another of the fundamental principles of English Jacobinism, that 'truth is omnipotent'. The English Jacobins declared that there was no such thing as evil, only error or prejudice; and that reason, sense, and truth must inevitably conquer error and so render all men virtuous. To an extent, of course, this moral was implied in *A Simple Story*, but in *Nature and Art* Mrs. Inchbald turned to new, more obvious methods of moral argument, ones more suited to the polemical times. But although it eschews for the most part the realism of *A Simple Story* and pertains to the sub-genre of the satiric rather than the psychological novel, Mrs. Inchbald's second work of fiction also has important affinities with her first. In a way *Nature and Art* translates the main themes of *A Simple Story* onto the social plane and into English Jacobin terms. By early in 1795 she seems to have revised her novel again, and to have called it 'The Prejudice of Education', a title which draws attention to its continuity with *A Simple Story* (Boaden, i. 346).

The Rousseauism implicit in the very title of *Nature and Art* was paralleled by another novel published in 1796, Robert Bage's *Hermsprong; or, Man As He Is Not*. Both novels were in the tradition of works such as *David Simple*, *Sandford and Merton*, and *The Fool of Quality*, which achieved their didactic purpose by means of contrasting moral values in a series of incidents. In Mrs. Inchbald's novel the simple and benevolent Henry, whose only skill is playing the violin (the same instrument at which Holcroft and Rousseau were so proficient), is contrasted with his brother William, who has the benefit of a gentleman's classical

---

[1] When she presented *Wives As They Were And Maids As They Are*, another echo of *Man As He Is*, and *Things As They Are*. Dates of performance of Mrs. Inchbald's plays are from G. Louis Joughin, 'An Inchbald Bibliography', reprinted from the *University of Texas Studies in English*, xiv (1934), 59–74.

education. Henry supports his brother through the proceeds of his fiddling, but when William begins to rise in the Church he also begins to disdain this brother who is a mere musician. William goes on to become a bishop while the neglected and heart-broken Henry is forced to leave the country and is lost on the coast of Africa. Both brothers have sons, and in the difference between the young Henry and William is found the real matter for the contrast of nature against art, sense against prejudice. William receives the fawning 'education' provided by tutors and becomes 'a foolish man, instead of a wise child, as nature designed him to be' (i. 45). He does not learn by the natural methods advocated in such works as the Edgeworths' *Practical Education* (1798) and the educational writings of Mary Wollstonecraft (1787–90), but he is made to learn everything by rote, with pre-dictable consequences. He 'could talk on history, on politics, and on religion; surprisingly to all who never listened to a parrot or magpie—for he merely repeated what he had heard, without one reflection upon the sense or probability of his report' (i. 46). Finally, William is allowed to bask in the flattery of the household servants—another aspect of the common domestic education strongly opposed by the Edgeworths and Mary Wollstonecraft. As a result of this indulgent and at the same time rule-bound education, William's thoughts and actions are, precisely, studied.

His cousin Henry on the other hand has not been trained into precocity, 'and from a simplicity spread over his countenance, a quick impatience in his eye, which denoted anxious curiosity, and childish surprise at every new object which presented itself, he appeared younger than his informed, and well-bred cousin' (i. 61–2). Having grown up on a desert island off the coast of Africa Henry has escaped the artificialities of civilization; like Hermsprong, who was educated among the North American Indians, he can see European 'civilization' as it really is, and his reaction to his cousin is meant to be our judgement on William's artificial education: 'A little man! as I am alive, a little man! I did not know there were such little men in this country! I never saw one in my life before!' (i. 67). The technique here suggests *Gulliver's Travels*, and Godwin had already revealed a considerable interest in Swift in the pages and footnotes of *Political Justice*. In Henry's reaction to William the phrase 'little man' becomes a moral criticism as well as a physical description, in a way quite reminiscent of Swift. Like Candide and Hermsprong, Henry has the education and common-sense outlook of a Houyhnhnm.

The education of women in *Nature and Art* is also presented by contrasts. Rebecca Rymer is the object of Henry's virtuous love; but since she is not beautiful like her sisters she is, like the young Elizabeth Simpson with her stammer, driven back on the resources of the parsonage library: 'She read—but more—she thought. The choicest books from her father's little library taught her to think; and reflection fashioned her mind to bear the slights, the mortifications of neglect, with a patient dejection, rather than with an indignant or a peevish spirit' (i. 133). Like Mrs. Inchbald herself, Rebecca is an autodidact and achieves that independence of mind so ardently advocated by Mary Wollstonecraft when she declared that 'those who reflect can tell, of what importance it is for the mind to have some resource in itself, and not to be entirely dependant on the senses for employment and amusement'.[1] In contrast, poor Hannah Primrose discovers the truth of Harriette Wilson's maxim that 'reading is a much more independent amusement than loving',[2] for her beauty, unlike Harriette Wilson's and Mrs. Inchbald's, is unguarded by a rational and independent mind. At the same time Mrs. Inchbald criticizes the dame- or charity-school education which was considered good enough for the lower classes.

In *Nature and Art*, however, a fashionable education like Miss Milner's is as bad as the inadequate one afforded the children of the poor. Miss Sedgeley, who usurps Hannah's rightful place as William's wife, has all the faults and vanities of a fashionable lady and, predictably, cuckolds her husband and is divorced, a much more severe fate for women in that day than this. Even before their arranged marriage takes place, William becomes aware of the sad contrast between his betrothed and the poor victim of his lust. Hannah's 'candour' is contrasted to Miss Sedgeley's artificiality, which is revealed, like that of Lady Wishfort, by her 'false face'—'the artificial bloom on her cheeks was nearly as disgusting, as the ill-conducted artifice with which she attempted gentleness and love' (ii. 6). This touch might be traced back as far as *The Spectator*, but, like so many other themes, it gained new colour and force from the times.

[1] Mary Wollstonecraft, *Thoughts on the Education of Daughters* (London, 1787), p. 48.
[2] *Harriette Wilson's Memoirs of Herself and Others*, p. 245.

Of course, Mrs. Inchbald did not just string out her ideas on education in a series of contrasts—that was the peculiar technique of Hannah More's Cheap Repository tracts. *Nature and Art*, like such novels as *Pride and Prejudice*, *Sense and Sensibility*, and *Patronage*, is not interesting because it is about the moral qualities stated in its title, but because it attempts to show those qualities as they inhere in characters who are interesting in their own right. Characters in satire, it is true, tend to be little more than functions of some grander scheme of virtue and vice, and to a great extent the characters of *Nature and Art* suffer from this limitation. But they also partake of the same moral world which was found in *A Simple Story*, and in Bage's novels and Holcroft's *Hugh Trevor*.[1] If her first novel could be given the sub-title 'Pride and Sensibility', thereby suggesting its affinities to the novels of Jane Austen, then her second work of fiction develops the moral argument a step further. The theme of education in *Nature and Art* is subsumed under the general conflict between the common sense which is the expression of Nature, and the Prejudice which produces artfulness and artificiality.

Such Things Are; or, Every One Has His Fault

This conflict between Sense and Prejudice, Nature and Art, is a part of what may be called the English Jacobin sensibility, and looked back to the literature of benevolence (including the novel of sensibility), as well as ahead to Romanticism. Mrs. Inchbald's treatment of the vices of society also looked back, to the satire and moral writing of the eighteenth century, to her own plays, and to the novels of Robert Bage. Luxury, the use of riches, and abuses of fashion are all topics which figured large in eighteenth-century discussions on how to live, and they appear in familiar enough form in *Nature and Art*. After returning from the coast of Africa[2] with his aged father the younger Henry learns of Lord Bendham's miserable end from Rebecca and her sisters: 'They told of Lord Bendham's death from the effects of intemperance; from a mass of blood infected by high seasoned dishes, mixed with copious draughts of wine—repletion of food and liquor,

[1] The first three volumes of which were published about the time Mrs. Inchbald was finishing the first version of *Nature and Art* in 1794.
[2] In the trip to Africa Mrs. Inchbald may have been alluding to the Sierra Leone expedition of 1791, a private venture by anti-slavery humanitarians.

not less fatal to the existence of the rich, than the want of common sustenance to the lives of the poor' (ii. 192–3). The concluding remark is hardly original, or the monopoly of English Jacobin writers; at the same time it can be imagined what effect such remarks would have in the 1790s, especially when it is remembered that the novel was published in the year after the terrible famine of 1795.

Lady Bendham too has suffered from the improper use of her wealth, as Henry also learns: 'They told of Lady Bendham's ruin since her Lord's death, by gaming—They told, "that now she suffered beyond the pain of common indigence, by the cutting triumph of those, whom she had formerly despised" ' (ii. 193). This is nothing if not a just novel, and the elder William's wife, Lady Clementina, has also succumbed to death, the only leveller countenanced by the reactionary in the 1790s, as a result of her rage for Fashion: ' "Yes," answered the stranger, "she caught cold by wearing a new-fashioned dress that did not half cover her, wasted all away, and died the miserablest object you ever heard of" ' (ii. 174).

The moral might have been taken from one of Hannah More's Cheap Repository tales, but all the while Mrs. Inchbald balances her satire and her moralizing with real sympathy for the poor, to which the Evangelicals only paid lip service. Like Mary Wollstonecraft, Mrs. Inchbald attempted to carry her sympathy beyond mere interest in philosophical and ethical considerations, without coming to consider the poor as they were often portrayed in sentimental novels, as objects on which the hero or heroine may exercise a becoming benevolence. The truth is that in her own life Mrs. Inchbald always preferred the humble circle of her domestic connections to the high society to which she, like Godwin, had access. 'To her lasting honour, she could live in this higher atmosphere without disdaining that from which she had no wish to remove—*that* in which her relations and humbler friends received her kind offices, and her darling independence was alone secure!'[1] Time and again Boaden attests to the charity which Mrs. Inchbald extended to her feckless brothers and sisters, and she knew, as did Mary Wollstonecraft, that the strictest economy was necessary if one were to enjoy the warm sentiments

---

[1] Boaden, ii. 290–1. The importance of 'independence' was the constant theme of most women writers of the 1790s.

attached to helping others. The use of riches was an issue of continuing importance in Mrs. Inchbald's own life, and so like Mary Wollstonecraft she condemned gamesters such as Lady Bendham simply because they wasted their wealth away from its proper objects, the poor.[1]

It is perhaps surprising, then, that Mrs. Inchbald concludes her novel with that sentimental view of the superior moral virtue inherent in poverty which was fast becoming one of the shibboleths of the Evangelicals and others who preached quietism against those who were beginning to ask why the poor are always with us:

After numerous other examples had been recited of the dangers, the evils that riches draw upon their owner; the elder Henry rose from his chair, and embracing Rebecca and his son, said,

'How much indebted are *we* to providence, my children, who, while it inflicts poverty, bestows peace of mind; and in return for the trivial grief we meet in this world, holds out to our longing hopes, the reward of the next!' (ii. 194.)

Perhaps prudence induced Mrs. Inchbald to soften the ending of her 'Satire upon the Times' to accord more with the political atmosphere of 1796 than that of early 1794; but the fact remains that this ending, with its note of 'uplift', is as adventitious as those of other English Jacobin novels which tried to reconcile some kind of happy ending with a radical *exposé* of 'things as they are'. Moreover the pious tone of the elder Henry's thanksgiving is quite contrary to the method of the rest of the book, of which the following dialogue, the attempt of dean William to instruct his 'ignorant' nephew regarding the condition of the poor, is typical:

'Come hither, child,' said the dean, 'and let me instruct you—your father's negligence has been inexcusable—There are in society' (continued the dean) 'rich and poor; the poor are born to serve the rich.'

'And what are the rich born for?'

'To be served by the poor.'

'But suppose the poor would not serve them?'

'Then they must starve.'

'And so poor people are permitted to live, only upon condition that they wait upon the rich?'

---

[1] e.g. Mary Wollstonecraft, *Original Stories* (London, 1788), p. 185.

'Is that a hard condition? or if it were, they will be rewarded in a better world than this.'

'Is there a better world than this?'

'Is it possible you do not know there is?'

'I heard my father once say something about a world to come; but he stopt short, and said I was too young to understand what he meant.'

'The world to come' (returned the dean) 'is where we shall go after death; and there no distinction will be made between rich and poor—all persons there will be equal.'

'Aye, now I see what makes it a better world than this. But cannot this world try to be as good as that?'

'In respect to placing all persons on a level, it is utterly impossible—God has ordained it otherwise.'

'How! has God ordained a distinction to be made, and will not make any himself?'

The dean did not proceed in his instructions; he now began to think his brother in the right, and that the boy was too young, or too weak, to comprehend the subject [i. 77–9].

The passage is worth quoting in full because it was obviously intended to expose the Evangelical defence of the *status quo* which was commonly couched in precisely the terms used by the elder Henry at the end of the novel. There are too many allusions to Evangelical doctrine, and too many obvious parodies of the manner and matter of the chapbooks of the Cheap Repository (the passage just quoted is one of these), for there to be any doubt that Mrs. Inchbald was mounting a comprehensive attack on those who were trying to justify 'things as they are'.

Dean William, for example, is to some extent a satirical portrait of the same Bishop Horsley who was ridiculed as Dr. Blick in Bage's *Hermsprong*, and as the gourmandizing bishop in the first part of Holcroft's *Hugh Trevor* (1794). Dean William helps himself to preferments by his pro-Government pamphlets, which praise the constitution in Church and State, and say nothing of the poor. They are therefore very like the sermon which Horsley had preached in January 1793, 'before the House of Lords at Westminster Abbey, depicting the dangers of the revolutionary spirit; as he began his peroration the whole assembly rose in rapt enthusiasm'.[1] In November of the same year, when Mrs. Inchbald was no doubt nearing completion of the first version of *Nature and Art*, Horsley received his reward, as it seemed, when

[1] *D.N.B.*, s.v. Samuel Horsley.

he was translated to the see of Rochester. Horsley's arguments were being widely disseminated at about the same time through the tracts of Cheap Repository, such as 'Village Politics', that were 'most extensively circulated, in 1793, to counteract the pernicious doctrines which, owing to the French revolution, were then become seriously alarming to the friends of religion and government in every part of Europe'.[1] The connection between the Establishment in Church and State is revealed in the fact that Dean William is also one of those clerical magistrates who played a large part in the repression of both political and religious dissent in the 1790s, and who found the quietism preached by the Evangelicals to be a handy substitute for real action to alleviate the condition of the poor.[2]

Mrs. Inchbald bluntly reminds the more powerful and privileged of the 'two nations' how their efforts on behalf of the poor are viewed by the humble themselves. When the dean and his household leave Anfield after the summer to return to the pleasures of the London 'season', there are few of the local inhabitants who regret their departure:

Those were not the poor—for rigid attention to the [religion and] morals of people in poverty, and total neglect of their bodily wants, was the dean's practice. He forced them to attend church on every sabbath; but whether they had a dinner on their return, was too gross and temporal an enquiry for his spiritual fervour. Good of the *soul* was all he aimed at; and this pious undertaking, besides his diligence as a pastor, required all his exertion as a magistrate—for to be very poor and very honest, very oppressed yet very thankful, is a degree of sainted excellence not to be attained without the aid of zealous men to frighten into virtue [i. 153–4].[3]

Mrs. Inchbald puts her finger on exactly the kind of hypocrisy which was breaking down the benevolent paternalism which was supposed to have prevailed in the eighteenth century, and in the 1790s there were increasing numbers of the poor who could see through Dean William's pious platitudes, and, like the poor workman in *Nature and Art*, they were beginning to speak out:

'I believe he meant well.' Said Henry.
'As to what he meant, God only knows—but I know what he *did*.'

[1] Hannah More, *Works*, 6 vol. edn. (London, 1834), ii. 221 n.
[2] Esther Moir, *The Justice of the Peace* (Harmondsworth, 1969), pp. 107–8.
[3] The words in square brackets were added after the first edition.

'And what did he?'

'Nothing at all for the poor.'

'If any of them applied to him, no doubt—'

'Oh! they knew better than all that comes to—for if they asked for any thing, he was sure to have them sent to bridewell, or the workhouse.—He used to say—"*The workhouse was a fine place for a poor man—the food good enough, and enough of it*—" yet he kept a dainty table himself' [ii. 176–7].[1]

Fair revenge for all the lectures read to the poor in the pages of Cheap Repository. Not only was Mrs. Inchbald aware of the hypocrisy of the Evangelicals' advice to the poor; she also recognized the insidious rationale behind many of their 'good works'. The young William rises to become a pillar of the law, and hence like his father a pillar of the Establishment. 'He was the president of many excellent charities; gave largely; and sometimes instituted benevolent societies for the unhappy: for he delighted to load the poor with obligations, and the rich with praise' (ii. 145). 'Charity' is even one of the words on which the young Henry is allowed to exercise his provocative naïvety, and he tells Lord Bendham, 'I thought it was prudent in you to give a little; lest the poor, driven to despair, should take all' (i. 127).

By the time she wrote *Nature and Art* Mrs. Inchbald had been amongst the rich and powerful a great deal, and her impression was probably much the same as that gathered by Francis Place in his years as a tailor to the ruling class. English society was dividing into the 'two nations' which the intellectuals and writers and politicians of the next century were to expend their efforts in trying to join together again. More than any other English Jacobin writer except Thelwall and Mary Wollstonecraft, more than Godwin the philosopher of political and social justice and more than Holcroft the writer 'sprung from the people', Mrs. Inchbald had an awareness of social realities in the 1790s which were the making of class consciousness in England.

Satire and Sentiment

However, in order to express her radical outlook on the corruptions and social realities of the age, Mrs. Inchbald did not rely on

---

[1] There is also an obvious reference here to the debate on the Poor Law in 1795. Cf. also Mary Wollstonecraft's *The Wrongs of Woman* (1798), which was begun in 1796.

her own experiences as Maria Edgeworth and Elizabeth Gaskell were to do. She turned back, diligent student that she was, to the satire of the previous century. She was, after all, dealing with the same theme as *Gulliver's Travels*, *The Fable of the Bees*, and the *Maxims* of La Rochefoucauld—the contrast between moral appearance and real motive.

Looking at conditions around her Mrs. Inchbald found much to satirize, but prudence was not the only pressure operating to induce her to alter somewhat her use of earlier models. It was characteristic of her in life and art to compromise extremes. Her satire is thus a mixture of the incisiveness of Swift and the geniality of Goldsmith, and her adaptation of La Rochefoucauld demonstrates her general approach. The French moralist was a favourite of women authors, and his maxims had been frequently quoted and imitated by Holcroft in his *Wit's Magazine*. Even in her first novel Mrs. Inchbald found some of the maxims appropriate to situations in *A Simple Story* where the self-delusions of love and pride were in question. Although in her second novel the maxims are much closer to the surface, Mrs. Inchbald modifies or even changes their import altogether. She chose, for example, to use only the first part of La Rochefoucauld's cynical definition of pity to describe young Henry's sympathy for the luckless Hannah Primrose:

La pitié est souvent un sentiment de nos propres maux dans les maux d'autrui; c'est une habile prévoyance des malheurs où nous pouvons tomber; nous donnons du secours aux autres, pour les engager à nous en donner en de semblables occasions, et ces services que nous leur rendons sont, à proprement parler, des biens que nous nous faisons à nous-mêmes par avance [Maxim 264].

Perhaps our *own* misfortunes are the cause of our pity for others, even more than *their* ills [ii. 76].

In another place Mrs. Inchbald even quotes La Rochefoucauld, only to use the quotation as a basis for her own, more temperate view:

It has been said by a celebrated writer, upon the affection subsisting between the two sexes, 'that there are many persons who, if they had never heard of the passion of love, would never have felt it.' Might it not with equal truth be added, that—there are many more, who having heard of it, and believing most firmly that they feel it, are nevertheless mistaken? Neither of these cases was the lot of Hannah. She experienced the sentiment before she ever heard it named in that sense in which she felt it—and she felt it as genuine love alone exists—joined with numerous other sentiments: for love, however rated by many, as the chief passion of the human heart, is but a poor dependant, a retainer upon other passions; admiration, gratitude, respect, esteem, pride in the object—divest the boasted sensation of these, and it is no more than the impression of a twelve-month, by courtesy, or vulgar error, termed love [i. 141–2].

Significantly perhaps, Mrs. Inchbald liberalizes and senti-mentalizes La Rochefoucauld, and she does so because Hannah Primrose is in some way involved. The Hannah who falls foul of young William the seducer is at least in part a portrait of Mrs. Inchbald's own sister Debby, who seems to have suffered a fate not unlike that of Hannah, ruin and an early grave.[1]

But the tendency to soften and sentimentalize her borrowings from the moral writers was general. It has already been suggested that the technique of the 'natural' character who questions the artful assumptions of the civilized is borrowed from Swift, and of course from Voltaire. An example of the young Henry's questioning has already been cited, in his inability to follow the dean's arguments on the inevitability of poverty, as well as an example of the way his lack of experience in the ways of society enables him to penetrate to the real meaning of Lord Bendham's 'charity'. There is clearly an influence from *Gulliver's Travels* in all this, and it is interesting that Bage should have used a similar technique in *Hermsprong*, his last novel, published in the same year as *Nature and Art*. What Mrs. Inchbald borrows from Swift especially is the way Gulliver, or one of his Brobdignagian inter-locutors, redefines words away from the sophistication of mean-ings which obscures brutal social reality:

In addition to his ignorant conversation upon many topics, young Henry had an incorrigible misconception and misapplication of many *words*—his father having had but few opportunities of discoursing with him upon account of his attendance at the court of the savages; and not having books in the island, he had consequently many words to learn of this country's language when he arrived in England: this task his retentive memory made easy to him; but his childish inattention

---

[1] Boaden, i. 258, 270, 296, 332. Boaden writes, 'The miserable fate of this sister, deeply regretted, pressed long and heavily upon the mind of Mrs. Inchbald' (i. 332). Debby died in 1794.

to their proper signification still made his want of education conspicuous.

He would call *compliments*, *lies*—*Reserve*, he would call *pride*—*stateliness*, *affectation*—and for the monosyllable *war*, he constantly substituted the word *massacre* [i. 80-1].

Mrs. Inchbald's *ingénu*, however, is too obviously on the side of right, and too obviously out of any moral peril to be considered a real descendant of Gulliver and Candide. Mrs. Inchbald manages to blend sensibility with satire, but at the cost of losing the ironic penetration and real sense of evil which distinguishes the fiction of Swift and Voltaire. Too much reliance is placed on simple goodness of heart—the influence of Rousseau and Mackenzie perhaps—to allow *Nature and Art* to take its place with the great satiric novels of the century. Alongside the radical *exposé* of the arrogance and ignorance of rich and powerful, and the angry sympathy for the plight of the poor, is a certain heart-warming *insouciance*, a desire to relinquish the battle with *l'infâme*, that is perhaps the real sign of the way Mrs. Inchbald had revised her satire after she had first completed it at the end of 1793. For by 1796 the battle had clearly been lost, or at best the hope of victory had receded far into the future. That this was recognized is shown by visible signs in the second part of *Hugh Trevor* (1797), and Godwin's *St. Leon* (1799).

If she diluted her satire with sentiment on the one hand, Mrs. Inchbald also vitiated it by making it too general on the other. Against the good characters who are all sympathetic, are ranged characters, such as Lord Bendham, who are Characters indeed, general portraits of vice modelled on the Characters of Theophrastus and La Bruyère:

A lord of the bed-chamber is a personage well known in courts, and in all capitals where courts reside; with this advantage to the inquirer, that in becoming acquainted with one of those noble characters, you become acquainted with all the remainder; not only with those of the same kingdom, but those of foreign nations; for, in whatever land, in whatever climate, a lord of the bed-chamber must necessarily be the self-same creature: one, wholly made up of observance, of obedience, of dependance, and of imitation—a borrowed character—a character formed by reflection [i. 120].[1]

This character of Lord Bendham is a reminder that much of *Nature*

---

[1] There is also an obvious pun in 'Bendham'; cf. the Cunninghams in Maria Edgeworth's *Patronage*.

and Art derives from the Augustan authors of England and France, in whose works, according to Boaden's testimony, Mrs. Inchbald was so well grounded. But her use of the radical satire of the Augustans is filtered through the literature of Sensibility on the one hand and the decline of English Jacobinism on the other. *Nature and Art*, however it may have shocked George Hardinge and the editors of *The Anti-Jacobin Review*, is already well on the way towards the nineteenth-century women novelists' rejection of revolution for romance.

Romance or Revolution

Mrs. Inchbald was a cautious author, and by preference or necessity she revised both her novels again and again, until she attained that high degree of technical polish which is the hallmark of her work. If *Nature and Art* is not as good a novel as its predecessor, either for us or for its first readers, it is probably in the nature of the thing. When writing about her own most personal feelings and experiences Mrs. Inchbald could be original; otherwise she could offer only a very high level of professional skill. In *Nature and Art* she was not (except in regard to Hannah Primrose, and her sympathy for the poor) writing about her feelings but about her ideas, and she was neither a deep nor an original thinker. Her reading and study showed her the models to follow, but she could not bring sufficient originality to transcend her particular task.

As a result the particular social and political conditions which inspired her novel became limitations rather than means to the kind of permanence achieved by Swift or Voltaire. The last chapter of *Nature and Art* retreats into a kind of Pantisocracy which is the logical ending for a book which certain events had inspired, and then passed by. The events of 1794, the Treason Trials and the nation-wide conservative reaction, made English Jacobin novels and English Jacobin ideas of general reform not only dangerous, but peripheral, and Pantisocracy was only one way out, a retrograde step seen in several English Jacobin novels of the time, a literary return to the ideal of rustic independence and sympathetic mutual help which had scarcely ever existed outside the world of fiction. That Godwin was interested in similar ideas we know—one of his earliest writings was a pastoral (*Imogen*, 1784) and both pastoral and Pantisocracy are linked to the emergence of Romanticism in England, Romanticism which was in part the real evidence of the defeat of English Jacobinism. The literary Jacobins followed the pattern of the end of *Nature and Art*, and their reluctance to engage in direct political action, to link up with the Corresponding Societies whose members were common working-men, was hastened into aversion by the failure of the French Revolution on the one hand and the obvious danger to their literary livelihoods on the other. As Raymond Williams said of the nineteenth-century 'industrial novelists', the 'recognition of evil was balanced by fear of becoming involved. Sympathy was transformed, not into action, but into withdrawal'.[1]

And yet sympathy had always been the characteristic response of women, and women novelists. Themselves powerless, and oppressed, they could feel with but not act for the poor and the distressed. Perhaps that is why so many novelists, in the 1790s as well as the 1840s, were women. Fiction is, after all, a kind of trojan horse for social and political propaganda, as Holcroft and Godwin, Bulwer Lytton, Kingsley, and Dickens all realized. But the sympathizer and the surreptitious reformer run a risk of being imprisoned in the belly of their vehicle; the wooden horse is an engine of assault, not construction. It is a fair assessment of *Nature and Art* to see it as deliberately offering a woman's solution to the ills of the age, the 'condition of England'. Other women novelists of the decade, such as Mary Wollstonecraft and Mary Hays, dared to be more radical, but not much more. At least Mrs. Inchbald, unlike Mary Robinson and Charlotte Smith, retained her English Jacobin loyalties. But like all the other women novelists of the decade, and some of the men, she turned away from the failed Revolution and escaped through the romance of sympathy.

In this act of aversion was the beginning of Romanticism, but women were also beginning to discover other trojan horses—the host of religious and philanthropic societies which enabled them to be as active in the world as men. Religion, philanthropy, and especially anti-slavery, became a kind of clandestine political action. Mrs. Inchbald also followed this route of retreat from Revolution and although her attitude to it was ambivalent, in this respect too her life imitated her art. As she grew older she was more and more affected by the kind of religiosity which was

[1] *Culture and Society 1780–1950* (Harmondsworth, 1961), p. 119.

practised by the very Evangelicals whose views she had attacked in *Nature and Art*.

At the same time she showed her adaptibility by becoming the foremost exponent in England of the drama of Kotzebue, with *Lovers' Vows* (1798). The quietist ending of *Nature and Art* reflected a real modification in Mrs. Inchbald's views between 1794 and 1796, perhaps it reflected a change in the outlook of English Jacobins in general. When Mrs. Inchbald renounced her 'Satire upon the Times' at the very end of the novel, she was renouncing the kinds of conclusions towards which a radical *exposé* of 'things as they are' must lead. She was always a feeling rather than a thinking liberal, and it is significant that her break with Godwin in 1798 should not be over a matter of principle, but over her friend's marriage to Mary Wollstonecraft. She had finally cut herself off from the philosophical basis of English Jacobinism, and her literary success after the break was, fittingly, as the chief English interpreter of Kotzebue's Romantic liberalism.[1]

Elizabeth Inchbald, therefore, along with Robert Bage, founded the English Jacobin novel. At a time when the English popular novel was going through a period of vulgar commercial formula and low critical esteem, Holcroft and Godwin, two of the most important novelists of the 1790s, had the benefit of direct acquaintance with both Mrs. Inchbald and her novel *A Simple Story*. They saw in *A Simple Story* and its author a prime example of the central English Jacobin doctrine, that circumstances form character. They felt in the novel what Lytton Strachey has called 'the living pressure of a human passion', and must have become aware of the connections between life and fiction which a successful artist could achieve. They saw too that a novel of ideas, to be effective, had to be effective artistically, as well as philosophically. Within a short time both Holcroft and Godwin had begun novels of their own. Not only did they imitate particular aspects of *A Simple Story*, they took up and made the most of the potential which Mrs. Inchbald's novel had made plain. Mrs. Inchbald had influence as a recorder of female experience, and as a novelist of ideas; but she had that influence primarily because she was a good novelist, rather than because she was a Jacobin one.

---

1 She wrote another novel sometime early in the next century, and showed it to Godwin, with whom she had for a time renewed something like the old acquaintance, at the time *Fleetwood* was published (letter from Mrs. Inchbald to Godwin, dated 7 Mar. [1805], in the Abinger collection).

CHAPTER III

THOMAS HOLCROFT

I. ANNA ST. IVES

The Rhetoric of English Jacobin Fiction

Thomas Holcroft was as close as an Englishman could come to being a *philosophe*. With the background and humour of Diderot and the scepticism of Voltaire he combined the studious generalizing mind of Montesquieu and the erratic passionate nature of Rousseau. But in particular, he alone of the English Jacobins resembled the French *lumières* in his persistent drive to popularize the 'New Philosophy' in a variety of plays, novels, periodical essays, reviews, biographies, histories, travels, and translations. A 'writer sprung from the people' (the phrase is Miss Mitford's), he was self-taught like Mary Wollstonecraft and Mrs. Inchbald, and he took his hard-won knowledge back to the people through every popular literary form he could lay hands on. Having been a shoemaker, stocking-weaver, stable-boy, and stroller, he knew the common people as Robert Bage, Elizabeth Inchbald, and William Godwin never could.

At the same time he had an ardent, penetrating, active, and stubborn mind. He had an opinion on everything, and he vociferated his opinions with passion and panache, although he is usually remembered as one of Coleridge's conversational victims. His translations and miscellaneous writings of the 1780s reveal an interest in science, philosophy, religion, history, and politics, as well as every aspect of contemporary literature; and his library contained works on all of these subjects as well as medicine, finance, chess, art and architecture, gardening, anatomy, grammar, law, theatre, music, geography, and literature in most of the living and dead languages of Europe.[1] He was also interested in books on onanism, pornography, and libertinism. His interests were as encyclopedic as his views. He also had a successful

---

[1] Sale catalogues of Holcroft's library, 1807 and 1809.

career as a dramatist in the 1780s, and when he was not reading, writing, or talking, he played the violin in a quartet made up of his friends (his favourite composer was Haydn, and he knew Clementi well), or added to his considerable collection of prints and pictures. He married four times, and when his son committed suicide in 1789, Holcroft could not shake off his grief for almost a year.

It would seem that no one could be more different from this active and passionate man than William Godwin, the philosopher and former Calvinist minister; but the two met in 1786, and Holcroft soon converted his new friend to scepticism. Godwin later described him as one of his 'four principal oral instructors'. Holcroft believed passionately in truth, virtue, and reason, and he opposed *l'infâme* with the same ardour as his admired Voltaire. If together he and Godwin gave the English Jacobin novel its philosophy, it was he who gave it its passion, its popularity, and its theory of form.

In view of his interest in the novel as a means of disseminating English Jacobin ideas it is somewhat surprising that *Anna St. Ives*, published in February 1792 at the height of revolutionary fervour, should be the only one of Holcroft's novels which did not have a preface. In his reviews for *The Monthly Review*, however, to which he contributed from November 1792 to February 1796, Holcroft continued to develop the views on the nature and uses of the novel which he had first formulated in the Preface to *Alwyn* (1780).[1] Brought together, these scattered opinions comprise the standard English Jacobin view of fiction. In his review of Bage's *Man As He Is*, for example, he emphasized once again the great effect which novels have on society: 'When we consider the influence that novels have over the manners, sentiments, and passions, of the rising generation,—instead of holding them in the contempt which, as reviewers, we are without exception said to do,—we may esteem them, on the contrary, as forming a very essential branch of literature.'[2] Holcroft was taking the neo-classical idea of the moral function of literature and applying it to the needs of his own time; and in other reviews he attacked aspects of the contemporary novel which, he felt, undermined this function. He criticized the increasingly fashionable Gothic gloom and misanthropy, for example: 'The continual tendency of the

---

[1] See Introduction.   [2] Op. cit., 2nd Ser., x (Mar. 1793), 297.

work before us is to persuade us that there is little else than misery on earth. Discontent, misanthropy, cowardice, apathy, debility, are each and all thus engendered; and we rise from reading, not with that animation which should make us happy in ourselves and useful to others, but with a sensation of the wretchedness of human existence.'[1]

Other aspects of the Gothic novel—revenge and recourse to the supernatural—were similarly condemned.[2] In this review the critic and the Jacobin combined to deplore the pessimism which was, in fact, increased in the later 1790s by the manifest failure of English Jacobinism to achieve reform.

Love and sensibility, as they were treated in the popular novels of the day, also drew down Holcroft's rationalist ire, and he appeared as the defender of the new image of woman as conjured up by Mary Wollstonecraft, when he described sarcastically the heroine of *Louisa Matthews*, written 'By an Eminent Lady': 'She is a sensitive plant, which shrinks, if the untutored finger of common accident approach it. We must warn the fair authoress, that this propensity of mind can neither conduce to her own happiness, nor teach happiness to her readers.'[3] Surely few novelists, except Jacobin ones, ever hoped that their performances would conduce to the happiness of their readers by any other means than entertaining them; it is ironical then, that the heaviest charge laid against Holcroft and his friends by the Anti-Jacobin reviewers was exactly the one Holcroft laid against the luckless author of *Louisa Matthews*. Years later, in the Preface to *Bryan Perdue* (1805), however, Holcroft declared that teaching female virtue, and therefore happiness, had been the chief aim of the novel which he had, at the time of the review of *Louisa Matthews*, already published, and which had dealt in detail with the English Jacobin view of those favourite themes in the popular novel, love and sensibility.

Holcroft was attempting in both his reviews and his practice as a novelist to broaden the moral and philosophical basis of the novel as literature. Like most of the English Jacobin writers he

---

[1] 2nd Ser., xii (Nov. 1793), 338. A review of *The Count de Hoensdern; A German Tale.*

[2] 2nd Ser., xiv (July 1794), 350–2. This was a review of the stage version of Ann Radcliffe's *Romance of the Forest*. See also *The Monthly Review*, 2nd Ser., xi (June 1793), 153–4.

[3] 2nd Ser., x (Apr. 1793), 459.

was more than just a novelist, and, because of his moral serious-ness, more than a mere miscellaneous writer. He conceived the writer's role and responsibility in very specific terms, those of English Jacobinism, and he set about putting his ideas into effect. By the time he came to offer his Jacobin definition of the novelist, once again in *The Monthly Review*, he had already made the definition into a description of his own most recent work. 'The labours of the poet, of the historian, and of the sage, ought to have one common end, that of strengthening and improving man, not of continuing him in error, and, which is always the consequence of error, in vice. The most essential feature of every work is its moral tendency. The good writer teaches the child to become a man; the bad and the indifferent best understand the reverse art of making a man a child.'[1] The role of the novelist is no different from that of any other writer; it is to teach; and in *Anna St. Ives* Holcroft anticipated all the major precepts which Godwin was to teach in his philosophical *Enquiry Concerning Political Justice*, published exactly a year and a week later.[2]

Holcroft, like all of the English Jacobin novelists, was a novelist of purpose, and he prepared his novels as he would have prepared any serious work, by studying the appropriate models. But for *Anna St. Ives* these models were not the same as those he had followed for *Alwyn*, and was to follow again for *Hugh Trevor* and *Bryan Perdue*. In order to 'teach fortitude to females' Holcroft turned away from the vigorous and masculine techniques of Fielding and Smollett to the gentler modes of sentimental fiction, as embodied in Richardson's *Clarissa*, Rousseau's *Julie*, and Mackenzie's *Julia De Roubigné*. These were, as it happened, the very same models Godwin turned to when he too wished to display the whole range of passions in conflict with reason and the moral sense.

The influence of Richardson in particular may be traced in the three first major novels of Mrs. Inchbald, Holcroft, and Godwin, and although the English Jacobin novelists rejected many points of Richardson's morality, their aims, as moralists, were essentially the same as his. It was not so much Richardson's matter as his manner of depicting psychological cause and effect which they

[1] 2nd Ser., ix (Nov. 1792), 337.
[2] According to Godwin's MS. Journal the novel was published on 7 February 1792, and *Political Justice* on 14 February 1793.

found of greatest interest. Even after Holcroft had returned to
Fielding and Smollett as his models in *Hugh Trevor* (1794–7),
he still accorded first place amongst English novelists to the
author of *Clarissa*, and pleaded for novelists of his own day to
study human passion as Richardson had done,[1] to 'develope the
emotions that preceded and the causes that produced the passion,
and, afterward, trace it through all its consequences'.[2] Holcroft
had certainly tried to do just this in *Anna St. Ives*, and even his
particular purpose in the novel, 'to teach fortitude to females',[3]
was also one of the main aims of *Clarissa*.[4] But the technical
interest of *Clarissa* for the English Jacobin novelists lay in its
brilliantly achieved 'concatenation' of events and character—
the 'unity of design' which Holcroft saw as the one feature which
distinguished the novel from romance.

To this achievement the English Jacobin novelists tried to join
their own particular themes and interests. If the English Jacobins
were to renovate the English popular novel, and make it a fit
vehicle for the dissemination of truth, they had to use the best of
English fiction and, as it were, bring it up to date. Richardson's
study of passion, his development of complex psychologies, and
his understanding of the way deep and hidden emotions reveal
their presence, were all of interest to novelists dedicated to the
'necessitarian' psychology drawn from Hartley and Locke; but
the English Jacobin novelists wished to do more than imitate
Richardson's portrayal of the relation between individual
psychology and action; they wished to show the relationship
between individual feelings and actions, and society at large.
It was a radical aim, and they seldom succeeded in achieving it,
but it was the real beginning of the social novel.

Teaching fortitude to females, then, was the particular aim of
both *Clarissa* and *Anna St. Ives*, as well as *La Nouvelle Héloïse*, but
it was also one of the aims of *A Simple Story*, and it seems probable
that Mrs. Inchbald's novel first stimulated Holcroft to imitate
Richardson. Even the form of the two novels was at one time the
same, for according to Godwin, he first read *A Simple Story*
'in alternate letters between two confidantes: Miss Woodley

---

[1] *The Monthly Review*, 2nd Ser., xvii (June 1795), 136. A review of Cumberland's
Henry.
[2] Ibid., 2nd Ser., xii (Dec. 1793), 393.
[3] Preface to *Bryan Perdue* (London, 1805), vol. i, p. iii.
[4] *Selected Letters of Samuel Richardson*, ed. John Carroll (Oxford, 1964), p. 124.

relating the story of Dorriforth, and the other the story of Rushbrook'.[1] But the real similarities between the two novels go beyond mere technique. Both novels show how a mind properly educated is proof against the excesses of passion and self-deception, and both contrast impulsive and passionate characters with those who, schooled in adversity, have the fortitude to endure the worst that can be offered by a world unregulated by English Jacobin morality. It is the fortitude which Miss Milner lacks which carries Matilda, Julie, Julia de Roubigné, and Anna St. Ives through their respective crises. Both *Anna St. Ives* and *A Simple Story* attempt to go beyond interest in the psychology and destiny of individual characters, and, by showing the various relationships between the characters of parents and children, to draw certain conclusions about society in general. But whereas Mrs. Inchbald only just brings her novel within range of the English Jacobin social philosophy by her emphasis on 'A Proper Education', Holcroft writes his novel in the midst of the same reading and discussion which soon produced Godwin's *Political Justice*.

For it is obvious that the aim of *Anna St. Ives* is much more than to 'teach fortitude to females'; it is a comprehensive preliminary statement of the principles of *Political Justice*, and itself induced Godwin, at least in part, to try his hand at novel-writing. It is proper, therefore, to regard *Anna St. Ives* in the same way that several critics have regarded Godwin's *Things As They Are*, as a fictive rendering of the arguments of *Political Justice*. However, the novel is more than just the usual timber of the 'English popular novel' embellished with liberal or even revolutionary opinions. Holcroft's Jacobin purpose informs every aspect of his technique—character, plot, theme, and not a few of the lesser ornaments. The 'unity of design' therefore comes from within rather than from without. *Anna St. Ives* is the most completely Jacobinical of all the English Jacobin novels, and it is nothing less than an attempt wholly to renovate that late eighteenth-century sub-*genre*, the 'English popular novel'.

English Jacobin Epistolary Art

In this attempt Holcroft recognized the need to follow only the best models available—in this case *Clarissa*, *La Nouvelle Héloïse*, and perhaps *Julia de Roubigné*, as well as *A Simple Story*. In his next

[1] MS. Journal.

attempt, *Hugh Trevor*, he would return to Fielding and Smollett and the picaresque method of depicting 'things as they are'; but in 1791 it was Mrs. Inchbald who showed the way. The adventures of Miss Milner and her daughter Matilda illustrated for English Jacobins the Godwinian doctrine of necessity—the argument that 'the characters of men originate in their external circumstances', and that the characters so formed then go on to influence events in a direct causal relationship. For this reason both *A Simple Story* and *Anna St. Ives* belong to the same variety of the *genre* as *Clarissa*—what Richardson called a 'dramatic narrative' rather than a 'history'.[1] By creating a sufficient degree of psychological realism the English Jacobin novelist could make the plot—his 'argument'—seem to be dependent on and almost identified with character, and thereby achieve that 'unity of design' which distinguished the novel from lesser forms of fiction.

In fact, by eighteenth-century standards Holcroft's epistolary art achieves a high degree of realism. There are, it is true, long conversations rather too well remembered, individual tricks of speech recorded with a too linguistic accuracy, and the usual breakings off for the postman's bell, a dramatic interview, or a crime. But on the whole Holcroft maintains a high degree of verisimilitude, and all of his correspondents write in a characteristic vein. Holcroft is especially adept at allowing a character's suppressed hopes and fears to betray themselves, by tell-tale repetitions, or Freudian slips. He is also good at allowing a hypocrite to unmask himself, as when Aby Henley writes a crude letter to his son followed by a creeping one to his employer (letters li and lii). He manages to create a great deal of suspense by allowing a crucial reply or account of a dramatic incident to be delayed by the interposition of letters from the lesser figures, or by opposing one account with another very different one. In the earlier part of the novel at least, there is hardly any part of any letter that does not serve a number of purposes at once. For his time, Holcroft was a skilled and vigorous dramatist, and he obviously had no trouble in transferring his talents to the form of epistolary fiction.

But then, he obviously went to the best models, and he chose the appropriate form. The intimacy and immediacy of the epistle were ideally suited to display the minute twists and turns of feeling, and hence to illustrate the chain of necessity in human

[1] Ian Watt, *The Rise of the Novel*, p. 217.

affairs. At the same time, overlapping accounts of the same event could display the slightest degree of a character's 'error' and self-deception. Holcroft never loses sight of his main task, and at every point he uses the epistolary form to establish his Jacobinical view of character and circumstance. And yet *Anna St. Ives*, like all other English Jacobin novels, carries its points largely by philosophical debates and discussions on a variety of subjects, and these debates naturally pose some difficulty of realistic presentation in an epistolary novel. From quite early in the novel some of the letters, especially those from Anna, contain lengthy reported dialogues—the sort of material which is usually considered utterly inimical to the maintenance of epistolary verisimilitude. But the relevance of the dialogues in *Anna St. Ives* must depend not on the subject matter but their appropriateness in a context, the skill with which they are dramatized, and their contribution to the larger themes of the novel.

A good example of the English Jacobin philosophical debate well contained by the letter form is Frank Henley's account of the discussion on the passions between himself, Anna, and Coke Clifton. Frank leads into the direct speech by an indirect report of the preliminaries:

> The interesting part of what passed began by Mr. Clifton's affirming, with Pope, that men had and would have, to the end of time, each a ruling passion. This I denied, if by ruling passion were meant the indulgence of any irregular appetite, or the fostering of any erroneous system. I was asked, with a sneer, for my recipe to subdue the passions; if it were not too long to be remembered. I replied it was equally brief and efficacious. It was the force of reason; or, if the word should please better, of truth.
>
> And in what year of the world was the discovery of truth to be made?
>
> In that very year when, instead of being persecuted for speaking their thoughts, the free discussion of every opinion, true or false, should not only be permitted, but receive encouragement and applause.
>
> As usual, the appeal was made to Anna: and, as usual, her decision was in my favour. Nothing, said she, is more fatal, to the progress of virtue, than the supposition that error is invincible.[1]

The debate proceeds, Anna affirming to Clifton's dismay that

[1] *Anna St. Ives*, ed. Peter Faulkner (London, New York, and Toronto, 1970), p. 98.

even the passion of love may be conquered by reason; but always there are reminders that the account is from Frank's point of view:

We seem to be convinced that we have fallen in love by enchantment, and are under the absolute dominion of a necromancer. It is truly the dwarf leading the giant captive. Is it not—(Oliver! She fixed her eyes upon me, as she spoke!) Is it not, Frank?

I was confounded. I paused for a moment. A deep and heavy sigh involuntarily burst from me. I endeavoured to be firm, but I stammered out—Madam—it is [p. 99].

Frank is in fact the living example as well as the reporter of Anna's views on the supremacy which reason should have over the passions. And so the debate, varied by Frank's interjections and parenthetical expansions, becomes a highly dramatic one, skilfully recounted within Frank's letter.

However, as the novel proceeds these debates sometimes prove too much for their epistolary context. Suspense is used to build up the impact of Anna's explanation of her principles to Clifton, and she retells every word of her speech in a letter to Louisa. The monologue runs to over two thousand words, and at the end of it all, Clifton can only promise lamely to make some notes, the easier to remember her arguments. There is a reason for the one-sidedness of this scene—Clifton has already resolved on Anna's ruin and since her letter closes volume four, his own enraged reaction is saved for the beginning of volume five; but this dramatic suspense seems artificial and is achieved at the cost of turning Anna into a self-righteous ranter. As a result she merely seems to be an over-zealous prig, the advocate of her own principles and virtues in a way dangerous in an epistolary novel—in a way which undermines her moral authority.

She does not always appear in this light. In her account of the attempt by her haughty relatives to force her into a reconciliation with Clifton, we see a real woman thinking and feeling, not a mouthpiece for the arguments of *Political Justice*, and a complex scene of conflicting wills and prejudices is presented with the immediacy of feeling of a deeply committed participant. Even her irritating habit of self-criticism is appealing for once, when she feels she has unjustly offended her aunt: 'I perceived that, though the spirit of my answer was right, the manner was wrong; and explained and apologised as became me' (pp. 360–1).

The scene and the dialogue are dramatic in the best sense here, and yet described and interpreted by one of the principals—a fine example of Holcroft's theatrical experience adapted to the needs of an epistolary novel. But in the latter part of the novel the epistolary techniques fail to carry the same conviction as they do earlier. They fail to sustain the complexity of characterization and this failure is crucial to the English Jacobin conclusions of the book, conclusions reached primarily in terms of the effect of the good characters on the not-so-good.

The Chain of Necessity: Character

'*The Progress of the Passions*': *Anna St. Ives*. In order to make his argument convincing Holcroft must establish the truth of his account of 'the progress of the passions'. This account is, in the first instance, dependent on Anna St. Ives herself. To some extent she is intended as a criticism of Richardson's Clarissa. By rejecting the erroneous attachment to 'honour' (a woman's reputation) in herself, she avoids the fate of the earlier heroine. At the same time, by overcoming the prejudices of rank and family pride in others, Anna secures for herself the love-match denied to Rousseau's Julie.

It seems, however, that Holcroft did not originally plan things to fall out so happily, that he planned an ending something like that of the story of Miss Milner or the romance of Julie and St. Preux. According to Godwin's manuscript critique of the novel, Anna's zeal to reform the rake Coke Clifton leads her and Frank Henley to fall victims to Clifton's revenge.[1] In the same way, Caleb Williams becomes the victim of Falkland, who is also attached to the erroneous code of chivalric honour. By enabling Clifton's arguments to triumph over Anna in the fourth volume Holcroft was, Godwin thought, destroying what he had achieved so far: 'I feared as much. I said at the end of the third volume; No; mortal man cannot support it; It would be better than Julie or Clarissa.'[2] Certainly in the earlier part of the novel Holcroft

[1] This pessimistic conclusion would explain why Holcroft may have named his heroine after Lady Anne (1456–85), daughter of Warwick the King-maker and wife successively of Edward Prince of Wales and Richard III. Once Anne erred in submitting herself to Richard's desires and his protection, her fate was sealed, even though she rose to be queen. Her adventures were recounted in Prévost's *Margaret of Anjou*, which Godwin read in 1793.

[2] The MS. critique in the Abinger collection is undated, and in quotes, which would suggest that it was Godwin's record of a conversation he had had with Holcroft.

succeeds both in showing how Anna's actions arise out of her character, and in making his heroine as interesting as Julie, if not Clarissa.

Even in the first of Anna's letters there are hints of her romantic suggestibility, and tendency to enthusiasm, qualities which Holcroft had already shown to be dangerous in *Manthorn*[1] and *Alwyn*. At first, Anna errs in regarding Clifton as a man of abilities whom it is her duty to reclaim for the use of humanity. At the same time she incorrectly ascribes too much weight to the world's opinion—her father and her relatives—in denying herself the prospect of a happy and 'useful' union with the low-born Frank Henley. She overestimates her own ability to reform Clifton solely by rational means, and she underestimates the strength of her feeling for Frank Henley, simply because she believes that love must be subject to reason's rule. The main interest in her character in the first five volumes, then, is in the conflict between her rational intentions and her unconscious yearnings and fears.

Here Holcroft reveals how much he had learned from *A Simple Story* and Mrs. Inchbald's skill at showing the force of feeling by the force necessary to suppress it. The psychological realism, in which every word, gesture, or action is related to some source in the feelings, was of a sort which struck contemporary readers as highly original, although it was not scientifically explained until Freud. The demands of subconscious feeling in Anna are manifested in her uncharacteristic fear of a candid explanation to Frank as to why she has rejected him in favour of Clifton. In fact the strain of repressing her real feelings becomes so great that she almost breaks down at the end of a letter describing her emotions after setting one of Frank's poems to music:

Indeed, Louisa, I could be a very woman—But I will not!—No, no!—It is passed—I have put my handkerchief to my eyes and it is gone—I have repressed an obstinate heaving of the heart—
Let her blame me, if I deserve it, but my Louisa must see me as I am—Yet I will conquer—Be sure I will—But I must not sing his song any more! (p. 122.)

At this moment all of Anna's qualities are combined—sensibility

[1] Published serially in the *Town and Country Magazine*, x and xi (1778 and 1779), but not completed.

and resolve, love for Frank and a dangerous tendency to repress unwanted but obstinate longings. Anna is woman before the Revolution, educated to submit herself to the masculine order of 'things as they are'; what she attempts to do is, like Mary Wollstonecraft, to struggle manfully for equality and moral and social independence.

Holcroft combines Mrs. Inchbald's technique with the epistolary form she herself rejected. Because the letter-writers reveal all, the reader sees the development of the 'necessary' chain of circumstances long before the characters themselves do, and because each incident is given from several points of view, a dramatic irony is established by which the reader can see the truths which the characters conceal from themselves and their correspondents. When Frank's alacrity saves the returning party from disaster whilst landing in a storm, for example, Anna records his presence of mind, but passes on to praise Clifton for his ready assistance, and she spends the rest of the letter trying to assure herself that Clifton's 'ardour' is a positive quality (p. 188). These self-quietings become more ominous than silence.

Meanwhile Louisa's persistent advocacy of Frank's cause and warnings of her brother's instability run parallel to Anna's anxiety, and contribute to the developing picture of Anna's self-deception. The final evidence is a kind of unconscious prescience by which Anna can understand things inexplicable to rational judgement. She can, for example, see through Clifton's habitual facetiousness to his fear of her reproval: 'to be too often encountered, by anyone whose intellects are more clear and consistent than his own, is a kind of degradation to which he scarcely knows how to submit' (p. 208). And yet her observation, slightly altered, could be applied to her own behaviour toward Frank Henley.

The reader has more than report to go by in this epistolary novel; there is something of Richardson's ability to let the reader read between the lines. But Holcroft is not interested in fine effects for their own sake. Anna's self-deception is an error, and to avoid the evil of unhappiness for herself and others, she must be 're-educated'. Luckily Clifton also errs, in supposing too much on his ability to use Anna's virtue against her, and he reveals his true character in attempting to extract conjugal 'rights' from Anna before the marriage ceremony has been performed (p. 326).

If Anna's sudden awakening is unspectacular, it is at least accurate, as she admits, 'I forgot, when passion has a purpose to obtain, how artful it is in concealment' (p. 346). The judgement is against herself as well as Clifton, and she has learned, not to doubt her own motives, but that candour and trust in truth are the only touchstones of virtuous conduct. If there is a flaw in this development, it is that Anna is not herself the agent of her enlightenment, but escapes, 'luckily', because Clifton overplays his hand; and luck is not an admissible feature of the plot-as-argument of the English Jacobin novel. On the other hand, it is a necessity of Clifton's character to overreach himself, and thus allow Anna to escape.

Once Clifton has been exposed the novel moves into a new phase, a test of Anna's and Frank's fortitude and ability to rely solely on their principles; and yet it is just at this point that Holcroft's characterization of his heroine begins to go wrong. In the early part of the novel Anna is like an idealized Elizabeth Inchbald, a beautiful and intelligent woman disposed to talk of virtue and philanthropy, but occasionally indecisive and fallible. After she becomes convinced of Clifton's duplicity, however, she becomes the philosophical 'goddess', and her role as a deity of virtue is underlined by the language in which she is described by both Frank and Clifton.

'*Don Cabbage-plant*': *Frank Henley.* A parallel development and decline occurs in Holcroft's characterization of Frank Henley. Frank's first letter displays him to the reader in a becoming state of sentimental distress over Anna's departure to visit London and Paris with her father, Sir Arthur. Frank's request for Oliver's copy of Petrarch is no whim, but the key to his relationship to Anna, a relationship designed at all times to contrast with Clifton's. After this introduction the second letter from him reveals a sensibility in full flight:

By the luckiest accident in the world, I have been allowed to accompany her thus far, have ridden all day with my eye fixed upon her, and at night have had the ecstatic pleasure to defend, to fight for her!— Would I had been killed!—Was there ever so foolish, so wrong, so romantic a wish? And yet it has rushed involuntarily upon me fifty times. To die for her seems to be a bliss which mortal man cannot merit! Truth, severe truth, perhaps, will not justify these effusions. I will, I do, endeavour to resist them [p. 15].

There is never any doubt that he will succeed, and where the self-struggle of Anna is somewhat interesting, in Frank it is perfunctory, a gesture to the requisite sensibility, which never poses a real obstacle to Frank. When Anna finally faces her interview with him, he apologizes for loving her, as though it were a kind of inebriation: 'I was unjust! A madman! A vain fool! An idiot!—Pardon this rude vehemence, but I cannot forgive myself for having been so ready to accuse one whom—! I cannot speak my feelings!—I have deserted myself!—I am no longer the creature of reason, but the child of passion!—My mind is all tumult, all incongruity!' (p. 130).

Frank's description of himself is interesting—he can be a madman and a child of passion, or else the creature of reason. In either case he would be a person passively at the command of one of two forces, in Freudian terms[1] a person or ego disastrously alienated from both libido and super-ego. It is not necessary, however, to describe Frank Henley in these terms; he can be seen simply enough in the terms of popular novel conventions. He is an English Jacobin St. Preux. He is created to worship Anna St. Ives and to reform Coke Clifton, and besides these two functions he is given the utterance of many of the novel's English Jacobin theories, and the performance of many of the novel's model benevolent deeds. He quickly overcomes his particular error and learns to moderate, though not to eradicate his love for Anna, and moves on to the English Jacobin task of reforming those about him, because this is a novel of 1792, a document in the debate on the principles of the French Revolution.

As often, though, Holcroft overstates his case. When Frank performs an act of benevolence to save a man from debtor's prison he is typically shy of accepting thanks from the man's wife for what he considers to be his duty: 'As for my name, I told her it was man. The quick hussey understood me, for she replied—No, it was angel' (p. 35). Even Milton, whose language Holcroft borrowed in places to assist his fable, could not make his angels as interesting as his devils; and if one of the functions of the character of Frank Henley is to show what Coke Clifton may become, the prospect is conspicuously uninviting. When

---

[1] The terms used by Ian Watt in his discussion of the psychology of *Clarissa* in 'Samuel Richardson', in *The Novelist as Innovator* (London, 1965), p. 13.

Clifton laughs at Frank as 'Don Cabbage-plant' (p. 283), the reader is only too ready to laugh with him.[1]

'*A Compound of Jarring Elements*': *Coke Clifton*. For it is a debilitating contradiction in the argument of *Anna St. Ives* that the villain is more interesting than the hero. The imbalance is borne out by volume of correspondence alone: Clifton has half as many letters again as Frank and almost as many as Anna herself;[2] but ultimately it is the character itself which is of greater interest, because it is mixed. Frank sees Clifton as 'a compound of jarring elements' (p. 108), and his opinion, naturally, is nothing less than the truth.

When we first meet Clifton interest has already been heightened by the delay of his first letter until the beginning of volume two; then we see a young man of fashion indeed, as his sister Louisa declared him to be, but no stage villain. He is in fact an exaggerated and humorous version of a later Jacobin 'man of honour', Godwin's Ferdinando Falkland. Like Falkland, Clifton has been on the Grand Tour where he has been indulging not in Petrarchan sentiment, but the more gentlemanly activity of knight of the bedchamber. He is a rake, a Lovelace, a follower of the fashionable and fleshly pursuits of the Restoration blood; he appreciates the beauty of the Alps (p. 61), and the beauty, not of Anna's mind, but of her person (p. 81); in short, he is an epicure, and he admires the Italians for their attitude of *carpe diem*; it is the only philosophy for *him*, at any rate, and it is the opposite of Frank Henley's stoicism—'The five senses are my deities; to them I pay worship and adoration, and never yet have I been slack in the performance of my duty' (p. 63).[3]

The contrast between Frank and Clifton, then, is a schematic one—the Stoic versus the Epicurean. On this 'philosophic' basis all other differences are built, and the competition for Anna provides most of the material. Clifton's first sight of her at Paris sends him into ecstasies:

I have found it, Fairfax! The pearl of pearls! The inestimable jewel!

---

[1] Clifton's nick-name for Frank refers, of course, to the Anti-Jacobins' characterization of schemes of reform as quixotic.

[2] The figures are: Anna 40 letters, Coke 37, Frank 23 plus the long 'Fragment', Louisa 13, Aby Henley 8, Sir Arthur St. Ives 7, Mrs. Clifton 2.

[3] The possibility of there being a coarse pun in 'slack' was by no means above the level of Holcroft's humour.

The unique! The world contains but one!—And what?—A woman! The woman of whom I told you!—Anna St. Ives!—You have seen the Venus de Medicis?—Pshaw!—Stone! Inanimate marble! But she!— The very sight of her is the height of luxury! The pure blood is seen to circulate! Transparent is the complexion which it illuminates!—And for symmetry, for motion, for grace, sculptor, painter, nor poet ever yet imagined such! Desire languishes to behold her! The passions all are in arms, and the mere enjoyment of her presence is superior to all that her sex beside can give! (p. 92.)

No description of Anna in the book makes her as real as this does, and yet it is typical of Clifton—ardent, enthusiastic, couched in connoisseur's language—and oblivious to Anna's mental qualities. To Frank, meanwhile, Anna is an ethereal Petrarchan ideal, a kind of Platonic deity whom he worships already in the kind of language that Clifton too will be using by the end of the novel: 'She soars a flight that is more than mortal! But she leaves a luminous track, that guides and invites, and I will attempt to follow. Thou shalt see me rise above the poor slavish wishes that would chain me to earth!' (p. 191).

As a mixed character Clifton can see folly in others perfectly well, and his wit, though frequently directed against 'Don Cabbage-plant', can also be turned on subjects more apt, such as the *Fête Champêtre* held by a French noble: 'The simplicity of the shepherd life could not but be excellently represented, by the ribbands, jewels, gauze, tiffany, and fringe, with which we were bedaubed; and the ragouts, fricassees, spices, sauces, wines, and *liqueurs*, with which we were regaled! Not to mention being served upon plate, by an army of footmen! But then, it was in the open air; and that was prodigiously pastoral!' (p. 116).[1]

Like the Italians he admires, Clifton is a character of extremes, and his vices are only the negative side of his virtues. It was one of the leading principles of *Political Justice* that criminals are often capable of great good if reformed rather than punished. And so, having established the lines of Clifton's character Holcroft sets about proving his English Jacobin thesis that truth and the example of virtue must conquer error. At the same time he wishes to make his thesis convincing by tracing the 'progress of the passions' in detail.

---

[1] The reference is to the notorious 'rustic' feasts held by Marie Antoinette before the Revolution.

Clifton, like Falkland, errs by over-valuing 'honour', the keystone of the chivalric system Burke had defended so strenuously in his *Reflections on the Revolution in France*. So it is appropriate that the seeds of Clifton's later crimes are planted at the Château de Villebrun, scene of the *Fête Champêtre*, and symbol of the folly and pride of the *ancien régime*.[1] His need to triumph over a social inferior impels him to leap rashly into the chateau's lake, and he is only saved from drowning by the man over whom he wished to exult (pp. 148–9). For this Frank earns his hatred, and from this point Clifton isolates himself from any open contact with Frank and Anna. The candour which is their code and the code of the English Jacobins is rejected by him for a Machiavellian duplicity. The failure of his scheme to use Anna's arguments against marriage for his own base ends is a further blow to his pride, for which he can compensate only by admitting his error, or by carrying his hostility to physical violence. Clifton is not interested in truth, and unlike Frank and Anna he makes no appeal for candid criticism from his correspondent Guy Fairfax. He is trapped, in a kind of solitary confinement, in a chain of error which he must follow to the catastrophe.

Holcroft's skill is to show how there is that within Clifton which struggles, like Anna's repressed passion for Frank, against the tyranny of error. Two themes run through his letters from the time he commences his plot against the happiness of Frank and Anna: reverence for her and admiration for him, and rage at the injury to his 'honour' done by the success of a rival.[2] To calm himself after one outburst, Clifton construes ten lines of Seneca (p. 286), a revealing, not to say Freudian slip. As his plot progresses his self-abhorrence increases, he becomes more and more misanthropic (pp. 364–5), and his hatred of his agent MacFane grows as the latter becomes more necessary to him (p. 375). At the same time his contempt for the weakness of pride in Lord Fitz-Allen (p. 364) and folly in Edward St. Ives (p. 407) also grows, so that he manifests ever-greater signs of self-alienation, even as he proceeds in his plot, until he is reduced to

[1] Villebrun is merely a French translation of 'Brunswick', name of the ruling house of Britain since the reign of Queen Anne, and hence synonymous with the system of 'Old Corruption'. The Duke of Brunswick was also the leader of the royalist forces attempting to crush the French Revolution.

[2] Holcroft plays on positive and pejorative connotations of 'honour', as Richardson does in *Clarissa*. To depict envy, Holcroft went to Gessner's *Mort d'Abel*.

alternating between despairing regret for the deities he has exiled himself from, and a mad haste for revenge.[1]

Echoes from *Othello* are by no means accidental in this part of the novel—Holcroft was a diligent student in finding out how best to achieve his literary purpose.[2] The ferment in Clifton's brain when first conceiving his plot is like that of Iago (pp. 235–6); and his description of Anna's virtues resembles Othello's despairing contemplation of Desdemona's apparent goodness (pp. 292–3). At one point Clifton even quotes from the play (p. 309). Like Othello, too, he comes to hate the 'cursed gnawings of the heart' which impel him to acts for which he will hate himself, and the language in which he expresses the extravagance of his jealousy is clearly Shakespearean: 'Oh that I were in the poisonous desert, where I might gulp mephitic winds and drop dead; or in a moment be buried in tornados of burning sand! Would that my scull were grinning there, and blanching; rather than as it is consciously parching, scorched by fires itself has kindled!' (p. 376). The echoes from *Othello* confirm the intent of Holcroft's characterization— a psychological portrayal of injured pride acting to vindicate belief in its own superiority. Clifton gradually comes under the sway of his supposed instrument Mac Fane, even as Othello's error gradually places him under the domination of Iago; but Holcroft intends to 'improve' on Shakespeare, and the outcome of his Jacobinical plot is a denial that error produces tragic consequences—Clifton is saved by the virtue and fortitude of Frank and Anna.

For the characterization of his villain Holcroft also borrows to some extent from Gothic fiction, as Godwin was to do for Falkland in *Things As They Are* and Bethlem Gabor in *St. Leon* (1799). At one point Clifton wishes he were Italian so that he could use the stiletto on Frank Henley without compunction or fear of consequences (p. 235). As his scheme of revenge matures he becomes more like a Gothic villain, but the dark imagery of his letters bears a real relation to his developing moral crisis. He uses the language of damnation—'All hell seems busy to blacken me!' (p. 391)—and when he prepares to violate Anna he wishes for solitude and darkness—'I could wish the scene were removed to the dark gloom of a forest; embosomed where none but tigers

---

[1] Letter cvii. The letter, significantly, is a reply to Fairfax's 'dissuasive epistle'.
[2] Godwin was to use the same play for his study of jealousy in *Fleetwood* (1805).

or hyenas should listen to her shrieks' (p. 412). This is not Gothic imagery for its own sake, but the extravagance of a mind divided against itself. And yet it is just this extravagance which makes Clifton interesting and which gives him a certain greatness lacking in Frank Henley. As Lavater put it, in his *Aphorisms on Man,* 'Who hides hatred to accomplish revenge is great, like the prince of hell.'[1] The allusion to Milton's Satan is by no means out of place in a description of Coke Clifton, since Godwin praised Milton's anti-hero in *Political Justice,* and exclaimed, as Anna might have exclaimed of Clifton, 'How beneficial and illustrious might the temper from which these qualities flowed, have been found, with a small diversity of situation!'[2]

Clifton's secrecy is forced on him by the error which cuts him off from the rational discourse and effect of persuasion, but finally the veil of error is torn away from his mind, after his repeated attempts to ravish Anna and break her will have failed. He thought her 'honour' could be ruined in such a way, but an English Jacobin heroine does not accept the convention of 'ruin', and the logic of Holcroft's argument is revealed: since they are free from the error which grips Clifton's mind Frank and Anna have a moral superiority over him, and therefore his revenge must fail, and the way be made clear for his eventual 'reform'. The character of Coke Clifton can be seen to have its place in the novel's argument, yet it survives mere function as the character of Frank Henley does not; and since Frank represents one half of the force of truth which defeats Clifton's error, the conclusion of Holcroft's Jacobin argument is seriously vitiated. Nor is it simply a case of contrast between Clifton's wit and Frank's solemnity. There is something actually repugnant about Frank's virtue, perhaps because any kind of asceticism 'represents a more or less permanent renunciation of any endeavour to secure certain types of satisfaction from life. Indeed, it implies an attempt—not, of course, always successful—to close one's eyes to certain possibilities, certain areas of experience.'[3] Clifton is more interesting precisely because he is open to experience, whereas Frank is not.

[1] Aphorism 496. The *Aphorisms* first appeared in English in 1788. Holcroft had translated Lavater's *Essays on Physiognomy* in 1789.

[2] Quoted in Roger Sharrock, 'Godwin on Milton's Satan', *Notes and Queries,* ccvii (Dec. 1962), 464.

[3] Simon O. Lesser, *Fiction and the Unconscious* (London, 1960), p. 53.

The War of the Angels. Nevertheless, the wider implication of the relationship between the three protagonists is obvious: circumstances form character; therefore, by changing circumstances in the right way, evil, which is another word for error, will be eradicated. Holcroft demonstrates this truth by the reform of Clifton, but he also broadens his 'argument' by setting up 'parties' of truth and error, thereby giving his conclusions the weight of general social truth at the same time that he adds to the richness and multiplicity of his characterization.

Since circumstances form character, and domestic education is one of the largest circumstances in an individual's life, the younger generation in *Anna St. Ives* all have their particular inheritance of virtue or vice. Mrs. Clifton, for example, has only two letters in the novel but is clearly of the party of virtue, like her daughter Louisa. Mr. Clifton, however, had been a rogue, and so it is no surprise that his son Coke turned out to be even worse. Similarly, Edward St. Ives only magnifies his father's foolish passion for 'improvement'—all the excesses of eighteenth-century landscaping—and develops his own fashionable vices into a comprehensive scheme to run through his patrimony. Lady St. Ives, on the other hand, had been as much of a saint as her daughter Anna. Frank Henley avoids taking after his money-grubbing self-righteous father only by finding a Mentor (*Télémaque* made its contribution to most English Jacobin novels) in the father of his friend Oliver Trenchard. Circumstances have formed these characters before the novel even begins, and the story itself is concerned to show that virtue can roll back error in the continual and inevitable progress of mankind towards perfectibility.

For it is part of Holcroft's 'argument', borrowed perhaps from *A Simple Story*, that the virtuous children can make reparation for the errors of their parents. To this end Holcroft presents a variety of minor vices in his minor characters. Sir Arthur St. Ives has the typical prejudices and follies of an eighteenth-century gentleman, such as a taste for 'improvement',[1] and hostility to the union of his daughter with a social inferior. He is redeemed from his errors by Anna's perseverance and Frank's undeniable moral superiority to all around him. With a little help from the realization that Frank's father Abimelech Henley has exploited his passion for

---

[1] Late in 1788 Holcroft had paid a visit to Strawberry Hill, with his friend Mercier. William Hazlitt, *The Life of Thomas Holcroft*, ed. Elbridge Colby, i. 307.

'improvement' to make a sizeable fortune,[1] Sir Arthur eventually admits that his steward's son may indeed be 'a gentleman by nature', if not by birth (p. 303).

If Sir Arthur represents the old aristocracy in decline, Abimelech Henley represents the new commercial man, whose only criterion of worth is money. Like the other characters in the novel, Aby is aptly named: Abimelech was either a king of the Philistines of Gerar (Genesis 26:1), or else a brigand (Judges 9).[2] Holcroft loved depicting a 'character', and Aby's letters are packed with slang and religious cant. The delightful vulgarity of his style can be traced back as far as a letter from 'Simon Saggittarius' in one of Holcroft's early 'Philosopher' essays,[3] and his hypocritical pietism may be found in the Motto family in *Manthorn*. No doubt his style also owes something to that of Tabitha Bramble in *Humphry Clinker*. However, Holcroft included no character merely for entertainment and Aby performs several roles in the novel. He effects his own version of the redistribution of wealth by bilking his employer of most of his estate and thus shows that right actions may have wrong motives. But the fortune he accumulates dishonestly later comes in handy when the selfish possession of wealth for its own sake is transmuted into a fund for general philanthropy through the union of the offspring of master and man, birth and money. Finally, by means of Frank's social success, Aby comes to see that virtue is not necessarily opposed to self-interest.

Perhaps because he had to portray them through their letters Holcroft succeeded in raising Sir Arthur and Aby above their mere functions; but even a character with no epistolary outlet of his own, such as the Irish villain Mac Fane, has a real presence in the novel due to Holcroft's ability to give him his 'appropriate sentiments and peculiar language'.[4] And although Mac Fane exists only by the report of others he has an important part in the argument of the novel, as the example of passions wholly uncontrolled.

Like the hero's father in Holcroft's last novel, *Bryan Perdue*

[1] A relationship perhaps based on that of the steward and his master, the fashionable beau, in *Gil Blas*, Book iii, Ch. iii. *Gil Blas* was a favourite with both Holcroft and Godwin.

[2] Both Holcroft and Godwin had Cruden's Biblical concordance in their libraries.

[3] *The Town and Country Magazine*, x (May 1778), 242–3.

[4] *The Monthly Review*, 2nd Ser., viii (June 1792), 155. Review of *Anna St. Ives*.

(1805), Mac Fane is an Irish gambler and crack-shot, whose errors, it is suggested, are the result of England's oppression of her un-happy sister isle. Clifton soon discovers that even a man like Mac Fane can speak up for his countrymen: 'He took offence, and retorted—"What did I mane by an Irishman? Becase he is a rogue you think he is an Irishman! By the holy carpenter you need not come to Ireland for that kind of ware! You have a viry pritty breed of rogues of your own! But he is not Irish. He is one of your own sulky English bugs" ' (p. 377). Like Clifton, Mac Fane cannot control his passions, and so is caught in a train of error which will lead him to disaster. Clifton sees this, and detests in his accomplice the very desire for revenge which he cannot control in himself (p. 375). It is Clifton himself who cuts Mac Fane down in the end, to prevent him taking the life of Frank Henley. Mac Fane dies with all his sins on his head, unlike his employer who has time to repent, and so serves as a reminder of another idea of the English Jacobins, that not every one can be reached by the reforming power of truth, that there must at least be a predis-position to truth and virtue.[1]

By now it will be clear that Holcroft's characterization in *Anna St. Ives* is wholly at the disposal of his English Jacobin argument about truth and its place in the world. The novel might as well have been dedicated 'To the Sacred Majesty of Truth' as Thomas Taylor's *Commentaries* of Proclus, published in the same year. Holcroft did not meet Taylor, apparently, until 1799, but both *Anna St. Ives* and *Political Justice* show a distant influence of contemporary neo-Platonism, assimilated to the ideas of the eighteenth-century Commonwealthmen. Truth, once known, must prove invincible, and it was every man's social duty to make the truth known as widely as possible.

The Chain of Necessity: Plot, Structure, and Allegory

The Necessity of Form. From the discussion of characterization in *Anna St. Ives* it will be clear that the plot of the novel is not merely a concatenation of events, but primarily a study of 'the progress of the passions'. There is a sequence of events, it is true, but Holcroft tries to make these dependent on the characters he

---

[1] B. R. Pollin, *Education and Enlightenment in the Works of William Godwin* (New York, 1962), p. 167.

has created, so that characters created by circumstance shape circumstance in their turn. First Frank and Anna clear up the error in their own minds, and then the other characters are re-formed by being drawn into contact with them. There are a few exceptions to the novel's Reform Movement—Lord Fitz-Allen, who is too haughty to be affected by truth and virtue,[1] and Mac Fane, who is too enmeshed in a life of crime—and these serve as dire warnings; but the rest of the characters are all eventually won over to the party of truth and virtue. Frank sums up the movement of the plot-as-argument near the end of the novel, when he simply declares 'Truth is omnipotent' (p. 458).

Holcroft meant this maxim to be the crux of his argument; and yet it is also the crux of his failure. Omnipotence is not a quality with much human interest or dramatic possibility, as Milton discerned. Holcroft's system is closed, a logical argument which operates like a syllogism, and the very unity of argument and 'unity of design' which he thought would ensure the general application of the novel's conclusions, in fact become its greatest defect.

The impression that the novel is unified but closed and abstract, is reinforced by an excessively symmetrical structure. The basic outline consists of two love-plots which overlap in the middle, the first concerning Frank's acceptance as Anna's suitor, the second Clifton's initial acceptance and eventual rejection as her betrothed. The turning-point occurs almost exactly in the centre of the novel, when Clifton declares war on Anna.[2] And connected with this structure in the love-plot is the pattern, already referred to, of correction of error in the three protagonists. Frank Henley overcomes his passionate love for Anna sufficiently to resolve on emigrating to America to establish a Pantisocracy amongst the Indians; whereupon Anna realizes, thanks to Clifton over-playing his hand, that she has mistaken her man. Finally, Clifton himself is made to see that he may after all cease to be 'a man of honour, a despiser of peasants, an assertor of rank' (p. 475). It is true that in the earlier stages of the novel, when the symmetrical lines of development are not so obvious, there is a sense of possibility vital to sustaining interest; but as the outline becomes apparent

[1] He is also too well-born. Baronets and lesser folk could be reformed in English Jacobin novels, but there were few peers who were not total villains.
[2] Letter lxxi; there are 130 letters plus Frank's lengthy 'Fragment'.

and the outcome obvious, interest wanes, at the very moment when Holcroft should be making his conclusions most impressive. Furthermore, the symmetry of structure is extended into a schematic grouping of characters arranged according to the demands of the 'argument'. Frank Henley is Holcroft's addition to Richardson's group of characters and he is obviously intended to contrast with Coke Clifton in birth, station, and views. Anna is caught in the middle and so a more elaborate if less subtle struggle of personalities and values develops than that seen in *Clarissa*. The contrast is meant to produce a conflict, but there is never any doubt of the issue. With Frank Henley by her side Clarissa too would have escaped her fate.

The characterization in the later part of the novel, especially, becomes so abstract that it is difficult to tell whether the conflict is between Frank and Clifton or Virtue and Vice. Holcroft deplored the intrusion of personality into debates on political and moral truth, and Anna rejects Clifton's invitation to hate him with the motto—'I hate only your errors! I scorn nothing but vice' (p. 422). So the conflict between characters is clearly meant to have a general application, but Anna and Frank are so impregnable in their stoic fortitude—they must be so to be exemplary—that Holcroft's argument has only one possible outcome; that is, it is not an argument at all, but a proposition. After Anna has told Clifton that she hates not him but his errors, she continues: 'On the virtues of which a mind like yours is capable my soul would dilate with ecstasy, and my heart would doat! But you have sold yourself to crookedness! Base threats, unmanly terrors, and brute violence are your despicable engines!— Wretched man! They are impotent!—They turn upon yourself; me they cannot harm!—I am above you!' (p. 422). But by being above him she is out of reach of more than his desperate schemes of revenge. To the schematic plot of the novel is added a degree of abstractness in the characterization of virtue in the last volume, and the result is a novel which is 'philosophical' in a bad sense. The novel's English Jacobin 'argument' attains all the suspense and interest of a syllogism.

And yet, in some ways the novel's argument is not uncompromising enough; for if *Anna St. Ives* was meant as a criticism of certain conventions of the popular novel, it fails to keep itself wholly uncontaminated by those conventions. The ending of

Holcroft's novel is a happy version of *Clarissa* because Anna refuses to accept the convention of 'ruin', and yet the happiness of the ending is increased by the acceptance of other conventions. Unlike Rousseau's Julie or Mackenzie's Julia, Holcroft's Anna does not have to deny herself her heart's choice. Frank is made acceptably wealthy thanks to his father's lifetime of embezzlement, and his low social status is compensated by a super-human virtue. Anna could choose a sinner if he is her social equal, but only a saint if he is her social inferior. The love conventions of this English Jacobin novel are as arbitrary as those of the novels Holcroft castigated in *The Monthly Review*: Anna never loves Clifton, for to do so would be an error of sentiment which is not allowed to a heroine, whereas an error of judgement is. Only in the novels of Mary Hays and Mary Wollstonecraft was there any real protest against the convention that an error of sensibility must be severely punished, and in their novels an inability to control technique vitiated the originality of their views.

Anna St. Ives is a philosophical novel in two senses then—it is a novel which, by plot and characterization, argues a certain case; and it is a novel which proceeds in large part by particular dialogues, debates, and discussions of a philosophical nature. In neither case is its philosophy necessarily a limitation; it only becomes so by Holcroft's inability to sustain through technique and diversity of material his overt attempt to make the novel of general and philosophical import.

English Jacobin Satire. Apart from the manipulation of character, dialogue, and plot, there are two additional ways in which Holcroft tries to diffuse his English Jacobin argument through *Anna St. Ives*. In spite of the fact that the novel is modelled on sentimental epistolary fiction some of its materials are also taken from the novel of manners,[1] and Holcroft uses a variety of traditional satiric themes and techniques. Some of his characters, Aby Henley and Sir Arthur St. Ives, for example, are based on the Theophrastan 'Character' which he admired so much, and which was a prominent feature of Bage's novels, of Mrs. Inchbald's *Nature and Art* (1796), and Holcroft's next two novels, *Hugh Trevor* and *Bryan Perdue*. The *Characters* of one of Holcroft's favourite authors, Samuel Butler, may especially have been in

---

[1] *Evelina* as well as *Cecilia* and *Camilla* were in Holcroft's library in 1807.

his mind, since he had borrowed from them to fill the pages of *The Wit's Magazine* which he had edited in 1784.[1]

In addition, *Anna St. Ives* contains a great deal of satire on the fashionable vices—the artificialities of French taste, 'improvement', gaming, pride of rank and station—which had provided matter for several generations of periodical essayists, and which the novelists of manners had plundered in their turn. This again was a truly popular literary form which Holcroft had practised with some skill as early as 1777.[2] Holcroft's own bent was for humour and satire, which he combined with a certain leavening of late eighteenth-century sentiment, and with this *mélange* he had already made a name for himself as a comic dramatist.[3] *Anna St. Ives* displays the same mixture of satire and sentiment to be found in his own plays and in those of his favourite authors, such as Sheridan and Foote. Holcroft blends these various modes with considerable skill in *Anna St. Ives*, and improves on Rousseau's clumsy attempts to make St. Preux into a social satirist in part two of *La Nouvelle Héloïse*. By making his villain his satirist, Holcroft shows that Clifton is reformable at the same time that he affords the reader comic relief from the moral seriousness of Frank and Anna. Other characters, such as Abimelech Henley and Anna's haughty relations, simply satirize themselves. But one way or another Holcroft manages to cut up a wide range of examples of pride, avarice, lust, wrath, gluttony, envy, and sloth—the English Jacobin moral scheme is not after all so different from the traditional Christian one. What is remarkable is that Holcroft succeeds so well in integrating satire with character, for the English Jacobins did not believe in sin, but only error. However deeply ingrained, the seven deadly vices are only bad habits, and so they are best laughed at rather than hated. However traditional the sources and the subjects of satire in *Anna St. Ives*, Holcroft still makes his satire collaborate with his English Jacobin argument. The novel's many satiric hits are part of a unified design—the struggle of truth against error—at the

[1] Some of Butler's *Characters* appeared in every issue edited by Holcroft (viz., *The Wit's Magazine*, i, Jan. to April 1784), as well as in several subsequent issues.

[2] In his 'Philosopher' essays in the *Town and Country Magazine* (Oct. 1777 to Feb. 1779). In 1780 he also contributed to the *Westminster Magazine*, in 1783 to the *English Review* and *Morning Chronicle*, and in 1784 he edited the *Wit's Magazine*.

[3] Virgil R. Stallbaumer, 'Thomas Holcroft: A Satirist in the Stream of Sentimentalism', *ELH, A Journal of English Literary History*, iii (1936), 31–62.

same time that they diffuse the novel's argument through the whole social sphere of 'things as they are'.

The proportion of satire throughout the novel remains low, however, especially if *Anna St. Ives* is compared with Holcroft's next two novels, or those of Bage. Moreover, the amount of satire and comedy diminishes in the later part of the novel, and does nothing to mitigate the growing solemnity and dogmatic narrowness of the 'argument'. It is as if Holcroft's vigorous sense of humour, as well as Coke Clifton's, were borne down by the increasing gravity of the moral debate, and he could not save the end of the novel from foundering into one of the century's other major modes, Gothic melodrama. The fact that he returned with redoubled vigour to his wonted vein of satiric humour in *Hugh Trevor* suggests that he recognized his failure.

English Jacobin Allegory. If Holcroft attempted to broaden the social scope of his novel by means of satire on manners, he attempts to widen its philosophic scope by means of moral, political, and historical allegory. He opposes stoic and epicurean language in a neo-Platonic framework, for example, to create a kind of English Jacobin theology. Behind this aspect of his fable, of course, is Milton. Clifton's epicurean delight on first beholding Anna's charms is expressed in images of precious jewels and objects of luxury, images and language which suit Clifton's epicurean philosophy of life, but this is not the only language used to describe the heroine. Writing to thank his sister for making him acquainted with such a paragon, he refers to her already as 'the divine Anna' (p. 84). As the novel progresses the use of such terms increases, and the language of the epicurean gradually dies away, until in the very midst of his rage over Anna's candid account of her design to reform him, Clifton extols her beauty and realizes that it was more than physical charm which had nearly won him over. 'Not that it was her arguments. What are they? It was her bright her beaming eyes, her pouting beauteous lips, her palpitating ecstatic bosom, her—I know not what, except that even this was not all!—No!—There was something still more heavenly!—An emanating deity!—The celestial effulgence of a divine soul, that flowed with fervour almost convulsive!' (p. 270). As if it were necessary, Louisa Clifton makes the point clear when she writes to blame her brother for the disappearance of her two friends. 'Did they not labour hourly, incessantly, with the purity of saints and the ardour of angels, to do you good? . . . Clifton!—You were not formed for this! You have a mind that might have been the fit companion of divine natures!—It may be still!—Awake! View the light, and turn from crimes, pollution, and abhorrence, to virtue, love, and truth!' (p. 430). Clifton is aware of the truth, if only subconsciously, and at the last he recognizes his desire to join the company of Saints. 'They are brave spirits, and will mock my power even to the last. I love their high courage. Perhaps they shall find I have a kindred soul!—Oh would they die forgiving me—!' (p. 442). Clifton moves from epicurean to neo-Platonist, and there is therefore an allegorical structure to the argument of the novel, as well as a satiric and philosophic one. It is the English Jacobin version of the redemption of the soul described by the neo-Platonist Thomas Taylor in 1805, but formulated before *Anna St. Ives* was written:

I . . . believe that as the human soul ranks among the number of those souls that *sometimes* follow the mundane divinities, in consequence of subsisting immediately after daemons and heroes the *perpetual* attendants of the gods, it possesses a power of descending infinitely into the sublunary region, and of ascending from thence to real being. That in consequence of this, the soul while an inhabitant of earth is in a fallen condition, an apostate from deity, an exile from the orb of light. That she can only be restored while on earth to the divine likeness, and be able after death to reascend to the intelligible world, by the exercise of the *cathartic* and *theoretic* virtues; the former purifying her from the defilements of a mortal nature, and the latter elevating her to the vision of true being. And that such a soul returns after death to her kindred star from which she fell, and enjoys a blessed life.[1]

It is love, Platonic love, which brings about Clifton's moral revolution. Clifton recognizes the purity and beauty of Anna's soul from the very beginning, but because he is ignorant of the truth he mistakes her spiritual appeal for physical allure. The frustration of his passion leads him into the dark night of hatred and revenge, but eventually he is brought back into the 'light', educated into a company of the elect (the Calvinist terminology is not inappropriate), and the end of the novel leaves us with

---

[1] From *The Platonic Philosopher's Creed*, in *Thomas Taylor the Platonist*, ed. Kathleen Raine and George Mills Harper (London, 1969), p. 444. Taylor uses 'daemon' the way Mary Shelley does in *Frankenstein*. Godwin first met Taylor in 1788, and, at the time he was reading *Anna St. Ives* in manuscript, Godwin noted in his Journal for 20 December 1791, 'Holcroft sups, talk of Plato'.

the prospect of some future Pantisocracy, a communal life based on candour and virtue and benevolence, in which the reformed Clifton is now entitled to share.

But even the neo-Platonic allegory only contributes to the impression of philosophical abstraction as the novel moves to its close.[1] The characters appear to be grouped as if they formed some Great Chain of Virtue, divinities such as Frank and Anna at the top, diabolical villains such as MacFane at the bottom, and erring 'mixed' characters such as Clifton somewhere in between. In describing Frank and Anna as 'divinities' Clifton makes them seem more than human, and so less than real. This philosophical language dominates the novel, moreover, in the volumes where the erosion of epistolary realism, the intrusion of melodrama, and a decline in subtlety of characterization have already vitiated the novel's persuasiveness. The weakness of *Anna St. Ives* is not that it is a philosophical novel, but that its philosophy is inadequately deployed and hence self-defeating.

The novel's allegory of love is both traditional and a text for the times. In the relationship between the three principal characters is clearly intended to be a paradigm of the political situation of the 1790s. Clifton's declaration of war on Anna brings this aspect of the novel into the open: 'Her pride shall first be lowered. I must command, not be commanded: and, when my clemency is implored, I will then take time to consider' (p. 236). The tyrannic sway he wishes to impose on Anna has in fact more relevance to the voluptuous decadence of the *ancien régime*, than to the English situation: 'Oh for a mistress such as I could imagine, and such as Anna St. Ives moulded by me could make! One that could vary her person, her pleasures, and her passions, purposely to give mine variety! Whose daily and nightly study all should centre in me, and my gratifications!' (p. 237). But then Clifton is a pre-revolutionary man. Anna, on the other hand, sees herself reforming Clifton, in terms which could have stood for the English Jacobin credo in the 1790s; and when eventually she succeeds, one of the crimes Clifton accuses himself of is having 'mimicked tyranny'. Holcroft's source, once again, was *Clarissa* and Lovelace's glorying in power; but he also drew on the sources of

[1] The novel fictionalizes almost every individual point made in the first four books of Plato's *Republic*, and Godwin prepared himself for reading Holcroft's MS. by perusing just these books of Spens's translation of *The Republic* on 6–7 September 1791.

Clarissa itself—the heroic drama of the previous age. Holcroft, after all, had read and acted in the same kinds of plays as Mrs. Inchbald, plays which, significantly, were beginning to enjoy a revival in the decade when issues and characters once more seemed larger than life.

The analogy between domestic and public affairs was a familiar one in the 1790s, but Holcroft also assisted his readers in making the connection by means of historical and literary allusions. It has already been noticed that Abimelech Henley's Christian name has obvious reference to either a king of the Philistines or a notorious Biblical brigand, perhaps to both; and that Anna's name and situation (in the original version of the novel at least) may suggest a parallel with Anne (1456–85), wife and queen of the historical villain Richard III.[1] Or, she may be named after the prophetess who spoke of the Lord to those who yearned for redemption (Luke 2: 38). It is certain that Coke Clifton's Christian name indicates his 'mixed' character. Clifton's epistolary style and epicurean philosophy are almost certainly modelled on the 'letters' of Thomas, second Baron Lyttelton (1744–79).[2] Although the letters were almost certainly written by William Combe, this made no difference to Holcroft; like Godwin he cared little for distinctions between fact and fiction if there was a moral at stake. Lyttelton's early career clearly inspired Clifton's. Son of the author of *Dialogues of the Dead*, Lyttelton was a promising youth, interested in the arts, a skilled painter, and well-educated; but the Grand Tour spoiled him. So readily did he indulge in the vices of Italy that his engagement with the daughter of General Warburton was broken off. Thereafter Lyttelton pursued a downhill course: he married a widow, left her for a barmaid, supported the Government during the American war, and finally died after a premonitory dream. 'Lyttelton's libertinism was exceptional even in his age and rank',[3] and yet he was a man of obvious abilities, like Godwin's Falkland in *Things As They Are*, denied his usefulness by the erroneous values of fashionable society.

Holcroft changed the ending of Lyttelton's history, and thereby made a characteristic joke. 'Coke upon Littleton' was one of the

---

[1] Godwin also drew the name of his villain Tyrrel from Richard's reign.

[2] *Letters of the Late Lord Lyttelton* (London, 1780). A new edition was published in 1792.   [3] *D.N.B.*, s.v. Thomas Lyttelton.

best known commentaries on those laws which Holcroft and Godwin believed responsible for the corruption of society, and Holcroft clearly based his own Coke upon another Lyttelton; but more interesting is the fact that Sir Edward Coke (1552–1634) was one of English history's most notable converts to the cause of truth and justice. After a brilliant career in law he became attorney-general in 1594, about two centuries before Holcroft wrote his novel, and then conducted a series of treason trials like those that were just beginning in England of the 1790s. 'In all of these he exhibited a spirit of rancour, descending even to brutality, for which no one has attempted a defence, his biographers one and all agreeing that his conduct towards Raleigh was simply infamous.'[1] But in the next reign Coke was transformed into an opponent of James's exaggeration of royal prerogative, and ended a brilliant career of resisting what he had once promoted when he developed the principles of Magna Carta into the Petition of Right. In the age of the Rights of Man there could be no more appropriate godfather for a reformed 'tyrant' (Clifton's own word), and Holcroft accordingly grafted this Coke upon his own Lyttelton.

For his surnames Holcroft seems to have indulged in some geographical jokes. Anna's surname for example, happens to be that of the sleepy village in Huntingdonshire where Oliver Cromwell spent a few years as a farmer and grazier in the 1630s, before he played his part in England's Revolution. Following Holcroft's line of thought it is also possible to speculate on the import of 'Henley' and 'Clifton'. England holds two Henleys, one in Oxfordshire and another, Henley-in-Arden, in Warwickshire. Another Arden was of course the refuge of the party of virtue in Shakespeare's *As You Like It*, and in Boiardo's *Orlando Innamorato* the fountain of Ardenne could transform hate into love.[2] If Holcroft's references here are well concealed, they are nevertheless similar to those in other of his novels. If his Henley is in Arden, it may be no accident that one of England's several Cliftons is in Eden, the Vale of Eden in Westmorland, where part of the action of his first novel *Alwyn* takes place. It is both ironical and just that Eden, as Paradise Regained, is the final object of Coke Clifton's desire.

---

[1] *D.N.B.*, s.v. Sir Edward Coke.
[2] Holcroft was quite familiar with Italian epic literature.

The Failure of Compromise. Godwin was to pursue Holcroft's allusive use of names in *Things As They Are*, with greater historical and philosophical rigour, and with less facetiousness. Cleverness was no part of Godwin's endowment as a writer, and he learned from Holcroft's mistakes. For Holcroft's allusive names seem to lack the prophetic resonance of Godwin's, and if Godwin's novels generally are less unified, less well-contrived than Holcroft's, it is ultimately to their benefit.

The Monthly Review was right to describe *Anna St. Ives* as 'well contrived',[1] but a contrivance is not a work of art. When the various elements of the novel fit together almost too well, when even the characters' names are contrived, the fiction seems to be merely a mechanical construction designed to illustrate a certain principle. An illustration is not an embodiment, and allegory is not symbol. *Anna St. Ives* pursues philosophical 'unity of design' so strenuously that it fails to achieve that symbolic embodiment of past and present in a domestic narrative which is the chief excellence of *Things As They Are*. Louisa Clifton provides the final explanation for the failure of Holcroft's novel: 'I, with my Anna, say mind can do all things with mind: truth is irresistible, and must finally conquer. But it has many modes of conquering, and some of them are tragical, and dreadful' (p. 154). *Anna St. Ives* fails because, after a certain point, it is seen to be closed to just this possibility of the 'tragical', a possibility which it was the great achievement of *Things As They Are* to realize.

2. HUGH TREVOR

The English Jacobin Picaresque

However, while Godwin took up the psychological line of fiction —*Clarissa*, *La Nouvelle Héloïse*, *A Simple Story*, and *Anna St. Ives*— Holcroft himself turned to the picaresque tradition, and tried to renovate it in the light of his English Jacobin philosophy, just as he had already tried to renovate sentimental fiction and the novel of manners. In the preface to *Alwyn* he declared that *Tom Jones* would never want admirers, and he obviously felt that Smollett merited the same admiration, for his next novel,

---

[1] *The Monthly Review*, 2nd Ser., viii (June 1792), 155.

The Adventures of Hugh Trevor, published in two three-volume parts in 1794 and 1797, teems with echoes from most of Smollett's fiction, but especially from *Roderick Random* and Smollett's translation of Le Sage's *Gil Blas*.[1] It could even be argued that the theme of *Hugh Trevor* is the same as that of *The Adventures of Roderick Random*, the reconciling of reason and passion.[2]

Although he obviously knew the major works of the picaresque tradition, Holcroft did not have to look as far as Smollett for a model. Just as Mrs. Inchbald had shown Holcroft the use that could be made of the achievement of Richardson, so Robert Bage showed him the use that could be made of Fielding and Smollett. In March 1793 he had reviewed *Man As He Is* for *The Monthly Review* and placed it in the highest category of 'useful' fiction, as a novel which had 'the power of playing on the fancy, interesting the affections, and teaching moral and political truth'.[3] So highly did Holcroft rate Bage's novel that he immediately passed it on to Godwin, who read it between 9 and 26 March 1793; and it may be that he passed on more of his reading as well, for Godwin then read through most of Smollett's novels in April, May, and June, although they did not bear much relation to the work of fiction he himself had in hand. For Holcroft, like his great predecessor, adapted the tradition to his purpose. He would naturally be interested in this representative form of the age of 'the invention of liberty', and he would also find very useful a form which enabled him to send his hero on a voyage through a corrupt society. He would appreciate the picaresque's opportunities for exploiting autobiography and confession, and he would see the obvious popularity of a form which emphasized the pleasures of freedom and the 'feeling of flux and variety' in human affairs.[4] But as an English Jacobin Holcroft could see that something had to be done about the picaresque's apparent formlessness. He would renovate the form by showing the moral reform of his picaro, not as a mere gesture at the end, but as

[1] Many of these echoes have been recorded in Rodney M. Baine, *Thomas Holcroft and the Revolutionary Novel* (Athens, Georgia, 1965), Ch. iv. The number of picaresque and semi-picaresque works in Holcroft's library is too great to list in detail.

[2] M. A. Goldberg, *Smollett and the Scottish School* (Albuquerque, New Mexico, 1959), p. 22.

[3] Op. cit., 2nd Ser., x (Mar. 1793), 297.

[4] See Maximillian E. Novak, 'Freedom, Libertinism, and the Picaresque', in *Studies in Eighteenth Century Culture*, vol. iii, ed. Harold E. Pagliaro (Cleveland and London, 1973), p. 45.

a gradual and inevitable process, a philosophic structure which shaped the whole of his novel.

In his effort to combine eighteenth-century empirical psychology with Revolutionary sensibility, Holcroft had already drawn on his French as well as English predecessors for *Anna St. Ives.* He continued this practice in searching out models for his new novel. For the first part of *Hugh Trevor* (1794) he also went to Marivaux's *Le Paysan Parvenu,* in order to learn how to soften his argument with sentiment at the same time that he enlivened it with sensibility. As could be expected, his collaborator William Godwin read Marivaux's novel in July 1793, only a month after he had had his first glimpse of Holcroft's new novel in manuscript. But the second part of *Hugh Trevor* is less wholehearted in its sensibility, at least until the end, and seems to replace sentiment with the more philosophical emotion of sympathy. Holcroft almost seems to be working in another mode of the picaresque, one more satirical and philosophical and less confident of ultimate truths and their inevitable triumph. It is interesting therefore, to find Godwin reading Diderot's *La Religieuse* and *Jacques le fataliste,* as well as the abbé Dulaurens's *Compère Mathieu,* in the very same months that he was reading the second part of Holcroft's novel (March–May 1797). In the sceptical anti-novel 'libertine' picaresque of Diderot and Dulaurens, Holcroft was already looking ahead to the mode of his next novel, which he may already have begun writing, *The Memoirs of Bryan Perdue* (1805).

The Chain of Necessity: Character

The English Jacobin Picaro. Whatever the particular sources of *Hugh Trevor,* Holcroft did not rest content with mere imitation. His aim was to spread the English Jacobin philosophy by means of the popular novel. To do so, artistic achievement was as important as philosophical truth, and both had to be combined in that 'unity of design' expounded in the preface to *Alwyn;* and so it is not so much the models which are of interest as the use he made of them, the way in which he renovated the characters, plot, and themes of picaresque fiction in his second attempt to fashion an English Jacobin novel.

Much as Holcroft was taken with Tom Jones, Gil Blas,

Roderick Random, Sir George Paradyne, Jacques, and Mathieu, they would not do as heroes of a thoroughly Jacobin novel such as he intended to write. *Hugh Trevor*, like *Anna St. Ives*, is affected throughout by its author's high sense of purpose, a sense which distinguishes the novels of the English Jacobins from the tradition of the popular novel as surely as their radicalism in politics distinguishes them from the tradition of eighteenth-century political opposition. And so Hugh Trevor is an English Jacobin picaro, and, in the second part of the novel he even has his Sancho Panza, named, appropriately, after one of the precursors of the English Jacobins' ethical rationalism.[1]

But Holcroft's picaro is no ordinary one. For example, Hugh is utterly unspotted by the lapses in sexual morality of Tom Jones, Peregrine Pickle, or Sir George Paradyne. In part, no doubt, Holcroft was simply falling in with the narrower proprieties of his own time; but he did so from somewhat different motives than Hannah More: the heroes of English Jacobin novels could not look back to the exploits of Tom Jones or Roderick Random without encountering the steady gaze of Mary Wollstonecraft and her demand for an end to the double standard, not only because it was a piece of hypocrisy in itself, but because it was a part of the same general system of social tyranny which the English Jacobins opposed in their pamphlets, plays, poems, and novels. Nor are the supposedly natural impulses of earlier novel heroes to be sublimated by surrender to sentiment. Hugh must learn to oppose passion of all kinds with reason, and only a few months before the first part of *Hugh Trevor* appeared Holcroft had censured a picaresque novel in *The Monthly Review* for preaching the omnipotence of love and justifying licentiousness 'by the consideration that it was irresistible'.[2]

In other respects, however, Holcroft was willing to accept the picaro, as he had been refined and developed by earlier novelists, as the ideal central character for an English Jacobin 'satire upon the times'. The leading characteristic of the hero in Smollett and Bage is his impetuosity, a tendency to rush into things which was often traced to an impoverished or unsettled childhood. Such

---

[1] i.e. Samuel Clarke (1675–1729). See also Godwin's use of the name of the necessitarian philosopher Anthony Collins.

[2] Op. cit., 2nd Ser., xii (Dec. 1793), 393. A review of *The French Gil Blas*. As a fair turnabout, *Hugh Trevor* was translated into French as *Le Gilblas Anglais* (Elbridge Colby, *A Bibliography of Thomas Holcroft*, New York, 1922, p. 71).

a tendency offers obvious comic and satiric possibilities. It also had a direct relevance to the changing attitude of the English Jacobins to contemporary political reality. The impetuosity of the French was proverbial in the eighteenth century, and the Revolution was seen as the final, most disastrous manifestation of that sad defect. English reformers too had been over-zealous in taking up the cudgels of controversy and by 1795 Godwin admitted that they had to bear some of the responsibility for the severity of the Government's repression,[1] and the hero of Godwin's novel of 1794, Caleb Williams, blames the tragical catastrophe of his adventures on the same 'precipitation' which is the major flaw of Hugh Trevor.[2] To Holcroft and Godwin the leading characteristic of the picaro was the same as that of the Revolutionary mob—an excess of liberty, passions unlicensed by reason, which the English Jacobin intellectuals feared as much as did the supporters of the Establishment.

Holcroft underlines dangerous impetuosity in several ways, besides actually showing Hugh in action. Like Caleb Williams, Hugh has a Welsh surname, and the Welsh too were subject to a national impetuosity of temper, according to the author of *The Spiritual Quixote*.[3] And like the narrator of one of Holcroft's translations, *The Life of Baron Frederic Trenck* (1788), Hugh finds it difficult to forget a grudge, and rushes from one misconceived scheme of revenge to another, until he learns the true principles of 'political justice'. There is even an easy transition from 'Trenck' to 'Trevor', and it is not surprising to find that Godwin also consulted this work whilst writing *Things As They Are*.[4] Blessed with sensibility and parts, but cursed with a fiery temperament, Hugh is a 'mixed' character, better suited to be the protagonist of a novel than 'Don Cabbage-plant'—Frank Henley—but especially suited for a novel about the correction of error.

There are, moreover, indications that the character of Hugh, like the hero of the *Bildungsroman*,[5] was drawn from that of his

[1] In *Considerations on Lord Grenville's and Mr. Pitt's Bills, Concerning Treasonable and Seditious Practices* (1795).

[2] *Caleb Williams*, ed. McCracken, p. 325.

[3] Richard Graves, *The Spiritual Quixote*, ed. Clarence Tracy (London, New York, and Toronto, 1967), p. 28.

[4] Godwin probably wanted to see how Trenck described his imprisonment, for volume two of *Things As They Are*.

[5] E. L. Stahl and W. E. Yuill, *German Literature of the Eighteenth and Nineteenth Centuries* (London, 1970), p. 101.

author. Hazlitt was the first to notice the autobiographical element, in his *Memoir* of Holcroft,[1] but whereas Holcroft drew on his own experience for simple raw material in *Alwyn*, in *Hugh Trevor* he carried the process a stage further, and moralized on his own life and character as he had seen Mrs. Inchbald do in *A Simple Story*. There is, it is true, a good amount of undigested experience, particularly in the long narrative of young Wilmot,[2] whose experiences as a would-be author are similar to Holcroft's own.[3]

However, the most interesting autobiographical passages are always related to the picaro's gradual abandonment of his naturally impulsive temperament. In the second part of the novel, published in 1797, Hugh's earlier determination to revenge himself on his persecutors, Lord Idford, the bishop, and the president of his Oxford college, is changed to pity when he sees Idford ruined by electioneering, and the bishop dying from a lifetime of gluttony. He decides to abandon his attempt to expose them in a pamphlet—'thus expired a production which had aided to drain my pocket, waste my time, and inflame my passions' (p. 422). Between publication of the two parts of his novel Holcroft had not shown his hero's good sense, and in attempting to vindicate himself from the charge of treason, and then from the slur of being called an 'acquitted felon', he published two pamphlets early in 1795,[4] neither of which was free from the intemperate language of which he accused his enemies. Hugh learns his lesson, and by 1797 Holcroft had learned it too.

The incident is but one example of the way in which Holcroft's English Jacobin picaro is a portrait, a 'confession', of his own virtues and vices. Hugh's impetuosity, extravagance, resentfulness, and self-righteousness, as well as his ardour, perseverance, magnanimity, and sympathy were in fact the attributes of Holcroft himself, as Godwin made clear in one of those candid communica-

---

[1] The index of Colby's edition of Hazlitt's *Memoir* lists passages in the novels thought to be autobiographical.

[2] Thomas Holcroft, *The Adventures of Hugh Trevor*, ed. Seamus Deane (London, 1973), pp. 231–51. As in Bage's novels, the inset narrative is set apart with a title, 'History of Mr. Wilmot'.

[3] e.g. the one-line review of Wilmot's novel is an almost exact quotation of *The Monthly Review*'s notice of *Alwyn* (1st Ser., lxiii, Sept. 1780, 233).

[4] *A Narrative of Facts, relating to a Prosecution for High Treason* (London, 1795); *A Letter to the Right Honourable William Windham, on the Intemperance and Dangerous Tendency of his Conduct* (London, 1795).

tions to which the English Jacobins were given.[1] This 'confessional' aspect, typical of most English Jacobin novels, was also a feature of the nascent *Bildungsroman* of which Holcroft, with his knowledge of German, was probably aware. In fashioning his picaro Holcroft borrowed now from fiction, now from the memoirs of others, now from his own experience, but always with a view to fulfilling the designs of an English Jacobin novel. And what Holcroft does at most points, in pursuit of his 'unity of design', is to demonstrate the same principle exhibited in *Anna St. Ives*, that 'the characters of men originate in their external circumstances'.

In Holcroft's attempt to illustrate this principle fiction and autobiography meet. Carrying forward from *Anna St. Ives* the idea that character is to some extent taken from parental influence, Holcroft displays Hugh's relatives as a feckless and irascible collection of interesting but unreliable eccentrics. His parents threw prudence to the winds, married, and earned the condemnation of Hugh's grandfather. Hugh's father, a carefree scapegrace who lacks the perseverance to make a success of anything, is probably a portrait of Holcroft's own; and his mother, though tender-hearted, is a weak character dominated by every changing emotion. Thus Hugh's character originates in that of his parents, not as an inheritance, but as an important influence in the events of his childhood, and Holcroft carefully traces out the relationship between those events and the growth of Hugh's temperament.

But Holcroft also prepares the ground for another, saving, aspect of Hugh's character. When the family fortunes collapse from death and debts Hugh has to endure hardship for a time, being put out to the lowest form of apprenticeship, that of farm labourer under a ferocious madman who is utterly unable to control his passions.[2] Finally this employer almost kills Hugh in a paroxysm of rage, and the youth decides to run away. In a scene which is reminiscent of the reconciliation of Dorriforth and Harry Rushbrook in *A Simple Story*, Hugh is received once more into his grandfather's household. But harsh experience has had its

[1] Letter from Godwin, unaddressed, but obviously to Holcroft, in the Abinger collection. Undated, but probably written in 1805.
[2] Holcroft's father displayed a similar failing. William Hazlitt, *The Life of Thomas Holcroft*, ed. Elbridge Colby, i. 31.

benefits: 'to use my father's language, the case-hardening I had
received tempered my future life, and prepared me to endure those
misfortunes with fortitude which might otherwise have broken
my spirit' (pp. 50–1).

Characteristically, a Prévostian pessimistic foreshadowing is
lightened with English Jacobin optimism, and not for the last
time does the hero thus draw the moral for the reader. For if
the novel is autobiographical, it is also strongly confessional.
Hugh, speaking for Holcroft, sees his past from the vantage point
of the reformed present. Hugh is the 'New Man' of the English
Jacobin New Jerusalem, and his memoirs serve the educative
purpose of spreading truth to his readers, so they too can become
fellow-citizens. The novel is a Dissenter's self-examination and
English Jacobin description of 'things as they are' all rolled into
one. The picaro is no longer absolutely free; he is bound by
the chain of necessity on one hand and his New Morality on the
other. He must draw the moral.

Redeemers and Redeemed.   Other aspects of the picaresque are
similarly Jacobinized. Truth spreads not by revolutionary mass
movements, but by individual communication and example.
Where the old picaro is taught new ways of profiting from 'man
as he is' and 'things as they are' the new picaro has a Mentor,
a conscience to shape his rebellious libido into a virtuous and
benevolent self. The heroes of Bage's and Smollett's and Fielding's
novels also have some kind adviser or wiser friend to counsel
them as they set off on their adventures, and to catch them when
they fall. Holcroft simply brings these types into line with his
own English Jacobin designs.

Hugh's super-ego for most of the novel is Turl, the self-
reliant engraver who is to some extent a portrait of Holcroft's
friend William Sharp.[1] Turl is the voice of reason, and practises
that candour which the English Jacobins saw as the most edifying
kind of converse, but which ordinary fallible mortals such as
Hugh Trevor often find too true to be comfortable. Turl is himself a victim of 'things as they are', and hence a warning to Hugh
of the ways of the world. Expelled from Oxford for his heterodox
religious views, Turl becomes Hugh's predecessor as secretary
to the Earl of Idford; but he cannot toady to a man of inferior

---

[1] Some of Turl's experiences are also based on Holcroft's own life, such as his
saving a man (Wilmot) from drowning. See *The Life of Thomas Holcroft*, i. 22–3, 227.

parts no matter how noble his birth, and so he takes up the arduous but independent employment of engraver.[1] When Hugh goes to him for praise of the political pamphlets he has written for Idford, he meets with criticism instead. Angered at first, Hugh eventually sees the justness of Turl's remarks, and gradually Turl becomes the moral yardstick against which Hugh's progress is measured, until he becomes capable of independent acts of virtue and wins Turl's sympathy as well as his praise.

Significantly, however, the idea of 'sympathy' only begins to operate in the second part of *Hugh Trevor*, published in 1797, after Holcroft and Godwin had begun to move away from the extreme rationalism of *Political Justice* and to give a larger place to the 'domestic affections'. It may be that Holcroft's ideas on sympathy were crystallized by reading Christoph Martin Wieland's *The Sympathy of Souls*, which seems to have appeared in English in 1795.[2] In any case, in the second part of *Hugh Trevor* Turl the rationalist is replaced by Evelyn the philanthropist and gentleman scientist, whose 'suavity of manners' (p. 360) is more effective in leading those about him to truth and justice than the ruthless, rationalistic candour of Turl. Evelyn represents the most virtuous kind of man, one who practises the principles of 'political justice' in his daily life, using his wealth for the advancement of learning, carrying out anatomical researches himself, and financing Hugh's study of law and his campaign to become a member of parliament. Such disinterested benevolence proves more effective than the stern exhortations of Turl, and after narrating his trials to his new friend Hugh exclaims:

Of all the pleasures in which the soul of man most delights that of sympathy is surely the chief. It can unite and mingle not only two but ten millions of spirits as one. Could a world be spectators of the sorrows of Lear, a world would with one consent participate in them: so omnipotent is the power of sympathy. It is the consolation of poverty, it is the cordial of friendship, it is the essence of love. Pride and suspicion are its chief enemies; and they are the vices that engender the most baneful of the miseries of man [p. 302].

Sympathy becomes the new measure of moral progress in the novel, and the chief reward of moral rectitude.

[1] Perhaps Holcroft also had in mind Rousseau's 'reform', when he gave up all ambitions and decided to earn an honest living as a music copyist.

[2] Trans. F. A. Winzer (London, n.d. Published in 1795 according to the British Museum catalogue).

Sympathy, inspiration, and reward come from another quarter too. In spite of the aid and encouragement of Turl and Evelyn, Hugh is finally defeated by his foes—the established system of 'things as they are'. When Evelyn dies suddenly, as a result of an accident during his experiments, Hugh is left greatly indebted to Evelyn's heir, Sir Barnard Bray, because he had insisted on giving Evelyn a bond to cover his election expenses. When Sir Barnard is bought out of opposition by the promise of a peerage, his erstwhile parliamentary protégé refuses to follow, and is flung into a debtor's prison. Hugh has reached the nadir of his career because of his own exaggerated principles of 'honour', the same error which had been attacked in *Anna St. Ives* and Godwin's *Things As They Are*. But at least, like the heroes of those novels, Hugh now has sufficient fortitude to bear all ills.

Moreover, like the hero of *Anna St. Ives* and many another English picaresque novel, Hugh is supported by the ennobling love of an idealized heroine, Olivia Mowbray. Jacobin and Anti-Jacobin novelist alike used such heroines as the final instrument of the hero's salvation, and in Bage's *Man As He Is*, for example, Sir George Paradyne is eventually rewarded for the intention if not the achievement of living virtuously. But even this will not do for Holcroft. Love is no substitute for reason and truth, and Hugh must be completely reformed and rational before he finally receives Olivia's admission of reciprocated passion. Like Anna St. Ives, Olivia is a goddess who has her part to play in the novel's moral argument, but unlike Anna she is merely a moral counter and has no personality of her own.

On one side of the hero, then, stand the redeemers and the guardian angels. On the other are those to be redeemed, and between the two groups the hero is a kind of English Jacobin gospeller spreading the glad tidings, a 'teacher' after the fashion of the Dissenting ministers from whom Godwin was descended. Holcroft recognizes, for example, that not all women are as perfect as Anna St. Ives or Olivia Mowbray. Lydia Wilmot is the novel's fallen woman, seduced and abandoned by the Mandevillean rake Wakefield, but rescued by Hugh Trevor when the latter agrees to surrender his estate according to the true principles of 'political justice' so that Wakefield can make an honest woman of Miss Wilmot. There is also a low-life counterpart to Lydia Wilmot in Mary, the farm-girl whom the young hero had saved from

murder at the hands of her seducer, and who later rewards Hugh
by helping in his *éclaircissement* with Olivia. In the English Jacobin
novel, virtue is always rewarded.

However, Hugh's real test, both as an individual and as a
missionary of the 'New Philosophy', is the redemption of Wakefield. Wakefield is known to Hugh only as the gay cynic Belmont,[1]
and is the Coke Clifton of this novel, a witty and attractive
epicurean, although he is less violent and less interesting than his
predecessor—Holcroft seems to have realized the danger in
allowing the 'villain' to steal the limelight. Since the hero himself
is a 'mixed' character in *Hugh Trevor*, his progress is measured in
part by his gradual abandonment of the desire to revenge himself
on the man whom he knows as Wakefield, the man who has
seduced Lydia Wilmot and besotted Hugh's own mother, but
who is also Hugh's gay companion, Belmont. It is precisely
because Wakefield/Belmont is a 'mixed' character that he is
dangerous, and from very early in their friendship Hugh admits
that 'though I even then conceived him to be a very bad moralist,
I thought him a delightful companion' (p. 223). Like Coke Clifton
and Aby Henley, Belmont often thinks or acts rightly, but for
the wrong reasons. Like Aby Henley, for example, he is a kind
of Robin Hood, battening on the vices of society according to
a coherent and frequently articulated Mandevillean philosophy.
But at the same time that he is encouraging the young hero to
adopt his own predatory views as Belmont, as Wakefield he
marries Hugh's widowed mother and proceeds to bilk her of her
estate. It is no surprise to discover that he is the son of the crooked
lawyer, Thornby, and had himself prepared for a career in the law.

Belmont's Mandevillean views are an essential part of the
novel's conflict of ideas. It may in fact have been Holcroft who led
Godwin to re-read *The Fable of the Bees* soon after the first part
of *Hugh Trevor* was published, in the summer of 1794; and in the
second (1796) edition of *Political Justice* Godwin inserted a
tribute to Mandeville as the chief exponent of 'the system of
optimism' by which all social evils are seen to be ultimate sources
of good:

It is not however easy to determine, whether he is seriously, or only

---

[1] Belmont is partly modelled after the rake Charles Belmont in Edward Moore's
play *The Foundling*; other minor characters are named from Goldsmith's *The Vicar
of Wakefield*.

ironically, the defender of the present system of society. His principal
work (Fable of the Bees) is highly worthy the attention of every man,
who would learn profoundly to philosophise upon human affairs.
No author has displayed, in stronger terms, the deformity of existing
abuses, or proved more satisfactorily how inseparably these abuses are
connected together.[1]

Hugh has to agree with Belmont's views, but in order to win
him over to reform rather than exploitation of 'things as they
are' he must show him an alternative philosophy. He does so in
a final test of his own virtue, as Belmont throws Hugh's arguments back at him in a challenge to abandon his claims to his
mother's estate so that he, Wakefield/Belmont, can abandon his
life as a gambler and make an honest woman of Lydia Wilmot:
'If I strictly adhere to the principle of justice, I must not singly
consider my own wishes; which may create innumerable false
wants, and crave to have them gratified. I must ask is there no
being, within my knowledge, who may be more benefited by the
enjoyment of that which I am desirous to appropriate to myself
than I can? If so, what right have I to prefer self gratification to
superior utility?' (pp. 434–5). It is *Political Justice* in a nutshell.
When Hugh decides to act by these principles he has completed
his moral progress. By opposing 'political justice' to Mandevillean
cynicism he effects the 'conversion' of both Belmont and Wakefield, and the 'villain' is redeemed just as he was in *Anna St. Ives*.

   Character and Satire. But for the most part *Hugh Trevor* lacks
the realism and depth of characterization found in its predecessor.
Holcroft's method is now more thoroughly satirical, and his
characters have become Characters, like the minor figures in
Bage's novels or Mrs. Inchbald's *Nature and Art*. Turning from
the psychological case-study demanded by necessitarian philosophy, Holcroft took up the techniques of characterization found
in the stage comedy, 'general' verse satire, and *romans à clef* of the
late eighteenth century. In the preface to *Bryan Perdue* Holcroft
declared that the purpose of *Hugh Trevor* was 'to induce youth
(or their parents) carefully to inquire into the morality of the
profession which each might intend for himself',[2] and most of the
Characters in the novel are indeed more appropriate to fable than

---

[1] *Political Justice*, ed. F. E. L. Priestley, ii. 490 n.
[2] Thomas Holcroft, *Bryan Perdue* (London, 1805), vol. i, p. iii.

fiction. As early as 1783 Holcroft had contributed a satire on the professions to the *Morning Herald*,[1] and he continues his work here. There is Councillor Ventilate, Glibly the critic, Stradling the half-demented and litigious law-printer, and Quisque the jargoning lawyer. These characters appear in the second part of the novel, but in the first volume there is a description of a fawning Oxford tutor which is presented as 'a short specimen' of the type. Like the 'Character of a Courtier' in Mrs. Inchbald's *Nature and Art*, the 'short specimen' of some species of hypocrite, flatterer, pander, or climber is one of the main techniques of Holcroft's English Jacobin satire.

However, *Hugh Trevor* is more than just a satire on the professions. It is a comprehensive attack on 'things as they are', and Hugh manages to encounter most of the embodiments of vice and folly already found in Bage's novels. Against the virtuous heroine and the redeemable female characters, for example, may be set the fashionable and worldly women, such as Mrs. Ellis and her daughter and Olivia's aunt, who are found at large in the comedy of manners, or the novels of Fanny Burney, Maria Edgeworth, and Jane Austen. But Holcroft had to look no further than Mrs. Inchbald's *Nature and Art*, a novel which he certainly had read before the publication of his own 'satire upon the times' (Boaden, i. 315). Like Dean William's wife and Lady Bendham in *Nature and Art*, the worldly-wise women in Holcroft's novel also have too much of an eye for the main chance in marriage and too much regard for 'person' and too little for 'mind'. Their conventional feminine education makes them as vain as Miss Milner but leaves them without her vivacity.

Holcroft's Characters from the Establishment seem to be drawn from both fact and fiction. For example, his portrait of the fat bishop who first patronizes Hugh, then steals his 'Defence of the Thirty-nine Articles', then becomes his persecutor, seems to have been borrowed from *Gil Blas*;[2] but he is also drawn after the same personage who appeared as Dr Blick in *Hermsprong* and the bishop in *Nature and Art*, namely Samuel Horsley, bishop of Rochester, who had preached a sermon before the House of Lords on the anniversary of the 'martyrdom' of Charles I, 23 January 1793, with the provocative text from Romans, chapter thirteen, 'Let

[1] 9 Oct. 1783, p. 920.
[2] Book vii, Chapters iv and v.

every soul be subject unto the higher powers.' By this sermon Horsley revived the whole controversy over obedience and resistance which had divided English politics since the Civil War, and in his remarks he added to the growing attack on English Dissent as a nest of potential traitors. Holcroft's bishop is certainly a generalized satiric Character, but most well-informed readers of the novel would probably make the contemporary application.[1] Holcroft had, after all, to avoid prosecution. Late in 1793 or early in 1794 Mrs. Inchbald had altered her satire, 'having Newgate before my eyes',[2] and Holcroft was obviously in a much more exposed position than she was as the tide of conservative reaction began to mount.

The other political Characters in *Hugh Trevor* are generalized in the same way as the bishop, but it is possible to see through some of the disguises. Hugh's sometime patron Lord Idford, for example, is a type familiar enough in Bage's novels, and in the verse satire of the century. Idford's campaign of raising his opposition to Government to a saleable pitch was not unfamiliar in eighteenth-century politics, but in the summer of 1793 the Duke of Portland scandalized the English Jacobins and his erstwhile co-partisans the Whigs by joining Pitt's government, after he had allowed himself to be persuaded that the threat from French principles overrode the necessity for parliamentary reform. Rewards were immediately showered upon him—Secretary of State northern department (in effect Home Secretary), Knight of the Garter, lord-lieutenant of Middlesex.[3] Lord Idford is also supposed by everyone to be the author of the 'Letters of Themistocles'; Portland was thought by many to be the author of the *Letters of Junius*. Idford entertains the illusion that he is an able speaker; Portland too was in reality a poor orator. There may even be a clue in the name of Holcroft's political piebald. The only Idford in the British Isles is Ideford in Devon, which also happens to be almost exactly on a parallel with Portland. Holcroft's sense of humour was not above drawing such a parallel.[4]

---

[1] Cf. Rodney M. Baine (*Thomas Holcroft and the Revolutionary Novel*, p. 83), who states that the 'portrait of the bishop represents no particular English ecclesiastic'.

[2] Kegan Paul, i. 141.

[3] *D.N.B.*, s.v. William Henry Cavendish Bentinck, third Duke of Portland.

[4] It is also worth pointing out that the two Trevors in the British Isles are both in North Wales, one of the locales of projected Pantisocracy, and childhood home of Godwin's Fleetwood.

There are just enough clues, then, for contemporary readers to see Idford as Portland, and yet not enough to enable the new Secretary of State responsible for prosecuting sedition to be sure of it himself.

The character of Lord Idford could have been inspired by events of 1793 and therefore presented in the 1794 volumes of *Hugh Trevor*, but the corrupt politician in the 1797 volumes seems to have come from events of 1794–6. Sir Barnard Bray is a member of the parliamentary opposition, and undertakes to get Hugh elected to join his own faction.[1] He is longwinded in vindication of liberty and vilification of the Ministry, but quickly abandons his protégé and his principles when the long-desired peerage is dangled before him. Edmund Burke was the arch-apostate of reform in the mid-1790s. He had of course declared his position as early as 1790, but thereafter his early speeches in favour of reform were constantly thrown back at him. In 1793 he retired from active politics and was about to receive a peerage when the death of his son made him no longer ambitious of that honour. He did, however, accept a large pension and the liberal reactions to this act of venery may be seen in the bitter note Coleridge appended to his sonnet to Burke in *Poems on Various Subjects* (1796). Godwin himself compiled notes on Burke's pensions, and recorded one anecdote which he had from Tom Paine: 'Paine and Burke talking together observe what a government of pensions and corruption ours is—and distributed by such a fool, said Paine—I wish however, said Burke, this fool would give me one of his places.'[2] Moreover, Godwin had already fictionalized Burke's moral decline in 1794 in *Things As They Are*.[3] In his own way Holcroft too was disguising an important contemporary figure as a certain fictional type.

A character which Holcroft was less cautious about identifying is that of the leading opposition figure, Mr. ***. Every reader would immediately supply the name of Fox, to whom Holcroft had addressed his (probably unpublished) exhortation to persevere in the cause of reform in 1791, as a counterpart to Godwin's address to Sheridan and as a reply to the attack on Fox as 'Mr.

[1] There was, of course, the general election of 1796, to prove to Holcroft once again how corrupt the unreformed constitution had become.

[2] Abinger collection.

[3] James T. Boulton, *The Language of Politics in the Age of Wilkes and Burke*, pp. 227–32.

F**' in Henry Mackenzie's *Letters of Brutus* (1791 and 1793).[1]
It is possible, too, that Hugh Trevor's 'Letters of Themistocles'
were a fictional riposte to Mackenzie's *Letters*. In any case, Mr. ***
represents the real political world brought inside the world of the
novel, just as La Fayette, Baillé, Mirabeau, and Lally Tollendal
are brought inside *Man As He Is*, but whereas Mr. *** is only
an incidental figure in *Hugh Trevor*, in Bage's novel they are an
important influence in the hero's moral reform.

Holcroft, then, like Bage and Mrs. Inchbald before him, used
traditional techniques of the satiric Character to represent all
aspects of 'things as they are'. He generalized his characters
sufficiently to accord with the age's preference for 'general'
satire, and sufficiently, so he thought, to avoid following other
English Jacobins to Newgate and Botany Bay. The warrant for
Holcroft's arrest went out in the spring of 1794, some months
before the first review of *Hugh Trevor*,[2] and it would seem the
novel played little part in drawing the attention of Government
to him. But in *Hugh Trevor* Holcroft presented a complete gallery
of Establishment villains, and in his grouping of characters—
redeemers, redeemed, and irredeemable—he was clearly presenting another version of the novel as argument.

The Chain of Necessity: Plot and Argument

'*The Spread of Truth*'.   Just as Holcroft 'Jacobinized' the stock
characters of the picaresque novel, so too he tightened up the
rather loose unity of the picaresque plot, which was normally,
or apparently, a series of miscellaneous adventures united only by
the character of the hero. But the picaresque plot, with its emphasis on moral freedom and freedom of action, had always been
latently 'philosophical'. Robert Bage had given a new militancy to
this form by the seriousness of his moral argument about the
conflict of freedom and restraint. In Holcroft's picaresque novel
the whole structure is thoroughly reconstructed into the usual
English Jacobin demonstration of 'the spread of truth'.

After establishing the moral foundations of his hero's character
in the events of childhood, and displaying his mixture of virtue
and vice, truth and error at Oxford (volume one), Holcroft sends

---

[1] [Henry Mackenzie,] *The Letters of Brutus to Celebrated Political Characters* (Edinburgh and London, 1791); *Additional Letters* [1793].

[2] Elbridge Colby, *A Bibliography of Thomas Holcroft* (New York, 1922), p. 71.

Hugh Trevor up to London to anticipate the social and literary life of the gentleman priest, which Hugh expects to enjoy once he has taken his degree and orders. After a volume of this he antagonizes his patrons, is refused a degree at Oxford, and decides to abandon a career in the Church for one in law, since this is the only way he can see which will obtain the fame and fortune he thinks necessary in order to claim the hand of Olivia. But while engaged in his new studies Hugh becomes disillusioned with the difference between law and justice, and his involvement with the rake and gambler Belmont leads to the loss of all his money gaming at Bath.[1] At the end of volume three Hugh has reached his nadir. Not only has he failed to fill a useful place in society; he has squandered the time and money which should have been used for service to others. The English Jacobin fable of wasted talents was a timely one: in the spring of 1794 a poem entitled 'The Two Foxes' drew an unfavourable comparison between one Fox, Charles James, and a namesake serving in the army:

> One Fox amidst the desp'rate strife,
> Of rattling cannon, stakes his life.
> T'other prefers the dice's rattle,
> And only with his tongue gives battle . . . .[2]

The second part of the novel, published in 1797, opens with Hugh setting out for London accompanied by his sentimental Sancho Panza, Clarke. By losing their way they meet Evelyn, who becomes Hugh's first honest patron and who sets Hugh once again in his path of legal studies. Hugh begins to feel the humanizing influence of sympathy and philanthropy, just as he learns to temper the desire to revenge himself on his foes, and as he comes to accept Turl's opposition to a legal career. Early in volume five Hugh abandons his studies and decides to play a more direct part in the spread of Truth by becoming a Member of Parliament. Evelyn introduces him to his cousin, Sir Barnard Bray, who is a leading figure in the opposition, and Hugh pursues the round of socializing that is indispensable to a fledgling politician. The problem of withdrawing his pamphlet *exposé* of his enemies gives Hugh a final taste of the hypocrisy of the law, and the volume ends with his relieved farewell to all the emotions of

[1] An incident obviously drawn from *Roderick Random.*

[2] *Anti-Jacobin Review and Magazine*, xxi (July 1805), 336, with a note that the poem was written in 1794. Holcroft had of course addressed a letter to Fox in the spring of 1791 exhorting him to persist in the cause of reform.

anger, hatred, and revenge which had afflicted him for so long. Volume six is the harvest of all of these miscellaneous adventures. Hugh decides not to prosecute Wakefield for embezzling his estate, and his disgust with the sordidness of an eighteenth-century election is capped by his amazement when Sir Barnard Bray sells out to the Government in return for a peerage. But in spite of his new wisdom and philanthropy Hugh is soon to be overwhelmed once more by 'things as they are'. The death of Evelyn leaves Hugh indebted to Sir Barnard, who persecutes his former protégé for refusing to become political turncoat. Hugh is imprisoned for debt, consoled only by love and friendship, until a man he had saved from death at the hands of highwaymen re-appears, and turns out to be his long-lost, and rich, uncle Elford. The novel ends predicting happiness for the good, and punishment for the bad.

Holcroft did indeed take the 'adventures' of picaresque tradition and give them a greater uniformity by his English Jacobin argument on 'the spread of truth'. And yet this argument depends to a large extent on the same kind of fortuitous events and coincidences he had abused in the preface to *Alwyn* and the pages of *The Monthly Review*. On the other hand Holcroft is at pains to point out the symmetry of his action: at each point in his progress Hugh stops to favour the reader with the moral of his particular adventure, or an explanation of his most recently acquired piece of English Jacobin philosophy. The first person narrative form is itself brought under the English Jacobin banner as Hugh becomes the commentator as well as the narrator of his adventures.

It can be no accident that Caleb Williams is given the same double task, but Holcroft's hero lacks the complexity of Godwin's, and there is none of that dramatic irony and consequent heightening of interest that results from the reader's perception of discrepancies between the narrator's account of the facts, and his account of his own reaction to them. That kind of dramatic irony was evident in both *Anna St. Ives* and *A Simple Story*, but in *Hugh Trevor* and Bage's novels it is all straightforward narration, and the novel is no more than the sum of arbitrarily joined parts. *Hugh Trevor* and *Man As He Is* are series of adventures; but there is no accumulation of significance and suspense, merely the interest in succession and change.

There is a certain movement, it is true, and the turning-point is at Bath, that microcosm of all that was artificial and corrupt in the system of 'things as they are'. But even this part of the novel is artificially contrived. Holcroft drags his hero off to the place, for no real reason, and, like the plethora of coincidences in the novel, the doing of things 'for no real reason' is contrary to the novel's English Jacobin argument. The principle of necessity in *Hugh Trevor* really only operates within each successive incident or 'lesson' to which the hero is subjected, and there is no necessary connection between the incidents except their relation to the central theme. The novel's ending, and its argument, have no real conclusion.

Bage had greater success with this type of structure because it suited his more humorous and digressive approach. Holcroft too tried to have the freedom of picaresque form as well as the logical, 'necessary' form of the novel as argument, but he had to reconcile the contradiction by placing a commentary after each of Hugh's adventures. Bage simply narrates, and lets the facts generalize themselves; or if he does draw a moral, he mitigates the effect by means of a self-conscious irony. Since Bage retains the narrator's voice rather than surrendering it to his hero, he is free to comment, as Fielding does, and so can combine serious matter with comic manner. Once again Holcroft found that an over-zealous attempt to Jacobinize a traditional fictional form only led to its stultification.

Debates and Dialogues. Another technique by which Holcroft tried to bridge the gap between picaresque freedom and English Jacobin purpose is the debate or dialogue. He obviously admired the way Bage handled this method, since he quoted the whole of the debate on religion from *Man As He Is* in his notice of that novel in *The Monthly Review*. But ever since Lucian the dialogue form had been a model for writers who wished to present serious matter in an entertaining way and Holcroft had numerous works of this kind in his library. Lyttelton's *Dialogues of the Dead* popularized the form in England, and Wieland's *Private History of Peregrine Proteus* (translated 1796) had contrived to stretch the dialogue form to two lengthy volumes.[1] Influenced perhaps by Bage as well as Lyttelton and Wieland, Holcroft carried forward

---

[1] This work was in Holcroft's library, and Godwin read it in November–December 1797.

the method, so much in evidence in *Anna St. Ives*, of airing his novel's 'philosophy' through talk.

In *Hugh Trevor* the dialogues follow the pattern of 'the spread of truth' and chart the hero's moral progress. The dialogues are of three sorts, depending on the nature and extent of his participation: dialogues in which he learns something, those in which he teaches something or defends some correct point of view, and those in which he merely listens and records the arguments. In the early part of the novel Hugh is either an observer, or under Turl's tutelage, and Turl's explication of the virtues and vices of Oxford (pp. 80–1), for example, forms a suitable epilogue to Hugh's own disillusionment with the place. The next phase of Hugh's tutorial course involves literary criticism, for once in London employed as Idford's secretary, he carries his writings to Turl for praise, but receives instead some just but mild criticism, which is nevertheless too strong for his vanity (p. 123). On reflection, however, he sees that the film has been partly removed from his eyes, and silently accepts his friend's strictures. And so it goes on, as the curtain of error is rolled back in one dialogue after another, until, in volume four, Hugh's attitudes are identical to Turl's.

Meanwhile Hugh has himself been spreading Truth, in a number of debates on the nature of law and justice, that central theme of the English Jacobin philosophy. After Turl has expressed the essential truth of the matter (pp. 254–6), Holcroft presents a number of Characters to tease out Hugh's own thoughts on the subject, until finally, towards the end of volume four, he pulls all his ideas together into a rousing defence of the French Revolution (p. 339). The debate on law is enlarged at the beginning of volume five, as Hugh plunges into his legal studies under Hilary, a relation of Evelyn's who may be a portrait of Erskine, the chief counsel for the defence in many prosecutions against English Jacobins in the early 1790s, including the Treason Trials of 1794. The debate now becomes a potted version of *Political Justice* (pp. 350–3), merely a tract crudely knocked into the fabric of the novel; but Hugh has finally become an instructor himself.

He does not, however, win this particular series of debates. His opponents, Characters of the cynical and worldly-wise, remain unconverted. By the time the second part of *Hugh Trevor* was published the English Jacobins had to admit that Truth was not always omnipotent. The real contest is between Hugh and Belmont, and from the latter's first appearance in volume three he is one of Hugh's chief disputants. Between them they develop the familiar distinctions between stoicism and epicureanism already advanced in *Anna St. Ives*. Finally, it is not words but deeds which convert Belmont, just as they convert Coke Clifton, but the debates along the way mark both the moral progress of the hero, and the gradual 'spread of truth' to the other mixed characters in the novel.

Unfortunately in these debates as in those of *Anna St. Ives* the cynic always has the advantage. Hugh Trevor comes to play Frank Henley—'Don Cabbage-plant'—to Belmont's Clifton. But Belmont is never as much of a threat as Clifton, and there is never a suggestion of real evil which may disrupt the inevitable 'spread of truth'. The dialogues between Hugh and Belmont, opposing the English Jacobin to the Mandevillean view of the nature of man, are only airings of attitudes before Belmont's inevitable conversion. Apart from this defect there is a general tendency for the dialogues to lose the kind of dramatic immediacy which they are given in *Anna St. Ives* and the early part of *Hugh Trevor*. In the second part of the novel the dialogues, like the characters, become more formalized, their function more obvious. As in *Anna St. Ives*, the philosophical purpose of the novel opposes, and eventually defeats, its quality as entertainment.

Compromise. Worse than this, however, is the obvious fact that the novel's logic is self-contradictory. If Holcroft undermined the validity of his argument by too little regard for what Godwin saw as the need to create dramatic interest, he demolished it altogether by making a bad compromise between his English Jacobin argument and the conventions of the popular picaresque novel. It has already been noticed that he falls back on too many coincidences in order to arrange for his 'chain of necessity' to work out properly. Coincidence was of course a common feature of the picaresque novel, but in a novel which also tries to argue the rule of necessity in human affairs and the formation of individual character, it must be an admission of defeat to allow the logic of the argument to depend on a fortuitous event.

Significantly, it is near the beginning of the 1797 volumes that the first important coincidence takes place. Benighted on their way to London from Bath, Hugh and his Sancho Panza, Clarke, lose their way and stumble on Evelyn's laboratory. The episode is meant to be a parody of the hair-raising ploys of Gothic fiction, but it also introduces Evelyn, the man who shows Hugh the value of 'sympathy', and who becomes his patron and supporter in virtue. The meeting is essential to Hugh's future moral development, and yet it comes about through the accident of being misdirected by a passing farmer (p. 283).

There are many other lesser coincidences, in both parts of the novel, but the most damaging one occurs at the very end. It is true that the sudden appearance of Elford to rescue Hugh from debtor's prison is partly the result of the hero's act of benevolence in helping an injured fellow-traveller (p. 443); but that the stranger should turn out to be Elford is only slightly less miraculous than that Hugh should have the opportunity to save him. Moreover, Elford reappears at the end of the novel to reward Hugh for his conversion to virtue, and the system of rewards was specifically rejected in *Political Justice* (ii. 229–30).

The popular novel convention of the happy ending wins out over the necessity of English Jacobin philosophy. For until Elford appears to save the day, the real conclusion to be drawn from the adventures of Hugh Trevor is pessimistic: in the unregenerate society of the 1790s a virtuous man is more likely to end in prison than to find personal felicity and social usefulness. But the English Jacobin philosophy insisted on optimism, and so the reformed hero must be given the opportunity to live a virtuous and useful life by the sudden reappearance of a fortune which he, like Frank Henley, had not to soil his hands in obtaining. The ending is adventitious, typical of what Holcroft would have seen as the 'romance' rather than the true novel. It is therefore counter to the English Jacobin doctrine of necessity, and strikes the final blow against the credibility of Holcroft's English Jacobin argument. Holcroft meant this argument to be universal, and exemplary; but he failed once again to reconcile edification and entertainment, and thus left his hero as merely a special case.

Perhaps the failure of the New Jerusalem to materialize undermined Holcroft's confidence in his role as a writer between 1794 and 1797, so that desperation moved him to make his whole fable more obvious. No doubt, in relation to the ordinary popular fiction of the day, Holcroft's novels appeared to possess a startling degree of candour and seriousness of purpose. But in spite of its obvious historical importance, *Hugh Trevor* is a failure. Its rhetorical techniques—character, dialogue, and incident—are too often and too obviously drawn to instruct, and this obviousness vitiates the novel's persuasiveness. Since the *raison d'être* of the English Jacobin novel was to convince, the failure could hardly be more damaging. And yet, the artistic inadequacies of *Anna St. Ives* and *Hugh Trevor* do not seem to have prevented them being admired by serious and literary young men such as Robert Lovell and Thomas Dermody in England, or William Dunlap in America,[1] and Crabb Robinson admitted that reading *Anna St. Ives* prepared him for *Political Justice*. Although he wrote no philosophical treatise Holcroft was equal with Godwin in influencing young intellectuals and leaders of the artisan reform movement such as Francis Place;[2] in fact Alexander Galloway, leader of the early working-class reform movement in London and later an important iron-master, seems to have owned a copy of *Anna St. Ives* and passed it on to his son.[3] Perhaps the greatest evidence that Holcroft, a mere novelist, was taken seriously as an influence on his time, is that some of his contemporaries decided to put him on trial for his life in 1794.

3. BRYAN PERDUE

The End of the English Jacobin Novel

Having failed to Jacobinize both the sentimental novel and the picaresque, Holcroft tried to fuse the two. In his last novel, *The Memoirs of Bryan Perdue*, he once again tried to expose the evils of 'things as they are' by leading his picaro through a series of 'adventures' in contemporary society. In order to dignify this new project Holcroft declared his purpose in some prefatory remarks which implied that he had a 'programme' of novels:

Whenever I have undertaken to write a novel, I have proposed to myself a specific moral purpose. This purpose, in Anna St. Ives, was to teach fortitude to females: in Hugh Trevor, to induce youth (or their

---

[1] *The Life of Thomas Holcroft*, ii. 83–4, 85–6. See also D. B. Green, 'Letters of William Godwin and Thomas Holcroft to William Dunlap', *Notes and Queries*, cci (Oct. 1956), 441–3.

[2] [Francis Place,] *The Autobiography of Francis Place (1771–1854)*, ed. Mary Thale (Cambridge, 1972), p. 187 n. Place first knew Holcroft in 1795–6.

[3] The copy of the 1800 edition in the Bodleian Library.

parents) carefully to inquire into the morality of the profession which each might intend for himself: and, in the present work, to induce all humane and thinking men, such as legislators ought to be and often are, to consider the general and adventitious value of human life, and the moral tendency of our penal laws.[1]

In fact, the new novel is much more than this. It is, at least in the beginning, an attempt to create a new kind of English Jacobin satire out of Fielding's *Jonathan Wild*, Gay's *Beggar's Opera*, Sterne, Lucian, and Wieland; as well as out of fiction that was very different—Rousseau, Prévost, and Mackenzie. It is hardly surprising that the result has as little 'unity of design' as Godwin's last English Jacobin novel, *Fleetwood*, published in the same year and constructed out of similar materials. Holcroft, like Godwin, failed to harmonize sentiment and satire, and admitted as much in his preface. After admitting that 'the ideas sportively scattered through the first volume, are intended either to satirize vice, ridicule folly, or suggest subjects that may peculiarly deserve the consideration of the wise and good', he offers the excuse that he allowed these ideas to die away in the subsequent volumes through fear that they might interfere with the story (vol. i, pp. iv–v). Such a fear had not been allowed to affect his method in *Anna St. Ives* or *Hugh Trevor*.

Certainly *Bryan Perdue* is in many ways a continuation of those earlier novels. The hero is one of those 'mixed' characters especially suited to demonstration of the English Jacobin thesis that circumstances form character, and that the spread of truth is inevitable. In fact in the middle of *Bryan Perdue* a member of the novel's party of virtue explains to the hero how his occasional good points make him all the more dangerous by enabling him to associate with and corrupt those who would otherwise become virtuous themselves (ii. 167). In the same way, the mingled contrarieties of Coke Clifton and Belmont make them especially dangerous. Holcroft has finally made the 'villain' the hero, and made the novel's Frank Henleys into mere secondary characters.

In other respects, however, the central character of the new novel is placed in a situation similar to that of Hugh Trevor. His background is similar—a rogue of a father (an Irish professional gambler), and an impulsive but tender-hearted mother whose character is amply suggested in her maiden-name, Lady Charlotte

---

[1] *The Memoirs of Bryan Perdue* (London, 1805), vol. i, p. iii.

Hair-Trigger (i. 44). Against the parental influence, however, is placed that of a Mentor who is a combination of Turl and Evelyn, a Roman Catholic priest who is Hugh's governor during his formative years. And just as Hugh Trevor is partly saved from the fashionable debaucheries of Oxford by the example of Turl, so Bryan is warned against the error of his ways at a fashionable public school by the trio of united Britons, Henry Fairman, Patrick Mac Neale, and Alexander Gordon (i. 142). Finally, Bryan is inspired to aim for virtue by love for Henrietta, a spotless—and characterless—'heroine' cut on the same pattern as Olivia Mowbray.

The plot of *Bryan Perdue* is also similar to that of *Hugh Trevor*. A young man is left with little but his abilities and a good education to make his way in the world. Torn between reason and passion, he encounters the temptations of fashionable society supported only by the occasional Mentor, reaches a certain nadir, discovers the joys of sympathy, friendship, and virtue, and wins his way back to a humble but useful place in human society. The difference in *Bryan Perdue*, of course, is that the hero and the 'villain' are united in the same character, who is a mixture of Frank Henley and Coke Clifton, Hugh Trevor and Belmont.

There is also a great deal of continuity in the themes of the two novels. The criticism of the professions is continued, although more attention is devoted to commerce. The condemnation of law is carried from *Hugh Trevor* through Holcroft's plays, such as *Hear Both Sides* (1803), to become a critique of capital punishment in *Bryan Perdue*. The Mandevillean self-interest of Belmont is duplicated in Bryan's father, and is opposed by the philosophy of political justice held by the novel's party of virtue. To some extent, however, the theme of 'the spread of truth' is less confidently presented than in the earlier novel. Imbibing error from his father, Bryan is then seen to spread it rather than truth, first corrupting his fellow school-mates, then other young men, such as Vaughan, who almost commits suicide after losing to Bryan a sum of money entrusted to him by his employer (ii. 151). Only when he has landed himself in Newgate does Bryan, following the criminal protagonists of Defoe, finally see the light (iii. 104, 107–8). Throughout, the impression is that Bryan is more dyed-in-wool than Hugh Trevor, and his conversion to the party of virtue is much more fortuitous. The mood of despondency pervades these

Memoirs. Far from the optimistic philosophy of 'perfectibility', which only enters the last pages of *Bryan Perdue*, there is through most of the novel almost an elegiac note, a sense that the opportunity to revolutionize the moral nature of man has been lost. Bryan errs partly out of despair at being balked in several attempts to live a virtuous life, and himself declares a real despair at the prospects for the improvement of mankind: 'What poor mortals are we! How confined, how contemptible, are our designs! How narrow, how selfish, how odious, are most of our motives: while ends of such moment, ends visible as noon day, by which not self alone but every human being that the spacious earth contains would receive benefit, force themselves upon us, and plead to be accomplished! Ah! Why am I writing these memoirs?' (ii. 191).

This pessimism obviously came from Holcroft's own experiences. After the Treason Trials of 1794 his career had run rapidly downhill. He attributed the poor success of his plays to party animosity, and, assisted perhaps by that extravagance which is like the besetting vice of Bryan Perdue, Holcroft was forced to leave England in 1799, partly to retrench his finances, partly to avoid the notoriety which he now felt followed him everywhere. He left for Hamburg, with his family, and eventually ended up in Paris, where he was considered to be in the pay of Napoleon to spy on the British there.[1] But in fact Holcroft detested Napoleon and all his works, as can be seen in the pages of one of his most interesting books, his *Travels from Hamburg, through Westphalia, Holland and the Netherlands, to Paris* (1804).

Like Holcroft himself Bryan Perdue eventually ends up as an exile and an 'acquitted felon' (iii. 166). Bryan has to win his way back to respectability by dint of hard effort, and it is a sign of the way Holcroft used his novels for personal wishful thinking that Bryan makes a better job of it than the author himself. For to a very great extent this novel, like many other English Jacobin novels, was inspired by a desire to explicate and interpret, to draw something useful from the author's experiences of the mid-1790s; and when this inspiration is properly controlled it adds considerable intensity and authenticity to the novel. However, there were elements of this experience which Holcroft could not control, and a sense of disappointment, bitterness, and frustration pervades a large part of *Bryan Perdue*.

[1] Elbridge Colby, *A Bibliography of Thomas Holcroft*, p. 82.

English Jacobin Satire

In *Bryan Perdue*, however, Holcroft tried to subdue his rancour in two ways, with sentiment and with satire. Unfortunately these modes are neither fused nor equally distributed throughout the novel. As he himself indicated in the preface, the satire occupies volume one and part of volume two, and then dies away. It is comprised of several elements, tone as well as theme, manner as well as matter, and would, had Holcroft carried it through, have resulted in a work as good in its kind as *Anna St. Ives*, in fact of a new kind altogether.

The whole method of this early part of *Bryan Perdue* is one of ironic indirection. Inspired no doubt by the comic possibilities in pretended fear of prosecution as an 'acquitted felon', the narrator makes extensive use of the device of *occupatio*. After explaining how his change of name to Bryan Perdue has enabled him to lose his bad qualities in the eyes of the world, the narrator gives the point a wider application:

for there are men who would have no characters of their own if they were not indefatigable in taking away the characters of others. They fish in troubled waters, and their nets come up loaded with titles, places, pensions, public thanks, statues of bronze for having done more wicked, destructive, and intolerable mis—

Bless me! I named nobody. I shall get entangled in their meshes, hurried into their pitfalls, maimed in their mantraps—I mean no harm. Pardon! Pardon, if I have said amiss! (i. 12.)

Holcroft was by no means a subtle ironist, but he was a vigorous one. The Hudibrastic vein was his forte, as he showed in his next regular publication, *Tales in Verse* (1806). The early part of the novel is full of digressive sallies of a crude kind of irony, very much like the wit of Coke Clifton, but directed, of course, against the Establishment. After describing how an over-worked hack may pitch its tyrannical rider into a ditch and break his neck, the narrator asks, with an air of transparent naïvety, if there can be any wrong in such an observation.

Surely, there can be no danger in saying this? A man may talk of riding a post-horse to death, or of the poor, over-driven, broken-kneed, broken-hearted devil dropping into a Scotch Slough, or an Irish Bog, or what is the devil indeed an English Pit at last, and dislocating the neck of the merciless rider, and—Well! And what?

Read the domestic occurrences of nations, east, west, north, and south, and you will find these were accidents common to them all [i. 218–19].

There are indeed enough references to 'English Pits' and 'pitfalls' to make the particular application clear.

Running through such miscellaneous asides is a conception borrowed from the satirical criminal biographies such as Fielding's *Jonathan Wild*, and anticipated in *Hugh Trevor* in Belmont's comparison of a gambling-den to parliament (p. 378). This is the conception that earns for *Bryan Perdue* a place with *Things As They Are* in the first chapter of Keith Hollingsworth's *The Newgate Novel*. Holcroft's narrator draws a parallel between the petty criminals, who are always punished eventually, and the greater ones, who escape punishment because their crimes are carried out on a national, or even international scale:

> In my course of reading, I have found (I beg it may be *seriously remembered*, I speak of times past) on comparing facts, that your social rogues may be silenced, perhaps by a little whipping; or, if not, by the hulks, the halter, or Botany Bay; but that your *Pestilential Rogues* have such effrontery that demonstration itself cannot hush their clamors. While they reign, every rash scribbler, every wretched prater, and every poor devil, who dares to grumble at the mischief which these *Pestilential Rogues* are heaping wholesale upon the world, is sacrificed without the smallest mercy. Death, transportation, and *solitary imprisonment*, are their favorite punishments; but, according to them, totally inadequate to such crimes! Yet, when they themselves have filled up their measure of wickedness, till it overflows, and they can no longer escape some small but very inadequate retribution, how do the caves of corruption resound with their cries! (i. 210–11.)

This is also the framework picked up by Bulwer Lytton for *Paul Clifford*, supposedly from Godwin. 'It is this conception which forms the link between the two objects of Bulwer's attack—the evil of the criminal laws and the general evils of the two old political parties. If this came solely from Godwin, Godwin's influence is at the centre of the book.'[1] It seems likely that the conception also came from Holcroft via Godwin.

It is fairly clear then, that Holcroft had *Jonathan Wild* and *The Beggar's Opera* in mind as models for *Bryan Perdue*, and it will be remembered that some lines from Gay's ballad opera appeared as the epigraph on the title page of *Hugh Trevor*. But as well as

---

[1] Keith Hollingsworth, *The Newgate Novel 1830–1847* (Detroit, 1963), p. 72.

drawing the sort of parallels between private and public vice which were drawn by Gay and Fielding and which were to be drawn by Bulwer Lytton, Holcroft's satire is aimed specifically at the forces of repression which, by the late 1790s, had driven English Jacobins into exile, into conformity, or underground. The ironic tone of the first volume of *Bryan Perdue* suggests origins in Sterne and the Lucianic mode of satire which was really the characteristic of the best of the Anti-Jacobin novels, such as Isaac D'Israeli's *Vaurien* (1797). The Anti-Jacobins drew from Lucian because the Greek satirist had himself vented his efforts in exposing the follies of one 'New Philosophy' or another in his own day. And at one point Holcroft's fictional mouthpiece attempts an ironic counter-thrust, and declares:

I do not live so entirely retired, but that I have heard of the danger into which the world has suddenly fallen, from ignorant, self-sufficient, and officious persons, who are very wittily stigmatized by the name of new philosophers, and who yet never once pretended to teach any thing that had not been taught ten thousand times before. The blockheads! It may be true that people may now fall into mistakes, as they always have done; but to remind them of such things may be very ill-timed: or, at least, if it be objected that truth can never be ill-timed, it may be very unfashionable, and indecent, nay, even insolent [i. 136–7].

And yet Holcroft is not incapable of going along with some of the Anti-Jacobins' satire: chapter twenty-three of this first volume is entitled 'A Morsel of Metaphysics which all Ladies and Lady-like Gentlemen, unless they attend Lectures, are advised to pass' (i. 167), and is something of a self-parody, directed against promulgators of systems. Bryan gives notice of his projected treatist 'A System of Practical Virtue'[1] and declares, 'No sooner shall my system be established then affliction, pain, and all evil shall instantly disappear!' (i. 168).

The real point of Holcroft's anti-Anti-Jacobin satire, however, is very much the same as that of Godwin's historical–allegorical novel, *St. Leon* (1799), and is made when Bryan recounts how his local vicar preached a sermon on truth advocating an end to controversy and persecution, and then was persecuted for it (i. 80 ff.). This similarity of theme helps to date the composition of the first volume of *Bryan Perdue* as sometime at the end of the 1790s, when Godwin was writing *St. Leon*, and additional proof

[1] An obvious reference to Wilberforce's *Practical Christianity*, published in 1797.

is found in the two anecdotes, at the end of volume one, concerning the two main historical personages of the first volume of Godwin's novel, Francis I and Charles V (i. 257–60). The religious dimension of the history of persecution was of course central to both the French Revolution debate and Godwin's *St. Leon*, and had been given a new impetus by the intervention of the Evangelicals in the propaganda war in England on the side of the Establishment. In *Nature and Art* Mrs. Inchbald had already tried to castigate their hypocrisy, and Holcroft too aimed a shaft at the Society for the Suppression of Vice for their zeal in stopping popular amusements while they turned a blind eye to the vices of the rich and powerful:

Have you not heard or read, in your parts, my good country gentlemen, how societies have sprung up, in the great city, for the reformation of morals and other things, which I am almost afraid to catalogue, lest I should unwittingly offend some well-meaning honest soul, and, notwithstanding my cottage retreat, be calumniated as a blasphemer, or at least an infidel? from which Heaven preserve me!

Have you not heard of the dancings they have put down, the opera singers they have silenced, and the fiddle sticks they have demolished?

In looking through the dictionary of the fashions, or the fashionable dictionary, you may or may not have stumbled upon the words fashionable brothels, fashionable clubs, women in high keeping, and many more, which, owing to my long country residence, escape my present recollection. Did you ever read or hear that any of these were put down? (ii. 31–2.)[1]

In general, then, Holcroft presents in the first volume of *Bryan Perdue* a lively and entertaining, if somewhat incoherent, satire. But the irony gradually dies away, and the novel becomes more like *Hugh Trevor*, an unironic account of the hero's encounters with various aspects of 'things as they are'. There is satire in the rest of the novel, but it is the kind of satire found in the first volume of Godwin's *Fleetwood*. Bryan's adventures in dissipated high society (volume three) are similar to those of the young Fleetwood in Paris, and are interrupted only when Bryan's expensive vices land him in Newgate, charged with forgery, made a capital crime in 1799.[2] There is also, in the portrait of Hazard, financier and speculator, a swingeing attack on

---

[1] The early part of volume two, in which Holcroft's narrator has not yet dropped the mask of irony, must be of the same date as volume one.

[2] Rodney M. Baine, *Thomas Holcroft and the Revolutionary Novel*, p. 102.

the corrupting tendencies of commerce to match that in volume three of *Fleetwood*. But in spite of these elements the tone of the rest of *Bryan Perdue*, like the bulk of Godwin's novel, is sentimental rather than satiric.

The New Man of Feeling

In the second part of *Hugh Trevor* Holcroft took up Godwin's revised view of the place of the feelings in common life, and anticipated the demonstration of the power of feeling which Godwin was to make in *St. Leon* and *Fleetwood*. Sympathy becomes the new motive force in the 'spread of truth', and in *Bryan Perdue* Holcroft continues the theme, portraying in Bryan's 'suaviloquent' tutor (ii. 19) a man like Hugh's friend Evelyn. Bryan also benefits from the kind advice of the British trio of Mac Neale, Gordon, and Fairman. Even before he commences his career of dissipation Bryan realizes that some impression had been made on him by these counsellors : 'That is, I suspect it to have been not so much my reasoning faculties as my feelings, which swayed me strongly on the side of goodness' (ii. 5). Holcroft and the English Jacobins had realized that although 'the mind is the sole seat of happiness' (iii. 13), it must be reached and reformed by warm sympathy rather than cold reason. Sympathy too is the chief element in the novel's argument on the reform of criminal tendencies. The English Jacobin view that all sin and crime is merely error and ignorance is developed into a scheme for redeeming the fallen by reform rather than punishment. And to illustrate 'the spread of truth' Bryan, saved from the gallows, becomes the agent of sympathy and reform himself when he is made a slave-overseer in the West Indies. His adventures there demonstrate that truth sweetened with sympathy is more effective than the crack of a whip.

This last part of the novel clearly owes a great deal to the adventures of Savillon in Mackenzie's *Julia de Roubigné*, a work which Godwin also used for *Fleetwood*. Once the influence of Sterne and Gay, Wieland and Lucian has died out of the novel early in volume two, the influence of Rousseau and Mackenzie and Prévost, authors who also influenced Godwin at this time, begins to increase. And yet it is one of the main aims of volume three to counteract the view promulgated by sentimental novels, plays, romances, and poetry, 'that love is an irresistible passion'

(iii. 1–2). Bryan recounts all the ridiculous excesses of his passion for Henrietta Saville, the daughter of his patron. No longer is such a frenzy a spur to virtue, as it is in *Hugh Trevor*. Rather Bryan's inevitable disappointment pushes him further into fashionable dissipation.

However, like Bage, Holcroft indulges in what he condemns. Bryan learns his lessons, but he is not left unrewarded for his conversion to virtue. In the West Indies he learns to entertain a more chaste and reasonable passion for Rachel Palmer, the daughter of Bryan's neighbour, and a Quaker. In true sentimental novel fashion Rachel's reciprocal love reveals itself only when she has to nurse Bryan through a dangerous fever, and Bryan realizes the highest form of passion. 'Love, when it is duly tempered by the understanding, and does not run into any of the wild extravagances, without which weak people imagine it cannot exist, is the most delightful affection of the heart; and, when it becomes mutual, when its sweet sympathies are all felt, it is then in its most pure and ecstatic state' (iii. 248). The point is given an extra Jacobinical fillip when Bryan stresses that he and his bride-to-be readily lay aside their religious differences, although she is a Quaker, and he a Roman Catholic (iii. 255–6).[1]

Just as the whole of the first volume is pervaded by pessimism and bitterness, so the last volume is dominated by a mood of naïve optimism, which may be a logical development of the former. In *Nature and Art* too, the Jacobin satire had broken down into a quietist and placatory conclusion, expressing the superiority of humble but virtuous poverty to meddling with the ways of the world. After the failure of the French Revolution and the success of the Government repression in England, the English Jacobins were looking for alternatives. Even Bryan's name and origins carry pessimistic import: his Irishness would put people in mind of the disastrous consequences of Ireland's 'year of liberty', 1798, and the surname Perdue indicates what was lost then. But alternatives there were. Some turned to Pantisocracy, which touches the last pages of this novel, as it does Mrs. Inchbald's *Nature and Art* and Bage's *Hermsprong*. Others took up a variety of new

---

[1] There is an obvious reference to the 'Catholic question' here. The issue of emancipation for Irish Catholics had been much agitated in the late 1790s, and in 1801 George III had managed once again to impose his own opposition to any such measures.

enthusiasms from the store of ideas and tastes that has come under the title 'pre-Romanticism'. It is no accident that, after his trial and before he goes to the West Indies, Bryan fits in a period as a monk in a French monastery (iii. 174 ff.), and some adventures with banditti (iii. 185 ff.). Others again took up some version of that enthusiastic religion which E. P. Thompson has called 'the chiliasm of despair',[1] and to which Holcroft's friend William Sharp, former English Jacobin and model for Turl in *Hugh Trevor*, fell victim.[2] Sharp came under the influence of Joseph Brothers and Joanna Southcott, and in 1806 he himself published a Southcottian tract entitled *An Answer to the World*, and so it is not surprising that Holcroft included a reference to 'Johanna Southgate' in the first volume of *Bryan Perdue* (i. 219). The cult of feeling of one sort or another was breaking up the English Jacobin connections of the 1790s and Holcroft had first-hand experience of the fact. But although he laid hold of many aspects of the changing times, and made a fair success, for example, as a writer of melodrama, Holcroft did not assimilate the new influences as Godwin did. *Bryan Perdue* is sentimental, whereas *Fleetwood* is Romantic. Just as Godwin had failed to master the new style in *St. Leon*, and had recourse to extravagant and cliché-ridden language, so too Holcroft fails, as he had failed in *Anna St. Ives* and *Hugh Trevor*, to make the language of English Jacobin sensibility carry conviction. The banality and sentimentality of the last volume of *Bryan Perdue* are in sad contrast to the ironic complexity of the first, and it is in fact the nadir of Holcroft's fictional writing. For example, there is Bryan's appreciation of the useful books with which his friends had fitted him out for his new life in the New World: 'The delight and the utility which these books, through my whole life, have afforded me, and the sweet associations of friendship which, till the hour that I die, will ever be connected with them, are pleasures such as can only be imagined' (iii. 206). The poverty of expression in 'till the hour that I die', and the vague trailing off into 'such as can only be imagined', are representative of these pages, as they would be representative of much of *St. Leon*. But Godwin left the ardent English Jacobinism of the 1790s behind and moved on to new endeavours and new enthusiasms in *Fleetwood; or, the New Man of Feeling*.

---

[1] *The Making of the English Working Class*, rev. edn. (Harmondsworth, 1968), p. 411.   [2] *The Life of Thomas Holcroft*, ii. 245–7.

In short, *Bryan Perdue* is utterly lacking in that 'unity of design' which Holcroft had declared to be the *sine qua non* of the novel twenty-five years earlier, in the preface to *Alwyn*. Sadly, Holcroft had come full circle. Like that very first novel, *Bryan Perdue* is an ill-digested mixture of satire and sentiment, Smollett and Mackenzie. *Fleetwood* too is a farrago, but Godwin had at least assimilated the new influences in order to create one of the first true Romantic novels. Holcroft abandoned the vigorous style, Hudibrastic humour, and quest for 'unity of design' which had been his outstanding contributions to the English Jacobin novel, and he failed to find any adequate substitute. If *Fleetwood* marks the metamorphosis of the English Jacobin novel into nineteenth-century fiction, then *Bryan Perdue* marks its demise.

CHAPTER IV

WILLIAM GODWIN

I. CALEB WILLIAMS

Things As They Are in 1794

To reviewers and readers alike, *Things As They Are; or, The Adventures of Caleb Williams,* Godwin's first work of fiction since 1784,[1] appeared to be an extension of the cold logic of his *Enquiry Concerning Political Justice* into the more popular and seductive form of the novel. *The British Critic* spoke of the work as if it were not a novel at all: 'This piece is a striking example of the evil use which may be made of considerable talents, connected with such a degree of intrepidity as can inspire the author with resolution to attack religion, virtue, government, laws, and above all, the desire (hitherto accounted laudable) of leaving a good name to posterity.'[2] Other, less severe, reviewers lamented the presence of 'the political reflections',[3] or debated the accuracy of one or other of them;[4] but the general feeling was clearly that such 'reflections' were there with intent.

However, as the revolutionary decade of the 1790s receded into the past, and as the Romantic Movement changed the taste of Europe, *Things As They Are* came to be viewed less as a piece of propaganda than as a Romantic study of individual psychology.[5]

---

[1] *Imogen, Italian Letters,* and *Damon and Delia* were all published in 1784.

[2] Op. cit., iv (July 1794), 70.

[3] *The Critical Review,* 2nd Ser., xi (July 1794), 290.

[4] *The Monthly Review,* 2nd Ser., xv (Oct. 1794), 145–9; *The Analytical Review,* xxi (Feb. 1795), 174–5.

[5] e.g. Robert Osborn, 'Meaningful Obscurity: The Antecedents and Character of Rivers', *in Bicentenary Wordsworth Studies,* ed. Jonathan Wordsworth (Ithaca and London, 1970). For different views, see Harvey Gross, 'The Pursuer and the Pursued: A Study of *Caleb Williams*', *Texas Studies in Literature and Language,* i (1959), 405; P. N. Furbank, 'Godwin's Novels', *Essays in Criticism,* v (1955), 218; James T. Boulton, *The Langauge of Politics in the Age of Wilkes and Burke,* p. 233; D. Gilbert Dumas, 'Things As They Were: The Original Ending of *Caleb Williams*', *Studies in English Literature, 1500–1900,* vi (1966), 584; Masao Miyoshi, *The Divided Self* (New York and London, 1969), pp. 23–9.

Godwin himself became imbued with the spirit of the new, post-revolutionary age, and although he never deleted the controversial passages from his novel, he changed its title for the 1831 edition from *Things As They Are* to *Caleb Williams*, thus acknowledging its changed status from tract for the times to prototype of the English novel's renewed interest in individual psychology.[1] Finally, almost four decades after its first publication, and in the year of the great Reform Bill, Godwin gave an account of the novel's origins, which was thoroughly Romantic in its emphasis on inspiration, and which completely ignored the political purpose proclaimed in the Preface of 1794.[2]

It is as *Caleb Williams* rather than *Things As They Are* that the novel has retained its place in the canon of English literature, and most modern studies continue to emphasize and attempt to explain the novel's strange psychological power;[3] and yet the novel's chief excellence, then as now, is precisely that balance between psychological interest and English Jacobin social criticism which most English Jacobin novels failed to maintain. *Things As They Are* continued to be read after most English Jacobin novels had been forgotten because of Godwin's success in reconciling several different purposes while most 'novels of purpose' managed to present only one. As a result Godwin preserved that sense of possibility which is so damagingly absent from Holcroft's *Anna St. Ives* and *Hugh Trevor*, Bage's *Hermsprong*, and Mrs. Inchbald's *Nature and Art*.

In the first place, the psychology of Caleb Williams exists within a definite and recognizable philosophical framework. As the hostile reviews proclaimed and the well-disposed reviews admitted, *Things As They Are* continued one of the central arguments of the *Enquiry Concerning Political Justice*. There are two main parts to the novel: the persecution of Caleb by his employer Falkland, which was the situation Godwin started from; and the parallel persecution of the Hawkinses and Emily Melville by Tyrrel, which Godwin later invented as a background. It is true

---

[1] I have chosen to retain the original title, though it is more cumbersome and less familiar, because it keeps the English Jacobin element, my main concern here, more in view. Jonathan Wordsworth has pointed out to me that the running title in the first edition was 'Caleb Williams'.

[2] Snppressed and published with the novel only in the second edition of 1795.

[3] e.g. Rudolf F. Storch, 'Metaphors of Private Guilt and Social Rebellion in Godwin's *Caleb Williams*', *ELH*, xxxiv (1967), 188–207.

that Godwin's imagination provided the first, most imaginatively interesting situation, and that reason contrived the rest, but both parts of the novel are clearly related to Book seven of *Political Justice*, entitled 'Of Crimes and Punishments'. Godwin was presenting a fictionalized case of that central aspect of the Enlightenment debate on political theory, the right of the state to punish, and to enforce its 'contract' by the sanction of the law.

Supporters of the Government were quick to point out this aspect of the novel, and an anonymous correspondent who claimed to be a practitioner of the law[1] favoured *The British Critic* with a detailed account of the legal errors to be found in the novel, and concluded:

Thus does it appear that a Philosopher who has already treated expressly of Political Justice, and has invented a Fable for the purpose of attacking the moral and political prejudices of his countrymen, and making them acquainted with the truth, in all the instances in which he has affected to state the law of the land, and to reason from it, has stated it falsely; and it is almost superfluous to say, that in so doing, he has outraged Philosophy, Reason, and Morality, the foundation, object, and end of which is Truth.[2]

Godwin, earnest seeker after truth that he indeed was, strove to reply to the particular criticisms, but claimed for his work a much more ambitious programme than a mere attack on bad laws: 'The object is of much greater magnitude. It is to expose the evils which arise out of the present system of civilized society; and, having exposed them, to lead the enquiring reader to examine whether they are, or are not, as has commonly been supposed, irremediable; in a word, to disengage the minds of men from prepossession, and launch them upon the sea of moral and political enquiry.'[3] His aim was twofold: to expose the evils that made political reform a necessity, and to eradicate prejudice and thereby effect the moral reform which must accompany the political. In the Preface published with the October 1795 edition, suppressed in 1794 'in compliance with the alarms of booksellers',[4] Godwin emphasized again that his novel was concerned with the political reform of society and the moral reform of the individual;

[1] Possibly the Queen's Attorney General, George Hardinge, who had found so much to dislike in Mrs. Inchbald's *Nature and Art*.
[2] *The British Critic*, v (Apr. 1795), 446–7.
[3] Ibid., vi (July 1795), 94.
[4] *Caleb Williams*, ed. David McCracken, p. 1.

it was the same task he had set himself in the *Enquiry Concerning Political Justice*.

But the novel's moral argument extends far beyond the subject of crime and punishment. The part of the novel which describes the early, happier period of the life of Ferdinando Falkland could, for example, be seen as an exposition of Book one of *Political Justice*, 'Of the Powers of Man Considered in his Social Capacity'. Through his discovery of the crime of Falkland and his subsequent flight Caleb Williams himself comes to learn of 'The Principles of Society' (Book two), 'Of the Operation of Opinion in Societies and Individuals' (Book four), and of course 'Of Crimes and Punishments'. So much of the action of the novel can be summarized by those aphorisms which were a feature of Godwin's style in *Political Justice* that it is tempting to interpret the entire novel in terms of the arguments of the philosophical treatise.

Yet this aspect of the novel was quickly forgotten as the controversies of the 1790s faded into the past and readers found in *Things As They Are* the psychological case study of a pursued criminal, Caleb Williams. Certainly Godwin acquiesced in this transformation—it was he, after all, who changed the title of the novel in the 1831 edition; but in the account which he included in his Preface to the Standard Novels edition of *Fleetwood* in 1832, he went even further, and ignored the political and philosophical aspects of the novel altogether.

I formed a conception of a book of fictitious adventure, that should in some way be distinguished by a very powerful interest. Pursuing this idea, I invented first the third volume of my tale, then the second, and last of all the first. I bent myself to the conception of a series of adventures of flight and pursuit . . . .

I was next called upon to conceive a dramatic and impressive situation adequate to account for the impulse that the pursuer should feel, incessantly to alarm and harass his victim. . . . This I apprehended could best be effected by a secret murder, to the investigation of which the innocent victim should be impelled by an unconquerable spirit of curiosity. The murderer would thus have a sufficient motive to persecute the unhappy discoverer. . . .

The subject of the first volume was still to be invented. To account for the fearful events of the third, it was necessary that the pursuer should be invested with every advantage of fortune, with a resolution that nothing could defeat or baffle, and with extraordinary resources of intellect. Nor could my purpose of giving an overpowering interest to my tale be answered, without his appearing to have been originally endowed with a mighty store of amiable dispositions and virtues, so that his being driven to the first act of murder should be judged worthy of the deepest regret, and should be seen in some measure to have arisen out of his virtues themselves.[1]

The process here described by Godwin is an impressive combination of reason and imagination, the latter supplying the central ideas and situations, the former devising the necessary conditions to give the whole 'an overpowering interest'. In fact, the way in which Godwin's reason worked in this case was similar to the way it had worked during the composition of the *Enquiry Concerning Political Justice*: it produced an 'elevation' of mind which Godwin himself described as a 'passion': 'I have a most unequivocal, perhaps unmitigated, passion for truth and right modes of sentiment, and therefore eagerly follow every light, apprehended to be such, that is presented to me.'[2] Only this kind of 'passion' could so combine reason and imagination as to enable Godwin to produce a novel as revolutionary in its effect as the *Enquiry Concerning Political Justice* had been: 'I said to myself a hundred times, The impression of my tale shall never be blotted out of the mind of him upon whom it has once been produced: he that reads it shall never again be as if he had not read it. I will not write for temporary effect: my purpose is, that what I say shall be incorporated with the very fibres of the soul of him who listens to me.'[3] If *Political Justice* had been designed to revolutionize the political views of the public, *Things As They Are* was just as clearly designed to revolutionize the sentiments of the individual. Godwin's MS. critique of *Anna St. Ives* objected to Holcroft's over-emphasis on reason, and on 24 March 1793, a month after he had begun writing his own English Jacobin novel, Godwin debated with his friend George Dyson the interesting question 'Which is most powerful, the moral inference fairly deducible from an interesting story, or its tendency to rouse?'[4] Clearly Godwin was coming to feel that only by arousing in his readers the same passions which had animated himself while he was enquiring after political justice could he achieve the greatest

---

1 *Caleb Williams*, ed. D. McCracken, pp. 336–7.
2 Autobiographical fragment, dated 28 Sept. 1798, in the Abinger collection.
3 Autobiographical fragment, dated 10 Oct. 1824, in the Abinger collection.
4 Supplement to Journal, in Abinger collection.

effect, and become as a novelist what Shelley later described as the true poet, the unacknowledged legislator of mankind.

Meanwhile, Godwin's *Enquiry Concerning Political Justice* was being subjected to a great deal of criticism from friend and foe alike, precisely because it ignored the power of feeling and imagination in human affairs. The very day before Godwin's interesting conversation with Dyson he had recorded the view of Joseph Priestley that 'mind will never so far get the better of matter as I suppose'. Godwin was, as he confessed in numerous autobiographical fragments, of an impressionable mind, and he soon recognized the justice of such criticisms. 'His eagerness to establish the supremacy of reason led him at first to underestimate the part played by the emotions; this was a fault which he remedied progressively'.[1] But, as F. E. L. Priestley, editor of the most complete edition of *Political Justice* also admits, the change in Godwin's views was not very evident in the second edition of 1796, and only became prominent in the third edition of 1798.[2] The best and earliest evidence for what can appropriately be described as Godwin's change of heart is the novel, for it is obvious from an examination of *Things As They Are* and especially its published and MS. endings that Godwin discovered in the very process of writing the work what he had already been told by friends and reviewers—that he, like Holcroft, had placed too much confidence in the power of reason to rule feeling and imagination.

The Problem of an Ending

If Godwin intended *Things As They Are* to fictionalize the *Enquiry Concerning Political Justice*, or to be an improvement on *Anna St. Ives*, then the fact that the MS. ending of his novel is radically different from the published version presents an obvious difficulty in interpretation. In the MS. Caleb's attempt to expose Falkland in a final public confrontation has failed, and he is imprisoned and driven insane by his experiences, and perhaps poisoned by his omnipotent oppressor.[3] The essential point in the MS. is that Caleb has failed to escape from Falkland's persecution—he is a

---

[1] *Political Justice*, ed. F. E. L. Priestley, iii. 12.
[2] Ibid., 85.
[3] The MS. ending is printed by McCracken, Appendix i, pp. 330–4.

victim of 'things as they are', and Falkland remains a complete villain.

Such was the ending of Godwin's original story, and such was the 'conclusion' of 'the adventures of Caleb Williams' when Godwin finished writing the novel on 30 April 1794.

Then, from 4 to 8 May he wrote a 'new catastrophe' in which, against all expectation, Caleb triumphs, forcing an admission of guilt from the dying Falkland, who is now pitied by his former victim. Caleb concludes his narrative with an expression of guilt and remorse at having been the inadvertent cause of the downfall of such a man (p. 325). Nevertheless, the import of the revised ending is optimistic: Truth can prevail, even against the combined forces of those who support 'things as they are'; the chain of necessity can be broken by one determined individual. As D. G. Dumas has claimed, this conclusion is clearly contrary to the principles of the *Enquiry Concerning Political Justice*.[1]

Such an abdication of principles was not, however, without precedent. Holcroft had come to a similarly optimistic conclusion in *Anna St. Ives*. The happy ending was not part of Holcroft's original conception either, and in fact, it appears that it was Godwin himself who persuaded Holcroft to change his plan. In his MS. critique of *Anna St. Ives* Godwin objected strongly to the original 'tragical catastrophe': '"How is the defect of your catastrophe to be cured? Of that judge for yourself. Perhaps by wholly changing it. By the ultimate rejection of Clifton, and the total success of Frank. I have a confused prospect of endless beauties consequent on such a change; and your total failure in your present catastrophe after such laborious study, leads me to suspect the tragical catastrophe to be radically wrong."'[2] By changing the ending of his own novel in May 1794 Godwin was in effect doing exactly what he had advised Holcroft to do some two years earlier. And yet important differences remain. Holcroft revised thoroughly, and prepared the way for a happy conclusion to his English Jacobin 'argument'; but as a consequence he gave the whole plot an air of inevitability which seriously detracts from its power to interest, and therefore also from its power to 'rouse'.

---

[1] D. G. Dumas, 'Things As They Were: The Original Ending of *Caleb Williams*', *Studies in English Literature, 1500–1900*, vi (1966), 584.

[2] Abinger collection. The critique is in Godwin's hand, and undated. Since it is enclosed in quotation marks it was probably a record of a conversation Godwin had had with Holcroft.

Godwin also revised his novel, right up to the last minute;[1] but he could not remove the considerable degree of surprise which attends the sudden triumph of Caleb Williams in the revised ending.

It must remain an open question whether he intended to remove that surprise, and perhaps Godwin was 'heeding his literary inspiration' in 'an effort to raise the novel from the level of propaganda and sensation to the heights of tragedy'.[2] What is certain is that in spite of 'certain unconvincing, even mawkish, effects'[3] the revised ending goes further towards making the novel as a whole what Godwin especially wanted it to be—'dramatic', 'impressive', and 'distinguished by a very powerful interest'.[4] Far from being a mere piece of wishful thinking in the face of a very gloomy outlook for the French Revolution and its English supporters, such a novel was, on the contrary, all the more necessary as Government repression increased late in 1793 and early in 1794. It became all the more important for Godwin to communicate to his readers some of his own sense of elevation and passion in the pursuit of truth. Artistic, moral, and political needs were served far better by the revised fable that emerged from those four days of rewriting early in May 1794.

There is, no doubt, a degree of sentimentalism in the revised ending, but there is in the MS. ending an even greater degree of 'Gothic' gloom and horror, as the novel ends with madness and poison as the fate of its protagonist. The sentimental excesses of the revision can be seen as the inevitable overwriting of an inexperienced novelist rather than as the signs of ideological uncertainty. And, in fact, the transformation of Falkland from persecutor and possibly poisoner of Caleb Williams (in the MS.) to converted admirer of Caleb's fortitude and innocence (p. 324) accords much more with the particular historical parallels which Godwin was developing, and which will be explored later. Finally, the guilt which Caleb feels for the destruction of Falkland can also be explained more easily than by recourse to the idea of ideological inconsistency. Caleb's remorse is certainly sudden, and profound: 'I have been his murderer. It was fit that he should

---

[1] The MS. of the novel in the Forster Collection of the Victoria and Albert Museum was the printer's copy, and shows many last-minute alterations.

[2] D. G. Dumas, op. cit., p. 594.

[3] Dumas, p. 595.

[4] Preface to the Standard Novels edition of *Fleetwood*, in McCracken, p. 337.

praise my patience, who has fallen a victim, life and fame, to my precipitation!' (p. 325).

The same error, too great an insistence on mechanical justice, too great a haste in securing reparation for every injury, was also a characteristic of the hero of Holcroft's second English Jacobin novel, *The Adventures of Hugh Trevor*. The first three volumes of this novel were published soon after *Things As They Are*, and showed Hugh Trevor at his most irascible and precipitate. By no accident, Godwin was reading the MS. of this very work at the time he was writing the last volume of his own novel, in April 1794, and he finished the perusal on 8 May, the same day on which he finished the 'new catastrophe' of 'The Adventures of Caleb Williams'.[1] There is thus a very real connection between the theme of Holcroft's second English Jacobin novel, and Godwin's first.

Since Holcroft, in criticizing the hasty resentfulness of his hero, was to some extent criticizing that quality in himself, it becomes necessary to ask what light the revised ending of *Things As They Are* may shed on Godwin's view of himself at this time. P. N. Furbank has argued that 'the novel is a highly dramatized symbolical picture of Godwin himself in the act of writing *Political Justice*'.[2] If so, then the revised ending of the novel must imply a certain degree of self-criticism and a certain element of autobiographical confession. In the draft Prospectus for a new edition of *Political Justice* in 1832 Godwin described himself as having delivered his thoughts in 1793 'with the same frankness that a Catholic penitent is bound to observe to his confessor'.[3]

It is a curious way of describing oneself in the act of writing a philosophical treatise; but as Godwin's description of himself in the act of writing and revising *Things As They Are* it has considerable interest. One critic has even argued that the novel's chief value is its psychological self-analysis: 'The fascination (and in a sense the greater value) of *Caleb Williams* lies in the fact that Godwin seems to have written a study of neurosis without being fully aware of doing so.'[4] But the revised ending is proof that Godwin was aware of what he was doing. In psychological terms

---

[1] The original subtitle of the novel, in its first four editions.

[2] P. N. Furbank, 'Godwin's Novels', *Essays in Criticism*, v (1955), 215.

[3] Abinger collection.

[4] Rudolf F. Storch, 'Metaphors of Private Guilt and Social Rebellion in Godwin's *Caleb Williams*', *ELH*, xxxiv (1967), 188.

it can be seen as a breakthrough towards recognition of the neurotic drive and guilt inherent in his own history of rebellion: his abandonment of the religion and belief of his father, his isolation from normal human contacts and sympathies, his sense of persecution for being too zealous in the pursuit of truth. It was a state of feeling Godwin shared with Holcroft and must explain, at least in part, the extraordinary sympathy between the two men. If Godwin had retained the MS. ending of his novel he would indeed have stifled any recognition of the subconscious roots of 'those energies of the individual mind which fuel overt social protest'.[1] As it is, the revised ending of the novel shows that he was at least partly aware of his own deepest motivations and guilts, and it marks a new departure in Godwin's emotional experience. For the next eleven years his writings were to reveal the gradual philosophic and imaginative assimilation of that new experience. As Wayne C. Booth has observed, 'To some novelists it has seemed, indeed, that they were discovering or creating themselves as they wrote.'[2]

But the life of the mind, whether in its rational or creative aspects, is never isolated entirely from its physical and social environment. The revised ending of the novel, with its recognition that there is no such thing as innocence when individuals or societies are at war, anticipates the judgement which Godwin had already passed on political associations in the *Enquiry Concerning Political Justice*, and which he was to pass again in the following year in *Considerations on Lord Grenville's and Mr. Pitt's Bills* (1795). Early in 1794 the intensity of political debate was increasing but the tone of argument was degenerating, and on 23 January he wrote to Joseph Gerrald advising him on how to conduct himself before his accusers at the Edinburgh Treason Trials: 'Above all let me entreat you to abstain from all harsh epithets and bitter invective. Show that you are not terrible, but kind and anxious for the good of all. Truth can never gain by passion, violence and resentment. It is never so strong as in the firm fixt mind that yields to the emotions neither of rage nor fear.'[3] Years later in 1832 Godwin proposed a new edition of *Political Justice* with the ob-

---

[1] Storch, p. 189.

[2] *The Rhetoric of Fiction* (Chicago and London, 1961), p. 71.

[3] MS. letter in Abinger collection, possibly meant to be published as a continuation of the 'Letters of Mucius' in *The Morning Chronicle* of February and March 1793.

servation that 'at the time when that work first appeared, the
advocates for a large measure of reform were too generally of
adust and sanguinary temperament, full of gloom and irritation'.[1]
He hoped for a more reasonable response from the generation of
the Great Reform Bill, but in 1794 and 1795 Godwin had seen
hope for political and moral reform fade as fears of social revolution, which the English Jacobins had themselves helped to aug-
ment, drove all but the most zealous reformers into the arms of
Government. For this disastrous state of affairs, and its consequent alienation of man from man, legal repression, execution,
and exile, Godwin could not but hold himself partly responsible.

Things As They Are, then, has a structure which is as argu-
mentative as that of *Anna St. Ives*, although less syllogistic and
more open. It is essentially an ironic structure. Godwin later
described his tales as 'adventures of flight and pursuit', and his
description concealed an unconscious ambiguity. For if Caleb
begins by pursuing his suspicion of Falkland's crime to a certainty, if he pursues an opinion into knowledge of a truth, he is
then persecuted for what he knows. The roles are reversed as
Falkland becomes the pursuer and Caleb the pursued, for Godwin
also wished to make his tale 'dramatic'. But it is not the reversal
of melodramatic and Gothic peripeteia. The reversal in roles also
contains a moral reversal—Caleb's realization that by pursuing
Falkland he is responsible for his own flight—and a social one—
Falkland succeeds in protecting his public reputation, his 'honour',
but only at the cost of self-alienation. The structure of these reversals has been described as 'contrapuntal',[2] but it is more appropriately described as ironic because it is an obvious commentary
on 'things as they are': in 1793 Godwin could not but feel ambivalent about the effects of pursuit of truth. Events were demonstrating with increasing and awesome clarity that the pursuit
ended in flight, or destruction. And so the 'new catastrophe' to
the novel *is* logical in a certain sense. Throughout 1793 and the
early part of 1794 Godwin saw the fate of reform in England and
Revolution in France hanging in the balance. What should he
recommend to his countrymen, to his fellow English Jacobins,
to the Revolutionaries? He intended to publish a terrible

[1] MS. Prospectus for a new edition of *Political Justice*, dated 9 Oct. 1832, in the
Abinger collection.
[2] Masao Miyoshi, *The Divided Self*, p. 26.

admonition: 'things as they are' destroy both Caleb and Falkland, rebel and ruler; the only alternatives therefore are liberty or death. But in May 1974, mere days before the suspension of Habeas Corpus, he called instead for a reconciliation, however remorseful, however coloured by guilt and sorrow. It was the only real liberation from an impossible situation, and that was the novel's concluding irony.[1]

There was, therefore, a conjunction of causes which decided Godwin radically to alter the ending of his novel. There was the desire to avoid a pessimistic conclusion, as Godwin had himself counselled Holcroft to do two years before. Then, Godwin realized that the ending as it stood in the MS. version was melodramatic rather than dramatic, horrific rather than 'impressive', and that it satisfied the demands of logic better than it 'roused' the feelings. Finally, by mitigating Caleb's triumph with remorse and sympathy for his persecutor, Godwin recognized the subconscious roots of his own social protest and passed judgement on the activities of the English Jacobins in the national crisis of 1793 and 1794. In the new ending was a new conclusion about 'things as they are'.

'*Adventures of Flight and Pursuit*'

Of course, the events leading up to the ending—the 'adventures of flight and pursuit'—are also important. It is clear that, on any reading of the novel, these adventures, like their conclusion, signify a great deal more than the mere surface events narrated by Caleb Williams. Godwin himself made this plain in the Preface printed with the 1795 edition of the novel and, before that, in his letter to *The British Critic*. In these statements he defined the meaning of Caleb's adventures as a narrative of and comment on 'things as they are'.

There was also a more personal allegory in the novel, a relationship between the kind of emotions (and emotional language) to which Godwin had become accustomed in his Calvinist upbringing, and the rebellion of Caleb Williams. Though Godwin may not have understood this relationship completely, he at least felt it clearly and strongly enough to transform it into the

---

[1] Cf. Stephen Gill's view that the novel lacks subtlety in comparison to Wordsworth's 'Adventures on Salisbury Plain', in ' "Adventures on Salisbury Plain" and Wordsworth's Poetry of Protest 1795–7', *Studies in Romanticism*, xi (1972), 62–5.

adventures of his fictional hero, for Godwin's interest in 'crime', pursuit, and punishment was psychological as well as social, historical as well as political, and drew together his own experience and that of 'protestants' and 'dissenters' throughout history. Even the fictional works with which he surrounded himself while writing *Things As They Are* reveal a combination of the fictional, the historical, and the psychological.

I was extremely conversant with the 'Newgate Calendar,' and the 'Lives of the Pirates.' In the mean time no works of fiction came amiss to me, provided they were written with energy. The authors were still employed upon the same mine as myself, however different was the vein they pursued: we were all of us engaged in exploring the entrails of mind and motive, and in tracing the various rencontres and clashes that may occur between man and man in the diversified scene of human life.[1]

Godwin's Journal confirms this statement. Acting perhaps on Holcroft's suggestions Godwin set out to explore fiction which presented social or political satire, or 'the diversified scene of human life'. The first novel he read after beginning *Things as They Are* on 24 February 1793 was, significantly, Bage's *Man As He Is*, published in the preceding year. He pursued this vein further by then reading three of Smollett's works (*Ferdinand Count Fathom*, *Roderick Random*, and *Peregrine Pickle*); but by May and June he had begun to turn to a more sentimental type of fiction, and read Henry Mackenzie's *Man of Feeling* and *Julia de Roubigné*, Richardson's *Sir Charles Grandison*, Fanny Burney's *Cecilia*, Sterne's *Sentimental Journey*, and certain passages of Rousseau's *La Nouvelle Héloïse*. At the same time he turned to a few satirical novels, and read *Jonathan Wild* and *Gulliver's Travels*, as well as Sarah Fielding's satirico-sentimental novel, *The Adventures of David Simple*. From July to October 1793, whilst he was writing volume two of his novel, Godwin continued to explore a wide range of fiction: Charlotte Smith's *Desmond*, Ann Radcliffe's *Romance of the Forest*, John Thelwall's semi-novel *The Peripatetic*, tales by Voltaire and La Fontaine, Prévost's *The Life and Adventures of Mr. Cleveland*,

---

[1] *Caleb Williams*, ed. McCracken, p. 340. Although McCracken has identified a work entitled *Lives of the Pirates* (McCracken 340, n. 4), Godwin's Journal only records his having read the *Lives of the Convicts* (9 Oct. 1793). McCracken does not note that the *Lives of the Pirates* was by Defoe, whose *Jack Sheppard*, *Roxana*, and *Colonel Jack* Godwin read in July, October, and December 1793.

Natural Son of Oliver Cromwell, Defoe's *Jack Sheppard*,[1] Mrs. Inchbald's *A Simple Story*, and Holcroft's *Anna St. Ives*. Clearly, that
sort of fiction which explored 'the entrails of mind and motive'
came to predominate. As he worked slowly through the early
part of his last volume Godwin perused *Colonel Jack*, another tale
of 'flight and pursuit' (he had already read the more sentimental
Roxana), and *Cecilia*, but read and wrote little in the early months
of 1794. April was decisive: in that month he wrote the bulk of
his last volume, including the MS. ending; and on 25 April he
began reading *Clarissa*.

Richardson was Godwin's most important fictional source, as
he had been Holcroft's, but Godwin characteristically took a more
philosophical approach to his models. If *Clarissa* provides the
pattern for detailed psychological observation, then *Sir Charles
Grandison* provides the pattern for Godwin's fable of man in
relation to society. He read *Grandison* in the eight-volume edition
of 1776, and got as far as the early part of the sixth volume before
he left off. During this time Godwin was writing precisely those
chapters of *Things As They Are* which display Falkland's character
at its most admirable, in the affair of Emily Melville (whose
character is based on that of Emily Jervois in Richardson's novel).
Falkland's early life, before he murders his rival in a fit of passion,
is clearly drawn after Richardson's example. Godwin was to return
to the theme of the ideal of a gentleman in his next novel, *St. Leon*
(1799), and he would then push his researches beyond fiction and
the eighteenth century; but for the moment at least he was content
to draw on the best known summary of the gentlemanly ideal of
contemporary society. He did so because he wished to expose that
ideal as a false substitute for the true principles of political justice.
Godwin wished to demonstrate that no code of gentlemanly conduct could prevent a man from becoming a murderer and perverting all his virtues into vices. Falkland the villain is the English
Jacobin's reply to Richardson's Christian hero.

In general, then, the evolution of Godwin's interest in fictional
models seemed to follow the evolution of his idea of *Things As
They Are*, from *exposé* of social and political corruption, to novel
of sentiment, to 'Gothic' narrative of fear and persecution, to

---

[1] *Jack Sheppard* provided Godwin with his descriptions of Caleb's escapes from
prison: he read Defoe's work just as he was writing vol. ii, Chs. xi, xiii–xiv. Defoe
comments on Jack's stoicism and attributes to him the 'Temper of a Philosopher'.

moral allegory of the 'triumph' of truth. And of course to some extent the three volumes of *Things As They Are* centre on the different phases of this evolution: volume one deals with the adventures of Falkland in society both at home and abroad; volume two with the confrontation of Caleb and Falkland, who has now assumed the qualities of the Gothic hero-villain; and the last volume deals with the flight and pursuit of Caleb Williams. Diligent student that he was, Godwin had simply set about studying how these things were managed by others.

But fiction did not provide the only models for the themes of *Things As They Are*, or for 'adventures of flight and pursuit':

I read over a little old book, entitled 'The Adventures of Mademoiselle de St. Phale,' a French Protestant in the times of the fiercest persecution of the Huguenots, who fled through France in the utmost terror, in the midst of eternal alarms and hair-breadth escapes, having her quarters perpetually beaten up, and by scarcely any chance finding a moment's interval of security. I turned over the pages of a tremendous compilation, entitled 'God's Revenge against Murder,' where the beam of the eye of Omniscience was represented as perpetually pursuing the guilty, and laying open his most hidden retreats to the light of day.[1]

The actual period of the adventures of Mlle de St. Phale, the Counter-Reformation and the French Wars of Religion, was to be reflected in Godwin's next novel, *St. Leon* (1799), but Mrs. Inchbald had already drawn a parallel between those times and the terrible events of 1792, in her play *The Massacre*, which Godwin had discussed with her on 29 October 1792, read on 1 November, and apparently advised her to suppress the next day. Throughout the last months of 1792 and the year 1793 events in France would have supplied Godwin with frequent illustrations of persecution, flight, and pursuit: Godwin actually began his novel within weeks of the execution of Louis XVI.

There can be no doubt that *Things As They Are* contains a provocative and complex contemporary historical allegory. Falkland, the sophisticated, polished, and gallant gentleman obsessed with the purity of his honour, could be seen to represent France of the Old Regime. Falkland's awareness of the value of chivalry

---

[1] *Caleb Williams*, ed. McCracken, p. 340. Godwin's reference to *God's Revenge Against Murder* confirms the influence of Holcroft: the work is not in either the 1817 or 1836 catalogues of Godwin's library, but is in the 1807 catalogue of Holcroft's.

as the most important social bond between rich and poor, strong and weak, had received its clearest statement in Burke's *Reflections on the Revolution in France*, and Godwin appreciated the cogency of Burke's arguments. Godwin disagreed with Burke on the value of the rationalist schemes which the Revolution was devising to replace the feudal system; in fact the character of Falkland is to some degree a lament for Burke's abandoned liberalism.[1] But Godwin also recognized the dangers in attempting to apply the rationalist theories of the Enlightenment with too much haste and intolerance. And yet truth must be pursued, even as Caleb Williams pursues the truth about Falkland's crime, the crime which must inevitably result from excessive attachment to chivalric values. And so Caleb is pursued in his turn, like the early and more moderate French reformers such as La Fayette, Dumouriez, and others of the Brissotin connection. Godwin knew their histories,[2] and knew that some of them, such as Dumouriez, were faced with the agonizing decision of having to join France's enemies and seek her downfall, or leaving the national distemper to run its course.

In fact, at the end of his *Memoirs*, which were translated by Godwin's friend John Fenwick, Dumouriez appealed to his followers and other *émigrés* to try a middle course, and described France in 1793 in terms which could have been applied by Caleb Williams to *his* former master:

She is labouring at this moment under a moral distemper, whose dreadful convulsions only render her a greater object of alarm. Foreigners may employ the sword, but her emigrant offspring should only approach her with the soothing accents of persuasion:—it is their interest to do so: their design of superinducing order on that confusion which has driven them from their country, will, otherwise, every month, and every week, become more perfectly hopeless.[3]

It is precisely by taking up the sword of justice and attempting to superinduce his own idea of moral order that Caleb destroys, in the MS. himself, in the published novel Falkland and his own

---

[1] James T. Boulton, *The Language of Politics in the Age of Wilkes and Burke*, pp. 227–32.

[2] Such memoirs, as well as accounts of the Revolution by English witnesses many of whom Godwin knew personally, formed a large part of his reading in the early 1790s.

[3] [C. F. Duperrier Dumouriez,] *Memoirs of General Dumourier* [sic], *Written by Himself*, trans. John Fenwick (London, 1794), Pt. 2, p. 262.

peace of mind. Dumouriez and the other moderate *émigrés* might have exclaimed with Caleb Williams:

Such has been the result of a project I formed for delivering myself from the evils that had so long attended me. I thought that, if Falkland were dead, I should return once again to all that makes life worth possessing. I thought that, if the guilt of Falkland were established, fortune and the world would smile upon my efforts. Both these events are accomplished; and it is only now that I am truly miserable [p. 325].[1]

By attempting to root out the evil of the old feudal regime Caleb Williams, and the French moderates, found they had helped to destroy the whole fabric.

In Britain too, it seemed by early 1793 that the activities of reformers and English Jacobins had raised controversy to a level which divided the nation, and consequently worked against reform. The Birmingham Riots of July 1791 had demonstrated that supporters of 'Church and King' could still manipulate the mob for their own, undemocratic, ends, and spread gloom throughout reforming and especially Nonconformist circles. The repression of liberal views and writings began in earnest, however, in the few months before Godwin began writing his novel. The formation of the Association for Preserving Liberty and Property against Republicans and Levellers had taken place in November 1792,[2] the trial (*in absentia*) of Tom Paine in December, and the break-up of the Edinburgh Convention at the same time. The forces seemed to be gathering to overwhelm those, like Godwin's friends in the Revolution Society, who hoped for an extension not of the French Revolution but of the Glorious Revolution of 1688.[3] The founding of the Association caused particular alarm, because it was seen as a clandestine Government agency operating under the guise of a voluntary and popular organization. It seemed to offer the prospect of just the kind of social and semi-legal persecution which Caleb Williams had to endure for daring to question the integrity of Falkland his employer; and the sentiments

---

[1] The same theme, and the same allegorical reference to the Revolution, helped shape Godwin's daughter's *Frankenstein*.

[2] Godwin addressed the second of his 'Letters of Mucius' to the Association's founder, Reeves, in *The Morning Chronicle* (written 17 Jan. 1793, published 8 Feb.).

[3] On 22 January 1793 Godwin wrote to the French National Convention on behalf of the Revolution Society, expressing the hope that their two countries would not go to war with each other. A draft of the letter is in the Abinger collection. See also Claire Tomalin, *The Life and Death of Mary Wollstonecraft* (London, 1974), p. 142.

expressed by another of Godwin's acquaintances, Joseph Towers, might with some alteration have been adopted by Caleb: 'Associations of private individuals, invested with no legal authority, but combined together for the purpose of exhibiting informations, or instituting prosecutions, against their fellow citizens, for what they may deem too great freedoms in speaking, or in writing, are certainly very inconsistent with the genius of a free people.'[1] The situation which Godwin conceived for his novel early in 1793 then became a prophecy, as a series of trials were instituted aimed at silencing English Jacobin preachers, publishers, and pamphleteers. These trials continued throughout the period in which Godwin was writing his novel, and he noted in his Journal or read accounts of most of them.

But one of the victims in particular seems to have made a deep impression on Godwin just as he was writing the last volume of *Things As They Are*. In January 1794 he saw a great deal of 'the unfortunate Joseph Gerald',[2] who was about to set off to be tried for sedition for his part in the 'British Convention' of December 1793, and whom Godwin described in 1832 as 'one of the most accomplished readers and excellent critics that any author could have fallen in with'. In March Gerrald was found guilty and sentenced to transportation for fourteen years. Godwin had already addressed one of his 'Letters of Mucius' to Gerrald in January 1794, and on 2 April he noted in his Journal 'dine in Newgate, with Gerald'. Throughout the month he continued to visit Gerrald and others, such as William Winterbotham, who were in prison for similar reasons, and on 29 April he saw Gerrald for the last time for many months. He finished the manuscript of *Things As They Are* on the following day. The ending of the novel as it then stood offered an astonishing parallel between the fates of Joseph Gerrald and of Caleb Williams.

It would seem, then, that the revised ending, written from 4 to 8 May, is even more difficult to explain, except as some sort of wishful thinking. Godwin must have known that there was little likelihood of a pardon or reprieve for Gerrald, for on 10 March he had seen Parliament crush the attempt by reforming peers to

---

[1] [Joseph Towers,] *Remarks on the Conduct, Principles, and Publications, of the Association* . . . (London, 1793), pp. 8–9.
[2] Preface to the Standard Novels edition of *Fleetwood* (1832), in *Caleb Williams*, ed. McCracken, p. 341. The name was often spelled 'Gerald' instead of 'Gerrald'.

raise the issue of Thomas Muir's sentence, which was the same as Gerrald's. And yet, if any one of Godwin's friends could have forced him to raise his sight above a gloomy contemplation of 'things as they are', it would have been Joseph Gerrald. Throughout his trials he had followed the advice of 'Mucius', and comported himself with the dignity of a Caleb Williams or a Frank Henley, exposing the mean prejudice of his persecutors, while remaining unshaken in his political faith: 'Campbell, the poet, heard Gerrald's defence, and, stirred by his eloquent and moving peroration, turned round to a stranger standing near him, exclaiming, "By Heaven, sir, that is a great man!" "Yes, sir," answered the stranger; "he is not only a great man, but he makes every other man feel great who listens to him." '[1] The effect Gerrald had on those auditors was precisely the effect which Godwin decided that Caleb Williams should have on Falkland in their final confrontation. And the Journal suggests that Godwin had been very moved indeed by that leave-taking of 29 April. On 1 May, the day after he had finished his manuscript, he supped with John Hollis, and noted 'talk of Gerald'. For the next two days he did little, except read Hooke's *Roman History*, in the pages of which he perhaps found some reference to those stoical heroes of antiquity whom he had admired ever since his childhood. On 4 May he began the 'new catastrophe', the revised ending of *Things As They Are* which raises the novel above the doctrinaire, above questions of the triumph of persecutor or persecuted, to a level which is humane and perhaps even heroic.

In fact, the example of Joseph Gerrald only confirmed for Godwin the lessons of history. Gerrald was only the latest of a long line of exiles and victims of 'things as they are', the corrupt system of politics and the vicious social values which arose after the last revolution, the Glorious Revolution of 1688. In talking to Gerrald, in reading French Revolution tracts, Godwin had the past always before his eyes. Too short-sighted to see objects clearly, his perception seized ideas with greater tenacity. When he addressed Gerrald and exhorted him to bear his martyr's part with dignity, he was speaking with the voice of modern history, and it was the voice of another martyr who advocated tolerance and moderation, Henry St. John, Viscount Bolingbroke. Burke

[1] W. Beattie, *Life and Letters of Thomas Campbell*, i. 88, cited in G. S. Veitch, *The Genesis of Parliamentary Reform*, p. 291.

treated Bolingbroke with contempt in the *Reflections*, and had parodied him in his first published work, the *Vindication of Natural Society*. But Godwin read the *Vindication* as no irony, praised Bolingbroke as a peace-maker,[1] read his works as a model for his own attack on faction (*Considerations*, 1795), and finally contemplated writing a biography of his ideal statesman (1800). In Godwin's powerful historical imagination there was no real difference between the victim of Walpole's system and the victim of Pitt's. The example of Joseph Gerrald showed Godwin that the moral of Bolingbroke's life, and the truth of his writings, still lived.

Godwin was a diligent scholar, a man whose life was spent amongst books; but he was, as he later confessed in a MS. autobiographical fragment, most influenced by individuals. There can be no question that, at a moment of crucial importance in the writing of *Things As They Are*, Godwin was greatly influenced by the character and the fate of Joseph Gerrald. It was an influence that came, moreover, as the climax to a period in which events in both Britain and France could be seen as giving additional colour and relevance to 'adventures of flight and pursuit'. By the early part of 1794 it seemed that the dogmatic approach of English Jacobins had become thoroughly counter-productive, and this was a lesson which Godwin took very much to heart. Subsequent events, including the miserable fate of Joseph Gerrald himself (he died five months after arriving in Australia in November 1795), proved that the original ending of *Things As They Are* was the more prophetic. That too was a lesson which Godwin took to heart. His next novel, *St. Leon* (1799), was also a tale of flight and pursuit, but it ends less happily than its predecessor. If Godwin were to continue to write fictional allegories of contemporary events, he ultimately had to accept the conclusions to be drawn from those events.

'Fictitious History'

There is in fact considerable evidence that from the very first conception of his novel he had attempted to do so, by including allusions to historical characters and events in order to reinforce the conclusions to be drawn from 'things as they are'.

Among Godwin's unpublished papers are a number of essays

[1] *Political Justice*, ed. F. E. L. Priestley, i. 13 n.; ii. 102.

'written while the Enquirer was in the press',[1] one of which contrasts 'Romance' and 'History' and sheds new light on Godwin's
concept of fiction, as he formulated it after *Things As They Are*
and before his first real historical novel, *St. Leon: A Tale of the
Sixteenth Century* (1799). The first part of the essay divided history
into general and individual (i.e. biography), following Prévost's
preface to *Margaret of Anjou*,[2] and declared the latter to be of
greater value to the cause of moral and social improvement:

Laying aside the generalities of historical abstraction, we must mark
the operation of human passions; must observe the empire of motives
whether groveling or elevated; and must note the influence that one
human being exercises over another, and the ascendancy of the daring
and the wise over the vulgar multitude. It is thus, and thus only, that
we shall be enabled to add to the knowledge of the past, a sagacity that
can penetrate into the depths of futurity.

His argument was typically utilitarian, and he brushed aside the
problem of historical truth: 'I ask not, as a principal point, whether
it be true or false? My first enquiry is, can I derive instruction
from it?' No doubt he had in mind his own translation of the
Memoirs of the Life of Simon Lord Lovat, a work which was also
published in 1797 and which may not have been strictly factual.

In the next part of his essay Godwin then went on to discuss
that species of writing called 'romance or novel':

The difference between romance and what ordinarily bears the denomi-
nation of history, is this. The historian is confined to individual
incident and individual man, and must hang upon that his invention or
conjecture as he can. The writer of romance collects his materials from
all sources, experience, report, and the records of human affairs; then
generalises them; and finally selects, from their elements and the
various combinations they afford, those instances which he is best
qualified to pourtray, and which he judges most calculated to impress
the heart and improve the faculties of his reader. In this point of view
we should be apt to pronounce that romance was a nobler species of
composition than history. . . .

The writer of romance then is to be considered as the writer of real
history; while he who was formerly called the historian, must be con-
tented to step down into the place of his rival, with this disadvantage,
that he is a romantic writer without the ardour, the enthusiasm, and the

---

[1] This superscription is in Godwin's hand. *The Enquirer* was published on 27
February 1797, according to the Journal.
[2] He read *Margaret of Anjou* in October 1793.

sublime licence of imagination, that belong to that species of composition. True history consists in a delineation of consistent, human character, in the display of the manner in which such a character acts under successive circumstances, in showing how character increases and assimilates new substances to its own, and how it decays, together with the catastrophe into which by its own gravity it naturally declines.

It is precisely this growth and decline of character which Godwin describes in the person of Falkland in *Things As They Are*, and it is generally true that Godwin's novels are strong in characterization but weak in plot and structure. Like the Romantic poets he was much more interested in situation and psychology than in narrative. Those historians whom he did praise were essentially biographers, and he praises Sallust, for example, as a modern critic would praise a good novelist: 'He seems to enter into the hearts of his personages, and unfolds their secret thoughts. Considered as fable, nothing can be more perfect. But neither is this history.' Godwin sought to merit the same praise, not by embroidering the facts of history, as Scott was to do, but by historicizing the facts of fiction.

The philosophical basis for Godwin's fable, was, as it had been for *Political Justice*, Montesquieu's *Esprit des lois*. The original conception of *Political Justice* had 'proceeded on a feeling of the imperfections and errors of Montesquieu',[1] and *Things As They Are* sprang from 'that temper of mind' in which the composition of *Political Justice* left him.[2] Montesquieu had argued that the spirit of monarchy was Honour, and Falkland is a kind of incarnation of the whole ideal of Honour. 'He is the spirit of Monarchy made visible.'[3] Against Falkland, as against the monarchy in France, are ranged the independent spirits such as Caleb Williams and Tyrrel.

But in order to find suitable historical parallels to the revolutionary age in which he was living Godwin had to cast his mind back to the seventeenth century, the age of the English Revolution in which lay his own intellectual roots as a republican and 'Commonwealthman':

The period of the Stuarts is the only portion of our history interesting to the heart of man. Yet its noblest virtues are obscured by the vile

---

[1] MS. autobiographical note, in Kegan Paul, i. 67.
[2] Kegan Paul, i. 78.
[3] D. H. Monro, *Godwin's Moral Philosophy* (London, 1953), p. 90.

jargon of fanaticism and hypocrisy. From the moment that the grand contest excited under the Stuarts was quieted by the Revolution, our history assumes its most insipid and insufferable form. It is the history of negotiation and trick, it is the history of revenues and debts; it is the history of corruption and political profligacy; but it is not the history of genuine, independent man.[1]

Godwin's novel was set in this age of corruption, it is true; but for his characters and his moral he went back to the Stuart age of social and political conflict, when 'that parliament again filled the benches in which Pym and Hambden [sic], and Falkland and Selden, and Cromwell and Vane sat together, to decide, perhaps for ever, on the civil and intellectual liberties of my country'.[2]

What Godwin's Ferdinando Falkland has in common with the historical Lucius Cary, second Viscount Falkland (1610?–1643) is a fatal devotion to that chivalric code of honour which Burke had described as the foundation of society in *Reflections on the Revolution in France*.[3] Viscount Falkland, for example, had fought a celebrated duel,[4] and the English Jacobins (particularly the Dissenters) execrated duelling as a Gothic and un-Christian barbarity. Not surprisingly, then, Godwin's Falkland has several affairs of 'honour' while on the Grand Tour in Italy, and if he shows self-government over a quarrel with Count Malvesi, it is only to underline his fatal surrender to passion after his eventual return to England. Both Falklands adhere to an aspect of the chivalric code which requires that the best representatives of culture and society risk their lives and social utility for the sake of trifles.

Of equal importance are the intellectual qualities which the two Falklands have in common. Both are possessed of minds at once profound and refined (part of Caleb's duties involve acting as his employer's literary secretary), and before his crime turns him into a misanthropic recluse Godwin's Falkland is the host to every local man of talent, just as Viscount Falkland received the best minds of the age at his house at Tew in Oxfordshire, so that the place was described as a second university. Joined to this scholarly but elegant turn of mind in both Falklands is a remarkable independence of thought and character. Viscount Falkland's religious

[1] MS. essay on 'Romance' and 'History', in the Abinger collection.
[2] *Fleetwood*, i. 143.
[3] Godwin's Falkland also takes his Christian name from the heroic and chivalric king of Spain.
[4] *D.N.B.* s.v. Lucius Cary, second Viscount Falkland.

opinions, for example, were similar to Godwin's own (nothing is
said of the religious principles of the fictional character): both
displayed the intellectual curiosity of the true Protestant and
Falkland, after resisting strenuous efforts by his mother to convert
him to Catholicism, became a Socinian, as Godwin himself had
once been, although in Falkland's day this creed was not the
specialized doctrine which it later became, but simply 'a habit of
applying reason to questions of revelation'.[1]

Both Falklands extend their independence of mind to resistance
to tyranny in all its forms. Godwin's Falkland opposes the local
tyrant, appropriately named Tyrrel, to the point of murder; Viscount Falkland spoke out vehemently against the attempt by Laud
and the bishops to impose their will, and when he had reluctantly
accepted the post of Secretary of State on the Royalist side he
could not bring himself to employ spies or open letters.[2] After the
battle of Edgehill he even intervened to save the lives of those of
the enemy who had thrown away their weapons. In spite of their
many humane qualities both Falklands in effect destroy themselves
out of remorse after they have been compelled by honour to enter
into warfare with their fellow man. Godwin's Falkland, like Coke
Clifton in *Anna St. Ives,* becomes a victim of the high value which
he and society attach to honour and reputation, and, once Caleb
has discovered the secret of his murder of Tyrrel, Falkland must
become a tyrant and persecutor in his turn. But the effort of continually struggling against his better nature destroys him and at
the end he throws himself into Caleb's arms, admitting that his
victim's perseverance in the cause of truth has finally triumphed
(p. 324). Godwin's Falkland is, as one modern critic has put it,
'a tragic example of the manner in which the evil spirit of a corrupt
society will taint, discolour, and blight the fairest flowers of its
culture'.[3]

Lucius Cary, Viscount Falkland, presented to eighteenth-
century historians precisely the same moral. Drawn unwillingly
into the Civil War on the side of the Cavaliers, he soon began
to show the same melancholic apathy to life seen in Godwin's
Falkland.

[1] *D.N.B.* s.v. Lucius Cary, second Viscount Falkland.
[2] Andrew Kippis, *Biographia Britannica,* 5 vols. (London, 1778–93), s.v. Lucius
Cary, Viscount Falkland. Kippis was, of course, one of Godwin's tutors at Hoxton.
[3] David Fleisher, *William Godwin, A Study in Liberalism* (London, 1951), p. 26.

Called into public life, amidst all the attacks on regal usurpations he stood foremost, and displayed that masculine eloquence, and undaunted love of liberty, which, from his intimate acquaintance with the sublime spirits of antiquity, he had greedily imbibed. When civil convulsions proceeded to extremity, and it became requisite for him to choose his side; he tempered the ardour of his zeal, and embraced the defence of those limited powers, which remained to monarchy, and which he esteemed requisite for the support of the English constitution. Still anxious, however, for his country, he seems to have dreaded the too prosperous success of his own party as much as of the enemy; and, among his intimate friends, often, after a deep silence, and frequent sighs, he would, with a sad accent, re-iterate the word, *Peace*. . . . From the commencement of the war his natural chearfulness and vivacity became clouded; and even his usual attention to dress, required by his birth and station, gave way to a negligence, which was easily observable.[1]

At the first battle of Newbury[2] he in effect committed suicide, by deliberately riding into a hail of enemy bullets. In a time when civil strife again seemed imminent, when the bitterness of public controversy was again dividing man from man, turning some into persecutors and others into victims, Godwin's Falkland was meant to present the same moral that Hume and other 'philosophical' historians drew from the fate of Lucius Cary, the finest flower of his age and, according to Robert Beatson's *Political Index*, last prime minister of England before 'the Civil War commenced and all went into confusion'.[3]

Godwin's analogy was by no means original, however. By 1793 the comparison between the parties, doctrines, and personalities of the 1790s and those of the English Civil War had become commonplace. The Revolution Society, of which Godwin was a member, was founded in 1788 to celebrate the centenary of the Glorious Revolution and hailed events across the channel in 1789 as the long overdue seizure by the French of those liberties granted to Englishmen in 1688. At the annual banquet of the Society on 4 November 1789, Richard Price delivered his celebrated *Discourse on the Love of Our Country* expressing the hope that

[1] David Hume, *The History of Great Britain*, vol. i (Edinburgh, 1754), p. 361.

[2] Godwin's own ancestors came from Newbury, and were still there at the time of the Civil War, according to a note in the Abinger collection.

[3] Op. cit., 2nd edn. (London, 1788), i. 8. This edition was in Godwin's library at his death (Sale Catalogue 1836).

the political settlement begun in 1688 would soon be completed. To this *Discourse* Burke's *Reflections on the Revolution in France* was a carefully considered reply. Burke memorialized the Glorious Revolution as the final political settlement of England, and sanctified the Old Regime in France as the flower of that feudal system of social responsibility which had been shattered in the Revolutionists' demand for abstract 'rights'. With the appearance of *Reflections* as a reply to Price and other reformers the lines of the Revolution debate in England had been drawn. The Society for Constitutional Information printed extracts from the seventeenth-century republicans and commonwealthmen in support of the Rights of Man,[1] while Anti-Jacobins drew from the Tory writers and historians of the same period to display the evils of 'levelling' and the horrors of civil war. The editor of *Characters of Eminent Men . . ., From the Works of Lord Chancellor Clarendon* (1793)[2] drew the parallel neatly:

To the present age, it is presumed, this volume may afford an instructive lesson, in disclosing the ambitious views of the principal actors at a time when this country was involved in all the horrors of civil war, resembling those which so lately have laid waste the kingdom of France, and disturbed the peace of the nations of Europe: and as similar causes must produce similar effects, it no less becomes our duty, than our interest, to guard against the visionary projects of those who, in their endeavours to reform the English constitution, would endanger those substantial blessings which were secured to us, not by the fury of the times of Charles the first; but at the peaceable and glorious revolution in 1688 [pp. v–vi].

After the execution of Louis and the outbreak of war early in 1793 Godwin began to feel the same anxiety for national peace and harmony exhibited by the editor of *Characters of Eminent Men*. To that purpose he wrote his 'Letters of Mucius' in January 1793, and to the same purpose he drew his fictional Falkland after the gallant Cavalier martyr of the English Civil War.

The name and nature of his other characters were similarly drawn. Caleb's Christian name, for example, was obviously chosen with care: the Biblical Caleb was one of the spies sent by Moses into the Promised Land, and means either 'dog' or 'bold'. His surname is more significant still. Holcroft had already made

---

[1] Daniel Isaac Eaton advertised a series of 'Political Classics', which included Algernon Sydney, Milton, Locke, and Harrington.

[2] Ed. E. T[urner], London.

a covert reference to Cromwell in *Anna St. Ives*, and in Mark Noble's history of the house of Cromwell (the 1787 edition of which was in his library) Godwin would have come across the curious fact that at his marriage Oliver Cromwell was registered as 'Oliver Cromwell, *alias* Williams'. But if that 'Williams' was the archetypal rebel, there were others who were victims of monarchic power. John Williams, for example, resisted Laud's ecclesiastical encroachments, and was imprisoned for it (his *Life* was in Holcroft's library), and another of Laud's victims was Roger Williams, who was pursued as far as the New World. Godwin's mind, stocked with a Dissenting Academy education and years of private study, would have had no trouble picking out a number of victims of 'things as they were'.

Fictional parallels may also have influenced Godwin's choice of name for his hero: Caleb's surname, like that of Holcroft's Hugh Trevor and Richard Graves's Mr. Powell,[1] is Welsh, and all three 'quixotes' display that excessive impetuosity which is supposed to afflict the Cambrian race.[2] The implication in the two English Jacobin novels of 1794 is clear. By impulsively welcoming the French Revolution and raising the clamour for reform in Britain, the English Jacobins had destroyed the reasonableness of public debate, and handed their enemies a weapon with which to delay political justice even longer. That is the lesson which Hugh Trevor learns in part two of Holcroft's novel (1797), and it is the lesson which Caleb Williams learns in the revised ending of *Things As They Are*.

Godwin's method, as usual, was more historical and philosophical than Holcroft's. For example Barnabas Tyrrel, the villain and enemy of Falkland, is named after Paul's conservative apostle who refused to mix with Gentiles (Galatians 2: 13), and after Sir James Tyrrell, the murderer of the princes in the tower who appears in Shakespeare's *Richard III* and Prévost's *Margaret of Anjou*.[3] Tyrrel represents the rebellious spirit of the middle-class squirearchy, the independent country gentlemen who oppressed the peasant class and resisted the king. Between Tyrell and Falkland stands Mr. Clare, a moderator like Holcroft's Evelyn, and

---

[1] The vicar in *The Spiritual Quixote* (1773).

[2] Richard Graves, *The Spiritual Quixote*, ed. Clarence Tracy (London, New York, and Toronto, 1967), p. 28.

[3] Godwin read the former on 2 December 1793 and the latter in October 1793.

drawn after Godwin's friend Joseph Fawcett.[1] Clare is clearly a version of Clarendon, who tried to reconcile Charles I and his Parliament before civil war broke out. Elsewhere Godwin may indeed have borrowed from Holcroft's technique: Gines, the thief turned thief-taker, for example, has been traced to Gines de Pasamonte in Cervantes;[2] but this pursuer of Caleb Williams was named Gines only in the novel's second edition. On the whole, it seems that Godwin's ideas and allusions were clearest where he was developing them from history rather than fiction.

A final example of Godwin's use of names will demonstrate the extent to which his novel was a philosophical conception, an 'argument' like *Anna St. Ives*. A large part of the first volume of *Things As They Are* is taken up with the narrative of Falkland's steward, Collins, who is persuaded by Caleb Williams to give a full account of the manner in which their employer declined from philanthropist to misanthrope. Collins's inset story (a favourite device with Godwin, as with Bage and Holcroft), is not merely a by-plot, as it is in most eighteenth-century novels, but a tracing out of the necessary steps in Falkland's decline, and it therefore illustrates the English Jacobin proposition that circumstances form character. One of the clearest expositions of the doctrine of philosophical necessity was to be found in the *Philosophical Inquiry Concerning Human Liberty* (1715) by Anthony Collins, the work which first taught the doctrine of necessity to Joseph Priestley,[3] and which Priestley reprinted in 1790 as a work of outstanding philosophical interest. There could be no more appropriate name than Collins for the chronicler of Falkland's necessary change of character in *Things As They Are*.

The names are not a key to the novel, but the evident concern for moral significance with which they are chosen emphasizes the thoroughness of Godwin's attention to particulars and the historical coherence of his fictional attack on 'things as they are'. Furthermore, the sensitivity of Godwin's historical imagination helps to explain the prophetic quality of the novel, the way in

---

[1] M. Ray Adams, *Studies in the Literary Backgrounds of English Radicalism* (Lancaster Pennsylvania, 1947), p. 193.

[2] F. W. Chandler, *The Literature of Roguery* (Boston, 1907), ii. 338.

[3] *Autobiography of Joseph Priestley*, ed. Jack Lindsay (Bath, 1970), pp. 76 and 140. Godwin read Priestley's edition of Collins in April 1792, as well as Collins's controversy with Clarke, who of course had provided the name for Hugh Trevor's companion in Holcroft's novel.

which it illustrates not so much the persecutions that had begun by 1793 as those which were soon to follow. By revising the ending of *Things As They Are* Godwin showed that when rational debate broke down, toleration was no longer possible, and both oppressors and those who demanded their 'rights' had to share responsibility for the consequences.

Godwin interpreted the state of British society in the 1790s better than his critics or his colleagues because he knew Britain's past, and the past of all civil and religious persecutions, that much better. What he conceived as a tract for the times in 1793 became a prophecy for the future in 1794, and the change helps to explain at least some of the novel's power to interest.

Things As They Are and Protestant History

But *Things As They Are* is as much personal as public allegory, and this also helps to account for its impressiveness. Recent criticism of the novel has in fact concentrated on the psychological and confessional aspects at the expense of others; and this approach is certainly a fruitful one. R. F. Storch has argued that the novel is really an analogue for Godwin's own ambiguous state of mind regarding his rebellion against the Calvinistic religion of his fathers: 'Ultimately the source of rebellion is guilt, which in *Caleb Williams* is clearly Calvinistic.'[1] However this argument assumes that the novel gets much of its power from the fact that Godwin was largely unaware of the many parallels between filial, religious, and political rebellion: 'When Caleb runs away his reflections on tyranny and freedom are a curious blend of political, moral and religious ideas. The blend is not deliberate on Godwin's part, but is the result of the metaphoric opening up of the imagination.'[2] Godwin's deliberate use of names from the great epoch of English Protestant history indicates, however, that he knew very well what he was doing. It is true that the complex emotional relationship between Caleb and Falkland may reveal feelings in himself which Godwin was unable to express except through the sublimated form of fiction; but Mrs. Inchbald and Thomas Holcroft also 'confessed' some of their deepest feelings through their novels. And no doubt the particular colouring which Godwin gives to Caleb's feelings may, at many points, be traced to the Calvinist vocabulary of spiritual and emotional experience,

[1] Storch, p. 189.   [2] Ibid., p. 198.

a vocabulary which was, after all, the only one which Godwin knew at this time. He was still a 'philosopher' rather than a Romantic, and he had not yet begun that extensive reading in the literature of the picturesque, the Gothic, and sensibility, which was to shape his next novel, *St. Leon.* Nor had he become involved with Mary Wollstonecraft. He could describe Caleb's feelings towards Falkland in terms of the Calvinist's feelings towards God simply because these terms were the only ones which Godwin knew how to use in 1793 and 1794. In fact, his early 'Sandemanian' Calvinism had had a profound influence on *Political Justice* itself. It was precisely those 'novelistic conventions' resorted to by Holcroft and Mrs. Inchbald which were beyond Godwin's personal or literary experience, as can be seen in his very earliest fictional works, *Imogen* and *Italian Letters* (1784).[1] When he relied on such conventions he produced those conventional works, or else the extravagance of *St. Leon.*

In *Things As They Are* he was attempting something more original, something that would move the feelings as well as the reason, but something above the feeble eccentricities of the Gothic or the novel of sensibility. Godwin's novel was, from the evidence of the natures and names of its characters, an allegory of Protestant, not to say Dissenting history: the struggle for truth and for liberty, and the continual risk of incurring for that reason all the horrors of intolerance, persecution, and civil strife. In fact, John Middleton Murry entitled his essay on Godwin, which remains one of the most sympathetic and penetrating, 'The Protestant Dream'.[2] It was the English Dissenting community, after all, which Burke had singled out for special attack in his *Reflections on the Revolution in France.* The fate of Priestley and Palmer raised the spectre of another age of persecution as vicious as the Counter-Reformation or the French wars of religion to which Godwin was to turn for his historical material in his next novel. But with *Things As They Are* Godwin had already written an historical novel, set, paradoxically, in the present, but dealing nevertheless with the moral history of man.

---

[1] A third novel, *Damon and Delia,* published in 1784 like the others, has been lost.

[2] John Middleton Murry, *Heaven and Earth* (London, 1938), Ch. xix. In the New York edition (also 1938, but retitled *Heroes of Thought*), Murry brings the political element more to the fore by giving his essay (Ch. xx) the title 'The Independents' Dream'. His earlier essay, in *Countries of the Mind* (2nd Ser., London, 1931), is essentially a review of Ford K. Brown's biography.

2. ST. LEON

Old Philosophy and New: The Opus Magnum

In *Things As They Are* Godwin had followed up with a work of
fiction the attack on Burke's *Reflections* which he had initiated in
his *Enquiry Concerning Political Justice.* The novel was to present
a particular example of how the system of 'things as they are'
destroys the best representatives of a culture, separates man from
man, and creates a state of war within society. A character such as
Falkland is transformed from philanthropist to misanthrope, becomes a murderer and a tyrant, because of his devotion to that
very code of chivalric honour which Burke had praised as the
foundation of pre-Revolutionary French society.

In his next novel, *St. Leon: A Tale of the Sixteenth Century* (published December 1799), Godwin extended his fictional attack on
Burke, from an analysis of 'things as they are', to an examination
of how they got that way. His design was grand: a French noble-
man is educated in all the precepts of chivalry and puts them into
practice in the Italian wars of Francis I; but once the wars are
over, St. Leon finds himself ill-prepared in the arts of peace, and
he loses his estate through gambling. Pride induces him to leave
his native country, but in Switzerland he is overtaken by natural
disasters: he seems to be pursued by some malevolent destiny. He
then acquires the secrets of the 'philosopher's stone' and the *elixir
vitae*, only to be continually frustrated in his desire to use his supernatural powers for the benefit of mankind. Moreover, the mere
possession of such secrets makes him an outcast from his family
and from human society. He is doomed to wander through space
and time. Godwin's conclusion is a pessimistic one: the alchemist
or 'old philosopher', like the English Jacobin or 'New Philosopher', is fated to be misunderstood by his fellow man, denied
the social usefulness he craves, and driven forth to be a lonely
exile.

Like the natural philosopher, Godwin felt himself to be in
possession of great and terrible secrets—the philosophy of *Political
Justice*—which he could not use for the benefit of mankind, but
which, on the contrary, made him an object of fear and loathing.
By implying a parallel between the English Jacobin political
philosopher and the medieval philosopher who sought the 'philosopher's stone', Godwin was merely developing an aspect of the

'paper war' over the French Revolution. The terms 'philosopher' and 'philosophy' still had a variety of uses in the late eighteenth century. No doubt Godwin thought of himself as 'a lover of wisdom; one who devotes himself to the search of fundamental truth' (*O.E.D.*). Nor would he have thought of his own work as essentially different from that of his fellow English Jacobin, Joseph Priestley, who was a philosopher in the widest and original sense of that word, 'including men learned in physical science (physicists, scientists, naturalists), as well as in the metaphysical and moral sciences' (*O.E.D.*). To the Anti-Jacobins, on the other hand, both Godwin and Priestley were philosophers in a special, and pejorative sense: adherents 'of the sceptical or rationalistic views current in France and elsewhere in the [eighteenth century]' (*O.E.D.*). Godwin certainly knew of this abusive application, and it was perhaps with a touch of irony that he planned his English Jacobin novel about the adventures of a man wholly unable to govern his life by reason and who was a philosopher in an entirely different sense than Godwin himself: Reginald de St. Leon is 'an adept in occult sciences' (*O.E.D.*). But ultimately, Godwin's novel argues, the fate of the adept and of the lover of wisdom are the same, both are feared by the ignorant and persecuted by the powerful, and just as Joseph Priestley had his library and laboratory destroyed by a mob during the Birmingham Riots, so too St. Leon has his apparatus destroyed by a superstitious Italian mob—the two notions of 'philosopher' being, as the *O.E.D.* remarks, 'popularly identified'.

There is however a further dimension to Godwin's parallel between 'things as they are' and 'things as they were', one which is more directly related to Godwin's attack on Burke's historical argument in the *Reflections*. Although *St. Leon* seems to be thoroughly saturated with the picturesque and antiquarian oddities of Gothic fiction, it does in fact take its historical background much more seriously than does any Gothic novel of the 1790s, and it continues Godwin's exploration of the relationship between history and fiction. By the time he began writing the novel early in 1798, Godwin had moved a considerable distance away from the rationalism of the first edition of *Political Justice*, and was well on in the path that would take him to the Wordsworthian Romanticism of his third major novel, *Fleetwood: or, The New Man of Feeling* (1805). Nevertheless, in the late 1790s his historical view was still that of the Enlightenment, that of the 'philosophical historians' whose work he used for the background of *St. Leon*. This view was simply that man was essentially the same, in all times, and all places: in terms of human nature, 'things as they are' were the same as they always had been.

Godwin had planned his new novel as early as 1795, as part of a programme of philosophical, historical, and fictional books designed to explore new developments in his thinking. In a note dated January 1796 he gave a list of 'works projected in or before the year 1795, and not yet produced':

Dissertation on the Reasons and Tendency of Religious Opinion
Observations on the Revolution in France
New Edition of Political Justice
Life of Alexander the Great
Dunstan, a Tragedy
The Coward⎱
The Lover ⎰Tales
The Adept ⎰

He managed to complete a new edition of *Political Justice*, and 'The Lover' turned out to be *Fleetwood*; but in some sense all the other projects were combined in the tale of the 'Adept', for *St. Leon* exposes at once the myth of human greatness, the effects of superstition, the folly of precipitate attempts at human improvement, and the tragedy of the individual who, for whatever reason, sets himself above or apart from his fellow men.

To construct this new philosophical fable Godwin set about preparing his evidence with characteristic diligence. He drew on three basic kinds of source material: the works of the 'philosophical historians', works on the 'old philosophy' and those persecuted for practising it, and Gothic and sentimental fiction. It was an ambitious programme of reading for an ambitious novel; unfortunately Godwin did not succeed in blending these disparate sources into an artistic whole, a novel with that 'unity of design' which he and Holcroft deemed to be the distinguishing characteristic of this literary genre.

It is not that Godwin became too dependent on fictional models for the supernatural and terrible in *St. Leon*, for he had also immersed himself in novels as preparation for writing the adventures of Caleb Williams. Rather, the models that were available for drawing large characters and events—characters and events on a scale commensurate with those of a decade of Revolution—were not of the same order as those Godwin had consulted in 1793–4. The novels of Richardson, Prévost, Smollett, Fielding, and Goldsmith gradually gave way to those of Mary Robinson, Mary Hays, Mary Wollstonecraft, Rousseau, and Goethe, as well as lesser works in the Gothic vein. It is almost as if, like the hero of his new novel, Godwin thought to transmute these baser metals into largess for mankind by applying the 'philosopher's stone' of English Jacobinism. But in fact it was his own talent which was debased, and the sentimental and Gothic novels which he read only led him to indulge in an extravagance of language and repetitiveness of psychological description which wholly undermined the originality of his grand design.

Moreover, it was not these trifles of the fancy which first inspired the fable of *St. Leon*. The source which Godwin himself acknowledged was a curious satirical work published anonymously in 1744 and entitled *Hermippus Redivivus: or, The Sage's Triumph over Old Age and the Grave*.[1] Godwin first read this book on 2 May 1795, and it may, like many which Godwin read in the 1790s, have come from Holcroft's library, since it dealt with a theme dear to him—that reason and 'a better disposed world' could prolong the life of man indefinitely.[2] The book also recounted the adventures of several 'Adepts' or possessors of the *opus magnum*,[3] and in particular of Nicholas Flamel, who was, like Godwin's St. Leon, of a good family 'though much reduced in point of Fortune',[4] and who acquired his powers from an old Jew in the town of Leon in Spain.[5] Also like St. Leon, Flamel was hindered in his career of philanthropy by the suspicion created by his secret practices, although he succeeded in carrying out some of the charitable deeds projected by the hero of Godwin's novel.

A third of a century later Godwin returned to the lives of men like Flamel, to draw the conclusion in his *Lives of the Necromancers*

---

[1] Written by J. H. Cohausen, trans. John Campbell. According to *Biographia Britannica* Campbell considerably improved the work with additions (s.v. John Campbell, vol. iii, p. 210).

[2] *Hermippus Redivivus*, p. 17.

[3] When Godwin began his novel at the end of December 1797, he first called it 'The Adept', then 'Opus Magnum' and 'Natural Magic', and finally 'St. Leon' (15 July 1798, in MS. Journal).

[4] *Hermippus Redivivus*, p. 89.

[5] Hence, presumably, the name of Godwin's hero.

that the history of such superstitions displays the eternal ambition of man to transcend himself:

These sublime wanderings of the mind are well entitled to our labour to trace and investigate. The errors of man are worthy to be recorded, not only as beacons to warn us from the shelves [i.e. shoals] where our ancestors have made shipwreck, but even as something honourable to our nature, to shew how high a generous ambition could soar, though in forbidden paths, and in things too wonderful for us.[1]

It was a Romantic point of view, and an optimistic one; but in *St. Leon* Godwin's argument was more pessimistic, and reached the same conclusion as *Hermippus Redivivus*: only the rational independence of the true Stoic can ensure happiness: 'When I speak of a Sage . . . I mean that Kind of Man to whom alone the Title of Philosopher properly belongs. He has no Sort of Tie to the World, he sees all Things die and revive without Concern; he has more Riches in his Power than the greatest of Kings, but he tramples them under his Feet, and this generous Contempt sets him, even in the midst of Indigence, above the Power of Events.'[2] The 'Gothic' apparatus of necromancy and the supernatural has its English Jacobin point, then; and it was for the sake of that point that Godwin read *Hermippus Redivivus*, Gothic and German novels,[3] the works of Hermes Trismegistus, Bayle's article on Spinoza,[4] and a number of other works on the occult and the persecution of those who practised it.

There is another way in which the necromancer is associated with the English Jacobin. By several important Anti-Jacobin propagandists the French Revolution had been attributed to the thought of the Enlightenment working through secret societies such as the Freemasons and the Illuminati,[5] and those

---

[1] Op. cit. (London, 1834), pp. 6–7. The book included an account of St. Dunstan, whose 'tragedy' Godwin had planned to write, along with the tale of 'The Adept', in his list of projects of 1795. St. Dunstan's life offered several interesting parallels to the 1790s.

[2] *Hermippus Redivivus*, p. 99.

[3] He consulted a novel entitled *The Necromancer* (by Lorenz Flammenberg, trans. Peter Teuthold, London, 1794) on 25 May 1795, and another entitled *The Sorcerer* (by Veit Weber, trans. R. Huish?, London, 1795) on 24 July 1795.

[4] Both in June 1795.

[5] e.g., A. Barruel, *Memoirs Illustrating the History of Jacobinism* (4 vols., London, 1797–8). Godwin read this work from November to February 1798–9. Also, John Robison, *Proofs of a Conspiracy Against all the Religions and Governments of Europe* (Edinburgh, 1797). Godwin consulted Robison in November 1798.

organizations were associated in turn with political and religious dissent. Referring to the English reform societies John Robison declared in *Proofs of a Conspiracy* (1797), 'We know that the enemy is working among us, and that there are many appearances in these kingdoms which strongly resemble the contrivance of this dangerous Association.'[1] Robison also charged Godwin's friend Joseph Priestley with openly preaching 'Illuminatism' (p. 481), and Priestley, like St. Leon, had been especially suspect to the ignorant mob because of his scientific experiments. The destruction of his expensive apparatus and library in the Birmingham Riots was seen by liberals as a blow by superstition against their belief in rational human progress. It was the same curiosity which impelled Priestley, Godwin, Caleb Williams, and St. Leon to fly in the face of all received ideas, and which, under the system of 'things as they are', led to their persecution by the ignorant and the powerful. The destruction of St. Leon's house by a superstitious Italian mob[2] can be read as a direct reference to the Birmingham Riots.

Finally, St. Leon's possession of the philosopher's stone—the power of multiplying gold—may in itself have topical relevance. In 1797 the Bank of England had suspended payments, an event which affected the carefully nurtured investments of Godwin's friend Mrs. Inchbald; and St. Leon's deliberate description of the steps he takes to relieve the war-blighted economy of Hungary in the fourth volume of the novel may be considered as one of Godwin's first contributions to the nascent science of political economy. Moreover, economic policy was just one of the aspects of the 'paper war' over the French Revolution. The deplorable experiment of the *assignats*, the economic reorganization of the Republic, the effect of war on the British economy and on the domestic politics of France, were all topics which had been agitated in the continuing debate on the nature and effects of the French Revolution. On 12 May 1796 Godwin had read 'Paine on Finance', and in January 1797 he had talked of 'banks and labour and population' with his friend Nicholson, and then read a pamphlet entitled *Iniquity of the Bank*. Most important of all, in 1798 Thomas Malthus had apparently struck a mortal blow at the

---

[1] Robison, p. 478.
[2] William Godwin, *St. Leon: A Tale of the Sixteenth Century* (London, 1799), iii. 115.

philosophy of *Political Justice* when he argued that equality was impossible because population would always outstrip resources were it not kept in check by the effects of 'vice and misery'. Godwin was obviously stimulated by this criticism from a new quarter: after reading the *Essay on Population* on 5–7 August 1798, he discussed the subject with his friend Nicholson on 9 August, and on 15 August the Journal notes, 'Malthus breakfasts'. Eventually Godwin persuaded Malthus to add 'moral restraint' to 'vice and misery' as factors preventing the 'natural' rise of population.[1] However, Godwin's view of economic policy as the other side of efforts to raise the condition of man in the fourth volume of *St. Leon* remains inconclusive—St. Leon's schemes of philanthropy are lost between the unruliness of the mob and the machinations of the Turkish government—but at least Godwin was acknowledging that there were important and as yet unexplored relationships between political and economic theory.

Things As They Were

Godwin's tale of the adventures of a necromancer has, then, direct relevance to the major issues of the 1790s, and the *opus magnum* of the necromancers is a direct parallel to the philosophy of the English Jacobins. Godwin's choice of subject and setting was just as deliberate and Jacobinical in *St. Leon* as it had been in *Things As They Are*, and there are many similarities between the two novels.

The Holcrofts felt 'that Leon is a second Falkland',[2] and both characters are indeed formed by chivalric ideals which prove disastrously inappropriate for the post-feudal world. Both Falkland and St. Leon are raised as gentlemen and indoctrinated with the code of a gentleman.[3] They both absorb their ideals from Italian poetry,[4] and both find themselves in Italy in the early part of their adventures. With care Godwin illustrates the development of character in both novels, demonstrating the English Jacobin principle 'That the varieties of mind are the produce of education',[5]

[1] T. R. Malthus, *An Essay on the Principle of Population*, ed. Anthony Flew (Harmondsworth, 1970), p. 13.   [2] Kegan Paul, i. 343.
[3] Godwin read James Cleland's *The Institution of a Young Noble Man* in August 1799.
[4] Godwin met an authority on this poetry, his 'Della Cruscan' friend Robert Merry, several times by the end of 1797.
[5] Autobiographical notes in the Abinger collection.

that is, education in the widest sense. When, for example, the young St. Leon recounts how he was taken to attend that chivalric extravaganza, the Field of Cloth of Gold, he reflects that it was a spectacle which tended 'more than any other to fix the yet fluctuating character of my youthful mind' (i. 10).

St. Leon, like Falkland, is in part a portrait of the apostate Burke, the renegade reformer who, dazzled by the pomp of chivalry, abandoned the cause of humanity for an empty show. Burke had died in 1796, and Godwin's new protagonist is an even gloomier example of talents wasted and perverted by a corrupt society. On a more general level however the character devoted to chivalric 'honour'—Coke Clifton, Falkland, St. Leon—represents in English Jacobin fiction a reply to Burke's argument in the *Reflections* that chivalry was the finest product of Christian civilization, and the only true bond in human society.[1] Perhaps the most celebrated passage in the whole of Burke's writings described the 'insult' offered by the Revolutionary mob to Marie Antoinette, and concluded that 'the age of chivalry is gone. That of sophisters, economists, and calculators, has succeeded; and the glory of Europe is extinguished for ever.'[2] Godwin attacks this view in several ways, principally by showing the disastrous consequences of adherence to outmoded ideals in the adventures of his hero. From the very first he contrasts the chivalric ideals of the young St. Leon with the real horrors of war during the seige of Pavia by Francis I (i. 63). At the same time, Godwin denies Burke's view that chivalry characterized France up until the Revolution, and he has his hero declare that the defeat of Francis I by the Holy Roman Emperor wrought a fundamental change in the French king, and in French society: 'His genius cowered before that of Charles; and the defeat of Pavia may perhaps be considered as having given a deadly wound to the reign of chivalry, and a secure foundation to that of craft, dissimulation, corruption and commerce' (i. 67).

Apart from attacking Burke on philosophical and historical grounds in the early part of the novel, Godwin also presents an analogy to contemporary events. The Italian wars of Francis I had their parallel in the 1790s. In March 1796 Napoleon had been appointed commander in Italy, and after defeating Austria (which

[1] Godwin read the *Reflections* in June 1794 and September 1795.
[2] Edmund Burke, *Reflections on the Revolution in France*, in *Works* (London, 1882–4), ii. 348.

still called itself the Holy Roman Empire) had set up the Cispadane Republic in October. But after another year of fighting he had secured peace for France and popularity for himself by the treaty of Campo-Formio in October 1797, only a few months before Godwin began writing *St. Leon*. The wars of the French Republic were at last breaking up the European polity which, according to William Robertson, the greatest British historian to write on the period, had been established during the reign of Francis's great rival, the Emperor Charles V.[1] Godwin deliberately set his tale in that period, to illustrate his own view of the moral and political history of Europe. Having explored 'things as they are' in his novel of the early 1790s, Godwin set about showing how they got that way in a truly historical novel written at the end of the Revolutionary decade.

In order to achieve this end, and show the continuity between 'things as they were' and 'things as they are', Godwin followed the principles which he had outlined in his MS. essay on 'Fictitious History', written in 1797 but already put into practice in his first English Jacobin novel. Now Godwin had to go further than the analysis of individual psychology under persecution which he had presented in *Things As They Are*; he had to anticipate the achievement of Scott and show the relation between personal destiny and public events. After the defeat of France the young French nobles are deprived of the normal activities sanctioned by the chivalric code, namely war and fighting, and turn to profligacy as the only 'gentlemanly' alternative. St. Leon, too, follows the primrose path, and is eventually ruined by the passion for gaming which he had acquired during the post-war doldrums.[2] For although Godwin moved his historical perspective back one more century from that he had taken up for *Things As They Are*, he had by no means forgotten the parallels he had drawn between the 1790s and the age of Civil War and Restoration. St. Leon is not so much another Falkland, as Holcroft thought, as he is another

---

[1] William Robertson, *The History of the Reign of the Emperor Charles V*, 8th edn. (London, 1796), vol. i, p. viii. Godwin consulted this work several times while writing *St. Leon*, and had also used it for the background of his early novel, *Italian Letters* (1784). See *Italian Letters*, ed. Burton R. Pollin (Lincoln, Nebraska, 1965), p. xv.

[2] Godwin went to Debrett's several times in these years, and met Banastre Tarleton, hero of the American war and lover of Godwin's friend Mary Robinson. Godwin certainly knew of Mary's distress over Tarleton's large gambling debts.

Rochester, a man of great talents, loyal to his king, a gentleman, left by circumstances of the age with no outlet for his abilities but gambling, debauch, and the black arts. The Restoration was in fact a great age for revival in alchemy and the pseudosciences. Even Cromwell had dealt with the devil, according to one story which Godwin later included in *Lives of the Necromancers*; but it was the Restoration rakes, and their rakish king, who dabbled in transmutation of metals in an age of extravagance and financial instability.

St. Leon is rescued from profligacy by a virtuous woman, but his fate has farther to run than that of a Rochester, and makes him resemble a refugee Roundhead as well as a superfluous Cavalier. Since his aristocratic pride will not permit him to live humbly in his native land once he has lost his estate, St. Leon and his family become wanderers, persecuted by man and nature, and their plight comes to resemble that of the refugees and *émigrés* who fled the French Revolution.[1] St. Leon himself eventually becomes a solitary exile, bearing the burden of his secret powers but unable to use them for himself or others without arousing new suspicions and running into new dangers. Just as Hugh Trevor's attempt to find a suitable vocation enabled Holcroft to lead his hero through all levels of society, so the wanderings of St. Leon enable Godwin to trace all the varieties of persecution in most of the countries of sixteenth-century Europe.

However, Godwin's fable has a historical resonance which is entirely lacking in Holcroft's fiction. Once again Godwin is exploring in fiction the nature of 'protestant history'. Like Caleb Williams, St. Leon assumes the burden of superhuman knowledge, not of another's guilt this time, but of extraordinary powers over material nature. In both cases the characters are crushed by the weight of the godlike power which they acquire as a result of their curiosity, curiosity which is also the essence of dissent and intellectual progress in every age of human history. As the young St. Leon kicked his heels before the walls of Pavia, the Reformation was gathering its forces to overturn religious and secular authority in every corner of Europe. As William Robertson put it:

The reformation, wherever it was received, increased that bold and

---

[1] Godwin continued to read dozens of books on French Revolution history between 1794 and 1799; he may still have been planning the 'Observations on the Revolution in France' which he had projected in 1795.

innovating spirit to which it owed its birth. Men who had the courage to overturn a system supported by every thing which can command respect or reverence, were not to be overawed by any authority, how great or venerable soever. After having been accustomed to consider themselves as judges of the most important doctrines in religion, to examine these freely, and to reject, without scruple, what appeared to them erroneous, it was natural for them to turn the same daring and inquisitive eye towards government, and to think of rectifying whatever disorders or imperfections were discovered there. As religious abuses had been reformed in several places without the permission of the magistrate, it was an easy transition to attempt the redress of political grievances in the same manner.[1]

Godwin expressed the same view in a MS. prospectus of a history of the Protestant Reformation in which he declared, 'The grand characteristic of the Protestant Reformation is that it was the dawn of intellectual liberty to man.'[2] Godwin never wrote this history; but he did not need to. He had presented his conclusions in *St. Leon*. It was there that he pursued the aim which he had expressed in the prospectus of seeing 'human minds in the highest state of excitement', of examining 'the situations in which our fellow creatures are presented to us in their genuine colours, and stripped of every shred of concealment and disguise'.

In the light of these parallels between *St. Leon* and protestant history it is all the more interesting to observe the exact path through which Godwin leads his 'Adept'—from his lost estate in the south of France, through Switzerland, Constanz, Saxony, Tuscany, Spain, and Hungary. All of these places had particular interest for the student of religious persecution: Spain for its Inquisition; southern France, Switzerland, Saxony, and Hungary for their large numbers of Calvinists; and Tuscany for containing one of the Italian republics (Lucca) dear to the English Republicans and Commonwealthmen. It is to this republic that St. Leon and his family flee when, like Joseph Priestley, their house is attacked by the superstitious mob. If Holcroft had displayed an awareness of Civil War geography in *Anna St. Ives*, Godwin displays a similar knowledge of the geography of protestant revolt in *St. Leon*.

To these locales significant in the struggle for religious and political freedom, Godwin adds a sprinkling of real historical

[1] *The History of the Reign of the Emperor Charles V*, ii. 252–3.
[2] Undated MS. in the Abinger collection.

characters or names connected to those struggles. St. Leon attends
the Field of Cloth of Gold in the suite of his uncle, the Marquis
de Villeroy, who figured in history as the royal secretary during
the struggle between Henry of Guise and Henry of Navarre.[1]
Other names and characters from the period of the French wars of
religion appear later in the novel. At the home of his future wife,
Marguerite de Damville, St. Leon meets Morot (one of the
translators of the hymns sung by the Huguenot armies), Rabelais,
Erasmus, and Scaliger. De Damville himself played an important
role in the Religious Wars, but a more important figure was
Gaspard de Coligny, Calvinist, leader of the Huguenots after the
battle of Jarnac in 1569, and by 1570 the most powerful man in
France.[2] He was, in addition, classed by Burke with those men
like Cromwell and the leaders of the French Revolution, who
'sanctified their ambition by advancing the dignity of the people
whose peace they troubled'.[3] Not surprisingly therefore, Coligny
is portrayed in Godwin's novel as the representative of all that is
most honourable and illustrious in France (ii. 162). Finally, in the
last volume of the novel Godwin presents the Gothic villain
Bethlem Gabor, who was also a real historical personage, a leader
of the Transylvanian Calvinists, but, like Falkland, altered by
Godwin for his own purposes.

In *St. Leon*, then, Godwin uses real events and characters from
the age of the Reformation in order to broaden and develop one
of the novel's major themes, the persistence of error and intolerance in human society. He expands the use of historical allusion
in *Things As They Are* into a consistent and coherent historical
background in *St. Leon*; but his aim in both novels is similar: to
draw suggestive historical parallels to the situation of men and
nations in the decade of the French Revolution. In attempting to
do so Godwin displayed his usual diligence. In the two years he
took to write *St. Leon* he read or consulted over fifty works of
history, as well as numerous historical plays, many of them
directly related to the period in which the novel is set. He immersed himself in historical literature, and deserved more than
most novelists the courtesy title of 'historian' which many of them
claimed.

---

[1] J. H. Elliott, *Europe Divided 1559-1598* (London and Glasgow, 1968), p. 255.
[2] Elliott, pp. 121, 109, 124, 203.
[3] *Reflections*, in *Works*, ii. 321.

The historical parallels which Godwin tried to draw in *St. Leon* were by no means original. As early as the autumn of 1792 he had been made aware of at least one parallel between the 1790s and the period of the religious wars when he read the MS. of Mrs. Inchbald's *The Massacre*, and Burke had drawn a more general parallel when he denounced those who worshipped the memory of Henry of Navarre, and denied that the French nobility had degenerated since those times.[1] In *Thoughts on French Affairs* (1791) he made the same analogy and declared, 'The last revolution of doctrine and theory which has happened in Europe, is the Reformation.'[2] Moreover, the practice of using history of the past to comment on the politics of the present was a well-established one in an age when governments exercised strict control over opposition. Godwin had been a Calvinist, and he was also an eighteenth-century Commonwealthman; he was undoubtedly aware of the way in which the English Commonwealthmen had used history as propaganda in the previous century. When conditions made it dangerous or impossible to comment on contemporary events, criticisms could be made in the guise of history, as reformers, republicans, and Whigs used Roman history after the Stuart Restoration. In the 1790s many works from the controversies of the previous century were reprinted for similar purposes, and in 1796 Godwin's friend Thelwall brought out a new edition, with introduction and notes, of Walter Moyle's republican tract, *An Essay upon the Constitution of the Roman Government*. In fact, on 29 March 1793, just after he had finished *Political Justice* Godwin himself proposed a 'Roman History' to his publisher Robinson.[3] He intended to cover the period from the founding of Rome to Actium, a period which was, as he pointed out to Robinson in a significant comparison, a hundred years longer than the period of Hume's history of England from William the Conqueror to the Glorious Revolution; but he had already begun writing *Things As They Are* in February, and the Roman History was forgotten when he resumed work on the novel towards the end of April.

By 1797, however, much had happened to Godwin to break down the pattern of interests which had made him ambitious, in March 1793, to take his place alongside the 'philosophical historians' of the eighteenth century. By the late 1790s he had begun

---

[1] *Reflections*, in *Works*, ii. 407.   [2] *Works*, iii. 350.
[3] Letter from Godwin to Robinson in the Abinger collection.

to evince an interest in the Medieval and Renaissance periods which were to be taken up by the new generation of Romantic historians, poets, and novelists. Godwin had not, however, altered his Commonwealthman's view of history, although he had shifted the period of his interest; for, as Caroline Robbins has observed, 'Ancient and Medieval or Gothic history, the history of parliamentary institutions and of revolutions in Church and State, all afforded at various periods opportunity for political propaganda.'[1] The period Godwin chose for his new 'fictitious history' was precisely one of those centuries of 'revolutions in church and state' which were dear to the memory of Commonwealthmen—the age of the Reformation, and of the Counter-Reformation.

Revolution and Reaction

For by the late 1790s, in fact by the time he revised the ending of *Things As They Are* in May 1794, Godwin realized that all revolutions inevitably produce a reaction. In his political tracts of 1794–5 he had continued to argue for political justice, and to denounce arbitrary measures; but in *Considerations on Lord Grenville's and Mr. Pitt's Bills* (published anonymously in December 1795) he admitted that English Jacobin Societies, and political lecturers such as his friend John Thelwall, had to bear some responsibility for provoking the Establishment, and for attempting to carry the common people forward at too fast a rate. His mind went back to the Civil War, the Restoration, the Glorious Revolution, and the Whig supremacy. British politics, indeed the whole political and religious history of man, seemed bedevilled by faction and the persecution and counter-persecution which attended it. In particular, Godwin's mind went back to Henry St. John, viscount Bolingbroke. Bolingbroke was one of the most celebrated refugees of recent history, and a dabbler in alchemy; he was also the most ardent arguer for an end to 'party'. His ideas influenced the *philosophes*, and when Godwin came to write his own plea for the replacement of 'faction' by 'patriotism' he studied Bolingbroke's pertinent writings. As he was wont to do, he also identified strongly with their author: like Bolingbroke, he alone seemed to be striving for a new synthesis in politics that would

[1] Caroline Robbins, *The Eighteenth-Century Commonwealthman*, p. 18.

transcend the opposition of Establishment and Reform. Just as St. Leon unites characteristics of roundhead and cavalier, aristocrat and independent, so Godwin saw himself, like Bolingbroke, standing above party- and self-interest in the disinterested posture of the true philosopher. Unfortunately, Bolingbroke, Godwin, and St. Leon all ended as isolated and reviled individuals, rather than saviours of man; but essentially Godwin retained his new political position for the rest of his life. It is not surprising that, after he had finished *St. Leon*, he wrote to propose a biography of Bolingbroke to his publisher, Robinson. In some sense Godwin had already memorialized Bolingbroke in fiction.

Godwin was turning away from political reform to emphasis on the moral amelioration of individuals, the outlook characteristic of a depoliticized Romantic liberalism. In the historical year of the Great Reform Bill, Godwin looked back to the 1790s in a MS. draft prospectus for a new edition of *Political Justice*, and made a significant admission:

In all memorable crises of human affairs there is apt to be a reaction. Men began to fear that they had gone too far; they suspected that when they sought liberty merely, they were in danger of anarchy, that war and bloodshed (modes of obtaining even a laudable end that were specially protested against in Political Justice) threatened to become general, and that out of this confusion a tyranny might arise, more remorseless than that under which mankind had groaned for ages. The friends of inequality and oppression took advantage of this alarm; aristocracy and priestcraft again raised their heads; the superficial adherents of the cause of freedom seemed to apprehend that a long night of arbitrary rule might succeed to the glimpse of a more auspicious period with which their hopes had been flattered.[1]

The prophecy of legal persecution implicit in *Things As They Are* had been all too well fulfilled in both Britain and France. The Treason Trials of 1794, the suspension of Habeas Corpus and the outlawing of political protest, the exile of Joseph Priestley, the death of Joseph Gerrald at Botany Bay in March 1796, the bloody reaction of Thermidore, the shipwreck of the Republic amidst waves of persecution and legal murder—events such as these dashed the hopes of all but a few of those who had greeted the events of the early 1790s as the dawn of a new era. Godwin

---

[1] Draft prospectus in the Abinger collection, dated 9 Oct. 1832.

himself did not despond, though he tempered his expectations, and placed in the mouth of the character Filosanto in *St. Leon* an expression of the disillusionment he heard others utter:

He exclaimed, that no innocence and no merit could defend a man from the unrelenting antipathy of his fellows. He saw that there was a principle in the human mind destined to be eternally at war with improvement and science. No sooner did a man devote himself to the pursuit of discoveries which, if ascertained, would prove the highest benefit to his species, than his whole species became armed against him. The midnight oil was held to be the signal of infernal machinations. The paleness of study and the furrows of thought were adjudged to be the tokens of diabolical alliance. He saw in the transactions of that night [when St. Leon's house was destroyed by the mob] a pledge of the eternal triumph of ignorance over wisdom [iii. 115–16].

Godwin himself retained his philosophical confidence in the future of man, but there is no doubt that, on the personal level, the ending of *St. Leon* is pessimistic. St. Leon looks back over a series of frustrated attempts to improve the lot of his fellow man, and realizes that the most he can hope for is some modest felicity for his own son. The same sense of personal disillusionment marks the later volumes of Holcroft's *Hugh Trevor* (1797), although it is concealed by the conventional happy ending, and in *Bryan Perdue* (1805) Holcroft displayed the bitterness of *St. Leon* without any of the latter's alleviating elegiac sentiment. For Holcroft had come to a dead end in his own intellectual development, and remained devoted to the outmoded English Jacobin fiction of the 1790s. He had always been too passionately committed to fixed principles to be flexible in his thought or his writings. Godwin alone had sufficient philosophic detachment to rise above doctrinaire tenets in *Things As They Are*, *Considerations*, and successive revisions of *Political Justice*. From the middle of the decade he began to search for a more thorough and more radical solution to the syndrome of revolution and reaction. He thought he saw it in the life and writings of Bolingbroke; he thought he found it in a reconstruction of his own ideas and the feelings released by his contact with Mary Wollstonecraft. Godwin was more detached and more dispassionate than Holcroft or any of the English Jacobins; paradoxically, he was therefore more free to move with 'the spirit of the age', from English Jacobinism to the new synthesis of Romanticism.

'*The New Man of Feeling*'

However, *St. Leon* was only the penultimate stage in Godwin's intellectual and sentimental re-education. He had still to digest and refine his new ideas and new sensations. When he did so he produced what is perhaps the first Romantic novel in England, *Fleetwood: or, The New Man of Feeling*. Godwin subtitled his Romantic novel 'The New Man of Feeling', but even in *St. Leon* there are signs that this is what Godwin had already become. Romanticism was in part a reaction against the limited concept of man entertained by *philosophes* and Revolutionaries, and aimed at a new vision of the whole man which included feeling as well as reason, 'domestic affections' as well as 'civic virtue'. In the latter half of the 1790s Godwin's sentimental education paralleled his intellectual evolution, and the results are manifest in *St. Leon*.

On the most superficial level, for example, *St. Leon* is more 'romantic' than *Things As They Are* simply because it includes adventures of love as well as of 'flight and pursuit'. St. Leon's wife, Marguerite de Damville, is clearly an idealized portrait of Mary Wollstonecraft, whose lover and then husband Godwin had become, at the advanced and unromantic age of forty, and who had died from the complications of childbirth only a few months before Godwin began to write *St. Leon*.[1]

Once again there is a strong 'confessional' and autobiographical element in this English Jacobin novel, and St. Leon's elegiac tribute to conjugal happiness comes from the author's deepest and most recent experience; but Godwin was always a thinking as well as a feeling man. Experience and study were combined in his thought and imagination to become new impulses in both his philosophical and his fictional writings. In the preface to *St. Leon* he admitted that in the earlier editions of *Political Justice* he had been wrong to ignore 'the affections and charities of private life' (pp. viii–xi), and he illustrated his new view of human nature by quoting from his own *Memoir* of Mary Wollstonecraft. The *Memoir* had been written, with extraordinary precipitation, in the months between Mary's death and Godwin's commencement of *St. Leon*, and in that time he had indulged completely in grief and melancholy, finding, as usual, benefits even in suffering. He wrote in

---

[1] On Godwin's influence on Mary Wollstonecraft, especially her unfinished novel *The Wrongs of Woman* (published posthumously 1798), see the introduction to *Mary and The Wrongs of Woman*, ed. Gary Kelly (London, 1976).

reply to a letter of condolence: 'I hope to be made wise and more human by the contemplation of "the memory of a beloved object"; I find a pleasure, difficult to be described, in the cultivation of melancholy. It weakens indeed my stoicism in the ordinary occurrences of life, but it refines and raises my sensibility.'[1] He was prepared to learn the limitations of that antique stoicism preached up in *Anna St. Ives* and the early editions of *Political Justice*, but now an anachronism along with the rest of the 'Roman virtues' embodied in the ideals of the French Republic. In the last months of 1797 Godwin read Mary Wollstonecraft's letters and works, gave himself wholly to her warm and humane personality, and completed the re-education of his sensibility. Only a few days after her death he wrote to a friend and confessed, 'I love these overflowings of the heart and cannot endure to be always treating, and being treated by my friends, as if they were so many books.'[2]

Mary's death was, of course, only a catalyst, and Godwin's re-education had begun long before. It was signalled as early as 1794 in the altered ending of *Things As They Are*; but *St. Leon* was the first novel Godwin attempted to write entirely out of his reformed sensibility, and, as usual, he consulted the best guides to this unknown territory. Autobiographical novels, however unique the experiences they embody, are still novels rather than autobiographies, and seldom go far beyond the accepted fictional conventions of their time. It is no accident that Godwin was reading *The Sorrows of Werther* and the novels of Rousseau at the time of Mary's pregnancy and death: the feelings he found described there, and the manner of expressing them, he would have found in the pages of her own works; but Mary Wollstonecraft carried Rousseauism to extremes, as did other novelists, mostly women, such as Mary Robinson and Mary Hays, whom Godwin knew and whose works he read in 1796 and 1797. The extravagance of their language and the emotional intensity of their thinly disguised autobiographies were, unfortunately, all too easy to imitate, and it was their example which Godwin seems to have followed, rather than the philosophical restraint and chaste language of other novels he read at this time—*Clarissa*, or the novels of Fanny Burney.

---

[1] Draft letter in the Abinger collection, unaddressed and undated, but probably to Holcroft.
[2] Draft letter dated 19 Sept. 1797, in the Abinger collection.

Having vitiated the fictional expression of his new sensibility through three volumes of 'the sorrows of St. Leon', Godwin compounded his lapse of literary judgment by extending his novel to a fourth volume late in 1799, and by relying in that volume on the worst excesses of the Gothic novels which he had read in 1795–6, and the Heroic tragedies which he had read for his own play *Antonio* in 1798–9. Godwin was exploring the whole range of a new sensibility in the years which followed the fall of the French Republic of Reason, and it is not surprising that he did not always use the best models.

However, there were other aspects of nascent Romanticism which Godwin studied besides Gothic fiction and the novel of sensibility. A subject related to both of these was the debate on the sublime and the picturesque, first dealt with in Burke's *Enquiry* (1757), but renewed in Richard Payne Knight's *The Landscape* (1794). Godwin made a systematic study of the literature on this subject, discussing 'taste' with Holcroft on 10 June 1794 and reading Burke several days later, followed by Knight's poem (June 20) and, after returning from a trip to Norfolk, 'Hume on the standard of taste' (July 10). Mary Wollstonecraft then revived his interest in the subject some two years later. In all of her work she had developed a profound awareness of the civilizing effect of sublime and beautiful nature, culminating in the *Letters from Norway* (1796), of which Godwin wrote, 'If ever there was a book calculated to make a man in love with its author, this appears to me to be the book.'[1] Then in January 1798, when he had just begun writing his new novel, and when he was reading through a number of Mary Wollstonecraft's favourite books, Godwin also read Sir Uvedale Price's *On the Picturesque* (1794) along with the *Discourses* of Sir Joshua Reynolds. Her influence clearly helped Godwin to proceed in new directions of taste and aesthetic theory.

Holcroft also helped. Godwin's old friend cultivated an ardent connoisseurship of the arts of painting and engraving; moreover Godwin in the mid-1790s came to know a number of outstanding artists of the day. Throughout the 1790s he visited the Royal Academy exhibitions annually, as well as other special exhibitions,

---

[1] *Memoirs of Mary Wollstonecraft*, ed. W. Clark Durant (London and New York, 1927), p. 84. See also Gary Kelly, 'Godwin, Wollstonecraft, and Rousseau', *Women and Literature*, iii (autumn 1975), 21–6.

such as the Orleans Gallery (27 May 1793), the Raphael Cartoons at Windsor (20 August 1793), 'Hope's Pictures' (25 August 1796), 'Grave's Exhibition' (17 May 1798), the Italian pictures from the collection of the Duke of Orleans (16 April 1799), as well as the celebrated Shakespeare Gallery (10 March 1791; 11 April 1792) and Milton Gallery (20 May, 25 September 1799). In addition, he could always rely on the advice of his friends Opie, Barry, North-cote, and Lawrence;[1] but it was not the classicism of Reynolds's *Discourses* or the melancholy romanticism admired by Holcroft (one of whose favourites was Salvator Rosa) which influenced the mood of *St. Leon*, but rather the spectacularly emotional and dramatic style of his friends Fuseli and young Thomas Lawrence, especially as exemplified in the paintings of the Shakespeare and Milton Galleries.

New styles in painting coincided with new tastes in poetry, and with these too Godwin was familiar. He had not yet begun that intimate friendship with Coleridge which marked the final revolution in his ideas and tastes, but in the late 1790s Godwin was beginning to explore for himself the literature which also appealed to the younger generation of Romantic writers. Early in 1798 he read Bowles's *Sonnets*, he was already a close friend of Charlotte Smith, whose sonnets were admired by Wordsworth,[2] and on 11 April 1799 he glanced at *Lyrical Ballads* itself. He also began to explore the literature of the Elizabethan and Caroline periods, although his excursions here were limited to drama for the most part, since he was studying, as it were, for his own play *Antonio*. Godwin was writing the play throughout the period in which he was working on his novel, and in both he anticipated many of the themes, as well as the tone, of Byron's poems and dramas. He read Shakespeare, the French classical drama, Schiller, Jacobean drama, and especially those tragedies of Beaumont and Fletcher and the Restoration dramatists which have become known as 'Heroic'.

In fact no adjective could better describe the aims, themes, and style of Godwin's novel, for although he would qualify Reynolds's reverence for 'general Nature' with a taste for the 'local' peculiarities found in the Gothic and picturesque, he

---

[1] Godwin met Opie in 1795, Northcote in 1796, Lawrence in 1794, and attended Barry's Royal Academy Lecture as early as 18 February 1793.

[2] Mary Moorman, *William Wordsworth, The Early Years* (Oxford, 1957), p. 170.

obviously shared the belief of the President of the Royal Academy
that history painting was the highest form of art, that 'there is a
nobleness of conception which goes beyond anything in the mere
exhibition even of perfect form; there is an art of animating and
dignifying the figures with intellectual grandeur, of impressing
the appearance of philosophic wisdom, or heroic virtue'.[1] It is no
accident that Godwin read the *Discourses* at the same time he was
beginning a novel which aimed to paint a historical canvas of the
largest and most heroic dimensions.

The full effects of Godwin's new tastes in literature and the arts
was not fully evident until *Fleetwood*, because in 1798–9 Godwin
was still assimilating these new influences; but it is clear that
he was already beginning to explore, by trial and error, new kinds
of emotional, aesthetic, and intellectual experience. Significantly,
his new interests and new ideas only achieved the coherence of a
fully formed Romantic sensibility after he had become intimate
with Coleridge, the last of his 'four principal oral instructors'.
But when he met Coleridge again, within weeks of the publication
of *St. Leon*, Godwin had already prepared himself for this new
influence on his life, thought, and writings.

For in spite of the important changes that had taken place in
his taste and his feelings, Godwin remained primarily a philosopher, the author of *Political Justice*. Just before he came under
the influence of Coleridge Godwin began to write, in the spirit of
Rousseau, fragments of autobiographical 'confessions' which recorded what he had learned in the 1790s, and which explored the
psychological and emotional basis of his personality as it had
developed since childhood. He had to recognize that he was after
all a man of feeling, like other men, perhaps even the 'new man
of feeling' like the hero of his next novel; but his new interests
and new self-awareness did not diminish his essentially philosophical approach to the problems of man. There was a philosophical as well as a personal basis to the new sensibility which he
saw forming in himself in the late 1790s, in the years when he was
composing *St. Leon*. Every important point in Godwin's shift to
Romanticism can be traced to modifications which he felt it
necessary to make to the philosophical structure of *Political Justice*.
Towards the most philosophical of his works, Godwin felt something like the reluctance of the Romantic artist to consider the

[1] Sir Joshua Reynolds, *Discourses*, ed. Helen Zimmern (London, 1887), p. 35.

thing finished, and even after the third edition of 1798 he continued to ponder alterations. In March 1800 he drew up a summary
of his intellectual progress since earliest youth, and listed the
three chief errors in the first edition of his treatise: excessive
stoicism, or neglect of the argument that pleasure and pain are the
only basis of morality; 'Sandemanianism, or an inattention to the
principle, that feeling, and not judgement, is the source of human
actions'; and finally, 'the unqualified condemnation of the private
affections'.[1] He acknowledged that all three of these errors were
related to the influence of Calvinism, and ascribed the correction
of them to, in the first case, George Dyson (one of his four
principal oral instructors), and in the second and third, a perusal
of Hume's *Treatise of Human Nature* in 1795.[2]

It is therefore of the greatest significance to discover that at
about the same time—at least by the time he came to write the
Considerations in November 1795—Godwin also came to share
the views of Hume, 'the prophet of counter-revolution',[3] on the
danger of faction and the disastrous consequences of fomenting
civil strife, no matter how noble or just the cause. The moral of
Hume's *History* of the Stuarts is that of the ending of *Things As
They Are*; it is also the moral of *St. Leon*: those who wish to
reform mankind must move gradually to overcome mistaken
'habits and customs', for history shows that revolutions are
counter-productive.[4] Political events in Britain and France since
the publication of *Things As They Are*, confirmed this lesson, and
St. Leon's adventures in many parts of Europe lead to the pessimistic conclusion that the dawn of political justice was farther off
than had been thought when Godwin published *Political Justice*.
The novel is pessimistic because Godwin had not yet found refuge
in the Romanticism which was absorbing many disillusioned
young English Jacobins. Personal and public events conspired
in the late 1790s to hasten Godwin's transformation into a 'new
man of feeling', with new tastes, new ideas, new emotions. The
events of his personal life and the fate of the Revolution both
demonstrated the inadequacy of *Political Justice* as an account of
the moral world of man. Godwin had already suspected this when

---

[1] Note in Abinger collection.
[2] He perused the *Treatise* on 8 October 1794, and in July–August 1795.
[3] See Laurence L. Bongie, *David Hume, Prophet of the Counter-revolution* (Oxford, 1965).
[4] Godwin dipped into Hume's *History* on many occasions during the 1790s.

he finished *Political Justice* in 1793; his suspicion became a prophecy as he wrote *Things As They Are* in 1793 and 1794; and in the list of projects he drew up in 1795 he gladly embraced a whole new range of literary tasks to tax his talent, and tease out every point of his new 'New Philosophy', from the study of the Revolution's failure to an analysis of a superhuman historical leader (Alexander), from the tragedy of a Christian necromancer (St. Dunstan) to tales of human psychological types (the coward, the lover, the adept). Characteristically, Godwin thought to express his new ideas through a variety of 'writings', for writing, of whatever kind, was an experience as well as an expression of experience. Characteristically too, he saw that both he and his philosophy would have to change, through these writings. Like the true Protestant, he saw life and belief as one whole, and a change in one must inevitably produce a change in the other; like a true 'necessitarian' and English Jacobin, he believed that the individual and social life should also be one whole, and that revolutions in one produced revolution in the other. He saw the history of man as a series of such revolutions, progressing dialectically towards perfectibility; but in the earlier part of the 1790s events had led him to overemphasize one part of the dialectic, revolution, and to ignore the inevitable reaction. The events of the mid-1790s had forced him to correct his historical perspective towards an over-awareness of reaction. Now, at the end of the decade, with his wife dead and his children still to be looked to, with his reputation as man and author vitiated, with his 'fellow labourers' in the cause of truth falling off on all sides, personally embattled in an embattled world, Godwin began to look for the synthesis, to seek it in every aspect of his intellectual, emotional, and social life. *St. Leon* was to embody this romantic quest.

Design and Execution

In its own time Godwin's attempt to fashion a myth for a decade of Revolution was a success. His friends and his reviewers accepted his attempt to impress, even if some of them found it to be a cold kind of impressiveness. So august was the novel's design, that it could easily seem remote. By any artistic standard, moreover, the novel is a failure, because it lacks 'unity of design', and does not even have much unity of spirit.

This failure is signalled and signalized by the novel's reliance on foreshadowing, a device especially popular with writers of the poorest kind of Gothic fiction and German melodrama. Foreshadowing was to replace the hard-won rigour of necessary connections in plot and characterization, was to replace, in short, the English Jacobin philosophy of necessity as it operated through every aspect of fictional technique. It had been one of the achievements of the earlier English Jacobin novelists to eliminate Providence and blind fate from the novel, and replace it with a more authentic, if no less philosophical concatenation. The Providence that operated throughout the works of Prévost and the novels of sensibility had been taken up especially by women writers, no doubt because their own social position required them continually to submit to the will and the whims of others. In the mid-1790s Godwin was surrounded by a 'seraglio' of such women novelists, and he struggled mightily to imbue them with his own perfectibilian optimism. He also tried to get them to eliminate fatalism from their fictions, as they tried to eliminate it from their lives. With Mary Wollstonecraft, at least, he succeeded, before cruel fate ended her life, and blighted much of his.

In the aftermath of that disaster he himself succumbed to the pessimism and the fatalistic fictional ploys he had once deplored. What unity *St. Leon* has is in the first three volumes, conceived, probably, as early as 1795. This is an original and bold fable of the errors leading to moral and social isolation; but the fourth volume (St. Leon in Hungary) and the style of the whole, are derivative. Rather than reaching ahead to the style of Romanticism, as he was to do in his next novel, Godwin fell back on the conventions of sensibility and the Gothic. In the character of Bethlem Gabor he came as close as he ever did to plagiarism. He had lost the intellectual and hence artistic certainty of the early part of the decade, and he was not to find it again until he remarried, and submitted himself to a new influence (Coleridge) and the course of exhaustive researches which resulted in his *Life of Chaucer* in 1803. For the moment he, like his hero, was wandering and unsure. *St. Leon* marks the dissolution of one kind of unity, and suggests the beginnings of a new one.

The place which *St. Leon* occupies in Godwin's development towards Romanticism is in fact the most important thing about it. Godwin is in the process of reconstructing the interests and ideas

of the English Jacobins—interests and ideas shared by many
including Wordsworth and Coleridge in the earlier part of the
decade—and finding refuge from political and philosophical disappointment at the failure of Revolution and the success of reaction in new ideas, new tastes, new feelings. That the novel marks
a reaction of some kind seems to be confirmed by the fact that it
is expressed in such an exaggerated form of language and construction. The attempt to reform mankind by appeal to reason
had failed; the passions were now seen to be the real motive
forces in human affairs; the passions must therefore be given their
due. Hence Godwin's indulgence in the picturesque, in the
Gothic, and the heroic. Moreover, the control of contemporary
events had passed out of the hands of the many into those of a
few individuals, and history seemed to be dependent once again,
as it had been in the ancient and modern historians Godwin knew
so well, on a few extraordinary characters.

St. Leon, therefore, is a novel which sets out to be in every way
extraordinary—in theme, style, character, and plot. It is both an
exploration of and an appeal to the imagination, an examination
of the place of character in history, and an argument for it. Once
again Godwin conceived a grand design which managed to unite
a number of aims. He was still at the old task of questioning and
instructing the moral nature of man; it was just that his notions
of how this might be done had, since 1794, expanded in a variety
of ways. There is still the general outline of 'adventures of flight
and pursuit' which links St. Leon to Things As They Are; and there
is still the theme of guilt and remorse for the disaster which the
hero's curiosity and impulsiveness bring upon himself and others.
But to this English Jacobin fable Godwin now joins a Romantic
interest in the importance of feeling in human motive, and a
glowing account of the joys of the domestic affections. He gives
his protagonist powers on a Napoleonic scale, and finally, in the
last volume of the novel, Godwin adds the Gothic figure of
Bethlem Gabor, a character who anticipates the gloomiest of the
Byronic hero-villains. In St. Leon Godwin was continuing the
work of Things As They Are, but he was also exploring new
territory, new aspects of human nature. One modern critic
has described the novel as Coleridgean,[1] and even Godwin's

---

[1] James T. Boulton, *The Language of Politics in the Age of Wilkes and Burke*,
p. 247.

contemporaries had to admit that, whatever its defects, *St. Leon* was a novel conceived on the grand scale.

Although Godwin's conception anticipated Scott and Byron, his execution did not. Technically, *St. Leon* suffers from the same conflicting excesses found in other late English Jacobin novels, such as the second part of *Hugh Trevor* and *Bryan Perdue*. There is excessive control over plot in order to arrive at the required philosophical conclusion, and yet coincidence is necessary in order to maintain that control. And there is an exaggerated and repetitive use of language necessary to gloss over the fact that the hero's reactions suit the requirements of the novel's 'argument' rather than the realities of the novel's events. *St. Leon* manages to unite in itself the major defects of two very different sorts of fiction—the English Jacobin novel of purpose on the one hand, and the Gothic novel on the other. For example, the novel is marked by two different sorts of interruption in the narrative. There are philosophical reflections and dialogues typical of earlier English Jacobin novels, and there are lengthy outbursts of guilt and remorse typical of the worst type of Gothic fiction. The skilful narrator and manager of suspense in *Things As They Are* has, in *St. Leon*, been swamped by a diabolical concoction of sententiousness and sentiment.

In fact, Godwin admitted that he had lost control of his novel when he wrote to Tom Wedgwood in February 1800 and described how *St. Leon* had grown under his hand, requiring a fourth volume.[1] The story was probably meant to conclude with St. Leon's escape from the Inquisition and final visit, incognito, to his daughters. The story contained in these three volumes is a self-contained philosophical tale of one man's quixotic attempts to help mankind, and it ends neatly (and with a certain obvious relevance to Godwin's own life) with the hero's remorse at having been, through possession of his terrible secret, the cause of his wife's death. He can only find some small consolation in the quiet obscurity of his daughters' existence, as he sets off, like Ulysses, to continue his wanderings through eternity.

The fourth volume of the novel is something of a different kind, as St. Leon experiments in monetary economics and is once again rewarded with hostility and violence for his pains. He then encounters the extraordinary character Bethlem Gabor, who is

[1] Draft letter, dated 2 Feb. 1800, in the Abinger collection.

unlike anything in the first three volumes, and the novel ends
with a bizarre version of the romantic myth of the rejuvenation
of age by youth, as St. Leon takes the *elixir vitae* to become the
companion, and rival in love, of his own son Charles. From the
Journal it can be seen that Godwin began the fourth volume
sometime late in the summer of 1799. On 26 July he consulted
Robert Watson's *History of the Reign of Philip the Second*, obviously
for the third volume of *St. Leon*. Then on 3 August he noted
'Bethlem Gabor, çala',[1] on 8–10 August he consulted Robert
Townson's *Travels in Hungary*, and on the 10th he referred to
Révolutions de Hongrie, an anonymous work which contained an
account of the historical Bethlem Gabor, who had himself proclaimed king of Hungary in the early seventeenth century by
winning the support of the Calvinists of Transylvania. However,
the Bethlem Gabor who casts St. Leon into a dungeon and whose
sole motivation is hatred bears little relation to the character of
the histories, and the description of him is in fact lifted straight
out of a German Gothic novel which Godwin had glanced through
in May 1795, entitled *The Necromancer*.[2] The character is merely
a Gothic villain with the name of a real historical personage, and
as such has neither the weight of moral example of 'philosophical
history', nor the weight of authenticity lent by the historical
characters who are scattered through the first three volumes of
the novel. Not only did Godwin vitiate the possibilities of historical
fiction by relying on the supernatural (the *opus magnum*), but he
also debased the kind of 'fictitious history' he had created by
committing the cardinal sin of the historical novelist and presenting an entirely imaginary character—a plagiarized one at that
—under the guise of 'history'.

The whole of *St. Leon* is marked by such confusions and contra-
dictions. It is a novel half-way between the bold conceptions of
Things As They Are and the refined sensibility of *Fleetwood*, and,
not surprisingly, it fails to reach the standard of either. Its stylistic
defects—extravagant and at the same time hackneyed language,
lengthy and repetitive self-revilings by the hero, exaggerated
descriptions and moralizing 'perorations'—only expose the lack

[1] 'Çala' means 'ça et la'; Godwin used the word to indicate that he had merely
browsed through a book.

[2] Lawrence Flammenberg (i.e. K. F. Kahlert), *The Necromancer*, trans. Peter
Teuthold (London, 1794; reprinted with an introduction by Montague Summers,
London, 1927), p. 196.

of coherence in the over-all conception. At one moment (in the first volume) the narrator sinks from sight as the author describes the siege and battle of Pavia, at another he rapidly sketches his adventures only to bog down in morbid self-examination, or indulge in moral and philosophical digressions. Finally, the dialogue, which had a certain force in *Things As They Are*, is now stilted and artificial, an inept imitation of the supposedly sublime language of Heroic tragedy.

In all this the end was plain, to produce a work of such 'overpowering interest' that 'he that reads it shall never again be as if he had not read it'.[1] Unfortunately Godwin had not yet learned how to affect the imagination in this way except by exaggerating every technique he had already deployed in *Things As They Are*. As a result he lost that 'unity of design' which both he and Holcroft saw as the essential feature of the true novel, the novel which could take its place alongside the highest forms of literature. Through such novels Godwin meant to affect the moral nature of every reader, and in a MS. essay on religion (undated) he wrote: 'I am myself deeply convinced that imagination is the basis of a sound morality. It is by dint of feeling, and of putting ourselves in fancy into the place of other men, that we can learn how we ought to treat them, and be moved to treat them as we ought.'[2]

In observing himself and others and the world at large in the years since the publication of *Things As They Are* Godwin had come to realize the importance of the imagination, and had altered and adapted his philosophy accordingly. Unfortunately he had not, by the time he composed *St. Leon*, fully digested his new ideas, tastes, and feelings, nor had he yet found an appropriate language to express them. To complete the evolution and to refine his sensibility into Romanticism he seems to have required the influence of a new master, who knocked on his door in Somers Town only two days after *St. Leon* was published. Coleridge was the fourth and last of Godwin's four 'oral instructors' and probably the greatest 'oral instructor' of his time. It was he who helped Godwin to complete the process he had already begun, of becoming, like the hero of his next novel, a 'new man of feeling'.

---

[1] Note dated 10 Oct. 1824, in the Abinger collection. Godwin is describing the aim of *Things As They Are*. [2] Abinger collection.

3. FLEETWOOD

'The New Man of Feeling'

Fleetwood contains ample proof that Godwin had learned a great deal from writing *St. Leon,* and advanced the evolution of his mind and heart. As usual he supplied his new novel with a preface which set forth his intentions, and revealed that he had himself become the 'new man of feeling' of his sub-title. Whereas the events of *St. Leon* were 'of the miraculous class', *Fleetwood* 'consists of such adventures, as for the most part have occurred to at least one half of the Englishmen now existing, who are of the same rank of life as my hero'.[1] As well as claiming a new degree of realism Godwin also implied that his purpose was now less controversial than it had been in his previous novels, and he merely wished to add 'somewhat to the stock of books which should enable a recluse shut up in his closet, to form an idea of what is passing in the world' (pp. ix–x). It is as if Godwin had bid farewell to political controversy with his *Thoughts Occasioned by the Perusal of Dr. Parr's Spital Sermon* (1801).

In fact, as some of the reviews were quick to point out, the principles of *Fleetwood* were closer to those of *Things As They Are* than Godwin seemed to admit. The novel's sub-title was found particularly provocative, and most of the reviewers denied that the misanthropic Fleetwood was in any way the 'new man of feeling'. There was nothing which could not be seen to have political implications in those times; any kind of change in attitudes, taste, or style was seen in the light of the international struggle against Jacobinism and 'innovation'. In the same cartoon by Gillray which caricatured Godwin as a braying donkey and Holcroft as an 'Acquitted Felon', Sensibility is portrayed weeping, with the works of Rousseau in one hand and a dead bird in the other, and one foot resting on the head of Louis XVI;[2] and in a number of English Anti-Jacobin novels, Sensibility and Godwinism were also smitten with the same satiric shaft.[3]

[1] William Godwin, *Fleetwood: or, The New Man of Feeling* (London, 1805), vol. i, p. vii.
[2] 'New Morality;—or—The Promis'd Installment of the High-Priest of the Theophilanthropes, with the Homage of Leviathan and his Suite'. See M. D. George, *Catalogue of Political and Personal Satires Preserved in the Department of Prints and Drawings in the British Museum,* vol. vii (London, 1942).
[3] e.g. Charles Lloyd, *Edmund Oliver* (1798), George Walker, *The Vagabond* (1799), Charles Lucas, *The Infernal Quixote* (1800); Godwin read the first two of these.

The association was not unapt, but it made the mistake of seeing the 'new man of feeling' in terms of the old. Godwin had not adopted the ideas and attitudes of eighteenth-century sensibility but rather those of Romanticism, and Romanticism's 'new man of feeling' was a rejection of the old, as Wordsworth tried to show in his preface to *Lyrical Ballads* and in his 'Lines left upon a Seat in a Yew-tree' (written 1795–7). Godwin's new man of feeling was not a rejection, but rather a revision and reconstruction of the old. As his life changed so, inevitably, did his philosophy and his fiction. All three were intimately connected, all three were in constant flux, as Godwin pressed forward to perfect truth and the personal perfectibility which was to herald the 'new man'. Philosophy and fiction were not just the expressions of newness, they were part of its discovery. Godwin had discovered feeling at the end just as he had discovered reason at the beginning of the Revolutionary decade. The discovery of reason entailed a philosophical enquiry, the *Enquiry Concerning Political Justice*; the modification of that enquiry required a novel, which proved to be prelude to the discovery of feeling. Toward the end of the decade Godwin began to define and explore further, through autobiography. He wrote chronological notes, memoirs, self-portraits, and carried his findings into his fiction, where he combined them with his new philosophy, new tastes, new values. Soon he explored even further, in historical writing (*The Life of Chaucer*, 1803), the possibilities for wholeness and progress in human life, and finally fixed his own variety of Romanticism in a novel, *Fleetwood*. Godwin completed a programme of writing and a programme of personal evolution at almost the same time. Only his autobiographical writings, significantly, remained incomplete and unpublished; but by 1805 Godwin had established, by a variety of literary endeavour from philosophy, to polemics, to fiction, to essays, to history, and back to fiction, his 'autobiographical space'.[1] He had, in a sense, completed the search for meaning in his own existence.

The changes in life and modes of writing required a change of style and form. Although this change was not radical in the case

[1] See Philippe Lejeune, 'Le Pacte autobiographique', *Poétique*, no. xiv (1973), pp. 158–60. Lejeune defines 'l'espace autobiographique' as the dimension between an author's autobiography and his fiction; I would add to fiction a whole range of prose-writing, especially the polemical and philosophical prose of the 1790s, which often concealed autobiography in the form of political or philosophical discourse.

of Godwin's fiction, it was important. Godwin simply expanded his range and increased his refinement, improving his technique, altering and adapting here, innovating there, but still carrying on the task undertaken in *Things As They Are* and *St. Leon*. Unlike Mrs. Inchbald he had not abandoned novel-writing altogether; nor did he fall back on the tired plots and ploys of the past, as Holcroft did in *Bryan Perdue* (1805). Making the fullest use of his friendship with Wordsworth and Coleridge, Lamb and Hazlitt,[1] Godwin achieved in *Fleetwood* a kind of fiction which continued, and completed, the development begun in *Things As They Are* and continued in *St. Leon*. *Fleetwood* marks the metamorphosis of English Jacobin into English Romantic fiction.

Romanticism and Sensibility

Although *Fleetwood* contained many elements of social criticism and satire, these are incidental to the romantic adventures of the hero, just as they were in Godwin's great model for 'the new man of feeling', Rousseau's *La Nouvelle Héloïse*. Godwin's story was romantic in the sense that Rousseau's was—it dealt for the most part with love and its attendant passions. Such a story by no means excluded moral purpose, in fact it was a feature of Romanticism to attempt to deepen and broaden the moral importance of sentiment and feeling; but although they had always displayed an interest in feeling and the novel of sensibility the English Jacobins, especially Holcroft and Godwin, had been thorough-going rationalists. Their New Men and Women had feelings, but they were those of a Frank Henley rather than a St. Preux.

Now Godwin contrived a hero who was much more like the erratic protagonist of Rousseau's novel. Fleetwood's 'Romantic' disposition, formed amongst mountains and the wildness of nature like that of St. Preux, dominates the tone of the first part of the novel, just as the examination of conjugal love takes up the last part of *Fleetwood*, and *La Nouvelle Héloïse*. In the portrait of Fleetwood's jealousy, however, Godwin seems to have dipped into an English imitation of Rousseau's novel, Henry Mackenzie's *Julia de Roubigné*, from which Holcroft and Mrs. Inchbald also borrowed. There was a line of development running through *Clarissa*, *La Nouvelle Héloïse*, and *Julia de Roubigné*, to *A Simple*

[1] On 18 March 1800 Godwin recorded in his Journal, 'Sup at Lamb's with Coleridge; talk of style'.

Story, Anna St. Ives, and *Fleetwood.* It was a line to which Godwin had also attempted to contribute in *St. Leon,* in the romance and marriage of the hero and Marguerite de Damville; but the dominant sensibility of that novel was Gothic, and Godwin had not yet begun to approach the originality of the English Romantic poets in the exploration and description of feeling. *St. Leon,* therefore, was 'pre-Romantic' in both a technical and historical sense. In Godwin's intellectual evolution it represented an attempt to express new interests, the interests of the younger generation of Romantic artists, poets, historians, and critics; and in his artistic development it lacked the refinement of style and technique which he achieved in his next novel. *Fleetwood* shows that Godwin had made the fullest use of his friendship with Coleridge and developed the 'pre-Romanticism' of *St. Leon* into something like fully Romantic fiction, that is, fiction fit to take its place beside the new Romantic poetry. Curiously, Godwin was creating this kind of fiction at almost the same time that Walter Scott, also in full flight from the decade of Revolution, was working on the novel which would be published in 1814 as *Waverley.*[1] It is curious, because it was only after *Waverley* was published, and its author's fame established, that Godwin, in a spirit of rivalry, returned once again to the novel, and wrote *Mandeville* (1817).

However, *Mandeville* and Godwin's later romantic novels, *Cloudesley* (1830) and *Deloraine* (1831), were only remodellings of *Fleetwood,* and so have no claim to special treatment in a history of the English Jacobin novel, a history in which Godwin's reconstruction of English Jacobinism into Romanticism is the last episode. What is remarkable is that amongst the English Jacobin novelists Godwin alone made the transition to Romanticism. By 1805 Bage was dead, Mrs. Inchbald had abandoned creative writing altogether, and Holcroft, after dabbling in stage melodramas, could produce only the farrago of satire and sentiment that was *Bryan Perdue.* So it is that an account of the genesis of Godwin's *Fleetwood* is also an account of the demise of the English Jacobin novel.

Wordsworth and Coleridge. Although he drew on the novel of sensibility for *Fleetwood* Godwin produced a work which was essentially different in kind from both that particular tradition and the Gothic novel. It is an indication of Godwin's determination to

---

[1] J. G. Lockhart, *The Life of Sir Walter Scott* (London, 1893), p. 301.

avoid adventures 'of the miraculous class' that his new novel
contains no trace of the 'German' influence found in *St. Leon*. The
roots of the Romanticism of *Fleetwood* are almost entirely English.

Casimir Fleetwood, for example, is not related to the misanthropic hero-villains of novels such as *The Necromancer* or *The
Mysteries of Udolpho* and *The Italian*, nor to the larger-than-life
protagonists of Heroic tragedy, but to the romantic melancholic
described in Wordsworth's 'Lines left upon a Seat in a Yew-tree':

> He was one who owned
> No common soul. In youth by genius nurs'd,
> And big with lofty views, he to the world
> Went forth, pure in his heart, against the taint
> Of dissolute tongues, and jealousy, and hate,
> And scorn,—against all enemies prepared,
> All but neglect. The world, for so it thought,
> Owed him no service; and so his spirit damped
> At once, with rash disdain he turned away,
> And with the foot of pride sustained his soul
> In solitude.[1]

These lines are almost a résumé of the adventures of Fleetwood
until, after a marriage with a much younger woman, he learns the
lesson of Wordsworth's poem:

> The man whose eye
> Is ever on himself doth look on one,
> The least of Nature's works, one who might move
> The wise man to that scorn which wisdom holds
> Unlawful, ever. O be wiser, Thou!
> Instructed that true knowledge leads to love;
> True dignity abides with him alone
> Who, in the silent hour of inward thought,
> Can still suspect, and still revere himself,
> In lowliness of heart [lines 55–64].

Wordsworth's solitary inhabits the same locale—the English
Lakes—visited by Fleetwood in his misanthropic wanderings,
and where he meets his future wife and instructress in 'lowliness
of heart'. Much of the story, in fact, is set in favourite places of
the English Romantic poets—the Lakes, Wales, and Switzerland
—and Fleetwood's boat trip on the lake of Uri (i. 179 ff.) bears

---

[1] Lines 12–22 in *Lyrical Ballads* (1798). Wordsworth later altered this passage
considerably. Godwin consulted *Lyrical Ballads* on 11 April 1799 and (vol. ii)
1 March 1801.

a remarkable resemblance to an experience of Wordsworth's whilst travelling in Switzerland in 1790.[1] Godwin even used the same reference book for his Swiss scenes that Wordsworth had used for *Descriptive Sketches*, William Coxe's *Travels in Switzerland*.[2] The landscapes are not mere backdrops, however, as they are in *The Mysteries of Udolpho*; Fleetwood traces his character back to the same combination of solitude and rugged scenery that Wordsworth described in *The Prelude*: 'My earliest years were spent [in Merionethshire] among mountains and precipices, amidst the roaring of the ocean and the dashing of waterfalls. A constant familiarity with these objects gave a wildness to my ideas, and an uncommon seriousness to my temper' (i. 3).[3] Godwin keeps to the English Jacobin—and Romantic—principle that circumstances form character; but he has expanded the range of those circumstances.

The question of Godwin's influence on Wordsworth has been much agitated, but the more interesting question is Wordsworth's influence on Godwin, and although that influence was no doubt mediated by Coleridge,[4] it is evident in *Fleetwood*. In fact the adventures of Godwin's hero—his solitary upbringing in the wilderness, his youthful hopes, his distaste for fashionable city life, his disillusionment with politics, and final settlement for the domestic virtues—have a vague resemblance to Wordsworth's own life up to 1805. Godwin remained typical of the English Jacobins of his generation in that he never lost his love for London, but in other respects his life too followed a sequence of moral and philosophical revolution similar to that of the hero of his novel, and of Wordsworth.[5] *Fleetwood* is evidence of the willingness with which its middle-aged author became the pupil of men who had once, however briefly, been his disciples. Some time around 1800 Godwin had written in an autobiographical note,

---

[1] Mary Moorman, *William Wordsworth, The Early Years*, p. 144.

[2] Godwin read Coxe in June and July 1804, just after starting *Fleetwood*. See Moorman, p. 128.

[3] Godwin had passed through North Wales on his way back from Ireland in August 1800.

[4] Coleridge at this time was at the lowest point of his 'abasement' before Wordsworth.

[5] e.g. the changes manifested in Wordsworth's long composition of *Salisbury Plain*. See Stephen Gill, 'The Original *Salisbury Plain*: Introduction and Text', in *Bicentenary Wordsworth Studies*, ed. Jonathan Wordsworth (Ithaca and London, 1970), pp. 142–79.

'It is my peculiar character to strike out nothing, but to expand with no contemptible felicity the suggestions of others—I now brood on those of Coleridge.'[1] *Fleetwood* is the product of that brooding.

Rousseau. The 'new man of feeling' was not entirely the result of the influence of Wordsworth and Coleridge, however. The influence of the novel of sensibility has already been suggested, and events in Godwin's own life in the late 1790s, discussed earlier in relation to *St. Leon,* continued to have their effect on the evolution of Godwin's ideas. Moreover, he had already begun to explore the literary antecedents of Romanticism before Coleridge came along to act as a catalyst.

Rousseau in particular attracted his interest, and had done so since the early 1790s; but at that time it was the political writings which interested him. As early as December 1789 he had undertaken to translate Rousseau's *Confessions,* and from the time of his intimacy with Mary Wollstonecraft, who was a prodigious admirer of Rousseau,[2] Godwin turned to the sentimental and autobiographical works with renewed interest. In August 1797 and June to August 1801 he read the *Confessions,* and at the same time began to set down his own autobiographical musings. Not surprisingly, the long narrative of Ruffigny, the Swiss sage and friend of Fleetwood's father, seems to be patterned after some of Rousseau's adventures, and Fleetwood's own story is avowedly confessional, as he admits near the beginning of the novel: 'The proper topic of the narrative I am writing is the record of my errors. To write it, is the act of my penitence and humiliation' (i. 18). There could in fact be no better illustration of the English Jacobin principle that circumstances form character than the *Confessions* of Rousseau.

The narrative method in novel and autobiography is also similar, being an account not so much of adventures as of the occasions of particular sentiments, an individual enquiry into the growth of mind, a psychological study in the same class as *The Prelude.* Near the end of the first volume Fleetwood writes: 'In

[1] Undated note in the Abinger collection. Coleridge called on Godwin at the end of November 1799, and in early December they began to see each other regularly and became quite friendly. This period of their intimacy lasted until around 1803, and they exchanged numerous letters.

[2] An enthusiasm derived from Fuseli according to Godwin's *Memoir* of her (p. 59). See Gary Kelly, 'Godwin, Wollstonecraft, and Rousseau', *Women and Literature,* iii (autumn 1975), 21–6.

contemplation and reverie, one thought introduces another perpetually, and it is by similarity, or the hooking of one upon the
other, that the process of thinking is carried on. In books and in
living discourse the case is the same; there is a constant connection
and transition, leading on the chain of the argument' (i. 265). The
apparent formlessness of Godwin's novel has its sanction in the
apparent lack of structure in the *Confessions*. Moreover, Rousseau's
candid confession of the autobiographical content of *La Nouvelle
Héloïse* had an obvious interest for the English Jacobin novelists,
all of whom injected their own adventures, sentiments, and confessions into their fictional works. And so, when Godwin introduced into *Fleetwood* a character who discourses upon Rousseau
from personal acquaintance, he was merely completing the circle
of fact and fiction.

There can be little doubt too that Rousseau's fiction had an
even greater influence on *Fleetwood* than the *Confessions*. Godwin
consulted *La Nouvelle Héloïse* in October 1796 and August 1797,
and read it completely between May and August 1798. The sensibility of the young Fleetwood while in Switzerland is obviously
akin to that of St. Preux, and the trio of Julie, St. Preux, and
Wolmar is paralleled by Mary, Kenrick, and Fleetwood. Godwin
presents, as it were, the gloomier version of Rousseau's *ménage*,
since Fleetwood can by no means suppress the jealous passions
to which Wolmar is a complete stranger. Godwin's Fleetwood is
obviously a combination of Rousseau's Wolmar and St. Preux,
with touches of Shakespeare's Othello and the jealous king of
Otway's *Don Carlos*,[1] and it is surely no accident that the young
romantic enthusiast of Godwin's novel, Kenrick, has the same
name as the first translator into English of *La Nouvelle Héloïse*.

The influence of Rousseau's novel on the incidents and atmosphere of *Fleetwood* was considerable, then; but some at least of
the Rousseauism of Godwin's novel was received at second hand
from Henry Mackenzie's imitation of *La Nouvelle Héloïse, Julia de
Roubigné*, which Godwin had read as early as June 1793. In
Mackenzie's novel Montauban, a middle-aged man disillusioned
with the world, takes the much younger Julia as his wife, and
finds, like Fleetwood, that his domestic peace is disturbed by the

[1] Godwin read *Don Carlos* on 15 November 1798 and 22 January 1801. Godwin
seems to have been especially interested in the heroic drama's blending of domestic
and state affairs.

youthful frolicking of one of his wife's admirers, Rouillé, who is the equivalent of Godwin's Kenrick. Moreover Montauban first discovers his wife's supposed infidelity when he finds a miniature of her former suitor Savillon in her chamber, just as Fleetwood finds a miniature of Kenrick in Mary's room, although it has been planted there by the Iago-figure Gifford.[1] It is certainly true that the over-all effect of Mackenzie's novel is coarser and more melo-dramatic than that of *La Nouvelle Héloïse*, but the evidence is clear that Godwin was making deliberate use of two of the best known sentimental novels, just as Mrs. Inchbald and Holcroft had done before him, in *A Simple Story* and *Anna St. Ives*.

Romance and History. There is, however, much more to God-win's Romanticism than Rousseauism or the influence of Words-worth and Coleridge. Godwin, like the young Romantic poets and writers, found food for his new sensibility in the literature of his own country, in Shakespeare and Milton, in the Elizabethan and Jacobean poets and dramatists and miscellaneous writers, and in the poetry and romance of the Middle Ages.

Hazlitt thought that Godwin's taste in poetry was altered 'from an exclusive admiration of the age of Queen Anne to an almost equally exclusive one of that of Elizabeth' by the influence of Coleridge.[2] Although Godwin's protagonists Falkland and St. Leon were formed partly by reading the literature of chivalry, his own favourite poet before 1798 seems to have been Charles Churchill. However, in that year he began to explore different sorts of poetry, such as Cowper's *Task*, Hoole's Tasso, the poems of Shenstone, and the *Sonnets* of Bowles. To some extent he also touched on the Elizabethan and Jacobean drama whilst studying for his own tragedy *Antonio*. Then after coming under the influ-ence of Coleridge he set about a new course of reading with all the diligence to be expected from a product of Hoxton Academy. He read the criticism of Warton, the poems of Spenser and Chaucer, Percy's *Reliques*, the poems of Ossian, Scottish Ballads, Gower and Lydgate, and the plays of Shakespeare, Jonson, Beau-mont and Fletcher.

He was not just following a course of reading, however. As his moral and political philosophy began to change, he gained

---

[1] *Fleetwood*, iii. 203; *Julia de Roubigné* (London, 1777), ii. 126.

[2] 'William Godwin' in *The Spirit of the Age, Works*, ed. P. P. Howe (London and Toronto, 1930–4), xi. 28.

a new appreciation of Burke's celebration of the arts and institutions of medieval culture. He saw that romance and chivalry had positive virtues, and he admitted as much in his *Life of Chaucer*. More important, he began to appreciate the *form* of romance. In an autobiographical note written in 1818 he described how, in 1799, he had departed from a lifelong practice of regular reading from the best classical and modern English authors. He began 'accidentally' with Beaumont and Fletcher:

It was as if a mighty river had changed its course, to water the garden of my mind. I was like a person, who for many years had subsisted on a slender annuity, and had now an immense magazine of wealth bequeathed to him. I looked over the inventory of my fortune, and felt that these treasures would never be exhausted. . . . What a blessing, for a man at forty three years of age, a period at which we are threatened with the blunting of some of the senses from monotonous repetition of their gratifications to enter into the lease of a new life, where every thing would be fresh, and every thing would be young.[1]

This experience found its way into *Fleetwood* in the hero's extravagant praise of the joys of love and spring, after being rejuvenated by his young bride (ii. 284), and it is not surprising to find a tribute to Fletcher in the same part of the book (iii. 21–2); but most important is the way in which the novel comes increasingly to resemble a tragicomedy in form. After a youth passed in tracing all the corruptions of society, Fleetwood, like Wolmar and Montauban, finds love and comfort in marriage with a much younger woman, Mary Macneil, the daughter of a friend of Rousseau who has retired to the Lake District; but due to the machinations of his nephew Gifford, a villain motivated like Iago or Bethlem Gabor by pure misanthropy and Mandevillean self-interest, Fleetwood is led to believe that Mary is cuckolding him with Gifford's half-brother, the impulsive but candid Kenrick.[2] Gifford almost succeeds in his fell scheme, but the perseverance of Fleetwood's real friends finally enables him to see the truth and he and Mary are reconciled, both sadder and wiser for their sufferings. The form of this narrative is so close to that of *A Simple Story* that the resemblance can be no accident. Godwin, of course, re-read Mrs. Inchbald's novel in October and

---

[1] Note dated 3 May 1818, in the Abinger collection.

[2] The rivalry of Gifford and Kenrick may be derived from another of Otway's tragedies, *The Orphan*. The situation of Monimia in the play is also similar to that of Mary Macneil.

November 1804, while he was writing of the courtship and marriage of Fleetwood and Mary Macneil (another version of Mary
Wollstonecraft). It is in fact this last part of the novel which is
most like a tragicomedy; Mrs. Inchbald had used the same form to
bind together the two halves of her novel almost fifteen years
earlier. The form of tragicomedy, a romance of middle-age and
youth, of experience and innocence, is particularly appealing in
a post-revolutionary, post-heroic age, an age such as Godwin
found himself in when he began his new novel. That he was
conscious of this historical perspective will be seen when consideration is given to his method of 'fictitious history' in *Fleetwood*; but tragicomedy, the form of much Romantic narrative
art, also drew attention away from 'affairs of state' to the domestic
level of human experience, and often, as in plays by Beaumont and
Fletcher, Otway, and Lee (some of Godwin's favourite reading by
this time), argued that regeneration of the state could follow only
from a rejuvenation of the individual, through the 'domestic
affections'.

It is appropriate, therefore, that Godwin should have chosen
Jacobean tragicomedy as one of the patterns for a novel avowedly
based on domestic subjects, rather than the Heroic tragedy which
he drew on for the larger-than-life themes and characters of *St.
Leon*. The difference in models may also help to account for the
considerable difference of style in the two novels. Gone is the
extravagant language of *St. Leon*, the melodramatic foreboding,
and the gloomy self-revilings of the hero. Fleetwood at least
knows how to describe his joys and sorrows without undermining
sympathy by straining after the sublime. Stylistic control and
restraint was essential if Godwin was to temper his manner to
his matter, for he was no longer dealing with adventures of 'the
miraculous class', but with the common experiences of domestic
life.

Strange as it may seem, Godwin's re-orientation towards
'home-thoughts' was reinforced by his historical work for the
Life of Chaucer during 1801–3. Not only did Godwin have for the
first time seriously to devote himself to literary studies, and to
read a wide range of medieval literature and romance, he had also
to relate the life of an individual to his time. The work was
representative of eighteenth-century 'philosophical history' in
that it attempted to relate one man's life and writings to his social

and political background, but it also showed traits of the new
Romantic history in its interest in the origins of individual and
national culture.[1] In this respect, too, Godwin showed his
affinity with Romanticism in his determination to avoid the type
of antiquarianism practised by his friend Joseph Ritson. Like the
Romantic poets Godwin used the researches of the eighteenth-
century antiquarians for his own purposes, feeling that 'antiqui-
ties have too generally been regarded as the province of men of
cold tempers and sterile imaginations', men who accumulated
their dry facts in 'ignorance of the materials of which man is
made'.[2] And so, although his *Life of Chaucer* was modelled on
works of 'philosophical history' such as William Robertson's
Charles V and William Roscoe's *Lorenzo de Medici*,[3] Godwin
'saw the age of Chaucer through the spectacles of Romanticism'.[4]

It was my wish, had my power held equal pace with my strong
inclination, to carry the workings of fancy and the spirit of philosophy
into the investigation of ages past. I was anxious to rescue for a
moment the illustrious dead from the jaws of the grave, to make them
pass in review before me, to question their spirits and record their
answers. I wished to make myself their master of the ceremonies, to
introduce my reader to their familiar speech, and to enable him to
feel for the instant as if he had lived with Chaucer.[5]

As he had indicated in the MS. essay on 'History' and 'Romance',
Godwin wished to apply the imagination to history as it was
already applied in fiction, to discover and communicate moral
truth.

Godwin rejected generic laws for imaginative truth, and behind
or within all of his new literary endeavours was a new version of
the old myth of romance. In the first years of the new century he
read old and new romance, old and new history, and poetry and
drama which was romantic in spirit and form. This spirit is

---

[1] H. E. Barnes, *A History of Historical Writing*, 2nd rev. edn. (New York, 1963),
pp. 179–80.

[2] *Life of Geoffrey Chaucer* (London, 1803), vol. i, p. x.

[3] William Roscoe, *The Life of Lorenzo de' Medici*, 2nd. edn. corrected, 2 vols.
(London, 1796). Godwin read it in 1796, and part of it in 1798. Roscoe was,
of course, a close friend of Mary Wollstonecraft. Godwin read Robertson in 1798
and 1801.

[4] Thomas P. Peardon, *The Transition in English Historical Writing 1760–1830* (New
York, 1933), p. 247.

[5] *Life of Chaucer*, vol. i, p. xi.

touched with the elegiac mood of tragicomedy, but it envisions a new resolution in life and art. Godwin had married again (December 1801), to a woman who was a capable housekeeper and mother rather than a 'hyena in petticoats',[1] and his house was full of children.[2] Of necessity, his thoughts now were often home-thoughts; but he held to his vision of the wholeness of individual life and social experience; he pursued his task of arguing and enchanting others into harmony with themselves and other men.

It is no surprise that the new vision, the new philosophy of William Godwin, refined through a decade of revolution and a wide variety of literary experience both as reader and writer, should produce, or require, a new style. The style of *Fleetwood* is as much Godwin's as was the style of *Political Justice, Things As They Are,* or *St. Leon,* in fact it seems at times to encompass all three; but it is for the most part a Romantic style, more evocative, more naturally metaphoric, more subtle, and above all more refined than anything he had written before. It is difficult to be sure whether Godwin had primarily written himself into a new attitude, or whether his new attitude found its appropriate new style; certainly both were comprised of elements of the earlier attitudes and earlier styles. In any case, the transformation was complete: as a man, as a philosopher, as a writer, Godwin had changed from a *philosophe* to a Romantic.

English Jacobin Satire

The fact that the change was ahead to Romanticism, rather than back to Sensibility, can be seen by the way *Fleetwood,* for all its Rousseauism, retains much of English Jacobinism, and contains much that would not be out of place in *Man As He Is, Hugh Trevor, Nature and Art,* or *Bryan Perdue.* The early adventures of Godwin's hero, for example, closely resemble those of Hugh Trevor, as Fleetwood leaves the cradle of Nature in Merionethshire and encounters successively the fashionable debaucheries of Oxford, the refined licence of Louis XV's Paris, the fatuities of London literary life, and the hypocrisies and corruptions of a career in

[1] Horace Walpole's description of Mary Wollstonecraft.
[2] Mary Wollstonecraft's and Imlay's daughter Fanny, Mary Wollstonecraft's and his daughter Mary, Mrs. Clairmont's two children by her first marriage, and Mrs. Clairmont's and his son William.

Parliament.[1] On the other hand, whereas Holcroft's hero avoids becoming embittered, Godwin's hero, burdened with his excessive sensibility, becomes a misanthrope, and is only restored to a semblance of common humanity by his marriage to Mary Macneil.[2]

The Byronic disillusionment experienced by Fleetwood could also have been derived from *La Nouvelle Héloïse*, from St. Preux's observations on the superficialities of Parisian women and Parisian social life, or from the experiences of Sir George Paradyne in Bage's *Man As He Is*. Godwin had also re-read *Hugh Trevor* in October 1800, and *Nature and Art* in February 1802, so he was quite familiar with the modes of English Jacobin satire, which he himself practised nowhere else as extensively as in the early part of *Fleetwood*. But Godwin's satire in *Fleetwood* went beyond the merely literary types found in earlier Jacobin novels, and anticipated the social satire of nineteenth-century fiction, and of Byron's *Don Juan*. This satire was militant irony, but of a sort different from that of the preceding century. A political revolution had altered awareness of social and sociological realities, and the industrial revolution was beginning to make itself felt, spreading a new *malaise* amongst those with a social conscience.

Godwin was concerned with all aspects of society, and he was enough of a social scientist to make use of those of his friends and acquaintances who were directly involved in the new industrial and economic forces which were already changing Britain and British society. The most important of such friends was Tom Wedgwood, whose letters to Godwin show that he was well-schooled in the rational duties of 'political justice'. As early as September 1795 Wedgwood had written a long letter to Godwin setting forth his doubts about many of the new industrial and mechanical processes, and he asked, 'Will not the truly conscientious employ these destructive engines as sparingly as possible?'[3] Wedgwood described in detail the industrial diseases and hazards which he was himself familiar with, and other friends also contributed to Godwin's knowledge of the effects of industrialization. He had visited Etruria in 1797 (when he first met

[1] *Fleetwood*, i. 49 ff., 118 ff., ii. 115 ff., 127 ff. The literary club to which Fleetwood belongs 'had assumed to itself a Greek name' (ii. 115), and may be based on the Philomaths, a debating club to which Godwin belonged in the 1790s.

[2] One of Bryan Perdue's guides to virtue is called Patrick Mac Neale.

[3] Letter in the Abinger collection.

Bage), he passed through the industrial parts of the midlands visiting Erasmus Darwin, Bage, and others, on his way back from Ireland in August 1800, and when he revisited Norfolk in September 1803 he noted in his Journal, 'walk to Norman's manufactory'; but finally, to see factory conditions for himself and to assist in his description of the silk-factory in which the young Ruffigny is incarcerated (i. 241–2), Godwin actually visited a silkmill in Spitalfields on 12 July 1804. For Godwin it was not enough to attack *general* social abuses; he wished to expose the actual evils of 'things as they are', and authenticity was to be a part of his attack, as it was in the great nineteenth-century social novels.[1]

Fleetwood also anticipated the strenuous efforts of the 'novelists of the 1840s' to relate social criticism to wider moral issues. Godwin denounced child labour on the same grounds which were to assist legislation on this subject throughout the nineteenth century, that it deprived children of natural educational development. Ruffigny describes the poor automata who service the relentless spinning machines, emphasizes the 'stupid and hopeless vacancy in every face', and concludes, in a Rousseauistic vein, that 'Liberty is the school of understanding' (i. 244, 247). Godwin has simply extended his attack on 'things as they are' to new kinds of social evil, but his premises remain very much the same: circumstances form character.

Associated with this attack on the factory system is an attack on Evangelical religion which Godwin may have drawn from Mrs. Inchbald's *Nature and Art* and which anticipates *Hard Times*. Godwin went beyond Mrs. Inchbald in depicting the French Protestant Vaublanc: not only does this character preach the divine ordination of poverty, but as the owner of the factory in which Ruffigny is employed he is directly responsible for that poverty. As Ruffigny ironically remarks, according to people like Vaublanc 'the earth is the great Bridewel of the universe, where spirits, descended from heaven, are committed to drudgery and hard labour' (i. 248). The character of Vaublanc itself seems lifted from the satirical world of *Nature and Art*. His name, for example, might be translated as 'worthless' and is close enough to that of the

---

[1] Byron too was an early advocate of social reform. His maiden speech in the House of Lords in 1812 opposed a bill to give the death penalty to stocking-frame breakers. Leslie A. Marchand, *Byron, A Portrait* (London, 1971), pp. 112–14.

hero of Isaac D'Israeli's Anti-Jacobin novel *Vaurien*[1] to suggest
that Godwin was prepared to borrow from foe as well as friend.

It is certainly true that Godwin's satire in *Fleetwood* is as
effective as that of Mrs. Inchbald in *Nature and Art*, or of Holcroft
and Bage at their best. He reveals himself in a new guise in this
Romantic novel, a guise which he did not assume often. However,
it is also true that the mingling of satire and romance is not
complete, and increases the impression that *Fleetwood*, like all
of Godwin's novels, possesses 'unity of spirit' but not 'unity of
design', perhaps because Godwin's novels were always closer to
'romance'. On the other hand, much of the satire in *Fleetwood*,
especially the hero's sardonic reaction to the hypocrisies of high
society, has a Romantic cast, and looks forward to Byron's
Don Juan as much as it looks back to Holcroft's *Hugh Trevor* and
Bage's *Man As He Is*. Godwin's hero, like Byron's, experiences
all the hazards, glories, and ultimate disillusionment with the
intrigues of public and private life. After the Revolutionary
decade of the 1790s real moral and political reform seemed
further off than ever, and because hopes had been so high dis-
enchantment was all the more complete, and so to some extent
Godwin anticipated in *Fleetwood* the Romantic satire found in
Byron's greatest poems. Perhaps it is appropriate that when
Godwin published his next novel, *Mandeville*, in 1817, it called
forth a spurious sequel in which the poetry and influence of
Byron were evident in almost every page[2]—proof that Godwin,
perhaps somewhat unwillingly, had finally been enrolled amongst
the important writers of the Romantic movement.

In any case, Godwin's satire in *Fleetwood* is cousin german to
that of *Don Juan*; it is the necessary ground of Fleetwood's
mal de siècle, his elegiac yearning for a heroic past, and a heroic
situation, as he defines his misanthropy with the explanation that
'I felt what man ought to be, and I could not prevent the model of
what he ought to be from being for ever present to my mind'
(i. 162). Fleetwood ends, un-Byronically, in marriage, but like
Juan, he learns that virtue and a virtuous woman are the only

---

[1] Published in 1797. Godwin read it in the same year. On the other hand, Godwin
may have taken the term *vaurien* from Rousseau, who used it frequently in the
Confessions.

[2] [Anon.,] *Mandeville; or, The Last Words of a Maniac! A Tale of the Seventeenth
Century in England.* By Himself. Vol. iv (London, 1818); i.e., intended to be taken
as a satirical sequel to Godwin's novel, but in fact neither satiric nor a parody.

remedies for his Romantic alienation. Too good for the world, for 'things as they are', Fleetwood becomes a misanthrope, and his satire is misanthropic, however justified by his experience with the way of the world. Like the disillusioned Restoration rake, or the hero of *The Adventures of Faublas* (which Godwin borrowed from for Fleetwood's amorous adventures),[1] the 'new man of feeling' becomes vicious from lack of the opportunity, or the challenge, to be virtuous. Morally, he is in the same situation, though a different time and place, as St. Leon after the Italian wars. Godwin uses satire and satiric narrative to display the evils of 'things as they are', and to show the circumstances which form Fleetwood's Byronic character; but he integrates the satire into a broader argument and more comprehensive narrative form. It is the form of romance, or tragicomedy, but it is a form which attempts to transcend as well as encompass the form of his previous fiction.

'Fictitious History'

Godwin supports that form by 'historical' methods he had used before. In one respect Byron, more than any of the other major English Romantic poets, resembled Godwin, and that was in his historical imagination, his sense of history and his love for historical literature; and in a poem such as *Mazeppa*, for example, Byron too created a kind of 'fictitious history'. Godwin had not become so absorbed by the influence of Coleridge and Rousseau that he neglected to construct the same kind of 'fictitious history' in *Fleetwood* which he had essayed in his earlier novels. By setting his novel in a certain period and by using names with certain historical associations Godwin underlines the points made by the novel's Romantic satire.

The MS. Journal reveals that when Godwin began his novel in March 1804 it bore, for the first few days of its existence, the title 'Lambert'. Now, both Fleetwood and Lambert are names which figure in the histories of the English Civil War and Commonwealth, contemporaries of Milton, in fact, whose nephews were to be the subject of Godwin's next major literary biography, the *Lives of Edward and John Philips* (1815). Both Lambert and

[1] Godwin read parts of *The Life and Adventures of the Chevalier de Faublas* by Jean Baptiste Louvet de Couvray (trans. 1793) in June 1794 and May 1804.

Fleetwood were protégés of Cromwell, both outlived him and lived on into the age of corruption and debauchery which followed the glorious Commonwealth of the 'Saints'. Not surprisingly the MS. Journal shows Godwin consulting several histories of the period in the month after he began his novel.

Most important of these was Anthony Hamilton's *Memoirs of Grammont,*[1] a work written by an exiled Jacobite, and intended to glorify the wit, licence, and intrigues of the English court after the Restoration. In Godwin's eyes such a book could offer the most instructive moral lessons on the relationship between government and individual character, and he was soon referring to other histories of the period, such as d'Aulnoy's *Memoirs of the Court of England*, and a work with the self-explanatory title of 'Bagnio Court'. The direction of his historical perspective is indicated by the fact that he was soon reading amongst Milton's republican tracts, and referring to Ludlow and Whitlocke, to Hume on Cromwell, to Burnet's history, to Clarendon, and to Clement Walker's *History of Independency*. Once again he was dwelling on the contrast between the heroic age of liberty, the Civil War and Commonwealth, and the age of 'corruption, negociation, and trick' which followed.

He also consulted Prévost's *Life and Adventures of Mr. Cleveland, Natural Son of Oliver Cromwell,* which he had already read in September 1793 for *Things As They Are,* and which offered an interesting balance to Louvet's *Life and Adventures of the Chevalier Faublas.* Prévost's novel obviously provided Godwin with a pattern for his alienated and solitary misanthrope: a large part of *Cleveland* is taken up by the narrative of Lambert, a fictitious representation of the historical figure, who describes how he became disillusioned with the treachery of Cromwell and the viciousness of men, and sought refuge on a desert island. Godwin fictionalized Prévost's fictionalization, and placed him in the Romantic locale of the English Lakes, from whence he begins his regeneration. Godwin also changed his character's name, perhaps to conceal his debt to Prévost, but probably to suggest a parallel to the reader well instructed in both history and fiction: the historical Lambert and Fleetwood ran parallel courses, just as the fictitious ones do.

[1] Godwin read it from 20 to 22 November 1803, just before he began writing his novel.

Characteristically, however, Godwin added a further historical and moral resonance to his novel. He deliberately placed his hero in the age of Louis XV,[1] to suggest that his Fleetwood was a descendant of the historical figure of the golden age of English liberty. Having himself been presented with a son by his second wife in 1803 Godwin may have tried to imagine the adventures young William would be likely to face when he too went out into the world which had succeeded to the heroic decade of the French Revolution. In any case Fleetwood, like Godwin himself, reveres those heroes of the earlier period of the struggle for parliamentary independence, when 'Pym and Hambden [sic], and Falkland and Selden, and Cromwell and Vane sat together, to decide, perhaps for ever, on the civil and intellectual liberties' of England (i. 143).[2] Godwin had already denounced that period of history which followed the Civil War in his MS. essay on 'History' and 'Romance': 'It is the history of negotiation and trick; it is the history of revenues and debts; it is the history of corruption and political profligacy; but it is not the history of genuine, independent man.' He had studied the origins of that period in his readings in Bolingbroke, and seems to have accepted Bolingbroke's analysis of that system of 'Old Corruption' which prevailed down to the 1790s and which had, by 1805, already withstood the shock of revolutions in America and France. In fact, the lesson of Bolingbroke's life, as a refugee of faction and opponent of Walpole's system, continued to interest Godwin as it had for the past decade. When he described his project for a life of Bolingbroke to Coleridge late in 1800, the latter wrote back comparing Bolingbroke to Sheridan, and expressing curiosity about the 'moral temperament' of such characters.[3]

The novel's historical allegory may have given Godwin further reason to change his title from 'Lambert' to 'Fleetwood'. He may have been trying to multiply allusions, since those who knew their political and ecclesiastical history as well as the student of Hoxton Academy could also see the name Fleetwood as an allusion to a hero of liberty of conscience from the age of Bolingbroke himself, namely William Fleetwood (1656–1723), bishop of Ely.

---

[1] In fact, the MS. of the novel, in the Pforzheimer Library, shows that Godwin was uncertain whether to set his novel in the reign of Louis XV or XVI.
[2] A similar passage occurs in Godwin's *Essay on Sepulchres* (London, 1809), p. 70.
[3] Coleridge to Godwin, 6 Dec. 1800.

The 1737 edition of his writings was in Godwin's library, and was described by its editor, in terms which could have applied to Godwin's own works, as 'upon Subjects in which the publick Welfare is greatly concerned, and all of them in general extremely useful in the Conduct of private Life, and for the Good of Society'.[1] Bishop Fleetwood also played an active role in public affairs. Conscientiously fulfilling the duties of his office he withdrew from 'the Noise and Hurry of the City', but, recalled by Queen Anne, he rode out the storm of factional madness which broke in 1710, and preached a notable sermon on the same text as Horsley's notorious Anti-Jacobin diatribe of 1792, but to different effect, and pleaded for mutual forbearance.[2] The point, Godwin must have felt, applied as well in the reign of George III as in that of Queen Anne.

Clearly, it was one of Godwin's techniques as a novelist to seek out some figure in history whose name or character he could borrow for his fiction, in order to give a greater resonance to his view of contemporary events and his own place in them. In this case he chose, after a false start, a name which could refer both to the Fleetwood who had descended from an age of heroes, and the Fleetwood who had survived with honour and virtue in an age of rabid party hatred and political corruption. It was an appropriate fable to end Godwin's career as an English Jacobin novelist.

Domestic History

The very nature of these allusions marks Godwin's turn towards Romantic interest in the 'domestic affections' rather than the cataclysms of contemporary history. Both historical Fleetwoods, as well as Prévost's Lambert, survive ages of upheaval to find domestic quiet in old age.[3] Like Bishop Fleetwood, Godwin was a man of studious habits, who liked a quiet life, and in *Fleetwood* there is ample evidence that Godwin's own withdrawal from public affairs was well underway. The whole import of his novel is the elevation of the domestic and private affections above the false values of 'civilized' society—hence the novel's Rousseauism.

---

[1] William Fleetwood, *A Compleat Collection of the Sermons, Tracts, and Pieces of all Kinds* (London, 1737), p. i.

[2] Fleetwood, *A Compleat Collection*, pp. 484 ff.

[3] Fleetwood's Christian name, Casimir, is Polish and means 'proclamation of peace'. Godwin was perhaps being ironic; the 'Peace of Amiens' had ended in 1803. He had wanted to travel to France then, but was refused a passport.

In fact *Fleetwood* really consists of two parts: the hero's adventures in society, and his adventures in marriage; and it is the second part which is of greater interest and intensity. What Godwin seems to have done, in fact, was to quarry the domestic histories of himself and his friends to provide a new tale for the times, a story which would show his readers that personal salvation was to be found not through revolutions and political activity, or by quixotic schemes for improving mankind, but through the charities which properly begin at home. There is, accordingly, a much higher proportion of domestic incident in *Fleetwood*, incidents taken directly from Godwin's own life or those who were close to him. It is not surprising, therefore, that there was a real and significant connection between *Fleetwood* and *A Simple Story*. Godwin read Mrs. Inchbald's novel again in the early part of November 1804, just as he was about to commence writing his hero's adventures in domesticity. Fleetwood's paternal relationship to an orphan who is in effect his ward, and his insane jealousy after her supposed infidelity are obviously parallel to the main events of *A Simple Story*. At the same time, Godwin no doubt knew of the autobiographical basis of much of Mrs. Inchbald's fiction, and was prepared to follow her example. Once again, personal and 'fictitious history' meshed in a fruitful relationship.

Fleetwood's awareness of the burden of domestic responsibility, for example, obviously came from Godwin's own experience. He had married Mrs. Clairmont in December 1801 and was now responsible for five young lives. He had made a deep plunge indeed into domestic life since his celibate days before 1796, and the burdens and turmoils of this new life are reflected in the busy household described in volume three of *Fleetwood*. Fleetwood's realization that if he has escaped the pains of solitude, he has also lost some of its advantages, no doubt came from Godwin's heart, as he struggled to support his family by the kind of writing which required quiet study. It seems on the whole, however, that Godwin drew on his own experience for the happier aspects of Fleetwood's married life. For authentic accounts of domestic tribulation, on the other hand, he had many sources to draw from. He had already known Mrs. Inchbald for many years and no doubt knew of her marital problems before the death of her husband. Mary Wollstonecraft, Mary Robinson, and Charlotte Smith also provided him with tales of conjugal misery, seen from the woman's side, as *Fleetwood*, in part at least, sees it. In fact Mary Macneil's mother, who had been ostracized from 'good' society ever since an ill-advised liaison in her youth, is an amalgamation of Mary Wollstonecraft and Mary Robinson, who also appears in the novel as the retired courtesan Mrs. Gifford (iii. 96–8).[1] Godwin had consulted with 'Perdita' over several of her novels, and had collaborated with Mary Wollstonecraft in her unfinished *The Wrongs of Woman* (published posthumously by Godwin in 1798). From the latter especially Godwin learned much, not only about the 'wrongs of woman', some of which *Fleetwood* describes, but also about the complex problem of the relationship between character and circumstances, autobiography and fiction.

In obtaining authentic life-materials for *Fleetwood* Godwin seemed to range more widely and inquire more deeply than he had done before. The erratic and romantic Kenrick, for example, though named perhaps after the first English translator of *La Nouvelle Héloïse*, seems to be a portrait of one of Godwin's protégés, John Arnot. Arnot's experiences on a walking tour of eastern Europe in 1798 may have been of use to Godwin in *St. Leon*.[2] Certainly Godwin was blamed for his young friend's extravagant projects and revolutionary views,[3] and was placed in a difficult position by Arnot's romance with Louisa Jones,[4] an impressionable girl who was a servant in the Godwin household. That Godwin could have been made as jealous as Fleetwood by this little affair hardly seems possible, but Arnot's disruptive influence in the family's life seems accurately depicted in the novel.

At least one of Godwin's friends was convinced that he had been portrayed in the novel to his disadvantage, a fact which suggests that those who knew Godwin would not be surprised to find real persons and incidents depicted in his fiction. Holcroft thought he had been the model for Mr. Scarborough, a severe gentleman whose high standards in the education of his son

---

[1] Godwin may have obtained the name, if not the character, from Sir Thomas Grandison's mistress Mrs. Giffard in *Sir Charles Grandison*.

[2] Kegan Paul, i. 339.

[3] Letters from Arnot's brother and sister, in the Abinger collection.

[4] Kegan Paul, i. 313. In the novel, Kenrick also falls in love with a Louisa, the daughter of the misanthropic Scarborough (*Fleetwood*, iii. 293).

drive the poor boy into a decline and an early death. Scarborough learns through grief to temper principle with humanity, and communicates this lesson to Fleetwood in the last pages of the novel. Holcroft saw in this an allusion to the unfortunate relationship with his own son William, who had committed suicide in 1789.[1] Godwin denied the allusion, of course, and tried to show that the incident was really based on his own relationship with a young relative, Thomas Cooper. 'I wanted a fierce, stern, severe and awe-striking person for the conduct of my story,' he declared, 'and I invented him as I could.'[2] The remark reveals an important aspect of Godwin's method of composition. Certain personal ideas and obsessions preoccupied him at certain times no doubt, but he went on 'inventing' his fable, using fictional models here, and personal experience there; or it may be that a personal problem or dilemma threw certain characters and incidents in his reading, be it fiction or history, into a new or significant light.

Whatever the source, all of Godwin's materials were in a certain sense autobiographical. After admitting in the middle of the 1790s that he and all men were in fact men of feeling, he could accept the role of feeling and imagination with increasing confidence. Godwin recognized by 1805 that any experience could be profoundly moving, not a transport of sensibility and a passionate losing of oneself, one's reasoning self, but a momentary sympathy, feeling with another, while remaining one's self. The novel *Fleetwood* is proof that Godwin had such experiences—or rather that he could admit that he had them, for he had always had them, even as a child. The novel reveals, as perhaps the writing of it revealed to its author, that Godwin could enter sympathetically, imaginatively, into another person, be it a personage in history, a character in fiction or drama, or simply a friend. That friendliness and open fellow-feeling is the sign that Godwin was habituating himself to the 'domestic affections'. Now at home in the world and with himself, Godwin devoted the rest of his life to his friends—people and books.

Personal experience increasingly dominates *Fleetwood*, because such experience was the source of Godwin's new philosophy.

---

[1] Hazlitt, *Life of Holcroft*, ed. Colby, i. 304. Godwin had been with Holcroft on that occasion; see Godwin's account in a letter published by Edmund Blunden as *Tragical Consequences* (London, 1931).

[2] Letter from Godwin to Holcroft, dated 28 Feb. 1805, in the Abinger collection.

That in itself was nothing new: ever since *A Simple Story* the history of the English Jacobin novel was the history of the English Jacobin novelists. Their purpose had always been to use the novel to instruct, but as times changed and they themselves changed, so too did the instruction they had to offer. And although Godwin's purpose in *Things As They Are* and *St. Leon* had been somewhat different from what it was in *Fleetwood*, the way in which he worked up life and study into fiction had scarcely changed at all. Life had changed Godwin, and the changes reveal themselves in his fiction. Godwin's interest in Rousseau in the late 1790s was not accidental, nor was his renewed interest in Mrs. Inchbald and her 'simple story'. The English Jacobin novel had come full circle.

CONCLUSION

The English Jacobin novel was the product and the expression of a historical moment, and when that moment passed, so too did the English Jacobin novel. Or at least it seemed to. For some of these novels continued to be read, especially and appropriately those of Elizabeth Inchbald and William Godwin. One was the least and the other the most philosophical of the English Jacobin novelists, but both had the talent and the detachment to transcend the timely aims of English Jacobin fiction and appeal to the spirit of a new age. It is appropriate that in his last English Jacobin and his first Romantic novel Godwin should come back to *A Simple Story*, the most shapely of the novels of the 1790s. In her autobiographical novel, written so carefully over so many years, Elizabeth Inchbald had found the form of romance and tragicomedy ideally suited to the myth of reconciliation she wished to realize in her life and her art, and so she domesticated it and left it as a legacy for her fellow labourers and for later and more talented generations of English novelists.

Godwin saw the importance of that myth to a decade of Revolution, and as a fervent believer in the power of truth he saw the philosophical possibilities in the form of romance. The experience undergone in the romantic hero's quest was the most appropriate model for any writer, whether English Jacobin novelist or Romantic poet, who wished to display the necessity and the inevitability of moral progress through increase of experience, knowledge, and understanding. But Godwin carried the form further than Elizabeth Inchbald could do. His potent and subtle historical imagination fused the domestic fiction with 'affairs of state' by means of allusions and allegory, and the classical analogy between the family and the nation acquired new vigour from an age of Revolution. The novel, with its traditional devotion to domestic history and the 'domestic affections', was therefore the logical counterpart to the pamphlets, poems, sermons, and satires by which the English Jacobins mounted their attack on 'things as they are'. Ever since the novel had first been established as part of the bourgeois reaction to the chivalric and romantic national literature of the Middle Ages and Renaissance it had asserted the value of individual autonomy and domestic relations against the chivalric culture of king, court, and aristocracy. Since Elizabethan times and especially since Defoe novelists had implied that there was another 'nation' than the aristocratic and feudal one, that there were other kinds of heroism and greatness than those founded in war and blood, and other kinds of relation than those based on feudal power. The decade of the French Revolution gave new relevance to these subversive tendencies in the novel, but the repudiation of chivalric culture and chivalric literature had begun long before a thousand pens had leapt from their ink-wells to rebuke Edmund Burke.

In another sense, however, the assertion of the bourgeois domestic values of the eighteenth century undermined the Revolution's attempt to found a universal polity of man and nations, undermined, that is, the beliefs that men were potentially the same everywhere and at all times and that their rights could be established accordingly. Godwin, like Prévost and Rousseau, saw history as moral discourse and saw the highest form of history as biography. He exercised this view in his novels, but also in his historical and philosophical writings. His fascination for the fictitious or historical exemplar was but one form of the century's yearning for the universal and the immutable. It was one of Godwin's favourite writers, Bolingbroke, who defined history as philosophy teaching through examples, and Christian teaching also saw the eternal will working always through the local, the particular, the temporal and temporary. But such a practice could, if extended far enough, lead to a denial of the universal. Exemplars could become special cases; history could become atomic, the sum of many individual lives; and the unique, the exotic, the Gothic could become the highest form of truth. Truth itself could seem to be merely local and particular and temporal. Rousseau, in his *Confessions*, showed that this could happen. Hence the revulsion he and his writings (the two were identified in this respect) caused in so many breasts in the later part of the century. Hence too, one might argue, the enthusiastic partisanship he aroused in other breasts, those which prized the romantic quest for self-awareness above claims of social duty.

Between Romance and Romanticism lay a century of literary,

cultural, social, and political evolution of which Rousseau represented but one phase, and the touchstone for much of that evolution was the philosophy of necessity derived by Hartley and others from the writings of Locke. The debate on necessity and free will ran as an undercurrent through theoretical speculation and a great deal of practice in arts, sciences, politics, religion, and history, and brought them all together. But no one attempted to apply necessitarianism so thoroughly as the English Jacobin novelists, especially Holcroft and Godwin. Necessitarianism seemed to them to solve all moral and philosophical paradoxes and to reconcile all aesthetic and moral antinomies. It also seemed to solve the perennial problem of form in the novel, by uniting plot and character. In fact, the novel offered possibilities for a free display of the nature and operation of necessity which could not be found in any other form of writing except autobiography. By inventing or re-creating an individual life universal principles could be discovered after all. History was too bound to fact on the one hand and doubtful interpretation on the other; it was the province of antiquaries or party-men, not true philosophers. Philosophy itself, however, was too abstract. What Holcroft and Godwin were looking for was something like Collingwood's idea of history, but freed from the imperfections and incompleteness of historical knowledge. Their solution was fictitious narrative based on their own experiences, situation, and sentiments, but informed by their particular historical perspective on the relationship of past, present, and future.

This perspective was, of necessity, a belief in progress and human perfectibility. Since knowledge or truth was a kind of material substance and since men naturally desired knowledge, truth must continually increase. Philosophers or lovers of truth in all ages and all climes were participants in the compilation of one vast encyclopedia. Moreover, for the English Jacobins and for their French colleagues the Girondins, the prospect of indefinite progress towards perfectibility was all the more exhilarating because it seemed to be based on rational demonstrations which could be communicated to all. Popularization of philosophical ideas, of truth, became the noblest of vocations, and popular forms such as the novel assumed a new value. The philosophy of necessity, carried to its absolute limits in the early years of the 1790s, redeemed much that had once been despised.

Most important of all, it seemed to end forever the frightening possibility that moral values were merely historical and local, and therefore relative. It seemed to prove that men were not ineluctably unique and therefore alone.

Naturally enough, the failure of the Republic of Reason caused a reaction as intense as the enthusiasm it had originally inspired. The failure of the Revolution of Fraternity seemed to suggest that men were indeed essentially isolated, and essentially alone. The disintegration of the brotherhood of man in the nationalistic wars and resistances which followed on the Jacobin overthrow of the Girondins and Napoleon's take-over of the Republic caused a despondency which was also universal, and which may be traced in the progress through dejection of Wordsworth, or the philosophical restlessness of Coleridge. The English Jacobin novelists shared in this reaction. They tried to bolster their crumbling necessitarian philosophy with values they had once rejected, with sympathy and sensibility, without realizing that those values would finally subvert English Jacobinism itself. Ultimately, it seemed, the history of the French Revolution proved Burke to be right: society was based on irrational personal ties and not on rational principles. Man was a creature of passions and not a reasoning machine. The vindication of Burke's prophecy was as full of implications as the apparent vindication of philosophical necessity had once seemed to be, and men of talent, industry, and imagination turned more decidedly to the study of individual uniqueness, idiosyncracies, and differences. But necessity had left its imprint in certain habits of thought and method. Uniqueness, whether individual or national, was traced to its origins, which proved to be medieval, and once again 'romantic'. The novel too returned to the spirit of romance, but it had gained greatly from its brief alliance with the philosophy of necessity.

Of course the novel, as anti-romance, had participated in social as well as philosophical developments during the eighteenth century, since changes in taste were predicated upon changes in society. Richardson's novels in particular expressed those changes with unnatural acuteness and clarity, and Richardson's novels were essential precursors of those of the English Jacobins, especially those of Godwin and Mrs. Inchbald. In another direction, however, the novels of Bage and Holcroft reveal the humanizing eclecticism of the English Jacobins. Fielding and Smollett, with their vision of mankind's profusion of types that anticipated Dickens and Carlyle, celebrated the uniqueness of individuals at the same time that they asserted, confidently and without naïvety, the possibility and indeed the necessity of social integration. Both Bage and Holcroft exploited that vision to the full, and attempted to infuse it with English Jacobin philosophy. If the romance and the comedy end with a marriage then they seem to deny the solipsist tendency and destructive power of human individuality. The novels of Bage and Holcroft end this way, and Mrs. Inchbald envisaged first a personal reconciliation in *A Simple Story*, and then a social one in *Nature and Art*. Godwin, blessed and burdened with an honest and educated imagination, could not write comic novels in an age of Revolution. His sense of individual existence in the face of universal cataclysm was closer to Richardson's, closer to the tragic. His romance was not of youth and a new dawn for mankind, but of age, and society in decline, decadent culture destroying youth and perverting life. With his Dissenting Academy education in modern history, he was too aware of the past to be quite as sanguine as Holcroft about the future. At the end of his journey Godwin's picaro will be wiser, but sadder, and most terrible of all, alone. *Fleetwood* seems to break the pattern of solitude of *Things As They Are* and *St. Leon*, but shows the terrible cost in suffering for the final reconciliation, and leaves the re-union itself drenched in elegiac sentiment. Godwin's Necessity is as dark as Prévost's Providence, and in *Fleetwood* Calvinism anticipates Byronic Romanticism. This is not to say that Godwin became a Romantic by losing his English Jacobin optimism, that he has no affirmation. For what he came to affirm was the value and necessity of feeling in human life and society, and he could affirm this at the end of the Revolutionary decade precisely because he had contemplated throughout that decade the errors of his own treatise of necessary rational optimism. As the Republic of Reason foundered Godwin devised a new romance, a new optimism, and a new wisdom from study, a recognition of his past mistakes, and his relationship with Mary Wollstonecraft. This 'domestic' knowledge and 'domestic' wisdom, Godwin went on to assert in a whole range of new books, was of the greatest social significance, greater even than the wisdom of reason.

Like the Romantics, then, Godwin came to affirm the domestic affections as universal truth (although he seems always to have remained a spectator in the face of Nature); and like the Romantics and the heroes of romance he owed this wisdom at least in part to women. Indeed, there was always something androgynous about his cast of mind, as he himself admitted. Perhaps it was that continual striving for wholeness, in himself and in his view of man's world, which led him to abandon the tenets if not the tendencies of Calvinism, which kept him intimate with the liberal Dissenters such as Price, Priestley, and Fawcett, and which finally led him to two of the century's great androgynes, Rousseau and Mary Wollstonecraft. There can be no other explanation for Godwin's attractiveness to such a wide range of female characters as Elizabeth Inchbald, Amelia Alderson, Mary Robinson, Mary Hays, and Mary Wollstonecraft. For these women Godwin was more than a Mentor or a father-figure, more one might say, than a mere man. The letters and the novels of these women, if read with care and candour, witness their recognition of Godwin's candid and catalyzing personality. Bage and Holcroft also shared in the life of women, and although less is known about them in this respect, it is certain that they too schooled and were schooled by the numerous women in their lives. It was a time when educating seemed to be an essential kind of human relationship; when Rousseau could see education as love, love as education; when education was romantic. Bage, Holcroft, and Godwin learned from women that logic is not necessarily truth, and that facts are not the only knowledge. If they taught their female friends to add a new philosophical rigour and historical perspective to their fictions and their lives, they themselves learned that there were other ways of feeling, of philosophizing, and of writing, than those traditionally practised by men. They learned that virtue, originally designating manliness, had come to be expected only of women, and that the result was a disastrous alienation. They saw, with those women, the need for reconciliation and romance, and in spite of the fact that they were all lapsed Christians they saw that the Christian virtues offered practical salvation for mankind in the midst of a decade of aggression, warfare, and bloodshed, and that those most accustomed to the nurture, practice, and preaching of those virtues were women. *En route* to Romanticism, Bage, Holcroft, and Godwin learned from the female propensity for local observation, for the 'science of the heart', for self-exploration and self-awareness, and above all the female gift for combining autobiography with fantasy. These were gifts conferred by centuries of oppression and inferiority no doubt, but they were of critical importance in the new age of liberation, and the novels of Bage, Holcroft, and Godwin all show ample evidence that, however unsatisfactory their personal relations with women may at times have been, they fully appreciated the necessity of integrating the special knowledge, experience, and wisdom of women in their design for the New Jerusalem.

The necessity for romance at the mundane level, the experience of love, they certainly took to the heart of their fiction, even before they took it to the heart of their philosophy; and love in the widest sense, the necessity of philanthropy, was argued even in the earliest English Jacobin tracts and given its fullest expression in the first edition of *Political Justice*. The novels themselves inherited a wide range of love conventions, many of which had changed little since the heyday of those romances which novels were designed to replace; but the English Jacobin novelists, though eclectic, were not uncritical and they tried seriously to renovate the conventions just as they had tried to renovate most of eighteenth-century philosophy. Partly as a result of their reconsideration of that philosophy and partly through personal experience they gave greater and greater place to love, whether personal or social, as the Revolution came to embody more and more hate. The plot of romance was pitted with increasing desperation against the plot of the Revolution, and what was desired in history was the form of romance, the form promised by the New Testament. As could be expected, the literature of the seventeenth century came to be as important to the imagination of the 1790s as its history had been. In their constant search for an ideal form for their fictions, the English Jacobin novelists helped to bridge the cultural gap between Milton and Beaumont and Fletcher on one hand, and Wordsworth and Coleridge on the other, and they played a vital part in providing English Romanticism with a tradition and a feeling for form. Neo-Platonism was only one stage, and an early one at that, in the English Jacobin evolution towards Romanticism, but it suggested the direction of movement, and the vigour with which the search was conducted. Of this vigour all of the English Jacobins' writings are evidence, their plays as well as their novels, their pamphlets, treatises, and projects as well as their novels and plays. Some of these efforts—Holcroft's melodramas, Mary Wollstonecraft's unfinished novel *The Wrongs of Woman*, Godwin's *St. Leon*—were unsuccessful, but none the less instructive for that. English Jacobin fiction, like English Jacobin polemical writings and the serried array of English Jacobin political movements, has been seen for too long as abortive or premature versions of later glories. Godwin was not being fatuous when he imagined that a new edition of *Political Justice* might speak to a nation riven by the Reform Bill of 1832. Significantly, he at least managed to get his novels of the 1790s once again into print at that time. There were other works, lives, and experiences which might have spoken as pertinently out of time to the 'two nations'.

Some did listen in those times and after. The English Jacobins had changed the meaning of so much of the history, literature, and philosophy of the eighteenth century that they could hardly be ignored by serious minds in the nineteenth. Some tried, with fair success, to belittle the English Jacobin achievement, but increasingly it seems that their ridicule was itself a kind of tribute. It is only one of the paradoxes of the history of English Jacobinism that its greatest influence was through apostates such as Coleridge or opponents such as Scott. Through such as them the English Jacobin historical perspective profoundly altered the sensibility of an era by requiring them to devise Romanticism as a consolation and a substitute. Another line of indirect influence was through the Anti-Jacobin writers and novelists, the greatest of whom was Jane Austen, and it is becoming apparent how much of her achievement arose out of a desire to emulate and refute such as Mary Hays, Mary Robinson, and Mary Wollstonecraft.

The influence was direct as well, through Bulwer Lytton; through Robert Owen, Francis Place, and the reformers of the 1820s and 1830s; and through second generation Romantics such as Shelley who were as fascinated by English Jacobinism at a distance as their predecessors had been at first hand. The mechanism of historical and cultural transition seems little understood, and even where it is carefully studied, as in the relation between the Enlightenment and the Revolution, seems to end in paradox. But just as the French Revolution proclaimed itself to embody the Enlightenment at the same time that it inverted most of the principles of the Age of Reason, so Romanticism in England both absorbed and rejected English Jacobinism as the domestic manifestation of the Revolutionary spirit.

SELECT BIBLIOGRAPHY

The following is a list of the main published and MS. sources referred to in the text, as well as the most valuable or interesting sources which have not found their way into a footnote. No attempt has been made to list the wide range of books read by Godwin or found in the libraries of Holcroft or Godwin, although many of these have been used for this study.

I. MANUSCRIPT SOURCES

1. Robert Bage

Hutton-Beale Collection, number 29A–C, Birmingham Public Library, Local Studies Library. Copies of extracts of letters from Bage to William Hutton, and of a letter from Mr. Chavasse, surgeon of Walsall, to William Hutton.

Letters from Robert Bage to William Hutton, 1782–1801. Birmingham Public Library, Local Studies Library, catalogue number 486802. For the most part these are short messages written on invoices for shipments of paper sent from Bage to Hutton.

2. William Godwin, Thomas Holcroft, and Elizabeth Inchbald

The Forster Collection, Victoria and Albert Museum, London. MS. letters of Holcroft, Inchbald, and Godwin. MS. of *Political Justice* and *Things As They Are*.

The Abinger Collection, in the possession of Lord Abinger, Clees Hall, Suffolk. Microfilm in the Bodleian Library, Oxford, the Library of Duke University, and the Pforzheimer Library, New York. MS. letters and copies of letters of Godwin, Mary Wollstonecraft, Holcroft, Inchbald, and many others. MS. notes of Godwin.

3. William Godwin

William Godwin's MS. journal, 1788–1834, in the possession of the Bodleian Library. Microfilm in the Bodleian Library, the Pforzheimer Library, and available from Duke University.

Autograph MS. of *Fleetwood*, in the Pforzheimer Library.

Autograph Catalogue of Godwin's Library in 1817, in the Library of the Keats–Shelley Memorial House, Rome. Microfilm in the Keats House Library, Keats Grove, London.

II. BOOKS

1. *General*

(a) *Historical*

Association for Preserving Liberty and Property against Republicans and Levellers, *Association Papers* (2 parts, London, 1793).

BRIGGS, ASA, *The Age of Improvement* (corr. edn., London, 1960).

—— 'Middle-class Consciousness in English Politics, 1780–1846', *Past and Present*, ix (Apr. 1956), 65–74.

BRINTON, CRANE, *The Political Ideas of the English Romanticists* (1926, repr. Ann Arbor, Michigan, 1966).

BROWN, FORD K., *Fathers of the Victorians* (Cambridge, 1961).

BROWN, PHILIP A., *The French Revolution in English History* (1918, repr. London, 1965).

BURKE, EDMUND, *The Works* (6 vols., London, 1882–4).

CHRISTIE, IAN R., *Wilkes, Wyvill and Reform* (London and New York, 1962).

CLÉRY, JEAN-BAPTISTE, *A Journal of the Occurrences . . . During the Confinement of Louis XVI*, trans. R. C. Dallas (London, 1798).

COBBAN, ALFRED, ed., *The Debate on the French Revolution 1789–1800* (2nd edn., London, 1960).

COLERIDGE, SAMUEL TAYLOR, *The Watchman*, ed. Lewis Patton (London and Princeton, New Jersey, 1970).

—— *Lectures 1795 on Politics and Religion*, ed. Lewis Patton and Peter Mann (London and Princeton, New Jersey, 1971).

CONE, CARL, *The English Jacobins* (New York, 1968).

CREASEY, JOHN, 'Some Dissenting Attitudes Towards the French Revolution', *Transactions of the Unitarian Historical Society*, xiii, no. 4 (Oct. 1966), 155–67.

EATON, DANIEL ISAAC, ed., *Politics for the People* (4th edn., London, 1794).

FINK, ZERA S., *The Classical Republicans* (2nd edn., Evanston, Illinois, 1962).

GEORGE, M. DOROTHY, *Catalogue of Political and Personal Satires Preserved in the Department of Prints and Drawings in the British Museum*, vol. vii (London, 1942).

HAVENS, GEORGE R., *The Age of Ideas* (New York, 1955).

MARSHALL, DOROTHY, *Eighteenth Century England* (London, 1962).

MARTIN, KINGSLEY, *French Liberal Thought in the Eighteenth Century* (3rd rev. edn., New York, 1963).

PLACE, FRANCIS, *The Autobiography of Francis Place (1771–1854)*, ed. Mary Thale (Cambridge, 1972).

PRICE, RICHARD, *A Discourse on the Love of Our Country* (London, 1789).

ROBBINS, CAROLINE, *The Eighteenth-Century Commonwealthman* (1959, repr. New York, 1968).

ROBISON, JOHN, *Proofs of a Conspiracy Against All the Religions and Governments of Europe* (Edinburgh, 1797).

RUDÉ, GEORGE, *Wilkes and Liberty* (Oxford, 1962).

STAROBINSKI, JEAN, *L'invention de la liberté 1700–1789* (Geneva, 1964).

THOMPSON, EDWARD, *The Making of the English Working Class* (rev. edn., Harmondsworth, 1968).

[TOWERS, JOSEPH,] *Remarks on the Conduct, Principles, and Publications, of the Association* . . . (London, 1793).

VEITCH, G. S., *The Genesis of Parliamentary Reform* (1913, repr. London, 1965).

WILLIAMS, E. N., ' "Our Merchants are Princes": The English Middle Classes in the Eighteenth Century', *History Today*, xii (1962), 548–57.

WILLIAMS, GWYN A., *Artisans and Sans-Culottes, Popular movements in France and Britain during the French Revolution* (London, 1968).

WILLIAMS, RAYMOND, *Culture and Society 1780–1950* (Harmondsworth, 1961).

(b) *Literary*

BAKER, ERNEST A., *The History of the English Novel* (London, 1934), vol. v.

BIRKHEAD, EDITH, *The Tale of Terror, A Study of the Gothic Romance* (1921, repr. New York, 1963).

—— 'Sentiment and Sensibility in the Eighteenth Century English Novel', *Essays and Studies*, xi (1925), 92–116.

BOULTON, JAMES T., *The Language of Politics in the Age of Wilkes and Burke* (London and Toronto, 1963).

CRANE, R. S., 'Suggestions toward a Genealogy of the "Man of Feeling" ', *ELH A Journal of English Literary History*, i (1934), 205–30.

FOSTER, JAMES R., *History of the Pre-romantic Novel in England* (London and New York, 1949).

FUSSELL, PAUL, *The Rhetorical World of Augustan Humanism* (Oxford, 1965).

GIDDINGS, ROBERT, *The Tradition of Smollett* (London, 1967).

GREGORY, ALLENE, *The French Revolution and the English Novel* (New York, 1915).

HOWE, IRVING, *Politics and the Novel* (London, 1961).

JOHNSON, JAMES W., *The Formation of English Neo-Classical Thought* (Princeton, New Jersey, 1967).

LEJEUNE, PHILIPPE, 'Le Pacte autobiographique', *Poétique*, no. xiv (1973), 137–62.

LLOYD, CHARLES, *Edmund Oliver* (2 vols., Bristol, 1798).

LUCAS, CHARLES, *The Infernal Quixote* (4 vols., London, 1800).

McCLELLAND, E. M., 'The Novel in Relation to the Dissemination of Liberal Ideas, 1790–1820', unpub. Ph.D. diss., London University, 1952.

NANGLE, B. C., *The Monthly Review First Series 1749–1789, Index of Contributors and Articles* (Oxford, 1934).

—— *The Monthly Review Second Series 1790–1815, Index of Contributors and Articles* (Oxford, 1955).

NICOLL, ALLARDYCE, *A History of English Drama, 1660–1900*, vol. iii, *Late Eighteenth Century Drama 1750–1800* (London, 1952).

PROPER, C. B. A., *Social Elements in English Prose Fiction Between 1700 and 1832* (Amsterdam, 1929).

PYE, HENRY JAMES, [Essay on the Imitative Arts,] *The Artist*, vol. i, no. xviii (11 July 1807), 1–12.

RODWAY, A. E., *The Romantic Conflict* (London, 1963).

STEEVES, H. R., *Before Jane Austen* (London, 1966).

TOMPKINS, J. M. S., *The Popular Novel in England 1770–1800* (1932, repr. Lincoln, Nebraska, 1961).

WALKER, GEORGE, *The Vagabond* (3rd edn., 2 vols., London, 1799).

WILLIAMS, IOAN, ed., *Novel and Romance 1700–1800, A Documentary Record* (London, 1970).

WITHYCOMBE, E. G., *The Oxford Dictionary of English Christian Names* (2nd edn. corr., Oxford, 1963).

2. Robert Bage

(a) Sources

[BAGE, ROBERT,] *Mount Henneth* (1782, 2nd edn., 2 vols., London, 1788).

[——] *Barham Downs* (2 vols., London, 1784).

[——] *The Fair Syrian* (2 vols., Dublin, 1787).

—— *James Wallace* (1788), in *Ballantyne's Novelist's Library*, ed. Walter Scott, vol. ix (Edinburgh, 1824).

[——] *Man As He Is* (4 vols., London, 1792).

[——] *Hermsprong: or, Man As He Is Not* (3 vols., London, 1796).

BARBAULD, ANNA L., Preface to *The British Novelists*, vol. xlviii (London, 1820).

COWPER, WILLIAM, *The Poetical Works*, ed. H. S. Milford, with corrections and additions by Norma Russell (London, 1967).

DISRAELI, BENJAMIN, *Sybil, or The Two Nations*, Bradenham Edn., vol. ix (London, 1927).

HOBBES, THOMAS, *Leviathan*, ed. C. B. Macpherson (Harmondsworth, 1968).

(b) *Secondary Sources*

BOULTON, JAMES T., and KINSLEY, JAMES, eds., *English Satiric Poetry Dryden to Byron* (London, 1966).

CLARKE, DESMOND, *The Ingenious Mr. Edgeworth* (London, 1965).

The Critical Review, lxvii (Jan. 1789), 76–7. Review of *James Wallace*.

CROUCH, WILLIAM, 'The Novels of Robert Bage', unpub. Ph.D. diss., Princeton University, 1937.

DENENFELD, PHILIP S., 'Social Criticism in the Novels of Robert Bage', unpub. Ph.D. diss., Northwestern University, 1957.

The English Review, xx (Dec. 1792), 437–43. Review of *Man As He Is*.

FAULKNER, PETER, 'Robert Bage', *Notes and Queries*, ccxii (Apr. 1967), 144.

GEORGE, M. DOROTHY, *English Political Caricature* (2 vols., Oxford, 1959).

HARTLEY, K. H., 'Un Roman philosophique anglais: Hermsprong de Robert Bage', *Revue de littérature comparée*, xxxviii (1964), 558–63.

HUTTON, WILLIAM, *The History of Derby . . . to 1791* (London, 1791).

—— *The Life of William Hutton, . . . written by himself* (London, 1816).

—— 'Memoirs of Mr. Bage', *Monthly Magazine*, xii (Jan. 1802), 478–80.

The Monthly Review, 1st Ser., lxvi (Feb. 1782), 129. Review of *Mount Henneth*, by Samuel Badcock.

—— 1st Ser., lxxvi (Apr. 1787), 325–9. Review of *The Fair Syrian*, by Andrew Becket.

—— 2nd Ser., x (Mar. 1793), 297–302. Review of *Man As He Is* by Thomas Holcroft.

—— 2nd Ser., xxi (Sept. 1796), 21–4. Review of *Hermsprong*, by William Taylor.

MUSSON, A. E., and ROBINSON, ERIC, *Science and Technology in the Industrial Revolution* (Manchester, 1969).

OSBORNE, E. A., 'A Preliminary Survey for a Bibliography of the Novels of Robert Bage', *Book Handbook*, i (1947), 30–6.

SCHOFIELD, ROBERT, *The Lunar Society of Birmingham* (Oxford, 1963).

SCOTT, WALTER, 'Prefatory Memoir to Robert Bage', in *Ballantyne's Novelist's Library*, vol. ix (Edinburgh, 1824), pp. xvi–xxxiv.

SMITH, G. BARNETT, 'Robert Bage', *Dictionary of National Biography*.

STEEVES, H. R., 'The Date of Bage's "Mount Henneth" ', *Notes and Queries*, ccx (Jan. 1965), 27.

SUTHERLAND, JOHN H., 'Bage's Supposed Quaker Upbringing', *Notes and Queries*, cxcviii (Jan. 1953), 32–3.

—— 'Robert Bage: Novelist of Ideas', *Philological Quarterly*, xxxvi (1957), 211–20.

SUTTON, C. W., 'Sir Brooke Boothby', *Dictionary of National Biography*.

3. *Elizabeth Inchbald*

(a) *Sources*

ADDISON, JOSEPH, and STEELE, RICHARD, *The Spectator*, ed. Donald F. Bond (5 vols., Oxford, 1965).

AUSTEN, JANE, *Mansfield Park*, ed. John Lucas and James Kinsley (London, New York, and Toronto, 1970).

Cheap Repository for Moral and Religious Publications [a prospectus and list of subscribers], n.d. [c. 1795].

EDGEWORTH, MARIA, *Letters for Literary Ladies* (London, 1795).

EDGEWORTH, MARIA and RICHARD LOVELL, *Practical Education* (2 vols., London, 1798).

ELIOT, GEORGE, *Felix Holt, The Radical*, Illustrated Copyright Edn. (London, n.d.).

—— *Daniel Deronda*, Illustrated Copyright Edn. (London, n.d.).

HAYS, MARY, *Memoirs of Emma Courtney* (2 vols., London, 1796).

INCHBALD, ELIZABETH, *Such Things Are* (London, 1788).

—— *Next Door Neighbours* (London, 1791).

—— *A Simple Story* (1791), with an introduction by G. L. Strachey (London, 1908).

—— *A Simple Story* (1791), ed. J. M. S. Tompkins (London, 1967).

—— *Nature and Art* (2 vols., London, 1796).

I[NCHBALD], E[LIZABETH], [Essay on Novel Writing,] *The Artist*, vol. i, no. xiv (13 June 1807), 9–19.

[—— A Defence of the Stage,] *The Artist*, vol. ii, no. ix [1809], 138–53. Signed 'A Christian, but no Fanatick'.

JOHNSON, SAMUEL, *Lives of the English Poets*, ed. G. Birkbeck Hill (3 vols., Oxford, 1905).

KOLLONTAI, ALEXANDRA, *The Autobiography of a Sexually Emancipated Communist Woman*, trans. Salvator Attanasio (New York, 1971).

LA ROCHEFOUCAULD, FRANÇOIS DE, *Réflexions ou sentences et maximes morales. Réflexions diverses*, ed. Dominique Secretan (Geneva, 1967).

MORE, HANNAH, *Works* (6 vols., London, 1834).

WILLIAMS, HELEN MARIA, *Julia, a Novel; interspersed with some poetical pieces* (2 vols., Dublin, 1790).

[WILSON, HARRIETTE,] *Harriette Wilson's Memoirs of Herself and Others* (London, 1929).

WOLLSTONECRAFT, MARY, *Thoughts on the Education of Daughters* (London, 1787).

[——] *Mary, A Fiction* (London, 1788).

[——] *Original Stories from Real Life* (London, 1788).

[——] *A Vindication of the Rights of Woman* (London, 1792).

—— *Letters Written During a Short Residence in Sweden, Norway, and Denmark* (London, 1796).

[WOLLSTONECRAFT, MARY] *Posthumous Works of the Author of a Vindication of the Rights of Woman*, ed. William Godwin (4 vols., London, 1798).

(b) *Secondary Sources*

ADAMS, M. RAY, 'Mary Hays, Disciple of William Godwin', *Publications of the Modern Language Association of America*, lv (1940), 472–83.

BOADEN, JAMES, *Memoirs of the Life of John Philip Kemble* (2 vols., London, 1825).

—— *Memoirs of Mrs. Siddons* (2 vols., London, 1827).

—— *The Life of Mrs. Jordan* (2 vols., London, 1831).

—— *Memoirs of Mrs. Inchbald* (2 vols., London, 1833).

The Critical Review, 2nd Ser., i (Feb. 1791), 207–13. Review of *A Simple Story*.

GORDON, ALEXANDER, 'Samuel Horsley', *Dictionary of National Biography*.

HOBHOUSE, CHRISTOPHER, *Fox* (2nd edn., repr. London, 1964).

JONES, M. G., *Hannah More* (Cambridge, 1952).

JOUGHIN, G. LOUIS, 'An Inchbald Bibliography', *University of Texas Studies in English*, xiv (1934), 59–74.

LITTLEWOOD, S. R., *Elizabeth Inchbald and her Circle* (London, 1921).

McKEE, WILLIAM, *Elizabeth Inchbald, Novelist* (Washington, D.C., 1935).

MOIR, ESTHER, *The Justice of the Peace* (Harmondsworth, 1969).

SÉJOURNÉ, PHILIPPE, *Aspects généraux du roman féminin en Angleterre de 1740 à 1800* (Aix-en-Provence, 1966).

STAROBINSKI, JEAN, *J.-J. Rousseau. La Transparence et l'obstacle* (rev. edn., Paris, 1971).

TOMPKINS, J. M. S., 'Mary Hays, Philosophess', in *The Polite Marriage* (Cambridge, 1938), pp. 150–90.

WARDLE, RALPH M., *Mary Wollstonecraft, A Critical Biography* (Lawrence, Kansas, 1951).

—— 'Mary Wollstonecraft, *Analytical Reviewer*', *Publications of the Modern Language Association of America*, lxii (1947), 1000–9.

4. *Thomas Holcroft*

(a) *Sources*

CARROLL, JOHN, ed., *Selected Letters of Samuel Richardson* (Oxford, 1964).

A Catalogue of the Library of Mr. Thomas Holcroft ([London, King and Lochée,] 1807).

A Catalogue of the Library of Books, the Property of Thomas Holcroft ([London, King and Lochée], 1809).

COLERIDGE, SAMUEL TAYLOR, *The Complete Poetical Works*, ed. E. H. Coleridge (2 vols., Oxford, 1912).

GRAVES, RICHARD, *The Spiritual Quixote*, ed. Clarence Tracy (London, 1967).

GREEN, D. B., 'Letters of William Godwin and Thomas Holcroft to William Dunlap', *Notes and Queries*, cci (Oct. 1956), 441–3.

HARPER, GEORGE MILLS, and RAINE, KATHLEEN, eds., *Thomas Taylor the Platonist* (London, 1969).

[HOLCROFT, THOMAS,] *The History of Manthorn, the Enthusiast*, published serially in the *Town and Country Magazine*, x and xi (1778 and 1779). Not completed.

[——] *Alwyn: or the Gentleman Comedian* (2 vols., London, 1780).

—— *Anna St. Ives* (1792), ed. Peter Faulkner (London, New York, and Toronto, 1970).

—— *The Adventures of Hugh Trevor* (6 vols., London, 1794–7).

—— *The Adventures of Hugh Trevor*, ed. Seamus Deane (London, 1973).

—— *A Letter to the Right Honourable William Windham, on the Intemperance and Dangerous Tendency of his Conduct* (London, 1795).

—— *A Narrative of Facts, relating to a Prosecution for High Treason* (London, 1795).

—— *Hear Both Sides* (London, 1803).

—— *Travels from Hamburg through Westphalia, Holland and the Netherlands, to Paris* (2 vols., London, 1804).

—— *The Memoirs of Bryan Perdue* (3 vols., London, 1805).

LAVATER, J. C., *Aphorisms on Man*, trans. H. Fuseli (London, 1788).

LESAGE, ALAIN RENÉ, *The Adventures of Gil Blas of Santillane*, trans. T. Smollett (London, 1900).

LUCAS, E. V., ed., *The Letters of Charles Lamb, and Mary Lamb* (3 vols., London, 1935).

LYTTELTON, THOMAS, *Letters of the Late Lord Lyttelton* (London, 1780).

[MACKENZIE, HENRY,] *The Letters of Brutus to Celebrated Political Characters* (Edinburgh and London, 1791); *Additional Letters* [London, 1793].

The Monthly Review, 2nd Ser., ix (Nov. 1792), 337–8. Review of *The Castle of St. Vallery*, by Thomas Holcroft.

—— 2nd Ser., xi (June 1793), 153–60. Review of *Arabian Tales*, by Thomas Holcroft.

The Town and Country Magazine, ix–xi (Oct. 1777–Feb. 1779). 'The Philosopher' essays, i–xii, by Holcroft.

TRENCK, FREDERIC, *The Life of Baron Frederic Trenck*, trans. Thomas Holcroft (3 vols., London, 1788).

The Wit's Magazine, vol. i (Jan to Apr. 1784). Edited by Holcroft.

(b) *Secondary Sources*

BAINE, RODNEY M., *Thomas Holcroft and the Revolutionary Novel* (Athens, Georgia, 1965).

The British Critic, iv (July 1794), 71. Review of *Hugh Trevor*.
BRONSON, BERTRAND H., *Joseph Ritson Scholar-at-arms* (2 vols., Berkeley, California, 1938).
COLBY, ELBRIDGE, *A Bibliography of Thomas Holcroft* (New York, 1922).
DEVALDÈS, MANUEL [i.e. Ernest Lohy], 'Un Révolutionnaire anglais du XVIIIᵉ siècle. Thomas Holcroft', in *Figures d'Angleterre* (Paris, [1932,]) pp. 55–66.
DIBDIN, THOMAS, *Reminiscences* (London, 1827).
The European Magazine and London Review, xxii (Dec. 1792), 404. 'Account of Mr. Thomas Holcroft'.
GOLDBERG, M. A., *Smollett and the Scottish School* (Albuquerque, New Mexico, 1959).
HAZLITT, WILLIAM, *The Life of Thomas Holcroft*, ed. Elbridge Colby (2 vols., London, 1925).
HOLLINGSWORTH, KEITH, *The Newgate Novel 1830–1847* (Detroit, 1963).
LESSER, SIMON O., *Fiction and the Unconscious* (London, 1960).
MACDONNELL, G. P., 'Sir Edward Coke', *Dictionary of National Biography*.
MITFORD, MARY RUSSELL, *Recollections of a Literary Life* (3 vols., London, 1852).
The Monthly Review, 1st Ser., lxiii (Sept. 1780), 233. Review of *Alwyn*. The author of this one sentence review is not identified, according to Nangle.
—— 2nd Ser., xv (Oct. 1794), 149–53. Review of *Hugh Trevor*, vols. i–iii, by William Enfield.
NOVAK, MAXIMILLIAN E., 'Freedom, Libertinism, and the Picaresque', *Studies in Eighteenth Century Culture*, vol. iii, ed. Harold E. Pagliaro (Cleveland and London, 1973).
RIGG, J. M., 'Thomas Lyttelton, second Baron Lyttelton', *Dictionary of National Biography*.
STAHL, E. L., and YUILL, W. E., *German Literature of the Eighteenth and Nineteenth Centuries* (London, 1970).
STALLBAUMER, VIRGIL H., 'Thomas Holcroft: A Satirist in the Stream of Sentimentalism', *ELH A Journal of English Literary History*, iii (1936), 31–62.
STEPHENS, H. MORSE, 'William Henry Cavendish Bentinck, third Duke of Portland', *Dictionary of National Biography*.
STEVENSON, LIONEL, *The English Novel* (London, 1960).
THIEME, J. A., 'Thomas Holcroft as a Novelist', unpub. M. Phil. diss., London University, 1969.
TUCKER, SUSIE, *Protean Shape, A Study in Eighteenth-Century Vocabulary and Usage* (London, 1967).
WATT, IAN, *The Rise of the Novel* (1957, repr. Harmondsworth, 1963).
—— 'Samuel Richardson', in *The Novelist as Innovator* (London, 1965).

5. *William Godwin*

(a) *Sources*

[Anon.,] *Mandeville; or, The Last Words of a Maniac! A Tale of the Seventeenth Century in England. By Himself*, vol. iv [i.e. to be taken as a continuation of Godwin's *Mandeville*] (London, 1818).

Barruel, Augustin, *Memoirs Illustrating the History of Jacobinism* (4 vols., London, 1797–8).

Beatson, Robert, *A Political Index* (2nd edn., 2 vols., London, 1788).

Blunden, Edmund, ed., *Tragical Consequences or a Disaster at Deal; being an unpublished letter of William Godwin* (London, 1931).

The British Critic, v (Apr. 1795), 444–7. Anonymous letter regarding legal inaccuracies in *Things As They Are*.

—— vi (July 1795), 94–5. Godwin's reply to the anonymous letter.

—— vi (Aug. 1795), 213–15. The anonymous correspondent's reply to Godwin's reply.

Cameron, Kenneth Neill, ed., *Shelley and his Circle, 1773–1822*, vol. i (Cambridge, Massachusetts and London, 1961).

Catalogue of the Curious Library of William Godwin (Sotheby and Son, London, 1836).

[Cohausen, J. H.,] *Hermippus Redivivus: or, The Sage's Triumph over Old Age and the Grave*, [trans. John Campbell] (London 1744).

Collins, Anthony, *A Philosophical Inquiry Concerning Human Liberty*, republished with a preface, by Joseph Priestley (Birmingham and London, 1790).

[Dubois, Edward,] *St. Godwin, A Tale of the Sixteenth, Seventeenth, and Eighteenth Century, by Reginald de St. Leon* (Dublin, 1800).

Duperrier Dumouriez, C. F., *Memoirs of General Dumourier, written by Himself*, trans. John Fenwick (2 parts, London, 1794).

Flammenberg, Lawrence, [i.e. K. F. Kahlert,] *The Necromancer; or The Tale of the Black Forest*, trans. Peter Teuthold (1794), with an introduction by Montague Summers (London, 1927).

Fleetwood, William, *A Compleat Collection of the Sermons, Tracts, and Pieces of All Kinds* (London, 1737).

Gill, Stephen, 'The Original *Salisbury Plain*: Introduction and Text', in *Bicentenary Wordsworth Studies*, ed. Jonathan Wordsworth (Ithaca, New York and London, 1970).

Godwin, William, *Italian Letters* (1784), ed. Burton R. Pollin (Lincoln, Nebraska, 1965).

—— *Imogen, A Pastoral Romance* (1784), ed. Jack W. Marken (New York, 1963).

—— *Uncollected Writings (1785–1822)*, ed. Jack W. Marken and Burton R. Pollin (Gainesville, Florida, 1968).

GODWIN, WILLIAM, *Enquiry Concerning Political Justice*, ed. F. E. L. Priestley (3 vols., Toronto, 1946).
—— *Caleb Williams* (1794), ed. David McCracken (London, New York, and Toronto, 1970).
[——] *Considerations on Lord Grenville's and Mr. Pitt's Bills* (London, 1795).
—— *The Enquirer: Reflections on Education, Manners and Literature, in a Series of Essays* (London, 1797).
—— *Memoirs of Mary Wollstonecraft* (1798), ed. W. Clark Durant (London and New York, 1927).
—— *St. Leon: A Tale of the Sixteenth Century* (4 vols., London, 1799).
—— *Antonio: A Tragedy* (London, 1800).
—— *Thoughts Occasioned by the Perusal of Dr. Parr's Spital Sermon* (London, 1801).
—— *Life of Geoffrey Chaucer* (2 vols., London, 1803).
—— *Fleetwood: or, The New Man of Feeling* (3 vols., London, 1805).
—— *Essay on Sepulchres* (London, 1809).
—— *Lives of Edward and John Philips, Nephews and Pupils of Milton* (London, 1815).
—— *Mandeville. A Tale of the Seventeenth Century in England* (3 vols., Edinburgh and London, 1817).
—— *History of the Commonwealth of England* (4 vols., London, 1824–8).
—— *Cloudesley: A Tale* (3 vols., London, 1830).
—— *Deloraine* (3 vols., London, 1833).
GODWIN, WILLIAM, the younger, *Transfusion: or, The Orphans of Unwalden* (3 vols., London, 1833).
HAZLITT, WILLIAM, *The Spirit of the Age*, in *Works*, ed. P. P. Howe, vol. xi (London and Toronto, 1932).
HUME, DAVID, *The History of Great Britain*, vol. i (Edinburgh, 1754).
[HYDE, EDWARD, Earl of Clarendon,] *Memoirs of King Charles I and the Loyalists* (London, 1795).
[MACKENZIE, HENRY,] *Julia de Roubigné* (2 vols., London, 1777).
MALTHUS, THOMAS R., *An Essay on the Principle of Population*, ed. Anthony Flew (Harmondsworth, 1970).
MANDEVILLE, BERNARD, *The Fable of the Bees*, ed. F. B. Kaye (2 vols., Oxford, 1924).
PRIESTLEY, JOSEPH, *Autobiography of Joseph Priestley*, ed. Jack Lindsay (Bath, 1970).
REYNOLDS, SIR JOSHUA, *Discourses*, ed. Helen Zimmern (London, 1887.)
T[URNER], E., ed., *Characters of Eminent Men . . . From the Works of Lord Chancellor Clarendon* (London, 1793).
WOLLSTONECRAFT, MARY, *Mary and the Wrongs of Woman*, ed. Gary Kelly (London, 1976).

WORDSWORTH, WILLIAM, *The Poetical Works*, ed. E. de Selincourt, vol. i (Oxford, 1940).

(b) *Secondary Sources*

The Analytical Review, xxi (Feb. 1795), 166–75. Review of *Things As They Are*.

The Anti-Jacobin Review and Magazine, v (Jan. and Feb. 1800), 23–8, 145–53. Review of *St. Leon*.

BARNES, HARRY E., *A History of Historical Writing* (2nd rev. edn., New York, 1963).

BLUNDEN, EDMUND, 'Godwin's Library Catalogue', *Keats–Shelley Memorial Bulletin*, ix (1958), 27–9.

BONGIE, LAURENCE L., *David Hume, Prophet of the Counter-revolution* (Oxford, 1965).

BOOTH, WAYNE C., *The Rhetoric of Fiction* (Chicago and London, 1961).

The British Critic, iv (July 1794), 70–1. Review of *Things As They Are*.

BROWN, FORD K., *The Life of William Godwin* (London, Toronto, and New York, 1926).

CHANDLER, F. W., *The Literature of Roguery* (2 vols., London, Boston, and New York, 1907).

The Critical Review, 2nd Ser., xi (July 1794), 290–6.

DUMAS, D. GILBERT, 'Things As They Were: The Original Ending of *Caleb Williams*', *Studies in English Literature, 1500–1900*, vi (1966), 575–97.

ELLIOTT, J. H., *Europe Divided 1559–1598* (London and Glasgow, 1968).

FLEISHER, DAVID, *William Godwin. A Study in Liberalism* (London, 1951).

FURBANK, P. N., 'Godwin's Novels', *Essays in Criticism*, v (1955), 214–28.

GARDINER, S. R., 'Lucius Cary, second Viscount Falkland', *Dictionary of National Biography*.

GILL, STEPHEN, ' "Adventures on Salisbury Plain" and Wordsworth's Poetry of Protest 1795–7', *Studies in Romanticism*, xi (1972), 48–65.

GROSS, HARVEY, 'The Pursuer and the Pursued: A Study of *Caleb Williams*', *Texas Studies in Literature and Language*, i (1959), 401–11.

HART, JEFFREY, *Viscount Bolingbroke, Tory Humanist* (London and Toronto, 1965).

JOHNSTONE, ARTHUR, *Enchanted Ground, The Study of Medieval Romance in the Eighteenth Century* (London, 1964).

KELLY, GARY, 'Godwin, Wollstonecraft, and Rousseau', *Women and Literature*, iii (autumn 1975), 21–6.

KIPPIS, ANDREW, *Biographia Britannica* (5 vols., London, 1778–93).

LOCKHART, J. G., *The Life of Sir Walter Scott* (London, 1893).

LURIA, GINA, 'Mary Hays: A Critical Biography', unpub. Ph.D. diss., New York University, 1972.

McCracken, David, 'Godwin's Reading in Burke', *English Language Notes*, vii (1970), 264–70.

Marchand, Leslie A., *Byron, A Portrait* (London, 1971).

Miyoshi, Masao, *The Divided Self* (New York and London, 1969).

Monro, D. H., *Godwin's Moral Philosophy* (London, 1953).

The Monthly Review, 2nd Ser., xv (Oct. 1794), 145–9. Review of *Things As They Are*, by William Enfield.

Moorman, Mary, *William Wordsworth, The Early Years* (Oxford, 1957).

Murry, John Middleton, *Heaven and Earth* (London, 1938).

Osborn, Robert, 'Meaningful Obscurity: The Antecedents and Character of Rivers', in *Bicentenary Wordsworth Studies*, ed. Jonathan Wordsworth (Ithaca, New York and London, 1970).

Paul, Charles Kegan, *William Godwin: His Friends and Contemporaries* (2 vols., London, 1876).

Peardon, Thomas P., *The Transition in English Historical Writing 1760–1830* (New York, 1933).

Pollin, Burton R., *Education and Enlightenment in the Works of William Godwin* (New York, 1962).

—— *Godwin Criticism, A Synoptic Bibliography* (Toronto, 1967).

Preu, James, 'Swift's Influence on Godwin's Doctrine of Anarchism', *Journal of the History of Ideas*, xv (1954), 371–83.

Rodway, A. E., *Godwin and the Age of Transition* (London, 1952).

Sharrock, Roger, 'Godwin on Milton's Satan', *Notes and Queries*, ccvii (Dec. 1962), 463–5.

Sherburn, George, 'Godwin's later Novels', *Studies in Romanticism*, i (1962), 65–82.

Storch, Rudolf F., 'Metaphors of Private Guilt and Social Rebellion in Godwin's *Caleb Williams*', *ELH A Journal of English Literary History*, xxxiv (1967), 188–207.

Tomalin, Claire, *The Life and Death of Mary Wollstonecraft* (London, 1974).

Willey Basil, *The Eighteenth-Century Background* (1940, repr. Harmondsworth, 1962).

Woodcock, George, *William Godwin* (London, 1956).

INDEX